S0-DXH-319

EMMETT A. RICE was Professor of Physical Education at the Normal College of the American Gymnastic Union, now a part of Indiana University, when he wrote the First Edition of this book. A graduate of Indiana University, he also served as teacher and administrator in several public school systems and Director of Physical Education and Health for the Indianapolis Public Schools.

JOHN L. HUTCHINSON, Ed.D., Columbia University, is Professor of Recreation at San Francisco State College. He was previously Professor of Education at Teachers College, Columbia University. Dr. Hutchinson has served as President of the College Recreation Association and as Vice-President of the American Association for Health, Physical Education and Recreation.

MABEL LEE, LL.D., Coe College, D.P.E., George Williams College, is Emeritus Professor and former Director of Physical Education for Women of the University of Nebraska. Dr. Lee was the first woman to be elected President of the American Association for Health, Physical Education and Recreation, subsequently serving also as that organization's first Archivist. She was also the first woman President of the American Academy of Physical Education, and was the third President of the National Association of Physical Education for College Women.

A BRIEF HISTORY OF PHYSICAL EDUCATION

EMMETT A. RICE
Late, Normal College of the
American Gymnastic Union,
Indiana University

JOHN L. HUTCHINSON
San Francisco State College

MABEL LEE
University of Nebraska

FIFTH EDITION

THE RONALD PRESS COMPANY • NEW YORK

VR

Library of Congress Catalog Card Number: 75–84080
PRINTED IN THE UNITED STATES OF AMERICA

Preface

The history of any subject may be taken as a means of measuring its progress. It provides data for comparison of past and present with respect to the importance and influence of the subject. It constitutes a record of experiments and achievements, and demonstrates the relationship existing between certain elements in civilization and the status of the subject in a particular society. Only through the study of history can a broad and appreciative view of the subject be obtained.

This book is a history of physical education from early times to the present. Its purpose is to give the undergraduate student an overview of the position physical education has occupied throughout the years in civilized society. It discusses those political, social, and religious situations which determine the character of a given society and reflect the physical activities of its people. For example, the book explains why one religious group promoted the development of physical power while another stifled it, and why certain countries under the influence of a dominating political power supported a vigorous physical training program while others under similar influence had no program of any consequence. The theories and methods of the leaders, the heritages from early movements, as well as the relationship that physical education has borne to general education, receive attention.

The material of the book is organized in three parts. Part I highlights the beginnings of physical education in ancient oriental cultures, in Greece, and in Rome. Part II reviews the place physical education held in the Dark Ages, the Age of Chivalry, the Renaissance, the Age of Realism, and the Age of Enlightenment; and then it presents the background of physical education in various modern European countries and other selected countries of the world. Part III treats the history of physical education in the United States from colonial times to the present.

The history of the physical education movement in the United States is of considerable importance because its program is more highly organized than those in other countries. For this reason, the devotion of one half of the text to the development of the United States program seems warranted. The heritage from early movements, combined with the knowledge of current activities, afford the student of physical education a sound basis not only for an understanding of the present status of physical education but also for judging the trends that may occur in the years ahead.

Since the objective of this book is to give the beginning student an overview of the status of physical education, past and present, we have not prepared an exacting, detailed reference work, nor have we attempted to cover every country. Also, we have felt it unnecessary to include an elaborate bibliography. We have included, however, a chapter-by-chapter list of important publications in the history of physical education that have been used as sources of information in the preparation of this Fifth Edition. In addition, many of the old books and foreign publications cited by Emmett A. Rice, who wrote the original edition in 1926, have been retained for their historical value.

The Appendix lists the leading organizations in the development of physical education in the United States and their officers through 1969, and also lists persons honored for their service to the profession. In addition, the biographical sketches in Part III accord recognition to those whose contribution has been of major significance. Sketches of leaders born since 1880 have not been included, since their contributions are too near the present for appraisal as to their historical significance.

Because of new information from later research, this Fifth Edition includes much material for the earlier periods not contained in former editions, and also brings into historical perspective the more significant movements and trends that have been developing since the last edition.

We express our appreciation to those who cooperated in supplying information and illustrations. In particular we wish to acknowledge our indebtedness to *Mind and Body* and the *American Physical Education Review,* which through their many years of publication offer rich sources of historical materials; to the valuable pioneering historical research work of Edward Mussey Hartwell and Fred E. Leonard in particular; to the national offices of the National Recreation and Park Association, the Young Men's Christian Association, and the Young Women's Christian Association, for their kindness in furnishing historical data on their organization work; and to Lea and Febiger, Publishers, for the illustration of Harvard University's Hemenway Gymnasium.

For much data on the early normal training schools and later developments in colleges and universities we are indebted to the archivists, registrars, and heads of departments of the many schools who have supplied official information that has put the records straight.

JOHN L. HUTCHINSON
MABEL LEE

San Francisco, California
Lincoln, Nebraska
April, 1969

Contents

APPENDIXES

I

PHYSICAL EDUCATION IN ANCIENT CULTURES

1

Ancient Oriental Nations

Instinct and the opportunity to play are more pronounced among primitive people than among those of civilized nations. Foot racing as a competitive sport is as widespread as the human family. Wrestling and boxing are hardly less so. Throwing at a target with weapons, stones, or other objects occurs among nearly all peoples. With some it takes the form of bowling, with others hurling the spear, and with the Canadian Indians sliding the spear over the ice. Swimming is engaged in by nearly all. Ball playing with a bat or racket is less common but was well known among the American Indians. Lacrosse was invented by them. Fencing with sticks or spears, too, is widespread.

Labor, searching for food, dancing, games, and the outdoor life of primitive man are all conducive to the development of sound bodies. Civilization took from some, the body building labor of primitive man, and gave to others far too great a burden. The machine, requiring little skill, accuracy, or strength, had supplanted the crude tool of the savage. The search for food passed long ago; today it is delivered to the home. Until recent times, for the great majority, games were put aside with childhood. The primitive hut gave way to the airtight house, and the outdoor life, to indoor life. Many shortcomings known to all have followed in the wake of these changes and have given rise to the necessity for conscious purposive physical education.

No one geographical area receives recognition by all authorities as the birthplace of civilization. The development of a sequential approach to early education and physical education depends, therefore, upon an arbitrary selection of the earliest civilization. Some contend present records show that the first civilized people lived in Mesopotamia, "the land between the rivers," while others hold that Egypt deserves this distinction.

The authors of this text feel that these two civilizations probably paralleled each other and so, without unchallengeable authorities to rely upon, have decided to begin with the Egyptians.

EGYPT

Although Egyptian civilization reached its peak in approximately 1500 B.C., the oldest records relating to Egypt go back nearly to 5000 B.C. As Egypt transformed from a primitive to a civilized existence, formal education received much attention. Eventually, a trend toward the inclusion of physical education activities as an important aspect of the total culture became evident.

These physical activities included gymnastic exercises and wrestling, both performed to honor the gods. Wrestling became a favorite entertainment; children's games were plentiful, as excavations have revealed; lifting and swinging weights, swimming, ball games of men, women, and children (including racquets), and bull fighting represent other physical activities peculiar to this early civilization. The common people, when their work was finished, also participated in these activities. Wrestling, swimming, and gymnastics, along with other sports, became a part of vigorous training for war. Interestingly, the participation of women in many physical activities was a common rather than exceptional occurrence.

Dancing held a prominent place for all Egyptian people. While the upper class participated only in religious dances, the common people engaged in folk dancing, and professionals, both men and women, performed at royal festive occasions and dinners. Drums, the lyre, the flute, castanets, and other instruments often accompanied the many forms of dancing that were practiced so extensively in Egypt. The dancing of civilized people since that time often has been traced to these early Egyptians.

SUMER

Although others undoubtedly occupied lower Mesopotamia earlier, the Sumerians are usually recognized as the forerunners of the Babylonians. No concrete evidence seems available that indicates the Sumerians developed a system of physical fitness. However, their interest in wrestling and fishing and advocation of hunting as a means for keeping the upper class physically fit during peace time gives evidence of this people's viewpoint toward physical activity. The heroic tales of Gilgamesh tend to emphasize the importance of physical prowess, and the stories about

Fig. 1. Wrestling in Ancient Egypt. (Taken from drawings in Egyptian tombs.)

this famed hunter, the first of the Paul Bunyan stories, stress the importance of physical strength, skill, and endurance.

BABYLONIA AND ASSYRIA

These nations perhaps never gave sports and games as much emphasis as the Egyptians. However, these people that dwelled between the rivers did participate in dancing and singing as they related both to religion and to the amusement of the common people. Like the Sumerians, they hunted not only for food but also as preparation for war.

Ancient reliefs indicate that boxing and wrestling as physical contests occurred. Games and bow-shooting, too, had their place. Swimming was emphasized to a great extent. Although some swimming for pleasure perhaps did exist, most evidence uncovered shows that swimming formed a basic part of the training of warriors. Inflated skins were and still are used in Mesopotamia to aid the swimmer.

CHINA

The Chinese civilization is one of the oldest in the world. It is composed of people who are industrious and frugal. Until recently they also exhibited peaceful and docile characteristics throughout their long history. Very early they adopted a policy of isolation, and when the Himalaya Mountains proved an insufficient barrier, the Great Wall was built. When that failed, laws were passed forbidding foreigners to enter China.

This nonintercourse with other nations tended to crystallize the social order and prevent change. Chinese have had great reverence for their ancestors and the teachings of the past; these ideals are also partly responsible for the static society. The difficulty of writing or reading the Chinese language made universal education almost impossible.

Schools in China were private. Boys of the upper class paid tuition; girls were not educated. The aim of the school was to teach the sacred books of Confucius in such a way that pupils could repeat them or write them from memory. In higher schools the style and content of books were studied until pupils could imitate the ancient sacred literature. Officers for the nation were chosen by competitive examinations among students of the highest schools. Nothing was taught to develop individual capacity; on the other hand, everything was done to obliterate the personality and individuality of the students and make them fit into the static social order.

Very early Chinese history indicates a stress on physical activities. Archery, charioteering, and physical exercises apparently had a place in the very early Chinese civilization. With the advent of religions like Confucianism and Buddhism, intellectualism was stressed at the expense of physical education.

In the fifth century A.D., a priest made note of a series of medical exercises called Cong Fu which had been practiced in China since 2600 B.C. Diseases were thought to result from organic inactivity. Certain bodily movements combined with breathing exercises were intended to keep the organs functioning and to prolong life and insure immortality of the soul. The Swedish system of medical gymnastics has no connection with this but arose quite independently.

Boxing in China can be traced back to nearly 700 B.C., while its counterpart, wrestling, evidently started, according to modern records, much later or between 300 and 250 B.C. Wrestling became a familiar exercise for conditioning soldiers. Various forms of football or kicking games began to appear between the third and second centuries B.C.

As in all ancient cultures, dancing was stressed. Various forms of dance evolved—aggressive action, defensive action, worship, and agriculture were symbolized in some of these dances. Music as usual was combined with the dance in China, with both men and women participating individually and together. Some danced for pleasure; others were paid. Dancing became so important in the ancient feudal society that a man's prestige often depended on his prowess as a dancer.

INDIA

The civilization of India is as ancient as China's. While the warm climate in certain parts has made the inhabitants a dreamy and speculative people, this condition does not hold true for the entire country. India is a land of religious and mystic philosophies. The dominant teachings are Hinduism, Mohammedanism, and Christianity. The theory of Hinduism reduces the multiplicity of things in the universe to unity. That unity is Brahma. The aim of religion is to unite in Brahma. Meantime, man's soul immigrates from body to body through thousands of reincarnations. Ambitions, desires, and individuality combine to increase the reincarnations and postpone the time of self-liberation and absorption in Brahma. The surest way to attain that is to refrain from activity and the enjoyments of this life.

Brahmins were the only teachers, and the sons of Brahmins were the pupils. The sacred books were the texts, and memorization followed by a study of content and meaning was the learning process. Although India was attacked many times by enemies, the stable society, coupled with the prevalent philosophy, was undisturbed until relatively recent times.

The children of India did play games of their own invention and in imitation of the elders. Adults undoubtedly participated in hunting the elephant, archery, boxing, riding, running, and the like because it is known that Buddha specifically prohibited such activities. And it has been noted that during peace time those in the military pursued sports as a means of entertainment and diversion from the regular mode of living. Centuries later the game of polo evolved from the high military personnel.

IRAN

In the seventh century B.C. the Persians and their kinsmen the Medes formed the greatest nation of the Indo-European branch of the white race. At the dawn of history these people were living in a tribal and nomadic state, tending their sheep on the hillsides and valleys of Iran. They were a rugged, industrious, serious, religious, and progressive people. From early times the Medes and Persians were noted as intrepid hunters, expert horsemen, and brave warriors.

The Persian Empire began its separate independent existence when King Cyrus the Great revolted from Media in 558 B.C. and in turn subjected the Medes to his power. With the wealth of his conquered kinsmen and the valor of his own victorious army, Cyrus incorporated nation after nation into his rapidly expanding empire; the Bactrians, the Lydians, the Asia Minor Greeks, tribes along the Caspian Sea, and finally the powerful state of Babylonia. At the end of the reign of Cyrus, 529 B.C., Persia extended from the Indus River to the Aegean Sea. The astonishing success of these conquests was due in large measure to the education of the Persian boy and young man.

Persian education was primarily moral and physical. The three classes of society were composed of farmers, trades-people, and mechanics. Intellectual training was not thought useful and was therefore neglected. Boys were taught to shoot with the bow, to ride, and to speak the truth. Education began in infancy in the home. The mother demanded obedience and truth from her sons and instructed them in the teachings of Zoroaster. According to that religion, Ahuramazda, the god of light, truth, beauty, and goodness, is in constant conflict with Ahriman, the leader of the forces of evil, darkness, disease, and sorrow. All good Persians should take their stand with Ahuramazda, and the evils of the world will be eradicated. The truthfulness of the Persians was referred to frequently by the Greeks; their abhorrence of falsehood partly accounts for their reluctance to engage in trade to any great extent.

At about the age of six, boys were taken over by the state for physical and military training. The Persian lad was expected to rise before dawn and appear at a designated field where he exercised with other boys in running, slinging, shooting the bow, and throwing javelins. In about one year, his instruction in riding began. In addition to ordinary horsemanship, he practiced jumping on and off while in full gallop and shooting and throwing with accuracy while the mount was at top speed. After gaining some skill in these sports, the boy was allowed to participate in the hunt, which was also conducted by state officials. While on the hunt, boys were made to endure extremes of heat and cold, to make forced marches day after day, to cross streams without wetting their weapons, to eat very little food, perhaps one meal in two days, to support themselves by foraging, and to stalk and kill wild animals, such as the lion, leopard, wild boar, and antelope.

When not on the hunt, boys continued regular training in archery, riding, and athletic sports. Some time was passed in the manufacture of weapons, shields, and traps and in the pursuits of agriculture. From the age of six to twenty this training continued, although from fifteen to fifty the individual was subject to active military service. The educational system of the Persians produced the finest army in Asia. Nearly every able-bodied man must have remained in the service until the age of fifty, for Persians not only protected their own native land but also garrisoned and patrolled conquered neighbors as well.

In addition, Persian history reveals that dance for men and women was discouraged or suppressed by religion but flourished as an exhibition by professional dancers. Wrestling, feats of strength, acrobatics, hunting, and polo comprise other sports practiced in Persia.

The character of Persian education was determined by what the rulers might have called "manifest destiny," namely, to conquer and hold in subjection the alien races about them. To accomplish that aim, physical, military, and moral training was thought necessary. Intellectual, cultural, and industrial training and pursuits were neglected. The Egyptians, Phoenicians, Babylonians, and other subject nations surpassed the Persians in those activities and furnished the enormous empire with the products of their labor. When the high tide of Persian conquests had been reached, a period of stagnation ensued. Wealth, tyranny, vice, and corruption, foes which the Persians were unable to withstand, so weakened the army and destroyed the stamina of the nation that when the great Alexander invaded Persia in 334 B.C. he found it to be like a hollow shell. The Persians failed to take into account the values of intellectual, industrial, and scientific training, and education of the masses as a means of building and preserving a mighty empire.

2

Greece

The Greeks were the first people in Europe to attain a high degree of civilization. So advanced did they become that the modern world has received a rich heritage in literature, government, art, and architecture from them. Physical education held a more important place among the Greeks than in any society since that time.

The mountains of Greece served to divide the inhabitants into independent political groups called city-states which were, a great part of the time, more or less hostile to each other. The rugged coast line and the proximity of the sea lured the Greeks to maritime enterprise and colonization. A mild climate, beautiful mountain ranges, the quiet sea, and the blue sky kindled the inherent sense of beauty, proportion, delicacy, and refinement so abundant in Athenian achievement.

EARLY PERIOD AND THE HOMERIC AGE

Aegean Age

Excavations at Mycenae and Tiryns, by Schliemann, revealed that as early as 2500 B.C. the mainland of Greece and adjacent islands were inhabited by a short, dark people who were well along in civilization. Knossos and other sites in Crete, laid bare by Sir Arthur Evans, gave up remains of a splendid civilization and mighty government. Judging from the excavations, Aegeans kept written records, had enormous palaces, powerful governments, houses with plumbing, wall paintings, great varieties of art, and a thriving commerce with foreign nations. Popular gymnastics, such as the Greeks later practiced, seemed to be lacking. A painting of three acrobats and a bull was found in the Knossos palace. One performer hangs on the bull's horns, another leaps over his back, and another stands behind the animal to catch his partner who is in mid-air. Other vigorous physical activities in which the people of Crete engaged were grappling the bull as a hunting activity, acrobatics, hunting deer with the bow and arrow, hunting lions with the hunters armed like soldiers, swimming with some evidence of the refinement of certain strokes, and boxing and wrestling with indications of these activities being closely related to both religious affairs and physical conditioning for soldiers.

Women played a prominent part in dancing, especially those forms associated with religion. Also, dance depicting peasant life, war, and acrobatics received considerable attention.

Homeric Age

During the century preceding 1000 B.C. great numbers of tall, fair-haired immigrants came into the peninsula of Greece from the north. These invaders mingled with the comparatively few native Aegeans and formed the Greeks of the Homeric Age and of later times. Migrations continued until the islands of the Aegean Sea and the coast of Asia Minor were occupied. The Homeric Age continued from the migrations until about 750 B.C. and is a distinct period of Greek history though origins of later institutions can be recognized at this time.

When the reader distinguishes between myth and fact, which is not difficult to do, the great epics, the *Iliad* and *Odyssey*, said to have been written by the blind bard Homer, give a complete and accurate account of the life of this period. The Homerics lived a simple, rustic life; wealth consisted in flocks and herds. Labor, even among the nobility, was not despised. Gold, silver, iron, tin, lead, and copper were known and used in a crude way in manufacturing weapons and tools. Very few laws existed. A crime was avenged by the injured one or by his kinsmen; piracy was common and not considered as dishonorable. Women were considered inferior, and a double standard existed. Although the wives had certain rights denied the slave women, both were treated as if they were property. The men were brave and hospitable to strangers. Each small community had its king and nobility. The religion of the Greeks had its origin in this period.

Zeus was the supreme god of all things, Apollo the god of light and truth, Ares of war, Hermes a messenger and the god of commerce, Poseidon the god of the sea, and Hephaestus of fire. Hera was the wife of Zeus, Athena the goddess of wisdom, Artemis of the chase, Aphrodite of love and beauty, Demeter of the harvest, and Hestia of the hearth.

These twelve major deities formed the Olympic Council and resided on or near Mount Olympus from whence they guided the destinies of the Hellenic individual and political groups. Besides these, scores of minor spirits inhabited the earth, sky, and sea. The gods had all the faults and passions of humans but were immortal and endowed with miraculous powers. The Greek approached his deities with a friendly human understanding, seeking help for which he made proper sacrifice and offering. In their honor, temples were erected and festivals celebrated.

Importance of Sports and Exercises. The *Iliad* and the *Odyssey* reveal the prominent place which athletic sports held in Homeric society. Sacrifices to the gods, funerals, entertainments for guests, and even less formal occasions called for chariot races and tests in manly strength and skill. The *Iliad* is the story of the war of the Homeric Greeks against the Trojans. Agamemnon, the commander of the Greeks, quarrels with his great warrior, Achilles. The latter sulks in his tent and will not fight; consequently, the Trojans are victorious, and the Greeks sustain severe losses. Finally Hector, a Trojan prince, kills Patroclus, the friend of Achilles. The latter then seeks revenge, and by his hand Hector is slain.

The funeral of Patroclus related in the twenty-third book should attract attention. After much lamenting and mourning and after many oxen and prisoners have been slain and sacrificed, the funeral games, presided over by Achilles, begin. First comes the chariot race. There being no race course, they drive over the rough plain to a designated spot and return. Phoenix is placed at that turn "that he may note the running and tell the truth thereof." First prize consists of a "woman skilled in fine handiwork" and a tripod; second place receives a six-year-old mare; third prize is a large bright caldron; fourth place gets two talents of gold; and fifth, a two-handled urn. Five nobles enter their teams and cast lots for starting positions. The race is on; the gods interfere, helping some drivers and hindering others; spectators argue on who leads the race; finally Diomedes wins, closely followed by the other four. All entrants received prizes.

Next came the boxing match—a sturdy mule for the winner and a two-handled cup for the loser. Epeios, a famous boxer, arose and said, "The mule I say none other of the Achaians shall take for victory with his fists, for I claim to be the best man here." Euryalos answered the challenge. Friends girded them with belts and bound their hands in thongs, and they fell to. Euryalos was so completely knocked out that some of his comrades "led him through the ring with trailing feet . . . drooping his head awry, and they set him down in a swoon . . . and themselves went forth and fetched the two-handled cup."

For the wrestling match two prizes were offered: a tripod valued at twelve oxen and a woman, skilled in all kinds of work, valued at four oxen. The contestants were Aias, of great strength, and Odysseus, "of many wiles." Upright wrestling was used, in which one must throw the other down. Two attempts were made, and they were starting the third when Achilles stopped the affair and awarded them equal prizes. They seemed to be too well matched.

Three prizes were offered for the foot race. A rare and beautiful silver mixing-bowl, an ox, and a half talent of gold. Aias the son of Oileus, Odysseus, and Antilochos were the entrants. It was a close race, but the goddess Athena caused Aias to slip in the blood where the oxen had been killed, and Odysseus won the race. Aias was second, and Antilochos came in third. The races closed the games, and the assembly broke up.

The *Odyssey* is the story of the adventures of Odysseus in his wanderings from Troy to his home in Ithaca. During his long absence, Penelope, his faithful wife, is beset with numerous unwelcome suitors who frequently amuse themselves before the palace in "casting weights and spears on a leveled place" (Book IV). These trials are the predecessors of the discus and javelin throws.

During his wanderings, Odysseus comes to the land of the Phaeacians who entertain him with feasting and minstrelsy. After the banquet, King Alcinous says, "Let us go forth anon and make trial of divers games, that the stranger may tell his friends when he home returneth how greatly we excel all men in boxing and wrestling and leaping and speed of foot." Odysseus is challenged to participate in any sport, but he, being sorrowful and longing for home, does not wish to compete with them. One of the boldest begins to chide and mock him, whereupon he catches up a weight much heavier than those that were being thrown and casts it far beyond their farthest mark and then challenges them to boxing, wrestling, or a foot race, "for I am no weakling in all sports." No competitor is found, and so the Phaeacians boast of their skill in dancing and give an exhibition with which Odysseus is pleased (Book VIII).

When Odysseus returns home dressed as a beggar and unknown to all, he is provoked to quarrel with another vagabond before his own palace gates. The suitors, joyed at the prospect of a fight, urge them on offering choice dishes of food to the winner. Their rags are girded up, and, when the thighs and arms of Odysseus are seen, the outcome of the match is known to all, even to Irus, the opposing beggar. The common fist fights of this time were raised to the dignity of a boxing match by the sportsmanship of bystanders.

A company of Homeric Greeks were ever ready to test their strength and skill in sports and material activities; it was their recreation and amusement. No record exists of a gymnasium or even a permanent athletic field in this period. The place of meeting was determined by convenience, and contests were impromptu and not preceded by special training. In funeral games of the Homerics, athletic sports took on a religious aspect and gave rise to the custom of celebrating great festivals by means of gymnastic competitions.

Boys and girls participated in many games together that resemble some modern activities. As they grew older, boys participated in a great variety of sports and physical exercises. Hunting for sport, as well as food, thrived, and dogs were bred and trained to further this sport. Although physical activities of all kinds were fostered to a high degree, the Homeric contests were informal as contrasted with the Great Games that followed later in Greece.

Place of Dance. Dancing was an activity participated in by all Greeks from earliest times. Homer, in the first book of the *Odyssey*, in speaking of the suitors of Penelope, says, "Now the wooers turned them to the dance and delightsome song and made merry and waited until evening should come on." When Odysseus was being entertained by the Phaeacians, the king, Alcinous, ordered the dancers, "the best in the land," to make sport. "So they leveled the place for the dance and made a fair ring and a wide. And the henchmen drew near bearing the loud lyre to Demodocus who got him into the midst, and round him stood boys in their first bloom, skilled in the dance and they smote the good floor with their feet. And Odysseus gazed at the twinkling of the feet and marveled in spirit." From this evidence it appears that dancing was cultivated and enjoyed but that exhibitions were frequently as impromptu as athletic contests.

PHYSICAL EDUCATION IN SPARTA

The growth of wealth, increase in population, intercourse with Oriental civilizations, and natural progress and achievements caused the primitive, simple, and rustic age of Homer to pass into the brilliant and productive period of Greek history, the fifth and fourth centuries B.C. By the fifth century B.C. the city-states had democratic governments, public education, and considerable wealth and prosperity. The orators, sculptors, architects, legislators, and dramatists of this century equalled those of any subsequent period of the world's history. The political groups varied in many respects, but in one they were very similar, namely, their attitude toward physical and military training. Greeks excelled all people in the extent of national participation in gymnastics, in the importance attached to physical education, and in honors conferred on the victors. The words gymnastic, athletic, agonistic, antagonist, hippodrome, and stadium are of Greek origin as well as the activities to which they refer. In this work, space permits only a study of the two leading city-states, Sparta and Athens.

The Spartans were, from the beginning of their history, a very patriotic and warlike people. Their victorious armies reduced almost every city-state in southern Greece to submission. This warlike spirit and successful hegemony over her neighbors shaped Sparta's social and educational institutions, her military policy, and her philosophy. Every freeborn Spartan gave his life to the state.

At birth the child was examined by state authorities and if found to be physically deficient it was exposed in some remote place to die; if strong and healthy the parents were permitted to rear it. The mother cared for the training and rearing of the children from birth to the age of seven. Her aim was to give the child a well-disciplined character and a hardy, rugged constitution. The Spartan child had to learn obedience, respect for elders, bravery, resourcefulness, self-restraint, and the endurance of pain and discomfort. The stories he heard, the songs he sang, and the life about him were conducive to that end. The hardiness of body was attained through the simple and scanty food, little or no clothing regardless of weather or season, rough and dangerous games, and fatiguing sports.

Methods of Physical and Moral Training

In Sparta moral and physical training had the same end in view and differed only slightly in methods. At the age of seven boys left the roof of their mother and entered the public barracks, which became their school and home. There they were grouped into companies, and the boys who showed the most native leadership were made the captains. The training was supervised by elders. Each company had its own quarters and mess table. The barracks offered the rudest accommodation; the boys slept on the ground or on their own improvised pallets. One garment sufficed the year round. The daily activities consisted in free play, throwing the javelin and weights, jumping, wrestling, running, making long hikes, and swimming.

At about the age of twelve the companies were reorganized, and a closer supervision of training began. The elders attended the place of exercise daily, and instruction, encouragement, and chastisement were never lacking. A youth about twenty years of age took command of the company. In addition to a more intensive and varied training, the boys were now compelled to secure some of the food for the mess; usually it had to be obtained by theft from peasants, the market, or the dwellings. Thieving was not a crime, but if the thief were detected he was severely punished. The aim was to teach craftiness and courage. Plutarch says that scanty food made them grow tall. The story of the boy who stole the fox and concealed it under his shirt and, rather than be detected, permitted it to gnaw his entrails until he fell dead, may or may not be true, but it reveals the ideal Spartan character. During the festival of Artemis, boys were lashed before the altar of that goddess that they might learn to withstand pain; some are said to have died without uttering a cry.

The moral training in citizenship was also of great importance. Everything was done to teach by example and precept that the state of Sparta was all important and that the individual and his likes and dislikes amounted to nothing. Self was to be totally subordinated, and Sparta exalted. The captain frequently tested his company on moral questions. The question "Who is a good citizen?" is asked. The boy is to give an accurate but very short answer; the Spartans always aimed at laconic and pointed speech. All that needed to be said on whether Sparta should be fortified was "that city is well fortified which has a wall of men instead of brick." The whole of Spartan philosophy was couched in terse maxims and proverbs which were learned by all. These tests of morality and speech were attended by the elders, and if the captain did not give rewards and punishments justly he himself was chastised when the boys were gone.

At the age of twenty the youth was a trained soldier and ready for war. War was welcomed as a relief from the strenuous discipline of peace. At the age of thirty he was compelled to marry to produce children for the state. He still continued in the army, however, only seeing his wife when he visited her clandestinely. Spartan men remained in the service of the city until they reached sixty years of age. They remained in service even longer if the government had need of them.

Information concerning Spartan women and girls is not so abundant, however. They were not secluded, and they held a very honorable and important place in society. The girls were given physical training somewhat comparable to that of the boys but under the supervision of women. They exercised publicly in running, jumping, throwing the weights and the javelin, and in wrestling. The aim was to develop robust, healthy mothers of sturdy children. It is thought that physical training for girls began at about the age of seven and continued until the age of twenty unless there was an earlier marriage. The Athenian women recognized the superiority of the Spartans in beauty, strength, and social position.

Labor, commerce, and handicrafts were despised by all Spartans; Lycurgus, who is said to have originated all important Spartan institutions, is supposed to have made the coins of great pieces of iron to purposely hamper commerce. The necessary labor was done by the Helots, who were conquered neighbors reduced to serfdom; certain other subjugated cities paid tribute to the Spartans.

The Spartan system of physical and military training obtained the desired results: the army was the best in the world. Spartans never made the mistake of substituting specialization in athletics for the ultimate goal of specialization for war. For this pre-eminent military position they sacrificed personal liberty, individualism, home life, and the achievements of peace. Sparta did not contribute great drama, immortal verse, models of architecture, and inimitable sculpture but left such accomplishments to her more cultured neighbor, Athens.

Place of Dance

In Sparta dancing was a more serious affair than in most lands and was usually one of three kinds, gymnastic, festive, or military. The Bibasis, engaged in by both men and women, consisted in springing from the ground and striking the feet behind. Prizes were given to those who could do it the greatest number of times. Another dance was participated in by youths and maidens together. The youth led with steps and gestures of a military nature followed by the maiden who approximately imitated him but gave a feminine interpretation. The most widespread military dance was the Pyrrhic, supposed to have been originated in Sparta. It was danced by naked youths armed with sword and shield; the steps and gestures imitated the charge, the retreat, and the thrust and parry of real battle, all in rhythm to the music of the flute.

PHYSICAL EDUCATION IN ATHENS

The Athenian father—not the state—decided whether his offspring was to be reared. Deformed, weak, or sickly babies, as in Sparta, were exposed and let die. The children, boys and girls, spent the first seven years under the charge and instruction of the mother and nurses. They learned to obey and respect the elders and became acquainted with the stories of the heroes and gods. The life of the children of Athens was not far different from that of America; they had balls, hoops, swings, carts, and jackstones and played hide-and-seek, blind-man's-buff, and hopping games.

At the age of seven the boy began a more serious education, but the girl remained in the home. The aim of Athenian education was to fit the boy for social, political, military, and religious life in Athens; this demanded a training of mind, morals, spirit, and body to their highest capacities. Three main studies were pursued: gymnastics, grammar, and music. The pedagogue, a male slave, accompanied the boys to and from school daily, protecting them from harm and giving instruction concerning interesting things about the city. In addition, the slave oversaw much of the boy's social life, such as eating habits, behavioral conduct, dressing, attitude toward elders, and the like. He carried the boy's books, music, and whatever else was needed.

Methods of Physical and Military Training

The school of gymnastics was called the *palestra,* which originally and literally meant a wrestling ground. The *palestrae,* of which there were many in Athens, were usually located on the banks of a stream where facilities for bathing and swimming might be had. As the importance of these institutions increased, more and more conveniences and accommodations were secured. First of all, a room for dressing and undressing was erected because all exercises were performed without clothing; then a room where the body could be properly oiled was provided; then a sand room, where conveniences for sprinkling sand on the body were maintained; need was also found for quarters equipped with bathing facilities. Last of all, rooms for recreation with punching bags and balls of varying weights and sizes were added. The entire structure formed a hollow square; a court in the middle where jumping, boxing, and wrestling might be practiced was open to the sky. Running and throwing the discus and javelin usually took place in the open field outside the building if the interior court was too small.

Nearly all the *palestrae,* open to boys, were owned by private individuals who conducted them for profit, but like all other Athenian schools they were regulated by the government officials. Expert teachers in all varieties of wrestling, boxing, running, jumping, and the discus and javelin throw were employed. These sports were so universally taught in Athens that it was easy to arrange a track meet among boys at any time. The festival of Hermes was largely an exhibition of boys' gymnastic accomplishments. Many boys trained in the *palestra* for the great national games. At the age of eighteen the youth deserted the *palestra* and found recreation and amusement in the gymnasium.

Along with physical education the boy attended the grammar school (didascaleum) where he very early learned to read and write and to calculate simple arithmetic problems. In the latter part of his schooling he not only studied and memorized the *Iliad* and *Odyssey* and other selections of the national literature but also practiced public speaking and oratory. In addition to these studies, moral lessons and instruction for citizenship were not lacking; the father and the pedagogue were constantly guiding and correcting his manners and conduct.

At about ten years of age musical education began; it was presumed that every educated man could play the lyre and sing the songs of Greece.

When eighteen years of age the youth became a man. He was enrolled as a cadet or *ephebus*, and with the other young men he took the famous ephebic oath of citizenship.

> I will never disgrace these sacred arms or desert my companions in the ranks. I will fight for temples and public property, both alone and with many. I will transmit my fatherland, not only not less, but greater and better than it was transmitted to me. I will obey the magistrates who may at any time be in power. I will observe both the existing laws and those which the people may unanimously hereafter make, and if any person seek to annul the laws or to set them at nought, I will do my best to prevent him, and will defend them both alone and with many. I will honor the religion of my fathers. And I call to witness Agraulos, Enyalious, Ares, Zeus, Thallo, Auxo, and Hegemone.

Then began an intensive military training lasting for two years. The first year was occupied by considerable time in guard duty in and about Athens and, at the same time, practicing warlike exercises and sham battles. At the end of the year a great exhibition in athletic and military sports was held. The second year was spent in more training and actual military service in some outlying province. If no war was in progress the young man was freed at the end of his training and might become a philosopher, poet, dramatist, historian, sculptor, merchant, politician, or any one of the many callings to which the cosmopolitan life of Athens invited one. But whether he specialized in any one activity or not he remained always a gymnast; for gymnastics meant pleasure, sport, health, a handsome body, amusement, social intercourse, moral training and complete development, and even honor and fame.

This compulsory ephebic training as designed by the state indicated a lack of faith in the previous method of developing strength and loyalty through individual freedom, creativeness, and voluntary choice. This preparation became a paternalistic state effort to insure military security and efficiency.

Importance of the Gymnasia

To serve the men of Athens the three great gymnasia, the Academy, the Lyceum, and the Cynasargus were established and maintained by the state. The earliest gymnasium was merely an athletic field usually located near a stream. When buildings were needed the architectural form resembled that of the *palestra,* and the hollow square building in a gymnasium is frequently called a *palestra.* The information concerning the arrangements of these Athenian gymnasia is very scanty; there is just an allusion to them here and there in the literature. The excavations at Delphi and Olympia tell more about the gymnasia of those cities.

The Lyceum building consisted of the great hollow-squared *palestra.* Near the entrance was the large undressing room (*apodyterion*). Seats and benches were around the room, and there were hooks on the walls for hanging up clothing. Also some gymnasium equipment was kept in this room: perhaps strigils, halteres, and a discus. Around the inside of the entire structure was a colonnade connecting the different rooms. From the *apodyterion* the athlete might go to the oil room where he or the attendants oiled the body thoroughly. The youth was then ready for exercises or contests. Along one side of the colonnade was a covered running track (*zystos*) suitable for short sprints or running in bad weather. If he chose to wrestle or jump or hurl the discus, opponents could be found in the opening court. If he preferred to exercise alone he might go to the punching bag room where bags of various sizes and weights were suspended. Outside the *palestra* young men engaged in long runs and received lessons in riding.

After the youth had finished his exercises he proceeded to the bath. In the gymnasia of the fifth century, the bath was very simple. To remove the oil, perspiration, and perhaps dust, he used a scraper called a strigil. Large tubs and troughs of water were provided from which the athlete washed himself. Some gymnasia seem to have had cold plunge baths. All three Athenian gymnasia were on small streams where plenty of water was available. After dressing, the youth had, as further recreation, walks along the river or conversations with poets, authors, and sculptors in or about the gymnasium. The Lyceum was a place of recreation and amusement for the idle youth, a place of training for the gymnast who wished to enter the Pan-Hellenic games, and a place of exercise for the elderly gentlemen who gave thought to their physical welfare.

During the fourth and third centuries B.C. the Greek gymnasia became much more elaborate and magnificent as a result of the increase in wealth and luxury and, later, the Roman influence. Particularly there were added more attendants, beautiful interiors, several bathing pools of various temperatures, rooms for a sport similar to hand ball and other games of recreation, and commodious lounging quarters for poets, philosophers, and musicians. Aristotle conducted his philosophic teachings at the Lyceum, Plato at the Academy; so famous became these gymnasia as intellectual centers that both names have come to refer to places of mental rather than physical culture. The Cynasargus became the home of the Cynic philosophers.

Position of Women

The social position of women in Athens was similar to that in the Oriental nations, one of semiseclusion. Consequently no provision was made for their education. The girl was reared by her mother and nurses in the duties of the housewife. She was taught to spin and weave, sew,

Fig. 2. Scenes from the Greek Pentathlon, 500 B.C. Upper: Discus, javelin, and wrestling events. Center: Discus and javelin events. Lower: A javelin thrower, a jumper, an athlete, and a javelin thrower. Note the picks, disci, strigils, halteres, and javelin thongs.

cook, and care for the home. If she learned to read or write it was only through her mother's teachings. No provision was made for physical education other than the simple games of childhood. Athenians were superior to their warlike neighbors the Spartans in all the arts of peace except in the education and the social position of women.

PAN-HELLENIC GAMES

The individual city-states of Greece celebrated the festivals of the deities in dances, songs, and games. Among these were the Panathenaea, the Dionysia, and the Eleusinia in honor of Athena, Dionysus, and Demeter respectively. More important than these, however, were the four great Pan-Hellenic festivals, the Olympian, Pythian, Nemean, and Isthmian.

Olympian Games

Olympia, in Elis on the River Alpheus, was a sacred spot where religious ceremonies and athletic contests were given long before the Olympian games were organized. The first recorded Pan-Hellenic celebration at Olympia was held in 776 B.C. and thereafter every fourth year in late summer until abolished by the Roman Emperor Theodosius in 394 A.D. As the games became more and more varied and attracted more visitors and competitors, the site of Olympia became adorned with many magnificent buildings such as the Temple of Zeus, the great stadium, and the *palestra.* Their remains and the descriptions left to us afford means of locating them with accuracy.

Before the festival, heralds journeyed through Greece announcing a sacred truce among all the people, that visitors and contestants might go to and from Olympia unmolested. Zeus, who was being so honored, would punish the one who failed to heed the warning. The entire management was controlled by ten magistrates who lived in Elis. All entrants for the games had to undergo examination; they must be of Greek blood, must never have committed crime, must take an oath to compete fairly, must have been in training for ten months before the games, and the last month must have been spent at Olympia. Ritual and ceremony marked the opening and every important stage of the games. Women were not permitted to be present.

Events. The foot races were among the oldest and most-honored events. The actual distances depended on the length of the stadium. A stade race, one length of the stadium, was about 200 yards, the *diaulos* was double the distance, and the *dolichos* was any number of *stades,* perhaps as many as twenty-four. Boys were not expected to run quite so far; Plato says they should run only one-half the distance of men. Contestants for short runs were divided into heats of about four men each by drawing lots, then the winners of the heats ran to determine the final victor. Races in armor, but without weapons, were introduced in the sixth century, and, after the Persian wars, they became very popular.

The pentathlon consisted of competition in five events—running, jumping, throwing the javelin and the discus, and wrestling—to determine the best all-round gymnast. Jumping, and throwing the javelin and the discus, were practiced very much in the *palestra* and gymnasium and were popular sports throughout Greece, but at Olympia and in other national games they were only a part of the pentathlon. The broad jump and the hop-step-and-jump were the only forms of jumping contested and the latter only rarely. All competitors jumped from the same takeoff into soft, loose ground; the distance was measured with a rod. The jumpers generally used weights of stone or metal called *halteres;* several of them have been found.

Throwing the javelin was one of the most popular and practical sports in Greece. The art was necessary in war and in the hunt, and every boy learned it in the *palestra.* Javelins eight to ten feet long and of varying weights with dull points were used for competition. Thongs were wrapped near the middle, leaving a loop for the fingers. This method of throwing trebled the distance that the javelin might be hurled and imparted a rotary motion to it.

In the original weight-throwing contests, stones and rough pieces of metal were used, but later the object took on the form of the modern discus. The many disci that have been found differ in weight and size, not only because some were for boys but also because different regulations were in force at different times. The discus was hurled without using the modern method of completely turning the body. Music from the flute frequently accompanied both discus and javelin throwing as well as jumping.

Wrestling, one of the most popular sports, was considered the most effective exercise for all-round development. It occurred as a separate event and as a part of the pentathlon. Of the two forms of wrestling, the "upright" and the "ground," the former was more common. The aim was to throw the opponent to the ground without falling with him; it took three falls to make a victory. There were no binding rules on holds, but those that caused torture or permanent injury were not looked upon as fair or sportsmanlike. The Greeks preferred speed, skill, and science to brute strength or foul play. When there were several competitors the modern method of matching by lot and elimination was used. In the *palestra* and gymnasium "ground" wrestling was frequent; the aim was to throw the opponent to the ground and then continue the struggle until he admitted he was beaten.

In boxing events the men were matched as in wrestling. In the place of the modern gloves, the Greeks securely wrapped the fingers, knuckles, wrists, and forearms with thongs of rawhide to protect the hands rather than soften the blow. The blows and parries were very similar to those of today. No ring was provided except insofar as the spectators formed one, there were no rounds; the fight went on until one was knocked out or until they rested by mutual consent. Boxers were not ranked or matched according to weights.

In the seventh century B.C. a combination of boxing and wrestling called the *pankration* was added to the events at Olympia. It was a free fight with hands unbound and all the tricks of both sports permitted: hitting, kicking, twisting of limbs, and strangling. Biting and gouging alone were forbidden. The fight continued until one contestant admitted he was defeated. Toward the period of the decline of Greek athletics, the *pankration* for boys was introduced.

Horse racing, both with chariots and with jockeys, found place in the Olympian games in the seventh century B.C., and, although they were very exciting, they did not harmonize with the aim and purpose of gymnastics and national games and were not permitted to overshadow the importance or detract from the honor of winning in the more athletic events. Contests for heralds and trumpeters were also held at Olympia. Originally all contests were finished in one day, but as the number of events and contestants increased five days were found necessary.

Rewards. The victor in any event at Olympia received both a crown of wild olive branches which had been cut from a sacred grove and a palm branch as a token of victory. He was honored in the celebrations and banqueting at Olympia, and his journey home was a triumphal procession. Frequently a city whose son had been victorious made a breach in the walls, so that he might not have to enter by the common path. His fame spread throughout Greece; sculptors carved his figure in stone, and poets wrote odes commemorating his achievements. The Greeks could name the victors of the various events for several years previous; it was common practice to recall an event to another by saying it was so many years after so and so won the pankration or the diaulos.

Training of Contestants. In the earliest times scientific training for athletics was not known, and the Spartans, because of their severe military training, won most of the prizes; but when contestants from other parts of Greece began practicing under scientific trainers, the Spartans, who continued to hold to military rather than athletic training, fell behind. The Athenian boy learned all the events and the proper forms of executing them in the *palestra.* If he excelled there, he continued his training in the gymnasia under skilled and scientific tutors, many of whom had been victors in the games. Exercises, such as punching the bag, shadow boxing, and dancing, were considered good training methods for the boxers; digging in the ground with a pick and jumping was recommended for wrestlers; using the halteres as dumbbells was encouraged for both boxers and wrestlers; the runners practiced in deep sand. Some thought was given to dieting.

Other Pan-Hellenic Festivals

The Pythian games were given in honor of Apollo near his shrine at Delphi, in the third year after every Olympian meet. In addition to the usual athletic sports and chariot races, competitions in the flute and lyre and in musical composition were held. The highest reward was a crown of bay leaves plucked from a sacred valley.

The Nemean games were held in Argolis in honor of Zeus in the early part of every second summer. The events were almost the same as those at Olympia. A crown of fresh parsley was the reward.

The Isthmian games, in honor of Poseidon, were given on the Isthmus of Corinth in the spring of every second year; wreaths of dry parsley leaves were given the winners. These four Pan-Hellenic gatherings never coincided but frequently came very close together.

Decline of the Games

During the second century B.C. a marked decline in Greek physical education is noticeable. The conquering Romans did not enjoy or have much respect for strictly athletic or gymnastic contests, and the Greeks were unable to maintain a national enthusiasm for them. The old gymnastics which aimed at complete development, exemplified in the pentathlon winners, gave way to athletics which implied prize-winning professionals who trained for one event only. The more exciting and brutal events such as chariot races, boxing, and the pankration became the most popular. The boxers fastened lead and iron pieces to the thongs which were wrapped about their fists, and science gave way to brute strength. The best people of Greece did not enter the games. Corruption and bribery were common. The officials at Olympia held out determinedly against this destructive influence, but they could not remain entirely free from it.

Fig. 3. The Pankration. One attempts to gouge the other's eye and receives a beating from the trainer. (From a kylix, British Museum.)

In effect, professionalism destroyed the original concepts of physical education in Athens. Athletics which were carried to the extreme encouraged specialization in one sport, hero-worship, winning at all costs, large audiences, and the like. Trainers, often ex-athletes, trained their protégés to such an extent that amateurs experienced little or no success in competing against them. On the other hand, professionals often bought their victories and did not have to trust to superior physical strength and skill in order to win. These evils became so common that offenders were fined and punished, but nothing seemed to stem the tide.

Dance and Ball Games

The Athenians esteemed the dance almost wholly for its esthetic values and religious expression. In earliest times the gods were worshiped by large groups of dancers, including men of noble rank. The dances were very simple, but from them evolved the more complicated Dionysaic or Bacchic, which required a trained chorus. Nearly every dramatic production demanded the presence of a chorus of singers and dancers who, in the absence of scenery, gave the setting the proper atmosphere. The Pyrrhic was also danced in Athens by the Ephebi. Frequently professional dancers, girls and men, entertained the guests at the symposium or drinking bout.

The games that served as a means of physical education and recreation were all played with balls. The Greeks played a game very much like hockey. Another game, called episkuros, in which a large ball was kicked about, accounts for the statement that the Greeks played football.

THEORIES OF PROMINENT MEN

Any activity as popular as gymnastics would be sure to draw from the greatest minds opinions concerning its aims, values and theories. Xenophon reports Socrates as saying, "No citizen has a right to be an amateur in the matter of physical training; it is a part of his profession as a citizen to keep himself in good condition, ready to serve his state at a moment's notice. Finally what a disgrace it is for a man to grow old without ever seeing the beauty and strength of which his body is capable . . . And in all the uses of the body it is of great importance to be in as high a state of physical efficiency as possible. Why even in the process of thinking, in which the use of the body seems to be reduced to a minimum, it is a matter of common knowledge that grave mistakes may often be traced to bad health" (*Memorabila* III–12).

Plato is said to have been nicknamed by his wrestling teacher because of his very broad shoulders. He, in all his writings, advocates physical training for its educational and military values but deplores every tendency toward professionalism and competitions for the purpose of amusing an audience. In his *Protagoras*, speaking of children, he wrote, "Then they send them to the master of Gymnastic, in order that the bodies may better minister to the virtuous mind, and that they may not be compelled through bodily weakness to play the coward in war or on any other occasion." In Book III of his famous *Republic* are found the following ideas: "Gymnastic as well as music should receive careful attention in childhood and continue through life. . . . Now my belief is not that the good body improves the soul but that the good soul improves the body. . . . Gymnastics will incline him to have as little as possible to do with medicine. . . . I believe that the teachers of both (music and gymnastics) have in view chiefly the improvement of the soul."

Plutarch, the biographer and historian, in his *Morals* says, "In the next place the exercise of the body must not be neglected; but children must be sent to schools of gymnastics. This will conduce partly to a more handsome carriage and partly to the improvement of their strength. For the foundation of a vigorous old age is a good constitution of the body in childhood."

Euripides, although not entirely opposed to gymnastics, rebukes the nation for worshiping the athletes because of their victories. "Of all the countless evils through Hellas, there is none worse than the race of Athletes. . . . Whoever helped his fatherland by winning a crown for wrestling or for speed of foot, or hurling the discus or striking a good blow on the jaw? Will they fight the foe with disci in their hands or driving their fists through the foemen's shields?" (Fragment of the play, *Autolycus.*)

Aristotle thought that "the education of the body must precede that of the intellect, it clearly follows that we must surrender our children in the first instance to gymnastic and the art of the trainer. . . . Up to the age of puberty gymnastic exercises of a comparatively light kind should be applied, with a prohibition of hard diet and compulsory exercises, so that there may be no impediment to the growth."

Hippocrates and Galen wrote on the values of physical training and advised their patients to take exercises in the gymnasia as a means of recovering from ills and weaknesses. Galen said, "He is the best physician who is the best teacher of gymnastics." Medical gymnastics and massage were known to both Greeks and Romans. Hippocrates asserted that "friction (may) be so violent that the body is made hard; so light that it is relaxed; so long-continued that it is decreased; so moderate that it is rounded."

THE GREEK IDEAL

The Greek military, educational, and religious system promoted and strove for the physical perfection of its people. This ideal influenced every form of art and achievement. The finest odes from Pindar and Bacchylides are inspired by the victors of the games. A part of Pindar's *Seventh Olympian Ode* in honor of Diagoras of Rhodes, who won the boxing match at Olympia in 404 B.C., translated into prose, runs as follows:

> Of garlands from these games hath Diagoras twice won him crowns, and four times he had good luck at famous Isthmus, and twice following at Nemea and twice at rocky Athens and at Argos the bronze shield knoweth him and the deeds of Arcadia, and of Thebes and the yearly games Boeotian and Pellene and Aigina where six times he won; and the pillar of stone at Megara hath the same tale to tell.

The gods alone rivaled athletes as subjects for the Greek sculptors. Naked contestants offered the carvers of stone an opportunity to study nearly perfect human forms in action; the result was that their chisels produced that unexcelled if not unequaled statuary of all time. A great part of the knowledge concerning Greek athletics stems from the vase painter, who so universally used the scenes of the *palestra* and gymnasium and of the games as a means of decoration. In coin designs the athletes frequently displaced the statesmen and the gods. True Greek gymnastics, exemplified especially in Athens, discouraged professionalism, brutality, and excitement, and encouraged complete development of the individual, fair play, and nation-wide physical education for esthetic as well as utilitarian reasons. High ideals and noble objectives characterized the golden age of Greek gymnastics.

3

The Romans

Near the end of the Homeric Age of Greek history a small settlement of sturdy shepherds and shrewd traders gathered near the famous seven hills on the banks of the Tiber. They were industrious, frugal, and earnest; they were practical in their view of life, stern in dealing with their fellowmen, reverent to their gods, and patriotic to their state. This small political unit of Latium extended its reign to eventually unite the entire Italian peninsula. The Roman Republic slowly gave the people more rights in return for military service. Emphasis on war and conquest led to placing great stress on physical vigor and relatively less concern for intellectualism.

EARLY PERIOD

The Roman father had undisputed control over his children and his wife. Disrespect might be punished severely and disobedience with slavery or death, but such measures were seldom necessary. The Roman matron was charged with rearing the children; she was honored and respected and given more freedom than were Greek women, excepting the Spartans. These people seem to have come to the idea very early that some day their city would rule the world. The first duty of the family was to serve the nation and to that end rear robust children with true Roman ideals. Since there were no schools, the homes were expected to give both moral and physical training, and no homes ever discharged their duties more faithfully or more successfully. The parents in their daily and hourly contact with their children instilled in them pride of race, obedience, honesty, courage, industry, loyalty to the state, and reverence for the gods and the ancestors.

The Roman child, like the modern one, had his cart, tops, hoops, stilts, balls, and pets. The people were warlike and ambitious, and physical training was regarded as necessary to every Roman. The father, who was usually a soldier, was charged with the duty of training his son. The aim of physical training was to produce strength, agility, endurance, hardiness, and skill in the use of sword, spear, shield, and javelin, and in horsemanship and swimming. The Greek idea of gymnastics for grace, beauty, carriage, symmetry, or complete development of man could not have been understood by these early Romans. Virgil says (*Aeneid* IX–603), "We carry our children to the icy streams and harden them in the bitter icy waters; as boys they spend wakeful nights over the chase, and tire out the whirlwind, but in manhood, unwearied by toil and trained to poverty, they subdue the soil with their mattocks, or shake towns in war." In their play, boys competed with each other in swimming, wrestling, boxing, running, and jumping, although there was no *palestra* as in Athens. Ball games of many varieties were played by the early Romans. Throwing, catching, and juggling various sized balls was common practice, while a game similar to handball was popular. Many other ball games were also played, some being very vigorous and rough. Dancing was restricted to the royal families, religious ceremonies, funeral processions, and other public events.

The *Twelve Tables,* written in 450 B.C., summed up the social, political, and religious customs and ideals of Rome and made them the laws of the land. From that time, both in the home and in the schools, the tables became the basis for literary and moral instruction; all children memorized them.

Between the fourteenth and seventeenth year the boy laid aside the toga praetexta and other insignia of childhood. With ceremony and rejoicing he dressed in the toga virilis, and his name was inscribed as a citizen of Rome. He was then subject to service in the army.

The Campus Martius, a field dedicated to the god of war, Mars, lay outside the Servian walls. It was, first of all, a military parade ground and a training camp for soldiers. Male citizens, between the ages of seventeen and forty-seven, might be drafted into the army when needed and discharged when the war was over. Military training was very severe, and the discipline was strict. There were exercises in running, jumping, wrestling, riding, swimming (both naked and in armor), and sham battles. Wooden horses were used to train the recruit in leaping on and off the horse. They practiced long marches with heavy equipment, including intrenching tools, shield, helmet, sword, spear, breastplate, stakes for palisade, and food for seventeen days.

The Campus Martius served also as a resort for young men not in service. Here on any afternoon they competed with each other in the ordinary athletics, swimming, and games. Since boxing, running, jumping, and wrestling were not ends in themselves with the Romans, they never attained the skill and technique of the Greeks.

PERIOD OF EXPANSION

Rome owed her success in war to the moral and physical training of her youth. By 265 B.C. almost all Italy had submitted to Roman power, and by the end of the next century, Carthage, Spain, the Mediterranean islands, a part of Gaul, Greece, and Asia Minor lay prostrate before the conquering armies. By 31 B.C., which marks the end of the Republic, the whole of the Mediterranean world was governed by Rome and for Rome. These conquests had an important and marked influence on Roman civilization. Contact with older and more advanced nations gave the conquerors greater breadth of mind and opened the way for alteration if not destruction of old Roman ideals. Wealth displaced poverty; luxurious habits took the place of simple living; thousands of slaves, sent back by the armies, degraded free labor; cheap grain from Sicily and Africa compelled the Italian peasant to give up his farm and move to the capital, where he and others of his kind formed the idle and dangerous mob. The prolonged campaigns tended to develop a professional standing army rather than a citizen army.

Recognition of the Value of Schools

As Rome evolved into a world power and came in contact with nations of superior intellectual attainments, the need arose for schools to produce statesmen and orators; so the homes surrendered the duty of training the youth to these institutions and to the slave pedagogue. Elementary schools taught reading, writing, and calculation; grammar schools taught the literature of Rome and Greece as well as the Greek language; and schools of rhetoric gave instruction in oratory, composition, law, and other high subjects. Although the organization, the methods, and even the teachers and pedagogues were Greek, the Romans failed to accept the Greek idea that gymnastics and music were essential to a complete system of education. The Roman was too practical to see any value in music; and as for gymnastics, its real value was thought to be military. An ability to swim, however, was considered essential to every Roman. Complete ignorance was often expressed by the adage, "He has neither learned to read nor to swim."

Effect of Moral Decline

Toward the end of the Empire, the rich lived not only wantonly, but luxuriously. On the other hand, the contented small landowner of previous days faced both economic and political deprivations. The directions that both classes began to take marked the first steps toward undermining the patriotic and self-sacrificing attitudes of earlier days. This trend, in turn, caused many undesirable factors to arise, such as political corruption, a judiciary open to bribery, loss of civil freedom, emperors of a severe, despotic nature, and the like. An accompanying decline of the birth rate, increased divorce, and a loss of religious influence weakened the Roman Empire even when it was the great world power.

Rise of Games of Circus and Amphitheater

The growth of luxury, demands for intellectual training, and establishment of the professional army tended to destroy the slight favor which the Roman masses had shown for physical training. At the same time national sports arose, such as the games of the circus and of the amphitheater, which contributed nothing to the physical development of the nation. Conversely, these activities proved of great danger to the life and limb of the participants and of debasing influence on the audience.

The Circus Maximus was about 2,000 feet long and 600 feet wide and accommodated approximately 200,000 spectators. In the arena was a low wall called the spina around which charioteers raced. There were, as a rule, four horses to each chariot and eight chariots to the heat. Entrants lined up about 400 feet from the end of the spina in an arc so that all were equidistant from the end. At a given signal all dashed for the end of the spina to secure the inside position. The race was not fast, but very dangerous and exciting. The sharp turns at the ends of the spina afforded the collisions and overturned chariots which the audience came to witness. These hazards required caution, daring, and skill of the drivers. The races varied from two to four miles. There were no penalties for fouls; driving against another chariot, tripping the horses, and all kinds of trickery were encouraged. There were few races without casualties or deaths. The audience wagered large stakes on the success of their favorite driver or teams.

Gladiatorial exhibitions proved even more debasing and destructive of true sportsmanship. Here slaves and ruffians, trained for the purpose, fought their opponents, either man or beast, until death decided the issue. The emperors searched constantly for new methods of fighting, strange combats, and new varieties of wild animals, for the populace soon tired of the ordinary struggle between two soldiers. Men by the tens and hundreds were pitted against each other; authentic accounts state that the arena was often flooded and naval battles were staged, in which hundreds lost their lives. Training schools for gladiators have been found at Capua and Pompeii, consisting of a square field enclosed by buildings which contained trainer's quarters, kitchen, mess hall, property room, sleeping room, and guard house. The field was used for the exercises and combats.

The gladiator and the race driver (auriga) were idols of the populace and, in the decadent period of Rome, were honored by all classes. If they were slaves, they finally gained their freedom; if free, they received substantial rewards in money. Diocles, a Spaniard, entered 4,257 races, was victorious in 1,462 and won the equivalent of $1,800,000 in twenty-four years.

Importance of the Thermae

In early times, Romans were content with the sponge bath, usually cold, or a plunge in the Tiber for hygienic and disciplinary purposes. With the increase of wealth and luxury, the government built the most magnificent public baths ever erected. At one time there were about 700 government baths. Some, much larger and finer than others and usually called thermae, had arrangements for both recreation and social intercourse. The Therma of Diocletian accommodated about 1,600 bathers at one time and that of Caracalla about 3,200. These institutions are similar to the late Greek gymnasia except that more space was given to bathing and less to gymnastic facilities and they were more luxurious. Bathing privileges were usually free to all, but at times an admittance fee of less than one cent was charged. One of the best preserved thermae is in the city of Pompeii.

There were separate apartments provided for men and women. Near the entrance was the apodyterium or undressing room; pegs were in the wall on which to hang clothing, or slaves were present to care for it. A *palestra* with a field open to the sky was incorporated in the therma. Here exercises and competitions of a light nature were engaged in to heighten the enjoyment of the bath and the evening meal. A spheristerium was provided where balls of various sizes and weights were tossed about for recreation and amusement. At least one therma has remains of what appears to be a bowling alley. The unctorium was the room where the body might be oiled before the exercises and anointed after the bath. In the frigidarium was the cold bath with pool and basins. The tepidarium was a very warm room, sometimes without any water, where perspiration might be induced and where one might accustom himself to the heat before entering the still warmer caldarium. The caldarium was usually the hottest room in most of the baths, but some had the sudatorium in which the water was almost to the boiling point. After the hot bath the bather returned to the tepidarium and cooled slowly, then used the strigil and towels to remove the perspiration. From there he went to the unctorium for ointment and perfumes. He might then dress and stroll about the corridors or gardens with friends, or he might seek the company of a poet, musician, philosopher, or a politician.

Roman Influence on Gymnastics

It has been stated before that the conquest of Greece by the Romans had a bad influence on the Pan-Hellenic games. Unable to value gymnastics as a means of attaining beauty, symmetry of body, grace, complete development and harmony of body and soul, the conquerors hastened the decay of the games, which had already begun under the later Greeks. Professionalism was encouraged, the more brutal and exciting sports came to be the most popular, money was given as prizes, and corruption and bribery followed. The games ceased to have any connection with general education; the moral values to be derived from friendly competitions disappeared.

The first exhibition of Greek athletics occurred in Rome in 186 B.C., but they did not prove popular. In the first century A.D., Nero built a gymnasium and instituted the Neronia games in which athletics had a part. Domitian, a few decades after that, built a magnificent stadium in the Campus Martius for athletics. The Olympiads were abolished in A.D. 394 by the Roman Emperor Theodosius, and physical training was no longer compulsory. All writings about these institutions are in the Greek language, and the athletes and trainers were Greek. Romans were the spectators, many of whom attended the games merely from curiosity to see the foreigners engage in their exhibitions.

Dance and Ball Games

In ancient times the sons of the proudest families of Rome practiced religious and military dances in public. But in the time of the Republic it became a disgrace for a man to dance on any occasion. In the times of the Empire some emperors introduced the Pyrrhic dance, usually executed by Greeks or children, for the amusement of the Roman populace. At the sumptuous Roman banquets the guests were entertained by professional and slave dancers, usually girls. In the theatres the pantomimic dancing which interpreted the love stories of the gods was enjoyed by all.

The Romans, like the Greeks, played a game resembling hockey as well as harpastum, which was similar to soccer. Another game of throwing two balls at one time to an opponent who was supposed to catch both of them was popular. Many private homes and the thermae were provided with handball courts; the game was played according to rules which were similar to modern rules.

II

PHYSICAL EDUCATION FROM THE TEUTONIC INVASIONS TO THE PRESENT

4

The Dark Ages

Every phase of Roman society experienced a decay during the fourth and fifth centuries A.D. until the fall of the Roman Empire in the West in A.D. 476.

One of the many causes of the fall of Rome was depopulation. The numerous divorces, the few marriages, the low birth rate, and loss of manpower through incessant civil wars and gladiatorial games, as well as through suicide and homicide, tended to produce race suicide. A no less important cause was economic ruin. The decreasing number from whom taxes might be collected, the extravagance of the rich, the habit of giving grain to the populace, which not only wasted the public funds but also encouraged pauperism, the slave system which exterminated free labor—all contributed to the ruin of Rome's financial and industrial stability.

Finally, the eventual and almost complete moral and physical decay of the Romans was a contributing factor in the ultimate overthrow of Rome as an empire. The last decades of Roman history offer unequaled scenes of private and public extravagance and debauchery. From the emperor's court to the rabble, sensual excess seemed to be the aim of existence. The cry of the mob was for "bread and games," both of which were freely given. The period is memorable for its political corruption and dishonesty, and embezzlement of public funds. As one writer of the times said, "Virtue is the sentence of death." In early times the Romans had believed that virtue was the greatest and most valued thing in life. In the later era the moral and physical condition of the Romans changed. The long war tended to exterminate the vigorous, hardy, self-reliant young men who formed the early armies; those who were spared frequently fell victim to luxurious living and effeminate manners. As the Empire approached its final collapse, the young men, who should have borne arms in defense of the country, were enervated by luxury, wrecked physically by excesses, and frequently self-mutilated so that they might escape the rigorous discipline and the dangers of war.

SIGNIFICANCE OF THE TEUTONIC INVASIONS

Into this decaying Empire there migrated whole nations of Teutonic barbarians from Northern Europe. Through several centuries the Romans had met them in occasional wars and always managed to retain the Rhine and the Danube as the northern frontier, but they had never succeeded in conquering all Germany. In A.D. 376 the Visigoths began their successful invasion, and historians usually agree that A.D. 476 marks the end of the Roman Empire in the West. During that century the Visigoths occupied Spain, the Vandals seized Northern Africa, the Franks and Burgundians captured and settled in Gaul, the Angles and Saxons took Britain and the Ostrogoths occupied Italy itself.

The immediate result of the introduction of millions of victorious barbarians into a weakened though highly civilized nation was to produce the "Dark Ages." Literature and learning ceased to advance and, indeed, were only preserved in Europe by those who controlled organized monasteries. Bridges, roads, harbors, and even public buildings were neglected. Centralized government was destroyed; all great achievements of the ancients were endangered. Civilization has never before—nor has it since—experienced such a lapse.

Subsequent history demonstrated that the barbarian invasion of the Roman Empire was a fortunate thing for the world. What then was their contribution to the world's progress? Simply their own bodies. Mentally they were barbarians, but capable of assimilating a part of the conquered Roman civilization and ultimately progressing far beyond that civilization. Physically they were a young, vigorous, and stalwart race; the large families of sturdy children reveal their virility. Their simple but active life produced a race of giants in comparison to the Romans. The barbarian family, held together by almost unbreakable marriage bonds, lived in a rude log hut with thatched roof. Skins of animals and crudely woven cloth served as garments and provided the only protection against the disagreeable mists and cold winds of the forest. Herding cattle and sheep and primitive farming constituted the principal occupations. Hospitable to strangers but cruel to his enemies, loyal to his comrades, reckless in battle, he was a true barbarian unbridled and free.

This rugged people by their mode of living provided a rigorous training of the young. Boys learned early how to hunt, and the use of weapons became a part of their daily instructions. In addition, hawking, foot racing, wrestling, throwing spears and knives, ball games, and other physical activities were practiced. The endurance, strength, and skill required of their physical education fit readily into the vigorous life which these people led.

The world needed a young stock of humanity to replace that of the Romans. Although it took centuries for the Teuton to rise to the cultural level of the Roman and Greek, the newly reconstructed society rested on firm foundations; namely, that of strong, virile physiques, the broad shoulders and strong constitutions of the Teutonic invaders. The greatest civilized nations of the world today are partly or entirely their descendants.

INFLUENCE OF EARLY CHRISTIAN IDEALS

In the midst of the dissolute and immoral society of the declining years of pagan Rome was molded the theology and organization of the new religion of Christianity. Converts to the faith refrained not only from worshiping the gods of Rome but also from heaping adoration upon the emperor; they did not attend the games of the circus and the amphitheater or enjoy the luxuries of the bath; morally, they would not fight in the army. On the other hand, they must, if need be, die for their leader Jesus Christ. Because the new sect set itself off from Roman society, its members were misunderstood and despised by many and soon marked for persecution.

The revolting social evils and the persecutions, combined with a firm belief in the immediate return of Christ, gave rise to the doctrine that worldly and material things were not of God. The great emphasis which Christianity placed on the reward of eternal happiness in the hereafter minimized the importance of pleasure or social position in this worldly existence. The joy with which the martyrs died revealed that fact. If life for its own sake is not worth living but merely a time to prepare for the next world, all human culture is folly and one's life should be spent in prayer, penance, and meditation. The pagan Greeks and Romans promoted art, architecture, literature, and philosophy and sought the development and perfection of both mental and physical powers, but a Christian might endanger his soul in such worthless and foolish pastimes.

What is the status of physical education in a society with these doctrines and ideals? God deals with souls, not bodies. The degenerate Romans cater to their bodies; they wash them and ornament them; their every thought is of the sensual pleasure they derive from them. But bodies are mortal; the soul is immortal. The early Christian was concerned about his soul, not his body. The Greek theory that body and soul harmonize almost into unity was challenged by the Christian theory that the body was of Satan and the soul of God and therefore antagonistic.

Theodosius, one of the early Christian emperors, abolished the Olympian games in A.D. 394 because they were pagan in their influence. As Christianity triumphed, chariot races and other debasing sports of the Romans came to an end.

When the East, especially Syria and Egypt, accepted Christianity, the idea that all worldly pursuits which gave pleasure were evil fastened itself to the religion and became the basis of asceticism. Asceticism was the highest ideal of medieval Christianity. This ideal originally referred to the discipline and training which an athlete pursues in preparation for a contest. But in religious and modern usage it refers to a subjugation of the flesh with its passions and worldly desires so that the soul may rise unhampered to great spiritual heights. Nearly all Oriental religions have an ascetic phase, and the holiest adherents of the faith are the ascetics.

When it was found difficult to subdue the flesh, it was regarded as insubordinate and to be tortured. It follows, then, that asceticism and physical education in their treatment of the physical man are diametrically opposed. Even dancing, which temporarily was retained as a part of religious ceremonies, later was forbidden because of its worldliness and impiousness. The earliest Christian ascetics were the hermits of Egypt and the Near East, of whom St. Anthony was one of the most famous. In caves and in the desert, these holy men sought refuge from the evils of the world and spent their lives praying, fasting, and meditating on the hereafter. The more fanatical beat themselves until exhausted, burdened themselves with heavy weights or chains, lay constantly on beds of thorns, or sought out other extraordinary forms of torment. For example, St. Simon lived on a tall pillar for twenty years. Hair shirts, which constantly pricked the flesh, were worn by monks in more recent times. In those days uncleanliness was next to godliness, and the ascetics were frequently infested with vermin and often diseased, all of which added to their discomfort. Such treatment of the body, accompanied by incessant brooding and meditation, must surely have deranged minds and opened the way for hallucinations and visions similar to those which many ascetics are reported to have had.

INFLUENCE OF MONASTERIES

In about A.D. 529, St. Benedict organized monasteries in Europe where men who wished to lead a holy life might retire from the world with others who were similarly inclined. Monastic life was regarded as the ideal Christian life in the Middle Ages. The conduct of monks was regulated by detailed rules and enforced by strict discipline. Seven hours each day were devoted to manual labor and two hours to reading and study; time was specified for prayer, meals, and sleep. Manual labor was regarded as a means of subduing the flesh to escape the evils of idleness and thus gave rise to the maxim, "To labor is to pray." A new monastery was frequently situated in a swamp or on mountainous ground so that even greater labor would be required to construct it.

With the overthrow of classical civilization by the barbarians, the monastery, the church, and a few libraries became the sole depositories of learning. Monks rendered great service to subsequent centuries by preserving some classical learning, keeping records of the events of the time, and copying the works of many authors which might otherwise have been lost to modern times. Until the time of the universities, monastery schools and those of the cathedrals, which were usually staffed by monks, were almost the only institutions of learning in the Middle Ages. In these schools, reading, writing, and a meager knowledge of calculation were taught, all of which had a religious aim. In no school of the Middle Ages could physical education have found a place; education, in its aim, method, and content, was dominated by asceticism.

RISE OF MEDIEVAL UNIVERSITIES

In the twelfth century there arose, in some cases from the cathedral schools, a large number of universities. Among the most famous were the universities of Paris, Bologna, and Salerno. These institutions were quite free from civil and ecclesiastical control. Students numbered in the thousands and were of all ages. Many of them begged for a living; others did any work they could find. Many wandered from one university to another. The subjects—grammar, rhetoric, logic, astronomy, mathematics, law, medicine, and theology—were taught by the professors' lectures and debates by the students. All subjects were taught in accordance with, and supplementary to, the theological doctrines of the time.

No place was given for athletic sports or physical education; consequently, much of the students' leisure time was taken up in boisterous pranks, drinking, gambling, carousals, and riots in the town which finally ended in serious fights between "town and gown." These fights became so frequent that the method and place of trial of students came to be specified in the charter of the university. One of the arguments frequently given for the promotion of modern college and high school athletics is that such activities tend to prevent such things as these that happened in the medieval university.

5

The Age of Chivalry

With the invasions of the Teutonic barbarians, centralized government in Europe became impossible. Feudalism arose in its place and provided a social, economic, military, and political system for society. The feudal system grew out of the lawlessness and barbarism of the time. The weak sought the protection of the strong and provided additional strength for the already powerful. The great landed noble became the lord, and those who sought his protection, the vassals. In spite of the teachings of chivalry and the prohibitions of the Church, the mailed fist generally ruled Europe. The lord who had a great following of vassals, sworn to serve him as trained knights, defied the king and usurped royal prerogatives in his immediate locality with impunity. The great mass of landless people sank to the position of serfdom, and, in order that they might have land to till, they pledged to surrender to the lord a part of the product of their labor and to pay certain other dues and penalties. Their lot was to toil, that of the clergy to pray, and that of the nobility to fight, govern, and engage in sports. A feudal army consisted of a lord or several lords, their vassals and their vassals' vassals, and so on but did not include the serfs. Private warfare was so prevalent that the nobles built fortified dwellings, castles with moats, massive walls, and battlements.

The Middle Ages offered only two fields of endeavor to the young nobleman—the church and chivalry. The former required a literary and religious education pursued in the quiet atmosphere of a monastery or cathedral; the latter demanded a physical and military education and training in social conduct, pursued in the active, gay, and pleasurable life of the castles of the high nobles. Needless to say, the great majority chose the training for knighthood. Specific training for war accompanied this program. However, hunting the wild boar or stag, hawking, swimming, wrestling, rope climbing, and horsemanship were engaged in and proved pleasurable as well as good preparation for future combat.

TRAINING FOR KNIGHTHOOD

At the age of seven the noble's son left his father's home to take up residence and begin training as a page in the castle of his father's lord. Here, in company with other boys, he played ball, marbles, seesaw, chess, and, in the later period, tennis. He imitated the active life about him and learned by observation many rudiments of chivalry. The purposive conscious training was in the hands of a lady who took upon herself the responsibilities of training a page. In return for her attention the page devoted himself to her and served her at all times and in all capacities. Under her direction the page learned to sing and to compose songs, to play the harp and dance, to dress properly, to be polite and respectful, to speak correctly in social gatherings, to be tactful, to conduct himself properly at the various important ceremonies and occasions. He was given religious instruction, taught to say prayers, and to revere the Church and its officials.

The page learned his lessons in actual service about the castle. It was his duty to wait on table—to carry in the food and dishes, bring water and towels for the guests, carve the meat, and pour the wine. He was always the errand boy and frequently the messenger of important news. Although the food and bed of the page were rarely different from that of the remainder of the household, it seems that in some localities there prevailed a Spartan attitude toward the page; no doubt, in the main the lot of the varlet was no easy one.

Toward the close of seven years as page, he helped the court in their sports of falconry by scaring up the birds to be chased and carrying extra falcons. He learned to ride, for it might be necessary to send him with messages to the neighboring castles. With the other pages he practiced swimming, running, jumping, fencing, boxing, and climbing around the walls of the castle.

At about fourteen the boy reached the status of squire. He remained attached to his mistress and continued to serve at the table, but more and more emphasis was placed on training for the most important activity of knighthood—fighting. He attached himself to a knight who required him to polish and repair the armor and weapons, care for the horses, and do other general service. In time of war he accompanied his lord, prepared him for battle, and watched him through the fight. If the knight's horse was killed, the squire brought another; if the lance or sword broke, he replaced it; if the knight was captured, the squire attempted a rescue; if he was set upon by more than one opponent at once the squire would join in the fight; if prisoners were taken, the squire guarded them. These responsibilities demanded intensive training.

The squire's spare moments were spent in running long races on foot as a means of procuring endurance, in constructing ladders of crude material and practicing the scaling of walls with them, in scaling walls without ladders, and in swimming with and without armor. Practice in fencing and swordsmanship was engaged in. The most important preparation was for horsemanship and for mounted combat. Mounting and dismounting gracefully, both at a stand and at full gallop, were practiced. To manage the horse, to carry the shield, and to use the various weapons effectively at the same time required years of training. The lance was a long sturdy spear with a thick shaft and an iron point. When this weapon was fixed for action, it projected six or seven feet in front of the horse's head. It took strength of arm and accuracy of aim to ride at full speed and deliver the lance head against a moving opponent. The squires constructed various targets for tilting; the most common was some form of the quintain. It might be a cross with a sandbag on one arm. When the squires struck the target on the other arm the cross turned on a pivot and dealt the attacker a blow with the bag of sand unless he was quick enough to escape it. Other quintains struck back only when they were not hit squarely. Training for accuracy was also secured by thrusting at the ring. In this exercise an iron ring was suspended in the air, and the squires charged at full speed endeavoring to place the lance point through the ring and carry it free from its support. Along with training in the use of the lance came the exercises with the sword, mace, and battle-ax in sham combat both with an opponent and with a dummy. It was also understood that the squire should discipline himself to withstand heat, cold, fatigue, and loss of sleep.

If, at the age of twenty-one, the squire had mastered the arts of chivalry, the ceremonies to create him a knight were arranged. First, he cut off a lock of hair, took a bath of purification, and dressed in pure white. The night preceding the event he spent in prayer, meditation, and fasting before the altar of the chapel, with the new armor and weapons near. At dawn he made confession and took the sacrament. At the appointed hour the court assembled to witness the ceremonies. The squire knelt before the lord to receive the accolade which was bestowed with appropriate words charging him to be a true knight. Then the new knight was assisted into his armor and, last of all, the sword, blest by the priest, was buckled on; then came the exhibition in the courtyard, where he demonstrated that he was worthy to be so honored.

The knight practiced physical exercise neither to attain complete development and establish harmony between body and soul, nor for any other lofty Greek ideal. He had nothing in common with the national patriotism of the Roman; rather, he sought an ability that was to be highly utilitarian and individualistic. The law of the fist necessitated a vigorous training for self-protection and self-preservation. Society and religion approved of the brave and skillful fighting man; the leisure of the nobility made possible the long period of training. Sports served as another incentive to attain a high degree of skill in horsemanship and the use of the weapons.

During the feudal period, physical education was completely divorced from intellectual education. These two disciplines had neither aims nor methods in common. Intellectual education was for the scholar and clergyman, physical education, for the knight. Hygiene and sanitation were never practiced in the castle or hut; consequently, the death rate was extremely high, disease was always prevalent, and epidemics, which decimated a district, were frequent.

IMPORTANCE OF TOURNAMENTS AND JOUSTS

Medieval tournaments served both as training for war and amusement. The joust was an engagement of two knights, tilting with lances; it might be spontaneous, resulting from a chance meeting or a wager, or it might be held in the lists under the regulations of the sport. A tournament was a contest arranged by a king or high noble in which many knights participated to exhibit and be rewarded for chivalric skill and bravery and to provide sociability and amusement.

The place of combat, known as the lists, was an oval-shaped field with seats arranged on each side. The contestants were stationed at the ends. The gay court of ladies, noblemen, and clergy assembled in splendid medieval pomp and pageantry; knights wore a gift-token from their lady-love and fought for her favor as well as for their own honor and fame. Contending knights were prepared for the contest by their squires; lances were tested; and the man and horse were clad in armor. Heralds read the rules of the joust and tournament. No pointed weapons were used. The lance head was blunted; only the broad sword without point was permitted, and the mace and battle-ax might be barred.

If the event was a joust the contending knights placed themselves at opposite ends of the lists, set the lance firmly in position, and, at the blast of the trumpet, amid the cries of their admirers, they dashed forward at full speed, bent low in the saddle, aiming the hard spearhead at the helmet or breastplate of the opposing knight. If both failed to strike their mark, the horses were wheeled about, and another charge followed. If one rammed the other with sufficient force to unhorse him, the former was declared the winner. If during several charges, square hits were made with such force as to break the shafts but neither rider was unhorsed, the one who broke the greater number of shafts was judged the winner. Sometimes the rules prescribed that when one was unhorsed, the other must dismount and continue the combat on foot; since both were encased in armor and pointed weapons were not permitted, the fight continued for a long time without much result unless one had been wounded in the fall or became exhausted.

In a tournament proper, a group of knights galloped from each end of the lists to the middle; each quickly chose an opponent, then turned back to the position to await the signal for the charge. On signal, all dashed forward to attempt to defeat their opponents with one blow; the unhorsed were trampled under foot; those with broken lances drew their swords; those with lances charged again into the melee; furious and unregulated fighting took the field, resulting in many serious wounds and considerable loss of life. When a great tournament ended in more deaths than usual, the church endeavored to end the sport but always failed. Dancing, feasting, and awarding of prizes in the castle ended the day of tournament and joust.

EFFECTS OF METHODS OF WARFARE

In the sixteenth century, the tournament became little more than a grand pageant which served as a pretext to show fine horses and beautiful armor and hold a social gathering. The rules of the game were altered so that it became a safe pastime. The change came partly as a result of new methods of warfare. From the eleventh to the fifteenth century, the cavalry of knights was the best fighting force, but with the increase in the use of missile weapons and the invention of the musket, a serf, so equipped, proved to be a better soldier than a knight. For many reasons feudalism, the age of serfs, nobles, and castles, was past.

Common methods of warfare from the earliest times to the decline of the feudal period demanded, in addition to courage and self-reliance, training in bodily strength, endurance, and skill plus accuracy in thrusting, striking, parrying, and hurling. Conflicts were man to man and hand to hand; the stronger and more skilled won, and the weaker and less skilled met death. The aim of physical education was closely related to self-preservation.

With the invention of missiles and the machinery of war, hand-to-hand combat declined to minor importance; the enemy was now defeated at a distance, and victory depended on the numbers of men, the accuracy of shooting, and the amount of effective machinery of war in action. Death on the battlefield came as a matter of chance rather than as the result of physical weakness. Progress in warfare has led to an increasing divergence in the aims and methods of military training and those of physical training. One draws its objectives from the possibility of war and the other from peaceful society.

6

The Renaissance

The name Renaissance applies to the transitional period in European history between the Middle Ages and modern times. During the fourteenth, fifteenth, and sixteenth centuries, feudalism gave way to monarchy, private warfare to comparative peace, provincialism to nationalism, barter to commerce, ignorance of geography to discovery and exploration, institutionalism to individualism, superstition to investigation, faith to reason, asceticism to esthetics, preparation for the hereafter to enjoyment of the present, otherworldliness to worldliness, and, finally, handwritten manuscripts to printed books. At the same time, a widespread interest in the civilization of Greece and Rome arose. All who were touched with the Renaissance spirit found satisfaction in the study of classic philosophy, literature, and art. This emphasis upon things human rather than divine is called Humanism. The Humanists endeavored to revive and imitate classical literature both as to content and style.

In any society that promotes individualism and recognizes the worth of this life, the care and development of the body assume a place of importance. When the Humanists discovered the civilization of Greece and Rome, they were, of course, struck with the important consideration given to the physical man in these societies; consequently, nearly all Humanist educators wrote on the necessity of physical education.

The Renaissance gave to Europe a system of secondary education, and names for these institutions were taken from the Greeks, for example, the German gymnasium, the French lycée, and the English academy. However, these secondary schools resembled Greek gymnasia only in name.

In effect, the Middle Ages, characterized by rigidity and repressiveness of both body and mind, gave way to a more broad and liberal education. The values of physical exercise and hygiene were highlighted. The racket, bat, club (golf), and other equipment for sports became common. Archery, tennis, golf, fencing, swimming, skating, and a multiplicity of dances were part of the culture. Although later discouraged or banned, such sports as bull-baiting, bear-baiting, cockfighting, and hawking occurred in one or various countries throughout Europe and England. The invention of the printing press and the discussion of gymnastics, sports, and other games in some of the publications tended to encourage wider acceptance and participation in these physical activities.

HUMANIST EDUCATORS AND PHYSICAL EDUCATION

The earliest teachers with Humanist views taught in the schools of northern Italy during the fifteenth century.

Vittorino da Feltre (1378–1446) was called from the University of Padua to the court of the Prince of Mantua to teach children of the nobility. Da Feltre's methods and subject matter were in great contrast to those of the monastic and cathedral schools. The institution lived up to its name, "The Pleasant House," and enrolled forty bright and happy children eager to learn and anxious to please their schoolmaster who, instead of ruling them with fear, lured them to their lessons with kindness and understanding. Da Feltre, first because he was a Humanist and secondly because he was instructing boys who would one day be expected to bear arms, had great regard for health and physical exercise. The children were guarded in their diet and discouraged in the use of artificial heat. Daily exercises regardless of weather conditions were compulsory. In addition to playing the games of childhood, the children learned riding, fencing, archery, and ball playing. Competitions were held, and proficiency was encouraged in wrestling, running, leaping, and swimming. Teachers frequently took the children on long hikes through the country, both for the physical and the educational benefits to be derived from them. Da Feltre's aim in physical education was to discipline the body so that health might ever be present, the rigors of war endured, and weapons handled with good results. However, da Feltre understood that the hours spent in play and in games also served as rest and recreation and tended to promote the learning of other lessons. He was one of the first schoolmasters to discover that ability to learn is partially dependent on physical condition, and except for the Greeks, he was the first to devise special exercises for invalid children. Further, Vittorino emphasized the need not only for small classes but also for shaping the program around the capacities of each individual.

Pietro Vergerio (1349–1428), of Padua and Florence, wrote an educational treatise, *De ingenius moribus,* in which he discussed, first, education for character; second, liberal studies; third, bodily exercises and training in the art of war; and, finally, recreation. A few quotations from his work follow: "But where an active frame is conjoined to a vigorous intellect a true education will aim at the efficient training of both—the Reason that it may wisely control, the Body that it may properly obey. So that if we be involved in arms we may be found ready to defend our right or to strike a blow for honor or power. . . . Now war involves physical endurance as well as military skill." He then says that the boy must "be gradually inured to privations and grave exertion, to enable him to bear strain and hardship when he reaches manhood." Further, the boy should be "exercised in activity and courage by feats of strength or dangers of the field; in endurance by bearing both heat and cold, hunger and thirst. For as luxury enervates mind and body alike, so exertion fortifies both. . . . In choice of bodily exercises those should be adopted which serve to maintain the body in good health and to strengthen the limbs; and thus it will be necessary to consider to some extent the case

Fig. 4. Climbing exercises as illustrated in *De Arte Gymnastica*, by Mercurialis, 1672.

of each individual boy. . . . In childhood much care must be taken lest the growth be hindered, or the nerves of the body be strained by severe exertion; but, as youth develops, this may be slowly increased. The order perhaps to be observed is this; in childhood, learning first; in youth, morals, with physical exercises, varying in degree, for all." Then followed advice on specific training for war. Finally, "But as we are not so constituted that we are able to bestow ourselves all day long upon our ordered tasks, I will now set forth the true place of recreation." Vergerio then denounces "debasing games or such as cannot develop bodily gifts or powers of will." He favors "the sharp exertion of ball-play, the best refreshment alike for jaded spirits and for bodily fatigue."

Pius II, a pope of very marked Humanist ideas, wrote to a young prince concerning education as follows:

> As regards a boy's physical training, we must bear in mind that we aim at implanting habits which will prove beneficial through life. So let him cultivate a certain hardness which rejects excess of sleep and idleness in all its forms. . . . A boy should be taught to hold his head erect, to look straight and fearlessly before him, and to bear himself with dignity whether walking, standing, or sitting. . . . For such physical training not only cultivates grace of attitude, but secures the health play of our bodily organs and establishes the constitution. . . . Games, too, should be encouraged for young children—the ball, the hoop —but these must not be rough and coarse but have in them an element of skill. Such relaxations should form an integral part of each day's occupations if learning is not to be an object of disgust. . . . In respect of eating and drinking the rule of moderation consists in rejecting everything which needlessly taxes the digestion and impairs mental activity. . . . What but disease and decay can result from appetite habitually over-indulged? Such concessions to the flesh stand condemned by all the great spirits of the past.

Three outstanding leaders of the sixteenth century were Sir Thomas Elyot, Roger Ascham, and Hieronymus Mercurialis. Sir Thomas Elyot (1490–1546) was an English Humanist who wrote *The Governor*, a treatise on education. After discussing intellectual and moral education he discourses on recreation. Elyot agreed with all Humanists that the mind and body need recreation and that long hours of study should be broken by play and exercise. He was also aware of the physical benefit to be derived from games and exercises, for example, tennis, fencing, dancing, archery, wrestling, running, riding, swimming, and dumbbells. On the other hand, he questioned the value of football for "gentlemen," and he did not prohibit all forms of dancing. Elyot, however, saw little reason for idleness, and he continually stressed the importance of physical activities, especially those which led to better bodily development.

Roger Ascham (1515–68), an English Humanist and a professor at Cambridge University, wrote *The Schoolmaster*. He advocated a study of the Latin and Greek authors as a means of obtaining a liberal education and recognized the importance of physical education. Ascham urged that young men "engage in all courtly exercises and gentlemanly pastimes. . . . All pastimes joined with labor, used in open place and in daylight, containing either some fit exercise for war or some pleasant pastime for peace, be not only comely and decent but also very necessary for a courtly gentleman to use." Ascham also appreciated the value of exercises as a means of resting the mind that it may be sharper at a later time. "The best wits to learning must need have much recreation and ceasing from their books, or else they mar themselves, when base and dumpish wits can never be hurt by continual study."

Hieronymus Mercurialis (1503–1606), a famous Italian physician, wrote a treatise, *De arte gymnastica,* in which he called the attention of his contemporaries to gymnastics of the ancients. His work was historical and descriptive, and he recommended the revival of the practice of gymnastics for the sake of health and individual welfare.

REFORMERS AND PHYSICAL EDUCATION

When the Humanistic spirit crossed the Alps, the tendency to enjoy life became a desire to seek the meaning of life: education for self-realization became education for social uplift; the study of the classics for pleasure and culture gave way to their examination for the light they might throw on the meaning of the Scriptures; training for good manners and courage became training for piety and character; literary education was replaced by religious education, especially in those countries that experienced a Protestant reformation. In the lands of Luther, Calvin, Zwingli, Knox, and other reformers, emphasis was again placed on the salvation of the soul rather than on the joy of living and preparation for life, but they did not preach salvation through asceticism or even through the Church alone. The reformers taught that the Holy Bible was the only source of religious truth and that one's salvation depended on understanding of and faith in its teaching. To assure this, the Protestant sects were therefore logically compelled to organize schools for boys and girls where at least reading, writing, and religion could be taught. The Reformation may be regarded as the cradle of the elementary school system of Europe which gave the masses an opportunity to gain a basic education. After private tutorial instruction, wealthy youths attended Latin grammar schools, and many progressed onward to the universities. Thus, a dual school organization based on a caste system developed in Europe.

Luther was determined that schools should be established in every Lutheran parish. In his famous "Letter to the Mayors and Aldermen of the Cities of Germany" he outlined the course of study and the methods to be used in these schools. He believed in gymnastic exercises because they were good for both the body and the soul. He said, "It was well considered and arranged by the ancients that the people should practice gymnastics that they might not fall into reveling, unchastity, gluttony, intemperance, and gaming. Therefore, these two exercises and pastimes please me best, namely, music and gymnastics, of which the first drives away all care and melancholy from the heart, and the latter produces elasticity of the body and preserves its health. But the great reason for these pastimes is that the people may not fall into gluttony, licentiousness, and gambling as is the case, alas! in courts and in cities. Thus it goes when such honorable and manly exercises are neglected."

Johannes Bugenhagen and Philip Melanchthon, the great organizers of the Lutheran Reformation, became the founders of the Volksschule and the Gymnasium, respectively. They arranged no place in the course of study for physical education but encouraged games and athletic competitions when time permitted outside of school hours.

Following the models of Melanchthon, Sturm, an early pioneer in German education, organized and named the first German Gymnasium in Strassburg. His school organization remained almost unchanged until modern times. When John Colet organized the Humanistic school of St. Paul in England he formed the model for the English and American grammar schools. All these institutions soon lost their original aim, and the main course of study came to be the languages of Greece and Rome, not the literature or civilization. Instead of giving a liberal education and a preparation for life work, the schools prepared students only for institutions of higher learning. It naturally followed that training of the body was neglected and was not considered of sufficient importance to receive attention in the schools.

7

Realism

The name, "realist," is given to those educators of the later Renaissance period who revolted against the formal drill on Latin and Greek grammar which characterized the secondary schools of Europe after the true spirit of Humanism began to wane. They advocated, instead of the narrow study of Latin and Greek works, a study of the real things of life. The Humanist Realists agreed that art, architecture, medicine, law, mathematics, and agriculture could best be studied through the classic authors; but the classics must be read and studied for their content and not for their style. The Social Realists believed that the aim of education should be to prepare one for a life career. They held that there were many good things in the classics but that not all of the valuable knowledge was contained there; further, that knowledge was not the end of education, but rather that the training of the mind, judgment, and character should be regarded as the true aim. Stress was placed on providing a student opportunities to test and explore so that his judgments would assure him a better way of life. The Sense Realists were influenced by the new discoveries in science and emphasized the fact that nearly all knowldge worth having could best be obtained through the senses—from objects, not words about objects, and from observation and experience. Therefore, sensory training was advocated by this group.

As long as the schools were narrow in their curriculum and emphasized the mastery of classic language and Ciceronian style, and as long as the institution was regarded as a means of preparation for the university or at most a scholarly vocation rather than a preparation for participation in society, little place was to be expected for physical education. But the Realists, who advocated training the individual to meet the conditions of society, could not fail to restore physical training to an important position.

HUMANIST REALISTS

François Rabelais, one of the greatest of French educational theorists of the sixteenth century, wrote a satire on contemporary education and published his own views in a famous book called *The Life of Gargantua*. The hero Gargantua was first subjected to the methods and subject matter of the usual Latin grammar school, and after several years of such training, he "did profit nothing; but, which is worse, grew thereby a fool, a sot, a dolt, and a blockhead." Then an ideal tutor, Ponocrates, was secured, and after Gargantua was given a pill to make him forget all that he had learned, his education began again. Needless to say he studied the content of the classic authors and due care was taken for his physical welfare. Gargantua practiced difficult feats of horsemanship, the wielding of arms, the lance and the battle-ax, throwing the spear, exercises in swordsmanship, and the pastime of hunting. "He played at the great ball and made it bound in the air with both fist and foot. He wrestled, ran, and jumped. . . . He did swim in deep waters on his face, on his back, sidewise, with all his body, with his feet only, and with one hand in the air." He practiced diving "into pits and gulfs. . . . He did cast the dart, throw the bar, put the stone, practice the javelin, the boar-spear, or partizan, and the halbert." In addition to this he shot at targets with the strongest bows and crossbows; climbed ropes and trees and scaled the walls. When weather did not permit these outdoors activities, manual labor was to be provided indoors.

John Milton, the great English poet of the seventeenth century, wrote a "Tractate of Education" in which he set forth the ideas of the Humanist Realists. His famous definition of education, "I call therefore a complete and generous education that which fits man to perform justly, skillfully, and magnanimously all the offices, both private and public, of peace and war," reveals his realism. Milton first found fault with the contemporary education and then set up his own imaginary Academy for "gentlemen's sons" between the ages of twelve and twenty-one. The boys "should divide their day's work into three parts as it lies orderly—their Studies, their Exercises, and their Diet." With regard to the exercises, "therefore about an hour and a half, ere they eat at noon, should be allowed them for exercise and due rest afterwards. . . . The exercise which I commend first is the exact use of their weapon, to guard and to strike safely with edge or point; this will keep them healthy, nimble, strong, and well in breath, is also the likeliest means to make them grow large and tall and to inspire them with a gallant and fearless courage. They must be also practiced in all the locks and grips of wrestling, wherein Englishmen were wont to excel, as need may often be in fight, to tug or grapple and to close." Then while they are "unsweating themselves" he recommends recreation "both with profit and delight" in either playing or listening to the "solemn and divine harmonies of music"; he also advocates such recreation after meals.

At the giving of an alarm, all are called out to military exercises, either on foot or on horse, and are daily trained in the "rudiments of soldiership in all the skill of embattling, marching, encamping, fortifying, besieging, and battering, with all the helps of ancient and modern stratagems, tactics, and warlike maxims."

Like many other educators, Rabelais and Milton had in mind the training of gentlemen's sons only. The former thought solely of the tutorial method; consequently, physical training must be for gentlemanly sports, pastimes, and duties. The days of chivalry were not long past. The gentleman was still recognized as the fighting man and the leader in war; he should have knightly bearing and be ready to preserve his honor in duels if necessary. Milton wrote his tractate in the midst of the civil war between the Royalists and the Parliamentarians; he was partisan to the latter group, and it is likely that the conditions of the time are responsible for the militaristic tinge of his ideas on physical education. Even wrestling is to be taught, because fighting sometimes demands close quarters. The Humanist Realist failed to value play and games as a means of recreation, pleasure, and social training but thought of them as training in skill, alertness, courage, and similar attainments. Every hour of the day should be given up to some exercise or study of utilitarian value and its use must be obvious. The poetic and esthetic nature of Milton is revealed in the advocacy of the music hour; he said that the divine harmonies "have a great power over the dispositions and manners, to smooth and make them gentle." But not even the poet was able to see beauty in the human figure and its motions as the Greeks had done.

SOCIAL REALISTS

Michel de Montaigne, the great French sixteenth-century essayist, wrote *The Education of Children.* Space in this text will not permit an adequate exposition of the excellent educational theories of this writer. Suffice it to say that the modern nations have hardly reached the high level of his ideals, although many of his theories have materialized in recent times. According to Montaigne, boys should be taught to do and to be that which a man ought to do and to be. His education would include training for character, right habits, manners, morals, and he agrees with Cicero that the best of all arts is that of living well. In regard to physical education, he regrets that parents so frequently spoil their children because "it would grieve them to see their children come home from manly exercise, sweaty and dusty, to drink cold water when they are hot, to mount an unruly horse, or to take a foil in hand against a skillful fencer. . . . It is not enough to fortify his soul; you must also make his muscles strong. The mind will be oppressed if not assisted by the body. . . . Now to be inured to labor is to be able to bear pain. . . . Our very exercises and recreations, running, wrestling, dancing, hunting, riding, and fencing will be a part of his study. I would have his manners, behavior, and bearing cultivated at the same time with his mind. It is not the mind, it is not the body we are training; it is the man and we must not divide him into two parts. Plato says we should not fashion one without the other, but make them draw together like two horses harnessed to a coach. By this saying would it not indicate that he would rather give more care to the body, believing that the mind is benefited at the same time? . . . Accustom him to heat and cold, to wind and sun, and to dangers that he ought to despise. Wean him from all effeminacy in eating and drinking, clothes and lodging, that he may not be a gay fellow, a dude, but a hardy, sinewy, and vigorous young man. I have been of this opinion all my life and still hold to it." Montaigne commends Plato for providing recreation for the youths of his city and encouraging them in races, sports, leaping, songs and dances, and "a thousand exercises for both mind and body."

John Locke, the famous physician and educator of the seventeenth century, wrote the treatise, *Some Thoughts Concerning Education.* In this work, Locke gives these aims of education: first, vigor of body; second, virtue in soul; third, knowledge or mental acquisitions. His first concern is for the body, and the opening paragraph of his book is, "A sound mind in a sound body, is a short but full description of a happy state in this world; he that has these two has little more to wish for." Then farther on, "How necessary health is to our business and happiness, and how requisite a strong constitution, able to endure hardships and fatigue, is to one that will make any figure in the world, is too obvious to need any proof. . . . The consideration I shall have here of health, shall not be what a physician ought to do but what the parents should do for the preservation and improvement of a healthy, or at least not sickly constitution in their children." About one third of the book is made up of health rules, each supported by some argument or explanation. Locke advises that children be not too warmly clad, either in winter or summer, wear thin shoes and wash their feet in cold water daily, learn to swim, be in open air as much as possible, and become accustomed to heat and cold, sun and rain, and refrain from the use of tight clothing. Locke cautions against permitting children who are very warm from hard play to sit or lie on the cold ground and to drink cold liquids. Then follows a long discourse on diet, and eating habits, the values and dangers of various foods, value of thorough mastication, and the conclusion that simple foods are the best.

From what has been said it is plain that Locke's road to health and physical welfare is through a hardening and disciplining process; he has much to say about hygiene but little about the value of play. The remainder of his book emphasizes the importance of moral training, and indicates that physical development was of paramount importance in man's total development. Locke seems to be only lukewarm in his attitude toward the training in knightly sports. Horsemanship is of value insofar as it conduces to health and to giving one a firm and graceful seat on the horse. "As to fencing, it seems to me a good exercise to health but dangerous to the life," meaning that it tends to make duels more frequent. In speaking so against the arts of gallantry, he recognizes that he is not in harmony with the traditional view.

Montaigne and Locke had in mind the training of the higher class, largely through tutors. All Social Realists took into account the necessity of health and physical training and realized the tendency of all families of the upper class to pamper and spoil their children. The earlier educators, for example, Montaigne, believed in the knightly sports; the later ones, such as Locke, discouraged them. All believed in rigorous discipline of the body. They, like the Humanist Realists, failed to understand the esthetic and social values of exercise and sports; of course, as long as the child is to be isolated from others by the tutorial system, group competitions and games would be impossible. For the most part the Social Realists had very little immediate influence on the schools of

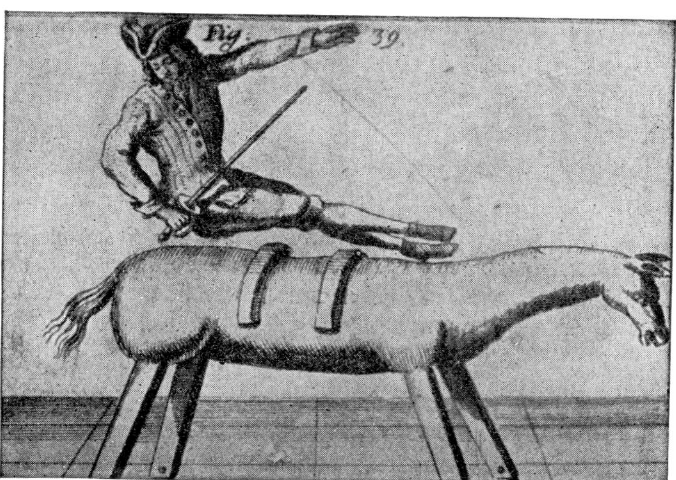

Fig. 5. Vaulting and fencing exercises in a school of arms of the seventeenth century.

the time; however, the Ritterakademieen of Germany and academies in France did provide education for the nobles' sons along the lines advocated. In England instruction was left to the tutors followed by a finishing education in a school of arms on the continent.

SENSE REALISTS

The modern nations in the last few decades have materialized some of the theories and followed some of the practices of the Sense Realists. A few of their beliefs were: all people, both sexes, rich and poor, should receive an education; the true end of education is to develop the faculties of both mind and body; teaching is best done through the senses of seeing and hearing, in short, experiencing rather than reading; to learn the mother tongue is more important than to learn Latin; the teaching process should be adapted to the learner and have a natural procedure; and teachers should be trained for the work of teaching.

The Sense Realists' school was filled with specimens, maps, charts, diagrams, pictures, and attractive textbooks. Because of their many new and radical ideas and methods, the Sense Realists were sometimes called Innovators.

Richard Mulcaster (1530–1611), the famous English schoolmaster of the sixteenth century, was for twenty-six years the head of the Merchant-Taylors school of London. He wrote one of the finest educational treatises of the English language, *Positions wherein those circumstances be examined, which are necessary for the training of children either for skill in their booke, or for health in their bodie.* He is among the first to call attention of the educators from the thing to be learned to the learner, thus laying the foundation for the science of education. There are forty-five so-called positions, and more than half of them deal with physical and moral training through games and exercises. Some of the chapter headings are:

> Of exercises and training of the body. How necessary a thing exercise is. What health is and how it is maintained. What a part exercise playeth in the maintenance of health. Of exercise in general and what it is. And that it is athletic for games, martial for field, and physical for health. Of the particular exercises. Why I do appoint so many and how to judge of them or devise the like. Of dancing. Of wrestling. Of walking. Of running. Of leaping. Of swimming. Of riding. Of hunting. Of shooting. Of the ball. Of the nature and quality of exercise. Of the bodies which are to be exercised. Of exercising places. Of exercising time. Of the manner of exercise. Why the training of the mind and exercising of the body should be assigned to the same teacher.

No writer on education in this period insisted on the importance of physical education more than Richard Mulcaster. He even recognized the importance of good school sites with available sunlight and adequate space for play and exercise.

John Comenius (1592–1671), the great Bohemian educational reformer and schoolmaster of the seventeenth century, is better known today than he was one or two hundred years ago, because only in recent times have his theories and methods been understood and generally accepted. His school attempted to carry out the entire realistic program, giving the pupil an encyclopedic knowledge in an entertaining and natural way. Comenius wrote several texts to be used in the schools; the most famous of his books was the *Great Didactic,* which dealt with both the methods and subject matter for instruction.

As for physical education, Comenius says that gymnastics and games, running, jumping, wrestling, ball playing, and ninepins are to be encouraged. The teacher is to take the pupils on long hikes both for recreation and study. Comenius apparently understood the value of play to children, and he visualized play as a natural and vital medium in which education of the young could be enhanced. He, like Locke and others, believed in physical discipline and simple food. He suggests that the day be divided into three parts, eight hours for sleep, eight for work, and eight for nourishment, recreation, and physical development.

Nearly all Sense Realists, except Mulcaster, believed in universal education, and he too would carry it further than many of his contemporaries. Therefore, to advocate knightly sports as a means of physical development or even recreation would be ridiculous, for the common people could not ape the nobles. Schools of the type of Comenius' could not hire fencing masters, dancing and riding masters, and did not care to do so. Youths who wanted that kind of training would not want to attend schools where the common and the poor might come. Mulcaster's program is not entirely free from knightly education, but Comenius' and later Realists' are entirely so.

The theory of the Sense Realist was that exercise is a means of obtaining and maintaining health, that properly directed play and exercise produces what is modernly called physical fitness; they agree with the Humanists also that exercise serves as a rest from study and ultimately furthers the learning process. Perhaps one of the most important contributions of the Sense Realists was in the methodology of teaching they advocated. Stress was placed on such factors as moving from the simple to the complex, from present knowledge to the unknown; learning should be in proper sequence, and materials should be based on the child's capacity. Such concepts are commonplace today, but they were quite radical in the seventeenth century. Although the principles upon which they based their methods were not substantiated scientifically, many of them have proved sound according to modern psychological findings.

8

The Age of Enlightenment

The eighteenth century was a period of transition to modern political, social, religious, and educational ideals. This transition is perhaps more easily traced in France than in any other country. During the early decades of the century France was governed by an autocratic king surrounded by arrogant, proud, but worthless nobles; the masses were abjectly poor and oppressed; a corrupt but powerful religious system executed heretics and allied itself to the monarchical government. The schoolroom practices were unscientific and actually cruel to the children. The society about the court was artificial and hypocritical: etiquette governed conduct, and punctilious religious observances served to veneer the gross immorality. Before the century was over, the teachings of Voltaire (François Marie Arouet), who attacked the Church and State, and Jean Jacques Rousseau, who denounced the society and education of the time, had been heeded. The activities of these men and their followers, combined with other forces, caused the upheaval known as the French Revolution, which wrecked the entire social structure of Europe beyond repair and led to its rebuilding in the nineteenth century.

ROUSSEAU'S EDUCATIONAL THEORIES

The emotional Rousseau (1712–78) was affected by the social inequality of man and the inhumanity of the upper toward the lower classes. He revolted against the artificiality and hypocrisy of life. He preceded Thomas Jefferson in the idea that all men are created free and equal. He believed that civilization was the cause of all the unhappiness in the world. He wrote *The Social Contract* and stated: "Civilized man is born, lives, and dies in a state of slavery." He advocated a return to nature and natural things. The essence of his teaching is, "All is good as it comes from the hand of the Creator; all degenerates under the hands of man."

Rousseau's *Émile* has had greater influence than any other educational treatise ever written: parliaments condemned it, the Church burned it and ordered its author arrested, philosophers praised it, and educators overlooked its exaggerations and adopted its sound principles. Rousseau condemned the contemporary practices of treating children as adults—dressing them in long, tight clothing and powder, paint, and wigs and compelling them to act as adults. He denounced the school for trying to teach them as though they were grown people and for flogging them when they failed to learn. "Nature wills that they should be children before they are men." Rousseau gives the imaginary boy Émile that which he considers to be an ideal education.

First of all, the boy is isolated from the contaminating influence of civilization by residing in the country. From birth to five years of age, the only concern for Émile is his growth and physical welfare. Accordingly he is placed under simple and healthful conditions; nature working in and through the boy is to have its way, unhampered by man. He is to be taught absolutely nothing. The second part of the book deals with the education or natural growth of the boy from five to twelve. Still no teaching of any kind is to be done, for Émile's nature demands that he continue to exercise his arms and limbs without interference. But at this age he becomes curious and desires to know things, to smell the flowers, to handle the rocks, to study the heavens and he "naturally" learns. "In order to learn to think, we must then exercise our limbs, our senses, and our organs which are the instruments of our intelligence." Émile wears very short, loose, scanty clothing, eats simple foods, accustoms himself to heat and cold; he swims, jumps, leaps over walls, scales cliffs, and grows into a healthy sturdy boy as naturally as he learns about his environment. After the age of twelve, the natural demands for physical activity have somewhat abated, and Émile is about ready to learn his moral and industrial lessons.

No educational theorist had conceived of education of mind and body as being so nearly the same thing as had Rousseau. Others were inclined to split the education of an individual longitudinally into two or more divisions—physical education, intellectual education, and moral education. But Rousseau had the idea of the continual growth of an indivisible entity, from birth until death. This growth might be cut into sections horizontally as nature had decreed. Physical and intellectual education are so intimately bound together that Rousseau found difficulty in determining when an activity ceased to be of physical value and became intellectual.

The following are some quotations from Rousseau's *Émile* which reveal his views on physical education. "The body must needs be vigorous in order to obey the soul; a good servant ought to be robust. The weaker the body the more it commands; the stronger it is the better it obeys. . . . A debilitated body enfeebles the soul. . . . If you would cultivate the intelligence of your pupil, cultivate the power which it is to govern. Give his body continual exercise; make him robust and sound in order to make him wise and reasonable; let him work and move about and run and shout and be continually in motion. . . . It is a very deplorable error to imagine that the exercise of the body is injurious to the operations of the mind; as if these two activities were not to proceed in concert, and the second were not always to direct the first." Rousseau seems to believe that a sound body makes a sound mind. "To spring from one end of the hall to the other, to estimate the bound of a ball still in the air, and to send it back with a strong steady hand, such sports do not befit a man but they serve to train a youth."

Rousseau understood the comparative educational values of different sports. He had little use for doctors, except when death was imminent, for then they could do no harm. "The only useful part of medicine is hygiene; and hygiene is less a science than a virtue." He resembles Locke in his ideas concerning clothing, food, sleep, and the general hardening process. Rousseau commends the writings of Locke and Montaigne on physical education and reflects that the vigor of mind and body of the ancients may be attributed to gymnastic exercises. He recommends games and outdoor activity for girls so that natural growth may produce healthy robust mothers.

During the last quarter of the eighteenth century, many of the theories and doctrines of the early decades were materialized and put into practice. This was particularly true of physical education. The theorists—Humanists, Realists, and Naturalists—had said enough; it was now time for action and practical reform. Since Rousseau's ideas were outlawed in France until after the Revolution, they received more immediate acceptance in Germany.

BASEDOW'S NATURALISTIC SCHOOL

Johann Basedow (1723–90) had been a teacher in a Ritterakademie in Denmark, where he saw students trained in the knightly sports and came to have some ideas of his own on the importance of physical activity. He was planning an educational reform when *Émile* appeared; he then determined to organize a naturalistic school along the lines of Rousseau, incorporating his own ideas. With the aid of the Duke of Anhalt he opened the Philanthropinum in 1774 at Dessau. So far as modern Europe was concerned, this was the first school admitting all classes of people to give gymnastics a place on the daily program. Although many of Basedow's ideas have eventually proved sound, the parents of his day did not accept his new methods of educating children. Because of poor enrollment and other factors he resigned in 1778, but others continued his methods until the school closed in the early 1790's.

Johann Simon was the first teacher of physical education in the Philanthropinum. During one hour of the morning and two hours of the afternoon the entire school engaged in a great variety of games, gymnastic exercises, sports, recreation, and manual labor. Some practiced the knightly sports of dancing, riding, and fencing; others, running, jumping, wrestling, and throwing. Ditches were dug of varying widths to leap across, and high-jump standards were constructed. There were also exercises in balancing as the pupils walked across a ditch on a narrow beam. The children played games, for example, shuttlecock and tennis, under the supervision of the teacher; the hoops and the seesaw were assigned to the younger ones. Later on, Johann DuToit, who succeeded Simon, introduced exercises on the ladders, swimming, skating, and archery. Manual labor—turning, cabinet making, and gardening—were also engaged in. The Philanthropinum won the favorable comment of the greatest men of the time and became the model for many similar schools. Basedow, its founder, is to be regarded and honored as the first modern educator to place physical education in an important position in the school.

Basedow's ideas of physical education were similar to those of Rousseau: nature and natural growth demand that the child be given time for play and bodily exercise; normal physical growth is more important in early years than mental training, and there are intellectual and moral values to be derived from the playing of games. These ideas were put into practice by Simon and his successors at the Philanthropinum.

GUTSMUTHS' INFLUENCE ON PHYSICAL EDUCATION

The Schnepfenthal Educational Institute, organized by Christian Salzmann in 1785, was modeled on the Philanthropinum. Rousseau himself could not have found a more ideal location for a naturalistic school than the Schnepfenthal estate near Gotha. A small court among the trees was prepared for the daily lessons in gymnastics, and Christian André was chosen to direct the exercises. Nearly all exercises that Salzmann had seen at Dessau were reproduced at Schnepfenthal and, in addition, throwing at a target racing up and down hill, and pole-vaulting were practiced. In bad weather there were indoor exercises for correct posture and good carriage, which might be taken as the origin of free exercises. Sunday afternoons were spent in games and gymnastic sports.

Johann Friedrich GutsMuths (1759–1839) succeeded André as teacher of physical education after one year and remained at this school for fifty years. Although GutsMuths was not the first physical education instructor he is regarded—because of his long service and valuable literary contributions—as the real founder of modern physical education and the "grandfather" of German gymnastics. Whenever weather permitted, activities were held outdoors in a field designated as a place for exercise. All exercises used by André were continued. Climbing ropes, masts, and rope ladders, swinging, balancing rods on the fingers, going through exercises while standing on one foot, and a great variety of "stunts" (used perhaps to retain an interest in exercise) were added. Swimming was taught and became one of the most valued exercises. GutsMuths kept an accurate record of the work done by the individual pupils in order to ascertain progress. The students at Schnepfenthal also received a course in manual training and gardening. Long hikes were taken with Salzmann and GutsMuths leading the way; frequently their excursions lasted as many as four days. The school sought to promote the health of pupils by providing light, airy rooms and wholesome but simple food.

GutsMuths' wide influence rests on his two best-known books, *Gymnastics for the Young* and *Games.* These are not only the first manuals published by a practical physical educator but also are of high quality. GutsMuths realized that the theory and practice of gymnastics should be based on a knowledge of physiology and medicine; that games and swimming have a place in a system of gymnastics; that some educational institutions are not aware of the value of gymnastics, and others are not deriving the maximum benefits from the physical exercises; that contemporary educators can learn much from the Greeks and Romans on the subject of complete education; that the nation should promote the physical well-being of its people. He was also aware that if buildings are not suitable for gymnastics, use may be made of the school yards and neighboring fields; that serviceable apparatus may be made by hand; that exercises in practice should be pleasant and enjoyable and have for their aim a strengthening and harmonizing of body and soul, the development of a complete person; that physical perfection produces self-reliance and courage, which every citizen should have; that nature demands that the growth and development of the body must come first, in childhood and boyhood; and that girls and women should engage in light gymnastics and games, but not in the heavy work of men. To look for the means of producing strong healthy girls and women in the doctor's medicine case is ridiculous. He agrees with Rousseau that to be refined and pleasing one need not be weak and sickly.

In addition to these views, GutsMuths classifies various exercises and describes them in detail and gives his ideas concerning the time for their practice. No one since the Greeks had handled the subject of physical education more intelligently either in practice or theory.

GutsMuths' influence was immediate and far reaching. Prominent families urged the tutors to instruct their children in gymnastics; the schools of many localities began to take an unprecedented interest in the work; swimming schools were organized; universities began to consider the value of gymnastics. Not only did this movement occur in the German states but also in Denmark and Sweden. GutsMuths' *Gymnastics for the Young* was printed in Philadelphia in 1802. Jahn, the physical education leader during his era, Spiess, the founder of school gymnastics in Germany, and scores of other prominent men visited his school.

A son of a tanner, GutsMuths not only became a well-educated man but also a real educator. He taught, in addition to physical education, subjects such as geography, French, and technology. However, GutsMuths' first love became physical education and, because of his wide contact with other scholars and his long service, he truly influenced the development of physical education. Had a period of political unrest and

Fig. 6. Jumping and climbing exercises as illustrated in GutsMuths' *Gymnastics for the Young.*

war not interfered, GutsMuths might have secured a prominent place for school gymnastics in general education, long before Spiess accomplished this.

PHYSICIANS' AND PHILOSOPHERS' CONTRIBUTIONS

While educators were coming to realize that physical education ought to be incorporated in the process of general education and that the need for physical welfare is no less important than the need for intellectual attainment, many physicians and writers were helping to mold public opinion in the same direction.

The *Medicina Gymnastica,* written by Francis Fuller (1670–1706), was published in England in 1705. The book dealt with the relation of exercise to disease. When translated into German, this treatise had as much influence in that country as it did in England.

In Germany, Friedrich Hoffmann (1660–1742), Professor of Medicine at the University of Halle, published a series of articles between 1700 and 1720. Among them were "On Motion, the Best Medicine for the Body," "The Incomparable Advantages of Motion and of Bodily exercises, and How They are to be Employed for the Preservation of the Health." These articles influenced GutsMuths some years later.

Johann Peter Frank (1660–1742), in his famous work, *A System for a Complete Medical Police,* by which he meant national policy, condemned the contemporary education for girls because of its seclusion and lack of physical activity. He further objected to the styles which tend to hamper bodily movements. He thought that the youth of Germany did not equal in vigor the youth of ancient Greece, and, therefore, he recommended gymnastics along Greek lines. Frank did not want the exercises to be too strenuous or too dangerous, and he objected to producing "athleten" or rope jumpers or jugglers. He demanded that open air places for gymnastics be provided, first of all for the school children. For inclement weather, a building should be ready for occupancy. He considered physical education a national problem that should be solved by the state.

As the eighteenth century closed, Gerhard Vieth (1763–1836), an expert gymnast and teacher of mathematics at the Haupte Schule in Dessau, was writing his third volume of the *Enzyklopädie der Leibesübungen.* The first volume dealt with the history of physical education, and the second with his own views. He contended that physical exercises promoted health, strengthened muscles, increased suppleness of the body, improved the carriage and physical beauty, stimulated courage and alertness, and "checked a too rapid development and misuse of the sexual instinct." He lamented that so few schools and universities promoted gymnastics among the students, and that they seemed rather to care only for the intellectual attainments.

Simon André Tissot (1728–97), a French physician, wrote *An Essay on Diseases Incident to Literary and Sedentary Persons.* He asserted that the life of the scholar entails much mental but very little bodily activity; consequently, there is no deep breathing, and the lungs always contain foul air. Very little attention is paid to food or drink, and, further, the sedentary life tends to seclude one from active and joyful companions. He recommended several exercises which would bring into play all parts of the body. With regard to children, he felt forcing them into hard study without regard for their physical welfare and growth proved injurious both to their development and health. He believed that girls should receive some kind of gymnastics also.

Clément Joseph Tissot (1750–1826), another French physician, exerted considerable influence in the cause of gymnastics through his work, *Medical and Surgical Gymnastics.* He complained that the gymnastics of his time had degenerated into mere games and pastimes and that the Greek sports were almost never practiced. Tissot discussed the effect of activity on the body and classified the exercises according to the result produced from a medical point of view.

Immanuel Kant (1724–1804), a famous professor of metaphysics and logic at the University of Königsberg, wrote at length on physical education in his *Pedagogy.* He emphasized the disciplinary value of physical education: a strong, sturdy body and a keen, alert, and fearless mind were to result from its practice. Running, jumping, lifting, carrying, throwing at a target, and wrestling were all good exercises in his belief. Many games were to be recommended, but they must have a definite aim. The purpose was to develop a body and mind that would be fit to lead in society. Many of Kant's ideas and statements showed that he was influenced by Rousseau and by the visits which he paid to the Philanthropinum.

PESTALOZZI'S CONTRIBUTION TO PHYSICAL EDUCATION

At the beginning of the nineteenth century the great Swiss educator, Heinrich Pestalozzi (1746–1827) laid the foundation for modern pedagogy. Although influenced by the negative doctrines of Rousseau, he reformed and improved them along positive lines; as he said, he tried to "psychologize" education. This necessitated a study of the child through actual contact and especially a study of the child mind; the resulting knowledge was used as the basis for educational procedures. Pestalozzi compared the child to an unfolding plant and held that the end of education was to assist in the natural, harmonious, and symmetrical development of the mental, moral, and physical powers of the child. The child's part in education was observation, sense perception, and self-activity; the teacher's part was intelligent and sympathetic direction. In effect Pestalozzi considered good education as a method which encouraged natural individual development through concrete experiences. Pestalozzi began his educational efforts among the orphans at Stanz; he then established a model school at Burgdorf and, finally, the institution at Yverdun, which attracted the attention of Europe and America. His school at Burgdorf was provided with separate teachers of singing, geography, history, language, arithmetic, gymnastics, gardening, and manual training.

Pestalozzi's aim and theories demanded that he promote games and physical exercises under the supervision of an instructor in all of his schools. In observing his own child in 1774, he noted that after playing in the open air for a time the boy could then sit and concentrate on his studies for an unusually long period. In addition to this recreational value, he believed that to give vent to the play and competitive instinct was a means of accomplishing the harmonious development of mind, heart, and body. The following ideas, also, are found in Pestalozzi's writings. The strength, skill, endurance, hardihood, and command of the body which are to be derived from physical exercise are desirable and warrant giving physical education an important place in general education. But physical education should not be separate in aims or methods from education in general, for the child is a unity. Nature uses the physical and mental faculties alternately for the development of each other. For example, instinct urges the child to motion, but the exercise may sharpen wits, produce skill and a desire for fair play. To be able to jump is not the only end in the practice of jumping; nor to swim, in the practice of swimming. The school should not neglect this vital principle.

In Pestalozzi's school, at Yverdun in 1807, one hour per day was given to prisoners'-base, ball, and other games, as well as to mountain climbing, skating, jumping, wrestling, and similar activities. Informal play and sport, however, were not sufficient for Pestalozzi; he sought to develop a system of bodily movements arranged according to their difficulty and according to their effect on the body; these were to be practiced under the direction of a teacher. In this work Pestalozzi anticipated the free exercises of Spiess; he had already preceded him in his advocacy of the close relationship that should exist between physical and mental education. Pestalozzi was not an imitator of GutsMuths or Basedow.

Pestalozzi's educational theories are explained in his *Leonard and Gertrude* and *How Gertrude Teaches Her Children*, but his specific views on physical education are found in his article "Concerning Physical Education" published in 1807 and now incorporated in Hirth's *Das Gesamte Turnwesen.*

Phillipp Emenuel von Fellenberg (1771–1844) appropriated the theories of Pestalozzi and developed the industrial phase of education. In his schools the students engaged in shop work, gardening, and various kinds of manual labor. The history of the manual labor school movement which was so popular in the United States in the 1830's traces its origin to these institutions. Fellenberg did not intend that manual labor should be regarded as a substitute for gymnastics; in all his writings he made it clear that systematic physical exercise and games were indispensable as a means of securing a complete education.

FROEBEL'S THEORIES

Friedrich Froebel (1782–1852) ranks with Pestalozzi as a founder of modern pedagogy. His educational experiences at Keilhau and Burgdorf resulted in the theory that education is acquired most efficiently through activity, self-expression, and social participation. Young children, he found, gave vent to self-expression most readily in their play. The kindergarten grew out of these theories, and Froebel presented the first well-organized program of education through play. Froebel's ideas and methods have been elaborated and accepted by the educational world. During the last few decades, volumes of literature on the subject of the educational values of play have appeared, and the world has, in a measure, ratified the theories of Froebel by the adoption of the play movement.

9

Germany Since 1800

The physical education programs in Germany paralleled to a great extent the political patterns of the nation. The leaders in the nineteenth century were Friedrich Ludwig Jahn, who championed liberalism and was most effective in his promotion of the turnverein, Adolph Spiess, who during a more conservative period organized gymnastics for school use, and Hugo Rothstein, who introduced the Swedish Ling system of gymnastics and attempted to impose it on the German army and schools. In the early part of the twentieth century, a reaction against formalism and militarism in the school program motivated the beginnings of the outdoor movement and participation in sports. But these more liberal and informal physical education programs were submerged about 1933 when the National Socialists came to power and imposed a strict militaristic pattern of exercise. After World War II, the pendulum swung back toward a program of sports and activities—this time, however, without political affiliation.

THE TURNVEREIN

The turnverein (German gymnastic societies) originated in the period of turmoil through which Germany passed in the first decade of the nineteenth century, and they are to a great extent the result of the labors of the patriot Friedrich Ludwig Jahn (1778–1852).

Contributions of Jahn to the Program

Jahn, though a Prussian by birth, felt that all Germany was his fatherland, and throughout his life he wrote, spoke, and fought for the political unity of the independent German states. When the citizen army of

Napoleon swept away the feeble resistance offered by the inefficient and unpatriotic professional troops of Prussia at the humiliating battle of Jena, 1806, Jahn learned that radical reforms were necessary before his fatherland could be freed from the French conqueror. He possessed no political or social influence, but was endowed with a rugged constitution, a fighting spirit, and a vision, and he began the tasks of arousing his countrymen to a realization of the disgrace of tolerating the foreign despot and preparing them to escape it when the time was ripe. His first important publication *German Nationality,* called attention to the excellence of German achievements and asserted that the Germans should unite in order to protect them and prevent them from being corrupted by foreign invaders.

In the spring of 1810, Jahn was teaching in Plamann's Boys School and also in the Grauen Kloster in Berlin. Wednesday and Saturday half-holidays were spent with younger pupils out of doors for games and exercises. Occasional expeditions into the surrounding country by teachers and pupils were customary before Jahn came to the Plamann school; he, however, became the most active promoter of these affairs. He met the boys regularly outside the city and went with them in a neighboring hilly and wooded stretch of ground called the Hasenheide. Here they competed in running, jumping, wrestling, and played the games popular at the time. Jahn's enthusiasm, his personality, and his stories increased the popularity of the trips. Crude apparatus was improvised; jumping standards and horizontal bars were constructed. Sometimes the company did not stop for the games but took a long hike through the country singing folksongs and enjoying the stories of Jahn. That winter the outdoor games and trips were discontinued, but Jahn gave some of the boys instruction in crossbow shooting and fencing.

In the spring of 1811, balance beams, vertical ropes, ladders, additional horizontal bars erected between trees and standards for high jumping and pole vaulting, a jumping ditch, and a running track were added to the open turnplatz (exercising ground). The games and exercises now took place four afternoons per week, and frequently as many as two hundred boys and young men were present. Schools other than those with which Jahn was connected were permitting the boys to attend. Jahn adopted a gymnastic costume of long trousers and short linen jacket, which caused no little jesting from the idle and unwelcome onlookers.

There was no program for the day; freedom of action and individual effort was the rule. A boy invented a feat and dared the others to do it. The boys determined the games to be played. Jahn thought that the great values to be derived from this activity were physical power and harmonious cooperation. With these rugged constitutions and just and patriotic minds the fatherland might be freed, then united and made worthy of democratic institutions. When the opportunity arose, Jahn let his charges know of his hopes for Germany's future. In the winter his most enthusiastic pupils continued the exercises indoors and studied the works of GutsMuths.

The year of 1812 was one of still greater success. A more spacious turnplatz was secured, and more apparatus was added, including vaulting bucks and crude parallel bars, which were originally used for exercises preparatory to vaulting. Jahn became more systematic and noted down the various exercises, named them, and described the methods of performance. The number of participants reached five hundred at times; on Sundays and specially appointed days adults were welcomed at the turnplatz. Jahn, unable to oversee and direct the entire group, appointed several leaders, called vorturner, who were to assist him.

The great War of Liberation for Prussia was declared March 17, 1813. Jahn was among the first to volunteer to help free his land from France. During his absence Eiselin managed the turnplatz which was now financed by the government. The battle of Leipzig ended French power in Prussia, and Waterloo ended Napoleon's career in Europe. Soon after his return from war, Jahn published his famous book, *Die Deutsche Turnkunst* (German Gymnastics). This book became the turners' guide throughout Germany.

Jahn began by encouraging schoolboys in the gymnastic exercises and athletic sports. However, his ideas were adopted by those who were past school age, and the turner clubs, which came into existence, were made up of youths and men. Volksturnen (peoples' gymnastics) came to be more widely practiced in Germany than anywhere else. Jahn never lost sight of the fact that the turnplatz and turnhalle (indoor gymnasium) should have an important place near a school or a group of schools and that it is the duty of every city to provide them. Here, on every national holiday, games should be played, gymnastic sports engaged in, and prizes awarded. Only very severe weather should prevent the exercises from taking place outdoors.

Jahn's faith and work in physical education originated from patriotic motives. He believed that the hope of German freedom lay in the development of strong, sturdy, and fearless youths and that the continuance of Germany's greatness rested on the vigorous minds of the next generation. A nation with such people, he thought, would not rest until they had secured unity and constitutional government. He was aware of the great power of games and sports to break down class distinctions and generate social democracy. Jahn differed from John Locke, the English philosopher, on the matter of discipline through physical education. Jahn held that exercise should be regarded as a means of growth and development of political powers rather than as a hardening process, and Locke in no wise arose to Jahn's ideas of the mental and moral training to be received from the turnplatz. Locke believed that the program of physical education should develop a strong constitution, sustain healthful living habits, offer recreational experiences, and develop sport skills essential for a "society gentleman." Jahn held that the turners should eat only simple food and refrain from overindulgence and intemperance. Tobacco and sweetmeats were forbidden near the turnplatz. He was aware of individual differences and did not expect all participants to do all exercises equally well. Jahn's methods were not based on the science of the human body but rather on a faith in physical education as a means of national regeneration. The sciences of anatomy and physiology were not fully understood and could not be applied to physical education.

During practice, Jahn says, the teacher should always be an example to the class. He should forbid bad conduct at the exercising place, be sociable and courteous to all, always be on time, observe all the rules, be enthusiastic about the work, learn the students' characteristics, and become their friend and advisor. When the exercises were to take up an entire afternoon, the participants chose their own activity for the first part; then, after a rest, came the orderly exercises in which all of certain age participated.

Die Deutsche Turnkunst contains a wealth of material on how to choose a location, how to lay out a turnplatz, and what apparatus to make. It describes many exercises, discusses the value and the methods of playing several games, and describes the general management of a turnverein. A large part of the German terminology of physical education originated with Jahn, for example, the word turnen (to practice gymnastics) and its derivatives and combinations.

Many of Jahn's contemporaries, for example, GutsMuths, thought that his ideas of physical education were somewhat narrow in that they were saturated with the patriotic motive; others, that his system was too heavy and difficult for children and defective because it had little or no free exercise and made no provision for the physical education of women. Spiess, of course, objected to Jahn's work on these grounds.

Jahn's gymnastics met with a ready acceptance throughout Germany, and in nearly all of the large cities, young men formed turnvereins using the *Turnkunst* as a guide. Hans Massmann and others who had been associated with Jahn assisted in the organization of these societies. The student clubs (Burschenschaften) whose aims were to unite Germany and secure a free government for the people, promoted the spread of turnen, and in due course their members usually became turners.

Fall of the Turnvereins

Because turnvereins arose in times of political stress, they had for their aims certain political achievements as well as the promotion of physical education. To free the German states from the French was an aim welcomed by kings, nobility, and commons. However, the idea of German unity was met by the kings with hostility and by the nobility with suspicion; to advocate constitutional freedom and government by the people was to tread on dangerous ground. But Jahn believed that all three were necessary to Germany's greatness, and turners in general were known to hold these ideas.

After Germany was freed and peace restored, the statesmen of Europe inaugurated a policy of repression and reaction to counter the spread of liberal political doctrines. At a conference of ministers in the fall of 1818, Metternich, the minister of Austria, declared—and all agreed—that the Burschenschaften and the turner organizations were hotbeds of revolution. In March 1819, Karl Sand, a turner, assassinated Kotzebue, a famous writer in the employ of monarchy. Jahn, although innocent of any connection with the crime, was accused of a conspiracy and arrested in July 1819. Immediately turnen was forbidden in Prussia.

Jahn was held in prison or under close guard during a long period of litigation and was not acquitted until 1825. Even then he was forbidden to live in Berlin or near a university or boy's school. He took up residence in Freyburg, and, although he was relieved of police restrictions and decorated with the iron cross by the new King Frederick William IV in 1840, he took no active part in turnen and died in 1852.

Some of the German states followed the lead of Prussia and abolished turnen. Others did not, but the years of 1820 to 1840 are barren of progress in physical education, though much was written concerning the subject.

Revival of Turnverein

Frederick William IV, who came to the Prussian throne in 1840, soon removed the ban on turnvereins and issued the order of 1842 that gymnastics are "formally recognized as a necessary and indispensable part of male education and received into the circle of means for popular education." The tendency that immediately followed—to provide facilities for physical education in the schools—encouraged the turnverein to become more adapted to adult gymnastics and sociability as well as independent of school organizations. There was a rapid increase both in membership and number of societies. The various organizations found need of a national organization of societies (the Turnerschaft), conventions and gymnastic meets (turnfeste), and the newspaper (turnzeitung) as a means of maintaining comradeship and cooperation.

The years of 1848 and 1849 were again years of European revolutions in which the people sought more liberal government and the turnvereins were suppressed because of their liberal political ideals. About 1860, signs of revival appeared, and turnen was encouraged by the government and flourished for many years. In 1870, the year German unity was practically achieved, the turner societies numbered 1,500; in 1880, 2,200; in 1890, 4,400; in 1900, 7,200; in 1910, 9,100; in 1920, 10,000. In 1915 the societies contained a membership of over 1,000,000, and in 1926 the numbers had reached more than 2,000,000. Adolf Hitler and the National Socialist Party, after seizing power in 1933, soon took control of all sports clubs and youth organizations as well as physical education in the schools. All such activities were placed under governmental control to further the movement toward a totalitarian state. In education there was a decline in emphasis in intellectual and liberal arts and a rise in emphasis in both the scientific and physical education.

THE OUTDOOR MOVEMENT

The environmental conditions present in the congested German cities led to the growth of a new activity. The hosteling movement spread rapidly in the early part of the twentieth century. Wandering throughout the German countryside became so popular with those who sought occasional refuge from the cities that hostels sprang up so that people could always find a hostel at the end of a day's hike. By the early 1920's, over 3,000 hostels existed and accommodated approximately one-half million visitors annually.

During the same period, many of the German sports organizations devoted to various competitions began to include activities which took enthusiasts far beyond the confines of cities. Cycling and rowing increased rapidly to the extent that special maps, guides, expense reductions, overnight facilities, and the like were provided for those actively engaged. Skiing, climbing, and gliding attracted many followers interested in wandering throughout various sections of the nation to secure their recreative pleasures. Until 1932, no nation excelled the Germans in their persistent travels throughout the country to enjoy nature.

The solidification or the unification of the underlying concepts of physical education has occurred to a marked degree in the Germany of today. A Study Commission in 1913 was initiated by authorities in Germany who sought an answer to the success of American athletes—German-born or otherwise. After seeing the playground movement in Chicago and other cities, this commission recommended vast additional play areas in all German cities. The spirit of the recommendations was adopted, but no legal acceptance occurred. Furthermore, the practices of American colleges and universities in physical education service and professional curricula were adopted in German universities.

Now, after years of chaotic conditions, the German sports teacher still moves forward. However, newer concepts—the social aspects of physical education and the development of self-discipline and perfection through physical education—are the objectives of the present German program. The creative aspects of sports and art have challenged the imagination of German educators.

GYMNASTICS IN THE SCHOOLS

The development of public schools for the masses came in the nineteenth century. The German turnverein did not immediately alter the school practices or introduce gymnastics into the educational institutions. They tended to supplement the work of the school rather than to secure a place for physical education in it.

Contributions of Spiess to the Program

Germany is indebted to Adolph Spiess (1810–58) for the successful development and organization of school gymnastics. When a boy, Spiess attended a Pestalozzian school where he came in contact with GutsMuths' gymnastics. As a university study, he became proficient in gymnastic activities, especially fencing. He was acquainted with Jahn, GutsMuths, Eiselin, and other leaders of the time. After a few years of teaching in Hesse, he went to Switzerland and remained from 1833 to 1848. During these years he organized his system of school gymnastics in the cities of Burgdorf and Basel. When, in 1842, Prussia's interest in physical education began to revive, Spiess went to Berlin in order to get his ideas before the authorities but failed to make a favorable impression and returned to Switzerland. Incidentally, Massmann, a leading turner, was chosen to devise a plan of physical education for all the Prussian schools.

While in Switzerland, Spiess wrote *Die Lehre der Turnkunst* (System of Gymnastics) and began his manual, *Turnbuch für Schulen* (Manual of Gymnastics for Schools). In 1848 he accepted the task of introducing his system into the school of the Grand Duchy of Hesse and began work in Darmstadt. He took personal charge of the teaching of physical education in the gymnasium, the realschule, and a mädchenschule (girl's school). An outdoor and an indoor gymnasium were provided and equipped with vertical poles, bars, ladders, giant stride, and bucks. Classes for boys and girls were organized.

Spiess's aim and achievement was to secure the adoption of physical exercise as a vital part of the child's education and develop a system suitable to the schools. To that end he advocated the following ideas:

1. An exercising hall and a turnplatz should be established as a part of, or very near, every school.
2. One period per day should be set aside for gymnastic work.
3. Pupils should be given marks according to their proficiency in the work.
4. Gymnastic material should be graded according to its suitability for different ages and sexes.
5. A special system of gymnastics for girls should be arranged.

In short, gymnastics should be recognized and treated with the same degree of importance as any other school subject. His motive was similar to that of the Athenians: physical education was to produce bodily perfection, beauty, and grace, and weld body and soul into a perfectly harmonious entity capable of ideal social participation. He wrote, in *Turnbuch für Schulen:* "The end of education is undivided, embracing the whole nature of the pupil, it is the school that divides the work and taking different courses aims in the same direction. . . . The intellect and physique constitute but one being." Spiess was also aware of the pedagogical value of physical exercise, its use as a rest and recreation and its moral and social lessons. The exercises and institutions of the turners were not considered satisfactory for the new theories of school gymnastics, especially for girls.

The material and classification of exercises used by the followers of Jahn did not seem satisfactory for children, and especially for girls of school age. Spiess's alterations and additions are explained in his books. In order to adapt gymnastics to the school methods, classes of pupils of approximately the same age were organized and directed by one teacher. Exercises suited to that age were engaged in for a specified period of time each day. In the interests of efficiency the gymnastic class accepted the usual school formalism. Since this program had to be carried out in inclement weather and in winter, an indoor gymnasium became necessary.

Spiess introduced the marching exercises into the German system and called attention to their value. Through their use the teacher was enabled to control a large group and to secure a desired position for the entire class without confusion and waste of time. For the pupil these exercises served as a training in discipline and erect carriage. Spiess also singled out free exercises for special elaboration and emphasis; he is frequently called the founder of that branch of physical education. His aim in this was to give to the entire class, in an orderly manner and in the short time available, a series of exercises designed to bring into play all those parts of the body whose activity was necessary to the ultimate complete development. Formalism was not practiced in Spiess's schools to the exclusion of games, sports, or dancing; the moral, recreational, and esthetic values of the latter were highly appreciated. He also called attention to the use of music; the rhythmical motions of marching and free exercise drills, indoors, offered an opportunity for the use of musical accompaniment.

Considerable stress was placed on gymnastic exhibitions; they were regarded as a means of holding the interest of the pupils as well as securing favorable public opinion. Spiess found that the excursions into the country, so enjoyed by turners, were also suitable for the school classes when time permitted.

Spiess was opposed to the Jahn system of teaching by vorturners (class leaders) and advocated the employment of a sufficient number of teachers who had training and experience equal to that of the teachers of other school subjects. To that end he established normal classes in Darmstadt in 1849.

Pestalozzi, GutsMuths, and Basedow antedated Spiess in the matter of fostering gymnastics in their schools, but he perfected the idea, stressed its importance, and attracted the attention of the authorities at an opportune time and is usually considered the founder of the system of German school gymnastics and of gymnastics for girls. His classes were visited by officials of nearly every state in Germany, and his methods were adopted so widely that his system became a part of the German system.

Fig. 7. The Basel Turnplatz.

Program Since Spiess

To carry out the Order of 1842, which advocated gymnastics for the schools, Hans Massmann (1797–1874), a turner of the Jahn type, was chosen to plan a system for all Prussia. Much to the disappointment of Spiess and most of the school authorities, Massmann clung to the old idea of a municipal turnplatz separate from the school and the school management, and very little advance was made in physical education in the schools. Massmann retired in 1850.

This period of stagnation was followed by one of strife. Hugo Rothstein (1810–65), while director of the Royal Central Institute of Gymnastics (Königliche Zentral-Turnanstalt) in Berlin, attempted to introduce the Swedish Ling system to the exclusion of some vital principles in the German system. Opposition was too great, and he withdrew in unpopularity in 1863. After several changes of name and location, the Royal Central Institute became the present Landesturnanstalt at Spandau, where thorough courses in gymnastics are given to prospective teachers of physical education.

Following 1860, Germany continued as a leader in school gymnastics and attached more and more importance to that subject. In that year, all schools for boys, from the elementary institutions to the universities, received orders to secure teachers of gymnastics and give additional time and emphasis to physical education. Two years later a manual for instruction in gymnastics in the elementary schools was published and attendance at the exercises made compulsory. In spite of the frequent revision of the manual and of official encouragement, the school authorities neglected to carry out the program through the eighties and nineties. This resulted because of a tendency to crowd the curriculum and to encourage an ever-increasing number of women teachers in the faculties.

By 1904, Germany awakened to the seriousness of this neglect and did much to combat it, partly through the playground movement and by insisting that women teachers prepare to teach the subjects of physical education. Following that date, the time allotted for physical activities increased to three hours per week and one play afternoon each week in nearly all schools. Some schools devoted ten-minute periods to deep breathing and correct posture exercises on alternate days. The boys' and girls' athletic clubs for the promotion of certain sports and games, supervised by teachers, supplemented the regular school work. The addition of gymnastics for girls in 1894 as a part of the curriculum in higher schools received continuing support, and a special manual of exercises for girls was published in 1913.

In addition to the Landesturnanstalt, the leading states of Germany established normal schools for teachers of physical education. Each state managed its educational system independently; therefore, each had its own individual history so far as dates, leaders, and events were concerned. However, their methods and objectives in physical education were very similar. This was partly a result of the efforts of the national organizations promoting physical education throughout Germany, for example, the Turnerschaft and the German Society of Teachers of Gymnastics. The latter organization, through its conventions and publications, tended to make uniform the best methods and aims in physical education.

EFFECT OF WORLD WAR I

The great mental and emotional strain during the war and the food famine which followed had a very detrimental effect on the physical welfare of German children. In addition to a rehabilitation movement which evolved to influence the total physical education program, more emphasis was placed on the games and athletic sports, and additional attention was given to health education. This rejuvenation related directly to the governmental support that physical education received from the Weimar Republic. Regulations required all schools to include physical education in the curriculum, and it received equal status with other school subjects. Athletic meets, graded performance, presidential certificates, increased facilities of all kinds, and other factors brought physical education in Germany to a new high level. Those phases of physical education which flourished before World War I were retained as excellent means for restoring the mental and physical health of an exhausted nation. The spirit of play manifested itself in the organization of athletic and recreation clubs for all ages, in playgrounds, summer camps, new courses on play in normal schools, greater emphasis on dancing, rhythmic gymnastics, and in sport publications of books and magazines. The employment of school doctors and nurses, vacation camps, nutrition classes, school clinics, open air schools, and sex education evolved as advancements in the health education movement.

PHYSICAL EDUCATION DURING NATIONAL SOCIALISM

In 1933 when National Socialism came to power, Adolf Hitler appointed a military officer as National Sports Commissioner. Amateur sports organizations and youth groups were either dissolved or reorganized. The Commissioner specified 16 unions to control all the sports that were to survive. In addition, these unions controlled the "Sports Physicians," teachers, and youth groups. A national representative association was developed which included one member from each of the 16 unions. In turn, corresponding groups were established on district and local levels. In addition to these major steps, approximately 165 unions were dissolved by Hitler, and the leisure time of the workers and employees was planned in accordance with Nazi purposes. As sports were adequately handled by the amateur clubs, competition with their efforts was avoided.

Physical education became a required subject in schools, and passing physical fitness tests became part of the requirements for graduation. Even entrance into secondary schools depended upon the ability of a student to pass physical as well as intellectual tests. Special schooling awaited those rated high in both leadership and physical capacities. The usual physical education requirements were two or three hours weekly for elementary school children and four or five hours for secondary pupils. Universities stressed physical education and prospective teachers met such classes daily.

At the end of the school day (1:00 P.M.), club activities for Hitler Youth were specified. At this time, hikes and drills continued to complete the physical fitness program while Nazi indoctrination and party work received a fair share of attention. To increase the physical vigor of out-of-school 14- and 15-year-olds, a compulsory program in a farm setting was required. The total program finally culminated in a half-year of service through labor followed by induction into army life.

EFFECT OF WORLD WAR II

Many schools, colleges, and training institutes let physical education die after 1945. This appeared as only a period of adjustment. The sports teachers aspect of Berlin University (dissolved by National Socialism) was replaced by a similar undertaking in 1947 called the Cologne Sportshochschule. This is a three-year course for men and women, which may be taken either separately or in conjunction with university studies at Cologne or Bonn. Primary teachers may also take a one-year postcertificate course.

The sports clubs began to reappear by 1946, but without political affiliation. Old and young alike met in the German Light-Athletic championship in 1946 in Frankfurt. The following year this same national event occurred in Cologne. The occupying authorites disallowed any central organization for sports, but nothing seemed to dim the desire of Germans to participate in sports.

Most schools in Germany have physical education classes which meet from 45–60 minutes twice each week. German physical education includes the native turnen, English games, Scandinavian corrective gymnastics, creative dancing, and other activities. In the spring and summer, outdoor sports receive major emphasis, and during the winter gymnastics and other indoor activities are stressed.

Although physical education has made many gains since 1946, it still must overcome two obstacles. There is a shortage of facilities and a lack of qualified teachers. In 1962, the National Olympic Committee initiated a plan to spend about two billion dollars in fifteen years for physical education and sports facilities. This program is slowly overcoming the facilities problem.

The physical education teacher is not considered on the same academic level as other teachers, and consequently recruitment of potential teachers of physical eduction has lagged. Efforts to raise the status of this segment of teachers have been effective, but the process is rather slow and tedious.

Sports clubs and turnverein abound everywhere. Over 10 per cent of the West German population belong to sports clubs. Nationwide special associations for each sport have been developed. Also regional sports associations have been organized at the state level, which in turn are divided into district sports associations. Thus from the local to the national level each of these sports organizations fosters the interests of the participants in every conceivable way.* All such organizations sponsor very active youth sections. Full-time instruction is usually provided. In most instances, schools do not have their own playing fields but depend upon the facilities controlled either by the clubs or the municipalities.

As previously mentioned, the movement back toward sports and other physical activities durng all seasons of the year quickly gained momentum following World War II. This trend has continued to flourish and the German child of today compares favorably from a physical standpoint with English children or other European children. In other words, few, if any, effects of the shortages resulting from World War II are visible.

The culmination of all this effort toward physical activities seems most apparent during week ends, vacations, and holidays when favorable weather prevails. Hiking, boating, hostelling, gliding, winter sports, aquatics, and other outdoor activities attract thousands of families and other groups to the parks and other natural areas. The love of the out of doors and the desire for enjoyable physical activity seem to be a part of the German culture.

* *Physical Education Around the World.* Indianapolis: Phi Epsilon Kappa, 1966. Pp. 27–28.

10

Scandinavia Since 1800

Denmark and Sweden have contributed much to the development of physical education. Throughout the years the interests of Scandinavian people have led to a continuous effort to improve the gymnastic system and develop fitness for all.

PHYSICAL EDUCATION IN DENMARK

The progressive nation of Denmark has occupied an important position in the over-all development of physical education. Danish interest and achievements in gymnastics began in the stormy Napoleonic period when Denmark suffered humiliation at the hands of the great powers. The evident need for strong national defenders, combined with the Danish love for sports and athletic competition, made Denmark a fertile soil for the growth of the institutions of physical education. So throughout the nineteenth century, Danish physical education emphasized programs which led to developing good soldiers and reverence for Denmark. The outstanding leader in the history of physical education in Denmark is Franz Nachtegall (1777–1847).

Contributions of Nachtegall

Nachtegall, when a university student, was a gymnast of the first rank. This proficiency and the reading of GutsMuths' works started him on the career of physical educator. He secured the position of teacher of gymnastics in a club of university students and later in a naturalistic school similar to that of Basedow. Nachtegall's career showed that he possessed boundless energy, tact, flexibility, and, above all, he was a good teacher with the ability to organize. In 1799, he directed his own private open air gymnasium in Copenhagen which proved to be very popular and the first of its kind. In 1804, Denmark turned its attention to the need for a larger and a better trained army and navy. The authorities recognized that the practice of gymnastics should be an essential part of that training and founded the Military Gymnastic Institute, the first gymnastic normal school of modern times. Nachtegall was made the first director. On his recommendation the government decided to extend the benefits of gymnastics to the schools and to encourage the participation of adults outside the military branches; to that end, civilians were permitted to attend the school.

In 1809 schools of the secondary grade were requested to give instruction in physical exercise. Five years later, in 1814, elementary schools were ordered to provide instructors and to secure grounds and equipment suitable for the practice of gymnastics. This is the first school ordinance establishing physical education as a part of general education in any European nation.

To prepare a large number of teachers for the work, courses in gymnastics were established in the various teachers' colleges in addition to the instruction given in the gymnastic institute. Nachtegall was chosen to fill the office of Director of Gymnastics for all Denmark. During the third and fourth decades of the century, progress was slow but worthy of notice. The Military Gymnastic Institute secured permission to establish practice classes for student teachers among the school children. A manual of gymnastics, published at national expense and distributed to the teachers of physical education in the various schools, became the guide. Gymnastics for girls was accepted and classes for women teachers of physical education were established in the Military Institute. Some localities far exceeded others in the practice of gymnastics; success or failure depended upon the attitude of the educators in a given community.

Revival of the Sixties

On the death of Nachtegall new and less able leaders took charge, and at times school gymnastics was threatened with extinction. The disastrous war of 1864 with Austria and Prussia aroused a renewed interest in gymnastics, especially as a means of augmenting national defense. The Danish Rifle Clubs, modeled after those in England, date from this period. At first all activities took place out of doors, but around 1871 the first of many buildings for exercise began to appear. Soon after they were organized these clubs took on the features of gymnastic societies. Members participated in, and encouraged others to engage in, gymnastics and games, and they held track meets and offered their buildings to classes of school children when no others were available.

Folk high schools, a Danish innovation, also evolved after 1864. These institutions, privately operated, were open to young men and women between the ages of 18 and 25. The majority who attended came from farms or rural communities. Many subjects have been or are taught (these schools still exist), but examinations are nonexistent. Gymnastics always have held an important place in the curriculum, and it was through the young adults attending these institutions that renewed interest in gymnastics took place in the nineteenth century.

Through the entire early period, GutsMuths' system, as altered by Nachtegall, and the Jahn-Eiselin system of the German turners prevailed in Denmark. During the eighties, the Ling system of Sweden, which was introduced in a folk or people's high school, began its invasion. The resulting controversies concerning the values of the Ling system increased the popularity of gymnastics in general and tended to revive school gymnastics, which had been neglected. A committee, appointed for the purpose, arranged a system thought to be suitable for Denmark and published a manual of exercises. This new *Handbook of Gymnastics* contained many innovations from Sweden but retained much of the material already current in Denmark.

Since 1900 the most noticeable movements have been the demilitarization of educational gymnastics, extension of teacher training facilities, national financial aids in the promotion of physical education, recognition of the value of sports and games, and the contributions of Niels Bukh (see p. 87).

Demilitarization of School Gymnastics

For nearly a century the leaders in gymnastics were military men, from the highest directors and inspectors to the class teachers. This condition was, of course, a survival of the originally dominant military aim of physical education. The disadvantages were that the aims, methods, and theories were not suitable to the school conditions and that the exercises did not become a part of the school but remained supplementary to it.

In 1904 school gymnastics was divorced from military gymnastics in every way. The University of Copenhagen in 1909 offered gymnastics as a subject and provided a laboratory. To provide civilian teachers, the normal colleges and universities established both complete and brief courses in physical education and an independent Central Institute of Gymnastics was opened in Copenhagen. By this means the opportunities for securing preparation as a teacher of physical education have been increased and made inexpensive. Consequently great numbers of well-educated teachers have gone from these institutions into the schools of Denmark and other countries.

An act passed in 1937 requires public elementary and secondary school education, which is compulsory between the ages of 7–14, to include physical education as a part of the curriculum. The official allocation of school time in Denmark to physical education follows: children between 6 and 11, 11 and 14, and 14 and 18 have a minimum of two, three, and four activity periods respectively each week. An annual mark for physical education is given each student, and it receives equal status with marks given for other subjects.

To meet the handicap which many localities experienced in not having sufficient funds to equip a gymnasium and employ an instructor, the national government makes significant grants and loans. A government order in 1946 required all country schools to erect a gymnasium and install various pieces of apparatus and equipment. In conjunction with these requirements for physical education, the School Medical Service Act of 1946 insures free or substantially free school meals, dental care, nursing, and various types of medical supervision.

The Play Movement

The comparatively recent world-wide recognition of the value of play and playgrounds is noted in Denmark in 1896. Earlier, however, many private schools had emphasized group games and outdoor sports, and the Copenhagen Playground Association had been established. Under the leadership of this organization, the national government appropriated funds to be used by a committee for the purpose of promoting group games among school children by furnishing playground equipment, giving consultant services, and helping prepare teachers. Hundreds of schools accepted the plan and were aided and financed by this committee. Teachers' courses have been altered to give time to the theory and managment of games popular in Denmark and suitable for physical education, such as Danish ball, cricket, football, and hockey.

Early in the 1900's many Danish children and youth recreation groups sprang up, such as The Boys' Voluntary League, Boy Scouts, Girl Guide Corps, and Y.M.C.A. programs. Hostelling became very popular in the 1930's with thousands of members joining and the necessary hostels being established. With at least twelve holidays for all working citizens, many clubs, schools, trade unions, municipal governments, and private interests cater to the leisure interests of the Danish people.

Primitive Gymnastics of Bukh

In 1921 Niels Bukh (1880–1948), the Director of Gymnastics in the People's School at Ollerup, Denmark, developed a new interpretation of the Ling gymnastics. Bukh recognized the many defects of the untrained body, the stiff round back, the forward projecting neck, the sets of overdeveloped muscles and underdeveloped muscles, and the like. His aim was to produce the perfect normal physique. To that end all bad postural habits, occupational deformities, and other defects must be eliminated first. Strength, suppleness, and coordination of the entire body must be obtained. The exercises for this purpose are called "Primitif Gymnastike." They differ from the ordinary exercises in that there are no "held" positions and no cessation of movement. In practice the work resembles a long memorized drill of big muscle exercises executed rapidly and with rhythm. His system does away with much of the old apparatus and relies mainly on wall bars, mattresses, and vaulting boxes. Marching (often while singing) accompanies the usual physical education sessions.

The ideas and methods of Primitive Gymnastics have influenced not only Denmark but Europe and America as well. Bukh and other Danish gymnasts have toured the United States and left their mark. However, the pattern of the American system of teacher education has been adopted by the Danes to a marked degree, even to the courses of instruction. Similar to the American system is the previously mentioned official allocation of school time in Denmark to physical education.

PHYSICAL EDUCATION IN SWEDEN

The history of physical education in Sweden runs parallel to that in Denmark. Although each exerted an influence upon the other, Sweden was more outstanding in her development of new methods and new objectives in addition to her international influence. Like Denmark, Sweden began with the military motive for national participation in gymnastics, and when the immediate danger of foreign attacks slackened, she continued physical education as a means of increasing national welfare and prosperity.

Contributions of Ling

The Swedish emphasis on the curative and corrective value of gymnastics, commonly known as medical gymnastics, has given the Swedish system adherents throughout the world. This movement resulted largely from the work of Per Henrik Ling (1776–1839), the founder of the Swedish system. As a university student, Ling showed great aptitude for foreign languages and literature. After attending the Swedish universities he went to Copenhagen, and remained from 1799 to 1804. While there he studied the old Norse literature, Danish and German languages, and took a course in fencing. He also visited Nachtegall's private gymnasium and very probably read GutsMuths' *Gymnastics for the Young,* which was popular in Denmark at that time. Apparently these events induced Ling to take up the work of physical education. His fencing exercises seemed to improve an arm affliction and he came to believe in the curative possibilities of gymnastics.

In 1804 Ling accepted the position of fencing master at the University of Lund, in Sweden. He required his students to supplement their fencing with riding, vaulting, and other gymnastic exercises. At the same time, he studied anatomy and physiology, because he believed that a thorough knowledge of the human body and nature's laws was a minimum for an intelligent understanding of physical education. As Ling became more and more acquainted with the science of the human body he came to believe that the medical value of gymnastics had been too little emphasized and that gymnastics for the weak were as important as gymnastics for the strong; that exercise must be prescribed for the individual rather than for a group; that a system of gymnastics must be based on an accurate knowledge of the effect of the various exercises on the human organism; that teachers and instructors must know the purpose and effect of every exercise; and that the aim must be physical harmony and perfection, "The one-ness of the human organism; the harmony between the mind and the body."

During these formative years of Ling's work, Sweden was defeated by the French and Russians, and, deserted by England, she lost the states of Pomerania and Finland. Like Jahn in Germany and Nachtegall in Denmark, Ling saw that the only hope for national honor lay in a brave and sturdy citizenry, and he set out to accomplish that through physical education. These political disasters also called from his pen patriotic verses and articles which rank high in Swedish literature.

When Ling became fencing master in the Royal Military School, he proposed that a national institute of physical education be established where teachers might be prepared for the ultimate purpose of the physical upbuilding of the Swedish people. The idea met the approval of the authorities, and the Royal Central Institute of Gymnastics was opened in Stockholm in 1814. Its most important immediate work was along the line of military gymnastics looking toward national defense. Ling and other instructors taught the soldiers in the Institute and in the neighboring barracks. Ling's system of bayonet fighting and his supplementary exercises and *Handbook of Gymnastics* were used in the course. The Institute became the center of this phase of military preparedness.

Ling laid the foundation both in the theory and practice of the Swedish system; his successors have added to and elaborated but never radically altered his original ideas. His *Gymnastikens allmänna Grunder* remains the cornerstone of the structure. In 1913, the centennial of Ling's proposal to establish the Central Institute, Sweden held a national celebration, including addresses, parades, gymnastic meets, and the decoration of Ling's grave.

On the death of Ling in 1839, Lars Gabriel Branting became the director of the Central Institute. The period of wars having passed, the military motive for gymnastics became less important, and Branting expanded the field of medical gymnastics. He pointed out that the greatest benefit of many exercises did not accrue to the muscular system but rather to the nervous and circulatory systems and to the viscera.

Medical gymnastic theories caused much controversy among medical men, but, in spite of the opposition, they were accepted in Sweden and had great influence in the leading countries of the world.

Physical Education in the Schools

The spread of gymnastics in Swedish schools came more slowly than in Danish. The earliest legislation on the subject was a law in 1820 requiring a course in physical education for the secondary schools for boys. The gradual adoption of a physical education program in all public schools did not result from compulsory legislation but rather from a genuine belief that physical exercise is an indispensable part of general education.

During the 1860's the Royal Central Institute of Gymnastics was reorganized, and three separate departments resulted, the pedagogical, the military, and the medical. Hjalmar Ling (1820–86), the son of Per Ling, became the head of the pedagogical department. The adaptation of Swedish theories to the school room is largely his contribution. This adaptation necessitated the construction of suitable apparatus, the arrangement of group exercises, grading, and progress of the work, and a classification of movements for young boys and girls. Through the work of H. Ling the rational "days order" of the Swedish system was evolved.

A healthy and gradual growth characterizes the history of physical education in Swedish schools during the last half century. Schools controlled by the Board of Education and the Supervisory Board of Trade Schools require compulsory physical education. The requirements apply to all state-supported elementary and high schools.

For school children between seven and nine years of age, either one forty-five-minute period or two shorter periods are required each week. The other elementary classes may have up to three required hours a week. The secondary school classes devote from three to four hours each week to physical education. The physical education program in Sweden deals, in the main, with gymnastics, games and sports, and winter activities such as skiing.

To supplement this phase of physical education, Swedish schools set aside outdoor days to further insure that the young people lead a vigorous outdoor life. These outdoor days amount to a half day being set aside so that outdoor activities in games and sports balance the other school subjects. Schools schedule these days at their own convenience, and some schools combine two half days into one full day of outdoor activity. The number of required outdoor days varies from a required ten to twelve per year in secondary schools to as many as sixteen to twenty-four in some elementary schools.

In the practice of physical education, the exercises of the Swedish system, supplemented by games and sports, form the foundation of the activities. The Long system always has been regarded in Sweden as superior to all other systems for its contribution to correctives. Also, its efficiency, orderliness, and adaptability to school methods are regarded highly. Stall bars and other wall apparatus prove functional in schools which have no gymnasia and where the classrooms or hallways must be used for physical education. Most high schools have well-equipped gymnasia, but many trade schools and elementary schools lack the necessary facilities for a well-rounded program.

The physical welfare of university students in Sweden receives as much attention as in any other country with the possible exception of the United States. The universities differ greatly in the facilities offered for gymnastics and sports. Some have abundant and well-equipped facilities, while others provide practically none. However, private gymnasia and gymnastic societies are readily available for those students desiring activity in gymnastics or sports.

A physical fitness program has developed in Sweden in which people voluntarily participate in gymnastics. The women began participation in this program in about 1942, and since that time thousands have begun to participate. As many as 5,000 women have participated in a Lingiad. Teachers are trained by the Gymnastic Association to circulate among working people and give them a few minutes of calisthenics.

The spirit of recreation play and sports competition has invaded Sweden as well as most other countries. Games have become a part of the physical and moral education program, and they have gained in importance in a program once dominated by gymnastics. Provision for outdoor games and sports is made at nearly every school at the present time. During the short summer the Swedes flock to the lakes and seashore for swimming, sun bathing, boating, and other aquatic activities. Skiing of all kinds, skating, curling, ice hockey, and many other similar activities predominate during the winter. Further, singing and dancing with participants dressed in colorful costumes are enjoyed throughout Sweden.

The Swedish system has done much to enrich the field of physical education both in theory and practice. Physical education has reached a high educational plane because of the insistence of authorities that prospective physical education teachers make a thorough study of the human organism through anatomy, physiology, and kinesiology. Exercises are then arranged with respect to that knowledge. Especially important are these basic sciences to the application of physical education in the corrective phase of the program. In all modern countries the field of corrective physical education has increased in importance in the past half century.

Preparation of Physical Education Teachers

Since its origin in 1814, the Royal Central Institute of Gymnastics has held a prominent position as a normal school. Three- and four-year courses are given and include both the theory and practice of physical education in the curriculum. Courses in physical education are given in all institutions which prepare elementary school teachers. Public schools provide the practice classes in which prospective teachers apply their skills and knowledges while learning. In the twentieth century the teacher education program is reflected in a new emphasis which the physical education teachers have made on caring for the needs of all age groups. By encouraging a broader program with additional stress on sports and games, the program gives less of the total effort to military aims.

11

Britain, Australia, New Zealand, and Canada

Throughout the various parts of the British Empire, the sports and games of England have become a part of the culture in the new lands. The English people, therefore, have had a profound influence on physical education and leisure activity among the countries of the world.

GREAT BRITAIN

While continental countries created systems of gymnastics and developed the science of physical education, the British people continued their participation in outdoor sports. Britain's isolated position and her powerful navy shielded her from dangerous foreign invasions and, consequently, made unnecessary the strict discipline and training to which the nations of the Continent subjected themselves for national defense. The conditions which prompted Jahn to advocate the physical development of his people never existed in England. Britain's free institutions, personal liberty, and individualism tended to give free rein to the play and sporting instincts of her people. Her large manufacturing and trading population found leisure time and inclination to imitate the nobles in their outdoor sports. The temperate climate was always inviting to outdoor activity. English nature had a bent for competitive sport, but, on the other hand, it rejected formal drill except for purposes of military training.

History of British Sports

All people, savage or civilized, engage in some kind of sport, and it goes without saying that English sport is as old as the English people. As early as the year 1200, writers were expressing opinions on the value of games in general and comparing the benefits to be derived from the different sports. A proclamation of Henry VII (c. 1500) read, "It ever hath bene of old antiquite used in this realme for all lustye gentleman to pass the delectable season of summer after divers manner and sundry fashions of disport," and established a series of athletic contests, the victors of which were to be rewarded. This national enthusiasm for play led to the invention of many games and to the adoption and alteration of several that were introduced from other lands.

In feudal England, the joust, tournament, and other knightly sports predominated. With the decline of feudalism and the rise to importance of the bowmen, archery became the most practiced sport and the one most encouraged by the royal authorities, both for nobles and commons. It was valued as a preparation for war—not as a means of physical education. Archery continued to have the royal favor and protection until the invention and common use of the musket lessened the importance of the bow as a weapon.

Golf probably originated in Holland, but when the game was introduced to the Scotch and English, it received such a welcome and added development that it is more commonly identified with Britain than with its native land. During the fifteenth century, laws forbidding the playing of golf were passed because it threatened to destroy the popularity of archery. This opposition did not long exist, for in the next century the nobles and the king himself accepted the game. Then golfing clubs were formed by the wealthy people of England, but it was not until the nineteenth century that this game was played by great numbers of commons. Since 1880 it has had a remarkable increase in popularity in England as well as in Europe and America.

Hockey was played by the Greeks and Romans and has been a sport of the nations of Europe since that time. The modern name seems to have come from the hooked sticks with which it is played. In Scotland the game was called shinty and in Ireland, hurley. Its recent popularity dates from 1875, when the English Hockey Association was established. Hockey clubs were then organized throughout the British Isles. Games between the teams representing England, Ireland, Scotland, and Wales were frequent. Since 1900 matches between England, France, and other Continental countries have been common.

Cricket originated in England about the thirteenth century and evolved in the direction of the modern game during the fourteenth century. In spite of the hostile legislation and the scorn of the nobility, the game became popular. In the sixteenth century the higher classes took up the sport, and, slowly but gradually, it took the position of the national game.

Bowling originated in the Netherlands and Germany but was soon carried over the world by the Dutch traders. The English and the Scotch "naturalized" the alien pastime but never accepted it with the popularity that golf received.

Pitching quoits became the pastime of the lower classes near the Scotch and English border in the fifteenth century. Neither laws against it nor Ascham's statement that "quoits be too vile for scholars" was sufficient to prevent its encroachments on archery. Rustics found that horseshoes were a good substitute for the regulation quoits.

Tennis seems to have had its origin in France and was played by kings and nobles of both France and England as early as 1300. It was forbidden to the peasant in both countries, but with the winning of political freedom it was taken up by the commons. Only in the last century, however, has tennis gained its great popularity.

Games resembling football were played by the Greeks and Romans and were probably introduced by Roman legions into northern Europe and Britain. In the twelfth century the young men of London were in the habit of going to the country green to play a similar game. Henry VIII and Elizabeth outlawed the sport, and Sir Thomas Elyot spoke against it in 1537. He said, "Foot Ball wherein is nothynge but beastlye furie and exstreme violence, whereof proceededth hurte; and consequently malice and rancour do remain with them that be wounded; where of it is to be putt in perpetuall silence." Another writer expressed his opinion: "For as concerning football playing I protest unto you that it may rather be called a friendlie kinde of fyghte than a play or recreation—a bloody and murthering practice than a fellowly sport or pastime.' In Ireland, on the other hand, a law of the sixteenth century forbade all sports except archery and "football." Because of its crude "rough and tumble" features, it became a game of the commons. Shrove Tuesday was regarded as a special day for playing.

During the eighteenth and nineteenth centuries some larger schools of England accepted it as suitable for boys and devised their own local rules for playing. Rugby purchased its first athletic field in 1749 and played the game there. It seems then to have been a kicking game rather than one of carrying the ball. An honorary tablet at Rugby explains how the game now known by the name of the school came to be developed. "This stone commemorates the exploit of Wm. Webb Ellis who with a fine disregard for the rules of football as played in his time, first took the ball in his arms and ran with it, thus originating the distinctive feature of the Rugby game A.D. 1823." The game of Rugby continued to be played, alongside the parent "football" (soccer), and in its turn fostered the game of football as played in the United States.

Hammer throwing competition is of Celtic origin and very early became popular in Scotland and Ireland. A common sledge hammer was used, and the trials were made for distance only. This was one of the few sports favored by the governing authorities. Changes in the rules of the game and the style of the hammer have altered the fundamentals of the competition very little.

Pole vaulting originated from the method of jumping canals and drain ditches in England; every homestead kept a pole for that purpose. It soon became a form of sport and was engaged in at the fairs and holiday gatherings. Pole vaulting found its way into Germany and was advocated by Jahn and GutsMuths as a valuable exercise.

Skittles, wrestling, boxing, fencing, pitching the bar, prisoners'-base, slinging, skating, rowing, and many more activities kept the nation physically fit. A greater number of people, men, women, and children, engage in these sports than ever before. Wherever the British go their games go with them, whether it be Australia, India, or America. Britain's position in this field has made her a center from which ideas and inspirations have been drawn in the international playground and recreation movements. Germany, the Scandinavian countries, and America have felt her influence.

The encouragement and development of many sports in England show, with few exceptions, that the English people did much more in the way of refining and popularizing these activities than in inventing new ones. Perhaps traditional British reverence for freedom and individuality proved a welcome environment for sports and a less likely context for gymnastics and other activities designed for military purposes. This observation does not deny the use and acceptance of gymnastics in schools, clubs, and the military, but it does point to the most valuable contribution England has made to physical education. Of added significance is the fact that in many of its colonies, such as Canada and Australia, the English successfully introduced both the sports and the sports attitude.

Gymnastics in Great Britain

Britain did not remain free from the theories and achievements of physical education in the Continental countries. First of all, an urgent need was felt in the army for a system of physical training that would combine the benefits derived from formal drill with those derived from competitive sports. In 1822 the government obtained the services of the Swiss army officer and director of gymnastics, Phokion Clias. He was given charge of all physical training in military and naval schools and also was employed to teach in the Charter House Public School. His theories and methods were largely those of GutsMuths and other Germans. Because of an accident he left England in 1825.

Gymnastics for the army and navy was continued, but no very important leaders appeared until the coming of the Swedes, Ehrenhoff and, later, Carl Georgii, about 1850. Both were graduates of the Royal Central Institute, and both opened private institutions in London. These leaders claimed so much for their system that the British people were brought face to face with the question of whether their sports were sufficient or whether the Continental systems had anything better to offer.

Contributions of Maclaren. Archibald Maclaren (1820–84), a Scot by birth, was on the Continent at that time giving considerable study to the whole question of physical education. On returning to England in 1858 he established a private gymnasium in Oxford. A few years later the government decided to reorganize and regenerate the system of military gymnastics, and Maclaren was placed in charge of the work. His ideas were incorporated in a manual *A Military System of Gymnastic Exercises* which was to be used as a text. There was sent to his gymnasium a group of officers who were to be instructed in the theory and practice of gymnastics; they were then to return to the military center at Aldershot, where a normal school for other officers was to be established. The entire plan was carried out, and Maclaren's system came to be used in the military and naval schools to supplement the games and sports as a means of increasing the physical fitness of the soldiers and sailors.

Maclaren was not satisfied with that; he believed that educational gymnastics was the direct and more important means of improving the physical standard of the British. His book *A System of Physical Education*, printed in 1867 and again in 1885, and again, by his son, in 1895, reveals the following theories:

1. Physical training should accompany the growing period of life.
2. Physical training and mental training should go hand in hand, and each should be of benefit to the other.
3. The much-practiced games in England will not produce a well-balanced organism, but on the other hand, they will tend to develop a one-sidedness.
4. Only trained instructors should be employed.
5. Health rather than strength and skill should be the aim.
6. "Mind and body should be viewed as two well-fitting halves of a perfect whole, designed in true accord mutually to sustain and support each other and each worthy of our unwearied care and unstinted attention."
7. School games, sports, and pastimes are recreational while systematized exercise is educational.
8. Exercises should be regulated by individual fitness.

9. Systematic exercise is not only good for children and soldiers, but for the men of the shops and factories.
10. Exercises must be progressive and organized in a rational manner.
11. Gymnastics must not interfere with the playtime in the school, but rather it should become a part of the regular educational program.
12. Gymnastics "mean a gradual progressive system of physical exercise, so conceived, so arranged, and so administered, that it will naturally and uniformly call forth and cultivate the latent powers and capacities of the body, even as the mental faculties are developed and strengthened by mental culture and exercise."

Maclaren found fault with the Swedish system because he thought it was too much limited by the medical and corrective aims, and he objected to the German system because of its music and rhythm and its efforts to attain precision in group exercises. However, he invented very little that was new, either in theory or practice, but rather culled from all systems those theories and practices that suited him. Maclaren was a pioneer in the study of anthropometry and kept records of measurements and weights of his pupils for the purpose of studying the results of exercise.

Period of Investigation. The system introduced by Maclaren did not prove a great success. Nearly all teachers of the Maclaren gymnastics were from the army, and school exercises looked very much like military drill. Various investigations resulted in many but feeble efforts to revise physical exercise in the interest of recreation and health.

Meanwhile, Danish and Swedish teachers brought to England the Swedish system of physical education. This system proved exceedingly popular especially with women and girls. In 1903 the Education Department of Scotland recommended to the school officials a new course which was based on the Swedish system. A year later the English Board of Education published a *Syllabus of Physical Exercise,* which was also founded on the Swedish system. This syllabus was revised in 1909 and again in 1919. During this period many educational laws favoring the spread of school gymnastics were passed, and several training schools for teachers of physical education were established.

Throughout the ensuing years, formal exercises have continued to be stressed. The reasons for this perpetuation of such a program seem to be threefold:

1. The general conception of physical education by both lay and professional people continues to be limited.
2. The stress on physical fitness during war periods has encouraged the continuance of the program.
3. Adequate facilities and space for a games and sports program are generally lacking in the English schools. This condition exists in spite of the fact that plans for the extension of hundreds of sites have been approved.

The Changing Concept

In England there has been an awakening among educational leaders which is bringing about a recognition of the connection between the school physical education program and the leisure program for those who have left school. Leaders now place a greater emphasis upon the recreation element. Athletics, games, swimming, canoeing, hiking, and dancing receive some emphasis in schools. In addition, the emergency schools (clusters of huts) built during World War II in rural areas are used by local school authorities. Children sent to these camps for a short period each year receive opportunities in many outdoor activities; however, regular academic work still continues during this outing. The relationship between many of these activities and those which people in England voluntarily select after leaving school may bring about general public understanding of the desired over-all program. Fortunately, the idea of a highly specialized coach employed to coach the few best players has not been readily accepted.

Physical Education in Schools

Primary schools develop their own curricula and physical education can be scheduled every day for as much as 35 minutes. These schools also have sufficient apparatus for such activities as hanging, swinging, and jumping. Although the primary schools do not all employ physical education specialists, there is a definite trend in this direction in the larger schools.

The secondary schools conduct physical education two to four 40-minute periods a week. There still remains some distinction between the activities taught within the gymnasiums and the games program held outside on the playing fields. Qualified physical educators conduct the gymnasium programs while non-physical educators as well as specialists may teach the games outdoors.

For about 25 years English schools have developed movement education in physical education in elementary and secondary schools. Most efforts in this respect have occurred in gymnastics and dance. Emphasis is placed on the individual development of each student through the use of his body in problem-solving situations.

Younger children are challenged with single concept problems by their teachers, while older students are presented more complex problems with two or more concepts. Individually, the students respond with movements of their bodies, which lead to better physical control as well as better understanding of their faculty for moving. The focus in the problem-solving context is a satisfying movement within each individual's capabilities.

Movement education has also been used to some extent in games, aquatics, and ball handling. In games and ball handling activities, the students advance progressively from individual movement to group undertakings in which two or more people are involved. In swimming, skills are also learned from general movement experiences. Many elementary schools have added swimming pools that are portable and shallow.

Movement education in England has been considered valuable for the following reasons: Improved body management skills, higher interest of students, freer movement; and each student realizes success and improved physical fitness. Of course, because of the individual approach to movement education, no two students will obtain the same values precisely.

These developments in elementary physical education in England have influenced the programs in both Canada and the United States. The future philosophy of elementary physical education may be altered in light of this trend.

Preparation of Physical Education Teachers

England has attempted to improve the quality of the physical education program by improving the teacher education curriculum and developing more competencies among all teachers. To improve the physical education competencies of these teachers, students in the two-year training colleges receive instruction in a course in physical training and hygiene. On the other hand, for the specialists, advanced courses of 400 hours are now offered and extended over a two-year period. Over a dozen training colleges now offer opportunities of this nature. A three-year course in physical education exclusively for women is now offered by several special colleges for women. On the whole, universities in England fail to recognize teacher preparation in physical education. An exception to this stand is Birmingham University, which gives significant emphasis to physical education in a general arts degree. Contrary to the elementary schools, the secondary schools tend to hire specialists in physical education or at least those classroom teachers that have undergone special preparation in physical education.

The aristocratic secondary boarding schools operate without governmental control of physical education, and their practices relating to the employment of qualified teachers of that subject vary from the public schools. These independent schools usually designate either a teacher (master) who formally participated in sports or a professional to organize and direct the program. School and national spirit appear as important aims of these instructors. In the universities, physical education is not required, so organizational help only is provided for those who voluntarily participate. Obviously, in the above type of boarding schools and universities, students who wish to participate find themselves in a position where they must use their own initiative to instigate and organize physical education activities.

AUSTRALIA

Australia, far removed from the mother country, is an island continent comprised of six states. The Dutch, who landed in Australia during the first decade of the seventeenth century, receive credit for being the earliest Europeans to do so. The Chinese, however, as early as the 1200's had a knowledge of this continent. In 1770, Captain James Cook landed at various places along the east coast and took formal possession for Britain by hoisting the Union Jack.

Australia is not a heavily populated continent, having only between seven and eight million people. The climate ranges from temperate cool to subequatorial. Alien immigration has been according to the "white Australia" policy, and the admission of southern Europeans and Orientals has been, in the past, seriously limited.

Each of the six states has developed and controlled education independent of the Commonwealth. An examination of Australia's public school system shows definite influences of both English and United States systems of education. However, the Australians do not establish school boards but put the control in the State Offices. Depending upon the state, education is compulsory up to the fourteenth or sixteenth year. Church schools and private schools, much like those in England, supplement the public school effort.

Culmination of the educational plan occurs in the universities in each state capital, the agricultural colleges in each state, the National University in Canberra, the teacher education colleges in each state, or in the technical colleges recently established. Extension courses, a form of adult education, and mobile libraries comprise other education efforts being made.

The Australians have emphasized the fitness aspects of physical education. Systematic physical activity programs have long been advocated as a means for producing a strong virile citizenry capable of protecting the nation from outside forces. Thus, the physical education programs in schools have stressed fitness and health purposes as major concerns.

Even though fitness has received considerable emphasis in schools, sports activities have not been overlooked. Teaching sports is well organized, and leisure time skills are stressed in schools. Schools develop their own sports and athletic clubs and associations. These organizations have developed in secondary schools in such sports as cricket, swimming, basketball, track, and rowing. The love for sport has carried on into the winter, and mountain areas near the cities play host to thousands who regularly visit them on week ends and holidays.

The Australians probably love sports more than any other national group. However true this may be, the vast number of spectators and the variety of sports played by the population show the distinct bent these people have toward physical activity. Their recent world-recognized feats in swimming, tennis, track, and other sports indicate that this relatively sparsely populated continent takes physical education rather seriously. Other sports such as golf, bowling on the green, boxing, field hockey, wrestling, and cycling have a long history in Australia and continue to interest both young and old alike.

The development of physical education in Australia originally stressed physical fitness, especially in the school programs. The fitness of Australian soldiers shows how vigorously this concept has been accepted. However, it must be realized that a broad program has developed in schools, as well as nationwide, and the sports activities have become an integral part of the total physical education program.

NEW ZEALAND

New Zealand is comprised of a group of islands which lie east of Tasmania and slightly over 1200 miles east of Sydney, Australia. The two main divisions of this British Dominion are the North and South Islands separated by Cook Strait. This channel varies from 16 to about 90 miles.

Polynesian canoe-men apparently came to the islands as early as the 1300's. But it was not until 1769 that Cook, the British navigator, visited the islands. New Zealand receives bountiful rainfall in most sections which encourages an abundance of evergreen vegetation. Fjords, rivers, waterfalls, fertile valleys, lakes, and mountains combine to make this Dominion as beautiful as any country in the world.

New Zealand has remained very close to England throughout the years. Many British customs prevail, and the people, from a social standpoint, remain quite conservative. On the other hand, social welfare legislation including social security, old age pensions, and a short work week (40 hours) have, to a great extent, been nurtured in New Zealand.

Education in this Dominion is controlled by a Department of Education on the national level. The local departments confine their major efforts to problems relating to educational areas and facilities. Secondary schools have more local autonomy than do elementary schools. Whereas local secondary schools employ their own teachers, elementary schools depend upon the National Education Department to do the hiring. The

National Department rates teachers biennially, advertises teaching positions, and attempts to fill the vacancies.

A National Superintendent acts as a dominion-wide administrator for physical education in both secondary and primary schools as well as universities. In physical education and in other subject areas, the influence of the British point of view is blended with the progressive educational philosophy of modern education in the United States.

The Maoris, natives of New Zealand, fought a ten-year losing war (1861–71) with the settlers. These natives showed bravery and tenacity but very little skill in warfare. The most visible contribution to physical education is in the area of rhythmical dances and related activities, which have been adopted by the school program.

Physical education in the elementary schools includes teaching the basic skills, such as running, jumping, and vaulting. Also taught are basic dance steps, both minor and major sports, and fixed-apparatus activities. Physical education at this level is scheduled for four half-hour periods each week, one of these sessions devoted specifically to games. Classroom teachers conduct physical education, and they have the aid of physical education specialists.

At the secondary level, two 45-minute periods of physical education are required each week, which stress strength and body development as well as skills and applied games. Students in the last two years of secondary school are excused from this requirement. All students have an additional 30-minute period each week in which organized games and sports are conducted. The program for both girls and boys have similar aims, and for the most part similar types of activities. Physical education specialists usually teach in the program at the secondary level.

Because of its geographical location, aquatic activities such as yachting, swimming, and boating of all kinds exist as popular recreation activities. On the other hand, many of the popular leisure activities of England have been wholeheartedly adopted. Such pursuits include horse racing, bowling on the green, tennis, and golf. Men and women alike participate, but interest in women's sports is not high.

CANADA

Canada is an autonomous political unit with Great Britain the nominal head. It is composed of ten provinces in which approximately 14,000,000 people live. The Canadian Parliament has the general powers of legislation and government, and the provinces legislate on factors relating to civil rights, education, and local affairs in general. Canada stretches from the Atlantic to the Pacific Ocean, is bounded on the north by the Arctic

Ocean from the border of Alaska eastward, and its southern border is the United States.

Canada is about 20 per cent larger than the United States, but the most desirable areas to live in lie relatively close to the United States border. Canada, originally noted for its fishing, furs, and lumber, now has a large pulp industry, hydroelectric power, and it has become a vast grain and agricultural center. In recent years, mining for aluminum, nickel, copper, gold, silver and other minerals has expanded. Petroleum resources are beginning to be exploited in Canada as well as uranium deposits.

The cultural problems have proved enormous in Canada. Native Indians not destroyed to the degree they were in the United States, a tightly knit French-speaking minority, and a large English-speaking population all combine to make patterns of living of Canadians complex. Since World War I Canada has increased in prestige considerably, and in the years following World War II her place in international affairs has developed rapidly.

The Dominion's responsibilities for education have been mainly limited to financing schools in federal areas, granting subsidies to those pursuing agricultural and vocational pursuits, sponsoring war emergency preparation programs, and stimulating health and physical fitness programs. The National Physical Fitness Act gave strong support to recreation. Provinces without adequate physical education and recreation programs were, through financial grants, encouraged to make agreements with the federal government. Some results included leadership education, cooperating with other interested governmental agencies, financial aid to localities, information services to communities, and the like.

Control from the federal government is avoided in all Canadian provinces and in all grades of Canadian schools. The purposes of physical education throughout Canada include development of organic vigor, health, leisure attitudes and skills, social habits and attitudes, and neuromuscular skills. These goals closely resemble those sought through physical education in the United States. As mentioned previously in this chapter, movement education in physical education at the elementary school level has begun to exert a profound influence on both the program and the underlying philosophy.

Elementary school physical education stresses physical fitness, fundamental skills, sports skills, and the social aspects of games and sports. Most provinces, however, have not developed well-rounded programs of physical education. This lack has been attributed to many factors, such as the lack of adequate gymnasiums, poor public support, and a serious lack of qualified professional personnel.

At the secondary level, physical education has made considerable progress in the last two decades—more in some provinces than in others.

Girls' physical education has emphasized "movement education" ranging from the basic motor skills through creative dance. In addition, gymnastics, and sports are offered in the girls' program.

Physical education for boys at the secondary level stresses physical fitness, and basic skills in various sports. The sports included in the program are very similar to those in secondary schools in the United States, except that ice hockey, lacrosse, skiing, and rugby are emphasized. Obviously, the climate of Canada encourages the inclusion of outdoor winter sports and gives the program a certain characteristic in various provinces.

In recent years the Royal Canadian Air Force developed exercise plans for physical fitness for both men and women. Actually, these plans aimed at helping Royal Canadian Air Force personnel to reach and maintain superior physical condition. The two exercise books, following a vigorous demand by Canadian citizens, became best sellers in that country.

The popularity of these books spread to the United States, and they were in such great demand that *This Week Magazine* obtained permission from the Queen's Printer to reproduce these books as a single issue for sale and distribution. The books have had a significant effect upon many programs of physical education in schools and colleges, as well as interested individuals in both countries.

Physical educators are prepared in a number of institutions of higher learning in Canada. McGill University in 1945 began offering a four-year course leading to the Bachelor of Science Degree in Physical Education. This culminated a series of adventures in the field which included participation by such prominent men as A. S. Lamb, R. Tait McKenzie, and James Naismith. The Universities of Toronto, Western Ontario, Alberta, and British Columbia represent some of those also offering the baccalaureate in physical education.

12

Other European Countries

In modern times, all European countries have programs in physical education. There appears to be, for the most part, a great similarity among these programs. The following short descriptions of the selected programs give a general over-all picture of the status of physical education in many European countries.

FRANCE

The effort to develop nationalism in France following the French Revolution included, among other factors, education of the child by the state. Napoleon gave strength to this movement, and he developed from the previous decentralized program a centralized educational system. From that time forward, much emphasis has been given to developing a strong nationalistic feeling in all youth who go through the curriculum.

The physical education program in France was developed, in the main, by borrowing from other countries those physical activities and concepts which seemed to fit best. Foreign teachers were also employed to carry out such theories and practices. Such leaders were selected usually because of their success in their own countries regardless of the peculiar needs of the French people. In the 1800's France followed the pattern of other European countries and developed numerous sports and gymnastic societies and clubs. To gain financial support from the government, these clubs often included training in preparation for military service. To accommodate the interests of the people in these clubs, many play fields, stadiums, swimming pools, and other facilities were constructed.

In spite of the foreign influence, a Frenchman, Baron Pierre de Coubertin (1863–1937), brought his dream of modern Olympic games into fruition. These games, with the accompanying spirit of amateur participation, have done much to mold the present and almost world-wide ideal of physical education. The modern Olympic games became a reality in Athens in 1894. These games still flourish, but often the spirit or ideal of De Coubertin is abused as various countries try to gain world-wide recognition through the prowess of their athletes. In reality De Coubertin visualized the revival of the games as one means through which he could focus on the necessity for improved health and increased physical vigor.

A dominant military flavor controlled the viewpoint on physical education following World War I. However, a gradual shifting of authority from the Ministry of War to the Ministry of Public Instruction began to appear before the 1930's. This trend included establishing a Physical Education Bureau, and eventually physical education received direction through a youth and sports section of that bureau.

France has experimented with a number of different physical education systems through the years. These programs have run the gamut from the Ling gymnastics, to the George Demeny system which aimed to improve posture and a vigorous body, to Hébert's system which stressed running, climbing, balancing, and other natural movements.

At the secondary school level a two-hour-per-week requirement in physical education exists. Included, also, is a weekly out-of-doors afternoon period usually scheduled for three hours.

Corrective physical education receives considerable emphasis with much attention being given to the development of large muscles through body building types of exercises. Games, dances, athletic skills practice, swimming, and track and field are included in the program. However, unlike the United States, the compulsory curriculum does not stress sports education and competitive events. Viewing the evolution of physical education in France over a period of years, the impact of the Olympic games and the many activities included, plus the concern for using leisure in a worthwhile manner, is revealed in the direction the program has taken.

RUSSIA

The development of a new social order in Russia, a country covering about 16–17 per cent of the earth's surface, has consumed the efforts of its people in the past few years. To help foster this change, education has been used extensively to indoctrinate all youth with the principles of communism. Much time is spent in schools to teach children the communistic viewpoint toward collectivism, work, cooperative groups, patriotism, and the like. In reality, the effort teaches the individual subordination of the self for the socialistic cause.

Tsarist Russia did not regard education as the important means for indoctrinating people as do the Communists. Similarly, physical education, which is now widespread throughout Russia, received little recognition before the development of the present socialistic state. Physical education, like education in general in Russia, should be studied as one way in which they strive to reach political and economic goals. Education for a free mind, or sports for leisure enjoyment, are ideals which Soviet patriotism does not embody.

Basically, the Soviet Union strives for mass participation in its physical education program as a means for attaining universal physical fitness. All citizens, not only those attending school, are encouraged to regularly take part in physical exercise and to follow approved health habits. Through these practices, the Soviet citizens are supposed to become more efficient and productive workers. On the other hand, this regimen is designed to intensify the patriotism of Soviet youth. Not to be overlooked is the emphasis placed on training for military life through the exercise program and the hygienic practices.

The Soviet Union has developed a very extensive and complex educational system. At the present time, compulsory education includes as many as seven years for children in urban areas. The present compulsory requirements are temporary, and the goal is for at least ten years of required education for all. Evening schools, correspondence courses, industrial trade schools, and technical high schools supplement the present basic educational plan.

Physical culture has become an integral part of the school curriculum at all levels. Lessons are usually about forty-five minutes in duration and, depending upon the grade level, range from once or twice to three or four times weekly. This formalized instructional program is supplemented by many extra class groups in athletic activities, dancing, and other forms of leisure interests. These groups or "circles" are centered in the school and meet two to four times each week following the regular school day. Education, the armed service, and trade unions support these activities. Many trips and excursions are planned for these groups on Sundays, holidays and vacation periods.

Youth organizations administered by the Communist party conduct many activities for children and youth, of which sports and games play a major role. These clubs are: (1) Octobrists for 7- to 10-year-olds, (2) Pioneers for 10- to 16-year-olds, and (3) Komsomoles for 16- to 25-year-olds. The Pioneers seem to be the best attended (about 80 per cent of this age group) and they conduct activities in Pioneer palaces, and in specially built camps.

The development by the Soviet Union of many recreation facilities such as camps, rest centers, travel stations, swimming pools, gymnasiums, ski areas, and the like makes it possible for adults as well as the youth to participate regularly. Adults become members of athletic clubs and by taking advantage of all facilities tend to continue participation in sports longer than people in many other countries.

Each summer Physical Culture Day highlights sports participation in a nation-wide celebration. This event not only permits the results of the fitness program to be exhibited, but also it provides an opportunity for the politicians to speak before the people and encourage greater attainments in physical activities in the future.

In considering the physical culture program as a whole in the Soviet Union, it is apparent, first, that gymnastics are stressed in the early school grades, then as a preparation for the military, and finally as a means both for keeping adults fit and for providing enjoyment during leisure. Athletics and sports of all kinds receive considerable attention also. Soccer seems to be the most popular sport, but basketball and volleyball both receive considerable emphasis. Swimming, boating, hiking, and bicycling are also very popular. Skiing, hockey, and skating comprise the major outdoor winter sports. In fact, in some areas, skiing becomes the only means of transportation for school children so they must learn this activity.

Testing for physical fitness receives considerable support with emphasis being given to sports and activities of a military nature. Examinations include health and hygiene factors, gymnastic exercises, track activities, swimming, riflery, skiing, and various military activities. The "Master of Sports" award is the end toward which all athletes strive. This award, granted by the All-Union Committee of Physical Culture and Sports, designates that individual athlete as outstanding.

The amount of emphasis placed on physical fitness and prowess is perhaps best appreciated by the way in which the Soviet Union trains its Olympic games competitors. Nothing is left undone to produce winners, and their skilled representation in a vast number of sports is significant. Irrespective of the motives behind their Olympic games effort, their successes indicate clearly that the development of physical strength and skill has become an important factor in the Soviet culture. In addition, the authorities believe strongly in competition for developing fitness and improving performance.

ITALY

Many changes have been wrought in Italy since the time of the Roman Empire, and among these has been the attitude toward physical education. The gladiatorial combats of course no longer exist, but a program of physical education seems to be well established.

The nationalistic feeling built up in Italy before World War I became more solidified as Italy engaged vigorously after that war in the politics of Europe. The Fascist party, which came into power in the early post-World War I period, began immediately to devise means for organizing the youth for eventual political purposes. A Department of Physical Education was established to conduct both in- and out-of-school activities as one means for inculcating the Fascist spirit in the youth. Physical activity for fitness and club activities dominated this program.

State manuals for both boys and girls outlined the program conducted in elementary and secondary schools. In the elementary school the classroom teacher handled the four required thirty-minute physical education periods each week, while a specialist in physical education conducted the required four-hour weekly program. Physical education teachers also taught in the out-of-school program directed by the Department of Physical Education. Athletics and track and field activities supplemented the calisthenics and gymnastic program.

The out-of-school program received government grants in addition to membership fees and local support. Youth organizations, two for boys and two for girls, were established. The age range for both sexes was eight to thirteen and fourteen to eighteen years of age. The political influence was carried to the extent that participants in these youth organizations even wore black shirts like those of the Fascist party. Sports, camping, gymnastics, winter sports, riflery, and work projects characterized the program. Many facilities and areas were developed throughout Italy to accommodate this program.

World War II abruptly changed the organizational character of the physical education program in Italy. However, the experimental work, the research in education in general and physical education, combined with the interest in physical activity, prevailed, and today Italian physical education has many fine features. Excellent work is being accomplished with the physically handicapped, gymnastics are directed toward meeting individual interests and needs, camping is stressed, and a fondness for sports is being instilled in the youth. Soccer, swimming, and other athletic teams are prevalent in schools throughout Italy and interschool competitions and tournaments are universal. Italians have continued to hold a prominent place in international sports, and they have produced many outstanding athletes. Among other activities, Italy has produced exceptional athletes in both fencing and soccer.

BALKAN STATES

Albania, Bulgaria, Rumania and Yugoslavia have experienced many conflicts either among themselves or with neighboring countries. This continual brush with war has placed emphasis on the need for physical fitness among the peoples of these countries. To attain a state of physical readiness for military service, various systems of gymnastics have been employed.

Albania has had a long history of being occupied and controlled by countries such as Serbia, Greece, and Italy. During World War II, its plight became even worse when the puppet government declared war against the Allies, but Albanian guerrilla forces fought viciously against the Axis powers. A Committee for Physical Education and Sports has been established to develop programs of physical education in the schools. This Committee reports to the Council of Ministers. Physical education in this small country has stressed developmental exercises which prove advantageous from a military standpoint. Naturally, the instillation of patriotism and a spirit of nationalism through physical activity has prevailed.

Bulgaria was once a dominant power which extended its rule over the whole Balkan peninsula except for Greece but eventually collapsed and came under the control of first Serbia and then the Ottoman Empire. Turkish rule was severe, and over a period of centuries the struggle of Bulgarians to free themselves created a strong nationalistic feeling. In 1915, Bulgaria joined forces with Germany in World War I. The restoration of peace resulted in Bulgaria losing much territory, but the climate of World War II gave Bulgaria the opportunity to restore its territory. After accomplishing this, Bulgaria once again joined Germany in its world conflict.

These associations with Germany, especially in World War I, resulted in Bulgaria's adopting the physical education methods and exercises of Germany. In the period between the wars, physical education progressed in Bulgaria. By the early 1930's compulsory physical education for all girls and boys below 21 years of age became a reality. At present, national championship competition is organized each year in various sports such as volleyball, basketball, skiing, and gymnastics.

A half-hour a day is set aside for physical education in elementary schools. Special teachers of physical education are employed in many of the large schools. In secondary school a daily game period is set aside, and gymnastics are required two hours weekly. Hiking and trips into the country supplement these programs. Also, university students meet a two-hour-a-week physical education requirement by belonging to student groups which sponsor sports.

Youth organizations are quite active in Bulgaria and they stress physical activity. The pioneers (10–14 years of age), for instance, had 250,000 numbers participate in the Dimitrov hiking event which marked the 20th anniversary of the socialist revolution. At the same event, over 240,000 secondary school students also attended.*

Those not in school or college also partake of systematic exercise. Organizations provide physical activity opportunities for the members. Industries are required to either provide the necessary facilities for employee physical education or pay the fees necessary for employees to join physical education organizations. Military and civic advantages go to those youth who pass an examination at the culmination of five years of physical education.

Rumania, too, has been plagued for centuries with military conflicts and occupation and rule from without. Although in 1916 Rumania entered World War I on the side of the Allies, it was forced by its geographical location to become a neutral partner of the Axis.

Although the Rumanians have been exposed considerably to German gymnastics, that system never took a firm hold. The Swedish system, with variations, has proved more acceptable to Rumania. The emphasis on development of physical fitness for military advantages has strongly colored the physical education program. Gymnastic activities seem to be the core of the program, but considerable attention is given to sports and various outdoor activities.

Three to four hours per week are devoted to physical training in the schools. "Sport schools" have been established outside of school hours, and these strive to develop better skills in sports in the youth of the country. Approximately 44 of these schools serve more than 16,000 pupils. Camping in the mountains, with emphasis on skiing and skating, also attracts thousands of students. In excess of 300,000 pupils have participated in the annual school championships in basketball, gymnastics, handball, swimming and volleyball. Finally, the Rumanian folk dances, performed extensively by both men and women in colorful dress, depict the customs of these people as they have developed over many centuries.

Yugoslavia as a state came into existence after World War I. Six small republics, two independent states and four states belonging to the Austro-Hungarian monarchy were combined to form Yugoslavia.

This country is noted for its native folk dances. Kolo, its national dance, is performed vigorously by both men and women. In fact many dances are performed in Yugoslavia, as well as in other Balkan countries, by men without women. The German and Danish programs of gymnastics apparently influenced physical education more than the Swedish type. Tumbling, apparatus work, games, and sports all receive considerable emphasis. The necessity for maintaining a large and rather power-

* *World Survey of Education III, Secondary Education,* New York: International Document Service, a division of the Columbia University Press, 1961. Pp. 288–89.

ful military force under the regime of Tito has influenced the direction in which physical education has developed in recent years.

Secondary schools in Yugoslavia require from two to three hours of physical education each week. This program is supplemented in out-of-school hours by pioneer and youth organizations, which stress gymnastics and various sports.

CZECHOSLOVAKIA

Like the Balkan countries, Czechoslovakia has experienced long periods of domination from without. The Czechs joined with the Allies in World War I and seemed to be in a favored position following that war. Hitler's rise in Germany led to eventual control of Czechoslovakia and the never to be forgotten slaughter at Lidice. A temporary Czech government was established in England during World War II, and Czech units fought with the Allies. In recent years the government has been dominated by the Communists.

The struggle to free themselves from the tyranny of the Hapsburg Empire during the 1800's caused the Czechs to develop a program of physical education that aimed to give the people physical and spiritual strength to gain their independence. The Sokol organization came into fruition early in the 1860's, and within a span of less than ten years a boys' branch and a girls' and women's division were added. This was a patriotic gymnastic movement that focused directly on strengthening nationalism. A festival, the Sokol Slet, is held at times to demonstrate movement, timing, precision, and form in large group activities. More than 95,000 school children and 270,000 men and women have participated in a Sokol Slet.

Physical education has become an integral phase of the educational system. Compulsory education exists for children to the age of fifteen, and a section on sport is included in the Ministry of education. In all schools, primary, secondary, college preparatory, and universities, two hours per week of physical education are required. The typical program consists of calisthenics, a variety of sports, track and field, aquatic activities, winter sports, folk dancing, and camping. Through the "sparks" (6–9 years of age), members of the Czechoslovakian Youth Union supplement school programs by conducting cultural and recreational activities including sports and games.

The colleges at Bratislava, Brno, and Olomouc plus Charles University at Prague offer specialized physical education programs for preparing teachers. All elementary teachers average an hour of physical education each day during their two years of study. Special physical education teachers for college preparatory schools receive intensive training in physical education, both practical and theoretical, during their four years of preparation. The great number of independent organizations, including the Sokol, also conduct training schools for their leaders.

FINLAND

Finland was completely under the control of Russia for over 100 years, but in 1920 the U.S.S.R. recognized Finnish independence. In World War II, after very stiff resistance to several attacks, Finland was able to avoid total capitulation to Russia, and to retain its independence, only at the cost of severe territorial, financial, and economic difficulties.

Finland's contribution to the physical education movement has proved significant. In building up the spirit of nationalism, the German and Swedish systems of gymnastics were introduced very early. This in part has led to their striving for perfection of execution of the exercises. Even though this emphasis exists, the Finns tend to seek fun and enjoyment in their physical education. In the same manner the dances of the Finnish people stress perfection, but a recreative atmosphere seems to persist throughout.

Physical education was introduced into the schools of Finland as early as the 1840's. Since the 1920's the Finns have expanded the exercises, marching, and gymnastics programs for pupils to include games and sports, track and field, and winter activities. Primary schools require two to three hours of physical education each week, while secondary schools have three to four hours each week. The program for girls stresses rhythmic calisthenics, other rhythmic activities, and games. Athletic competitions for girls receive little backing, and even the Finnish Women's Gymnastic Organization recommends no competitions or championships in highly competitive athletics.

The enthusiasm of the Finns for physical activity of all types is marked. Finland supports sports institutes which emphasize leadership in physical education. Such institutes are subsidized by the government from 70–84 per cent of their annual expenditures. These sports institutes attract over 11,000 students each year. The feats of some Finnish athletes have been outstanding in international competition and in the Olympic games, especially in track and field activities. People from many countries have studied the methods that Finnish athletes use for conditioning themselves. The Finnish people love festivals, which include many exhibitions of sports, gymnastics, dancing, and other physical activities.

The part that the Finnish women have played in furthering physical education deserves special mention. A modern program of gymnastics for women has been developed by Miss Elli Björksten, Helsinki University. A vital interest in individual needs led her to develop a system which varied markedly from the Swedish system. As in physical education throughout Finland, this system stresses, as far as possible, informality and joyful participation. Another woman, Miss Anni Collan, has spent considerable time in preserving the old native folk dances by introducing them in the school program and generally encouraging their preservation by stimulating people to engage in these dances.

Many voluntary organizations promote physical education in Finland. These agencies have done much to advance athletics throughout the country. For the boys their program has stressed competition and perfection in sports activities. The girls' programs offered by these voluntary programs have remained mainly noncompetitive.

NETHERLANDS

The people of the Netherlands support a complex school system that is on the elementary level predominantly private. However, both public and private schools are supported by the state. The influence of the churches (Catholic and Calvinistic) has been considerable, and marked support exists for the viewpoint that play and recreation are wasteful.

The formal school curriculum has left little room for physical education. Until 1940 physical education was not compulsory. However, since that time advances have been made in introducing physical activity and health into the school day. Secondary schools require three hours of physical education each week for both boys and girls. In addition teachers now receive opportunities in their preparation to study gymnastics, which, incidentally, are similar in nature to those of the Germans. The influence of natural gymnastics of the Austrians is prevalent.

The Dutch, in spite of the restricted school program and an unenthusiastic church attitude, seek pleasure through sports and games. The schools form many activity clubs, including sports clubs, which hold sports events outside the regular school program. Skating, hockey, boating, dancing, basketball, volleyball, and korfball (similar to basketball) represent a few of the more popular leisure sports. The accomplishments of the Dutch in international speed skating, and of the women in swimming and track in the Olympic games, have been outstanding. Further, the Dutch girls in their wooden shoes and colorful costumes as they participate in folk dances are a symbol of the Netherlands throughout the world.

BELGIUM

The Belgians are divided into two language groups. Flemish, a Dutch dialect, is spoken in the north. In the south, French is the official language, but considerable German is spoken. Almost the entire population is of the Roman Catholic faith, and thus the church plays a very important part in shaping the educational pattern. During most of the nineteenth century Belgium was free of foreign domination, but her neutrality was ignored by Germany in both World Wars. The country was not only dominated temporarily from without, but widespread destruction took place.

Belgium's school system adheres to certain state standards. All schools, private included, receive state aid when minimum requirements are satisfied. Swedish gymnastics dominate the physical education program, but the German gymnastic influence is strong in the northern part of the country. Games and sports as a part of the physical education program in schools have been gaining acceptance since World War I. Soccer, track and field, basketball, and volleyball represent a few of the more popular sports.

Physical education in Belgium has been viewed with regard to the contributions it makes to health. In fact, the Belgians seem very interested in personal and community health as evidenced by industrial health programs, welfare benefits, labor legislation, and the close cooperative work with the Red Cross and various voluntary health organizations. Research in medicine and physiology are often related either directly or indirectly to physical education. Remedial exercises make important contributions to the over-all physical education program.

SPAIN

Spain, whose civilization dates back to the Stone Age and whose role in international affairs has declined from a very significant to an insignificant influence, has done very little to develop organized physical education programs. Although Spain requires eight years of compulsory education, the regulation is often overlooked, and organized physical education receives little or no attention. Even though Spain through her military force was an international power at one time and now operates as a dictatorship, physical education for nationalistic and military purposes has never seemed to permeate the regular lives of its people.

At present, however, the curricula in the general secondary and vocational secondary schools include regular sessions weekly in physical education. The Ministry of Education supplements this program by conducting annual interschool championships in each province in various sports. State as well as private schools enter these competitions.

Bull fighting is the national sport of the Spanish people, yet few participate. Jai alai, a sport played in a large court (side, front, and back walls) and resembling handball except for a basket-type throwing implement attached to one forearm, originated in Spain. Spectators watch and bet on the results of this game. The people of Spain are also noted for their lively, colorful dancing which highlights many of their holiday and festive occasions. Fencing has remained popular in Spain, and considerable boxing takes place.

SWITZERLAND

The people of Switzerland have remained neutral during two world wars, yet all able-bodied men remain in the reserve army until they reach the age of 60. German dialects are spoken by most Swiss, but French, Italian, and Romansh (a Rhaeto-Romanic dialect) are official national languages. Not only do the languages differ, but the country is split from a religious standpoint with Protestantism prevailing over Catholicism in the ratio of about five to four.

Switzerland, which was the home of the League of Nations, is a confederation of twenty-five federal states or nineteen cantons and six half cantons. All these cantons have considerable autonomy, and consequently their educational systems differ. However, education is compulsory, and all children attend until they are at least 15 years of age.

Swiss education reflects the philosophy of the great educator Pestalozzi. Thus, physical education and play receive considerable emphasis. For the most part, special teachers usually conduct gymnastics three mornings each week and sports in the afternoon. Rhythmic group calisthenics tend to increase interest and add vigor to the exercises of the participants. Because of the differences of nationalities in Switzerland, other forms of gymnastics are prevalent such as the Jahn gymnastics with apparatus and the Delcroze movements accompanied by music.

A vast number of sports clubs exist in Switzerland. Many of the clubs include such activities as mountain climbing and hiking, soccer, basketball, rugby, rifle and pistol shooting, and skiing. Winter sports and hiking are particularly adapted to the geography and climate of Switzerland, and much attention is given to promoting tourist trade. Summer tourists are provided additional inducements in the form of well-developed beaches, swimming pools, parks, and other facilities in or near the larger cities.

13

Japan, China, India, and South Africa

Most Eastern countries, until about 1900, functioned at a rather slow pace, some operating as the European countries did during the Middle Ages and others as colonies of Western countries. The strong nationalistic feeling prevalent in Japan for a long time has been developing in many other Eastern countries in the twentieth century. Accompanying this phenomenon has been the introduction of gymnastics, games, and sports through such media as armies and occupation forces, visiting sports teams, the Young Men's Christian Association, missionaries, and tourists. Interest has developed in physical activities to the extent that the Far Eastern games have been organized, and many of these nations now participate in the Olympic games.

JAPAN

Japan, an overpopulated nation, is made up of four major islands and numerous smaller islands. Although contact with the West was made as early as 1542 and some trading took place, a repressive feudal government arose in the seventeenth century and continued for about 250 years to 1867. This date marked the Meiji restoration, which led to trading once again with the West. Also, many Japanese went abroad to study and returned to Japan with knowledge about foreign developments in military science, political institutions, and industrial developments. Japan also developed a strong army and navy.

With this surge to become a world power and with the continued trend toward a strong nationalistic feeling, physical education became an important factor. Military drills and gymnastics (later the Swedish type) have given way to a sports and games program. Following World War II, in which physical activity for military preparedness dominated, new education laws completely reorganized the school program including physical education. Six years of elementary school are followed by two three-year periods for junior and senior high schools. Physical education is required throughout this entire educational experience. In addition compulsory physical education exists as a part of the university general education plan.

Physical education in Japan at present resembles that advocated in the United States. An attempt is made to integrate physical education with other subjects. Individual interests, needs, and capacities receive attention as boys and girls participate each day in physical education. Sports, games, dancing, and forms of outdoor education comprise the major activities. Emphases are placed on improving health, personality, motor skills, and social acumen through wise selection of activities and proper methods of teaching.

Japan has always been noted for its wrestling and judo. The Japanese are very strong participants in the Far Eastern games, and they also enter the Olympic games. Swimmers from Japan have gained world-wide recognition, and their accomplishments in international competition have been outstanding. The development of after-school athletic programs and the activities of many clubs and organizations indicate that Japan will continue to produce outstanding athletes. Over 30 per cent of the students join sports clubs at their schools, and interschool matches and athletic meetings are quite common. For example, over 10,000 secondary students participate yearly in local baseball games, which lead to the all-Japan upper secondary school baseball meetings. Japan has adopted baseball as a major national sport and in the process has developed thousands of amateur teams and some professional teams.

CHINA

China has never been a closely knit country with a strong and influential central government. Great Britain, France, Germany, and Russia all had concessions for trading with China until the Open Door policy, advocated by the United States, gave all countries equal access to China's trade. This foreign influence has always been resented by the Chinese. At present China is controlled by the Communist party, and a militaristic atmosphere prevails throughout the country.

Physical education in China made little progress until the twentieth century. Missionaries and the Young Men's Christian Association introduced gymnastics and some games. American educators later encouraged the introduction of a sports program, and in 1929, a compulsory physical education law was passed. Physical education then became more organized, and standard programs were developed by the Ministry of Education for all levels of education, including college. Standardization becomes less rigid in the higher grades, and the informalized program of sports and games receives most attention. In fact the recommended college physical education activities resemble those advocated for a well-rounded American college program.

The Chinese have developed few professional sports, but a great amount of local amateur competition takes place. This practice grew in China despite the fact that there was no required physical education until relatively recent years. The Chinese National Amateur Athletic Federation conducts National Athletic Meets, and in many cities local competitions are held once or twice each year. In recent years women's events have been added to these meets in which general enthusiasm prevails.

This participation by girls and women has been increasing rapidly since the approach to education included girls. They were quick to take advantage of this opportunity, and as a result physical education also became a requirement in schools for girls. Popular activities for girls include swimming, volleyball, basketball, tennis, and softball. Many institutions have trained women physical education teachers throughout the past twenty-five years.

INDIA

India, lòng under the domination of England, has been a self-governing nation since 1947. The traditional caste system of India was legally abolished by the new constitution, but regardless of this important advance the country is involved with internal conflict. In addition the outmoded farming methods, lack of flood control, poor housing, dense population, many different languages, and other factors thwart attempts to move forward with social and economic reforms.

Education is hindered by all the above conditions, but the many languages, the lack of adequate educational facilities, and the sparsity of qualified people to teach loom as major deterrents. The central government gives some financial assistance to education and provides over-all leadership. Plans for educating the people of India include a compulsory free elementary education for all children which already is taking shape.

Also planned are limited secondary school and college programs plus a literacy program for all adults.

Although leadership comes from the central government, each province and the city councils therein assume responsibility for education. Thus the ascetic philosophy and the taboos and traditional practices may have definite effects on the development of the educational program at the local or state level. Some of the progressive states require physical education through all educational levels including college.

A few schools—some of which are located in Calcutta, Bombay, Madras, Amraoti, and East Punjab—offer teacher preparation programs in physical education. The affiliation of such schools with the universities is progressing slowly, and completion of this movement should result eventually in a better educated physical education teacher. Short-term courses for classroom teachers also help them in becoming better prepared to conduct the physical activities for children. Already India's educational leaders view physical education as a way of helping to attain the total educational development of the individual. Health, personality development, neuro-muscular skills, and social adjustments are some desired outcomes of the physical education program.

India seems determined to nurture the present physical education program and expand it considerably in the years ahead. Many voluntary and public groups are stimulating progress. The National Association of Physical Education and Recreation was formed in 1946 at the initial National Physical Education Conference. Advisory Committees on Physical Education exist in many states as well as on the central government level of India. A National Sports Club is in the process of planning and making available modern physical education facilites and areas. The Indian Olympic Association not only has many affiliates of sports groups with national governing bodies but also helps further sports which have no national governing bodies. Interscholastic and college athletic associations abound throughout the country, and sport and gymnastic tournaments are conducted by many private associations.

The emphasis on physical education in India has spilled over into community life. Communities throughout the nation have exercise centers, and some cities are setting aside recreation areas as centers for leisure pursuits. The establishment of leisure programs is being encouraged because individuals, local government, and some central government departments view recreation as the means through which people will be diverted from drinking alcoholic beverages.

Today, the program of physical education for India varies markedly from school to school, but regarded as a whole it is quite comprehensive. In most states in India, physical education is a regular compulsory course subject for students in classes V through XI. Some school camping, classical Indian dances, folk and modern dance, gymnastics, a variety of dual and individual games, team games, and swimming comprise major activity categories included in the school program. As India advances its social and economic programs and as the philosophy which supports subordinating the body to the spirit becomes less popular, physical education should attain a real place in the educational program.

SOUTH AFRICA

South Africa is bordered by the Atlantic Ocean on one side and the Indian Ocean on the other. A large country, almost a half million square miles, it is mostly plateau (2,000 to 5,000 feet high) although some mountainous areas exist in the east and some lowlands along the long coastline. South Africa is dry and warm, and irrigation is often necessary to supplement the rainfall. The Dutch were the first white settlers at Capetown, but the British took over in 1841. Finally, in 1910, following the South African War, the British established the Union of South Africa, a federation of four provinces: Natal, Orange Free State, Cape of Good Hope, and Transvaal. Mainly a farming and cattle country, South Africa also mines many products, such as diamonds, gold, copper, asbestos, and chromium.

South Africa has established an educational system organized on a basis of 12 grades, either 8–4 or 7–5. Education is compulsory from the ages of seven to fifteen or sixteen, depending upon the province. The various races and languages result in a complicated social structure which is reflected somewhat in the school systems. The European group is provided with fine teachers and superior school facilities. However, the colored and Asiatic groups receive less benefits, and the natives have been seriously neglected from an educational standpoint. This condition is of great consequence because approximately 10,000,000 natives, 2,500,000 whites, about 1,000,000 colored (i.e., part-white), 300,000 Indians, and a small group of Chinese make up the population of South Africa. This obviously leaves the vast majority of inhabitants without adequate educational opportunities.

The Union Department of Education is the central government authority, and it guides the physical education programs of universities, special and technical schools and colleges, and various governmental departments of the Union. The provinces control elementary, secondary, and teacher education institutions. Compulsory physical education exists on all education levels.

Dr. Ernst Jokl has contributed much to the advancement of physical education in South Africa. In 1938 he produced a film which portrayed the type of physical activities for use in physical education. The film was shown to various groups and it was generally well received. Two years later Jokl also developed a *Syllabus of Physical Exercises* for South African schools. Printed in both Afrikaans and English, it describes by word, sketches, and diagrams the activities ranging from simple children's games to complex activities. Jokl held the position of Director of the Physical Education Department at Wetwatersand Technical College, Johannesburg, the largest institution of higher learning in the country.

Physical education is usually held three 30-minute periods per week in the elementary schools. Both classroom teachers and specialists participate, and the emphasis is usually on teaching sports for boys and movement education for girls. On the secondary level, the emphasis is much as it is for the primary level, except skills are taught on a higher level. More specialists with university training are also used in secondary schools.

The goals of physical education in South Africa include organic fitness, desirable health habits, neuro-muscular skills, continued recreational interests, and desirable social habits and attitudes. To accomplish these ends, gymnastics are stressed, especially in physical education classes, but activities such as rugby, soccer, cricket, hockey, golf, tennis, and rhythms represent some of the other activities that are used extensively.

There are nine South African universities, but only five have established physical education departments. A Bachelor of Science or Arts degree is offered by these departments through a three-year course of study. A Senior Education Diploma is selected by most students as the goal of their fourth year of study.

South Africa has been faced with much criticism with regard to its racial segregation in sports. Many countries refuse to participate with them in international sports events, and great pressures from without the country are being exerted to bring about the elimination of this practice of apartheid.

14

South America and Mexico

The countries of Latin America have had many internal difficulties, and one of the consequences has been the failure to build strong educational programs. In recent years, these countries south of the United States give evidence of working toward educational goals which will provide educational opportunities for all. European influence has always been strong in these countries, and it is reflected in the physical education programs that have been developed.

ARGENTINA

Argentina, the second largest country in South America, is more than one-third the size of the United States. Approximately 23,000,000 people live in this country. Argentina has some of the finest cattle herds in the world, but it also produces wheat, corn, mutton, wool, wine, and lumber. Argentina has most every kind of climate and a varied topography that includes mountainous territory, a huge fertile plain, and tropical forests and swamps.

British, French, Germans, Italians, Swiss, and East Europeans have settled in Argentina and developed it considerably. Argentina is not only one of the world's granaries, but also considerable manufacturing has been initiated. The lack of power, resources, and power tools has tended to retard industrial developments.

The native Indian population, which caused the Spanish settlers to abandon Buenos Aires in 1841, five years after it was founded by the Conquistador, Pedro de Mendoza, has almost disappeared. In effect, the population is European, favoring French culture. Even though Argentina produces vast amounts of farm products and beef, almost seven out of ten people live in cities.

Education in Argentina is the responsibility of the national government, through the Department of Education, and the provincial governments. The provinces support elementary education often aided by federal funds, but secondary education is left to the federal government. Most provinces require children to attend school from ages six to fourteen. However, this requirement is not strictly enforced, especially for girls. The secondary schools, called national colleges, generally have a five-year curriculum. Normal schools have a four-year primary teacher education course or a seven-year secondary (national college) curriculum. Beyond this level a national university system exists.

The teaching in Argentina differs from that in the United States in many respects. The federal government appoints teachers to the schools it provides; local school councils have little or no authority with regard to federal schools; teachers in universities and secondary schools support themselves by holding an additional job; schools, especially those federally administered, have identical textbooks and other materials; and teachers on the elementary level are not required to have as much education as those on other levels.

Physical education on all levels is under the jurisdiction of the Ministry of Education and supervision is carried out to insure compliance with regulations. Physical education is required from elmentary school to the university. Classroom teachers instruct physical education on the elementary level, but special physical education teachers are employed above that level. Buenos Aires is the home of the National Institute of Physical Education, which has a three-year curriculum for preparing men and women teachers.

European influence has undoubtedly resulted in the emphasis given to gymnastics, and there is a trend toward Bukh exercises and away from Swedish gymnastics. In 1951 the National School of Dancing was initiated, and it provides prospective teachers with the opportunity to prepare in classical dance and Argentina folk-dancing. Rhythms and folk dancing also play an important part in the physical education program. Sports and athletics are very popular in Argentina; in fact, with few exceptions, most games popular in America are played enthusiastically. In addition to the required physical education program, extra class activities are organized for the children and youth.

Physical education in Argentina is viewed as the way to keep individuals fit. Further, the social values and the aspect of leisure education are stressed as very worthwhile outcomes. The leisure goal seems to be realistic because, in general, the people avidly pursue sports activities.

Many clubs with a variety of facilities for games, sports, and other activities serve the interests of people throughout Argentina.

Riding and handling horses has long been a favorite pastime in Argentina. Polo is a popular sport. Another game, el pato, is played with horses, but riders roughly contend for a six-handled ball which they attempt to throw through the opponent's basket. The gauchos, nomadic herdsmen of an earlier era, receive credit for inventing this game and passing it on to the present sportsmen.

BOLIVIA

Bolivia, like Paraguay, is an inland country in South America with a population of less than 4,000,000 people. It is part mountainous and part tropical. The mountains hold Bolivia's wealth—its minerals. Tin, silver, copper, zinc, lead, and gold are a few of the minerals mined. The tropical area in the east is unsettled, and its potential value has never been adequately appraised.

More than half the Bolivian population is pure Indian. In the east many tribes have not been influenced by white culture whatsoever. In the west Spanish culture and Catholicism prevail, but the Indians maintain their customs and language. Around 35 per cent of the population are mestizos, called cholos, and the remainder are white. The cholos and whites control business and politics, and the native Indians do the labor.

The Ministry of Education, Fine Arts, and Indian Affairs supervises Bolivian education. One of six bureaus is organized to direct and supervise physical education throughout Bolivia as well as many special institutions. Free, public elementary and secondary education exists, and all children between the ages of seven and fourteen must attend. A six-year elementary curriculum is complemented by a six-year secondary school which is divided into two parts. Another peculiarity of the educational system is that private secondary schools equal the number of public institutions.

Physical education is compulsory in both elementary and secondary schools. Two to three hours of activity are required each week. At the university level no physical education requirement exists. The curriculum in schools includes formal gymnastics, many sports such as volleyball, basketball, and rugby, and rhythmics and folk dancing. Education is conducted quite formally in Bolivia, and this holds true in the health education classes.

Boys before reaching eighteen years of age take training in preparation for two years of compulsory military service. Physical education is stressed during this training period.

BRAZIL

Brazil is the largest land mass by far in South America, and approximately 82,000,000 people reside there. Because of its size, Brazil has variety in its climate and topography. The people, too, come from diverse origins, and the new Bralizian "race" is an amalgamation of Indian, Negro, and European strains. Although Portuguese is the official language, German and Italian prevail in certain southern areas, while Indian languages are used in the north.

The huge Amazon River basin occupies much of the north and north central portions of Brazil. Here, the steaming jungles, although providing rubber, hardwood, and other products, remain virtually unexploited. The northeast is a farming and cattle region, while the east and southeast form the populous section of Brazil. Much industry is springing up in parts of Brazil as evidenced by the rapid growth of both the state and city of São Paulo. Brazil has the natural resources to eventually develop industry to the utmost. For instance, the iron reserves are considered as fine as any in the world.

By law, primary education is compulsory in Brazil, and the states are supposed to spend at least 20 per cent of their total incomes and the national government 10 per cent or more for education. Of course opportunities for education vary according to the economic wealth of a state. The federal government directly supervises secondary schools and institutions of higher learning, while the states, for the most part, maintain primary and normal school education. About three types of normal schools exist: (1) those offering four years beyond elementary school, (2) those having two- or three-year post junior high school curriculums, and (3) those maintaining a five-year course emphasizing cultural and professional education.

A Minsitry of Health, developed in 1930, has a physical education office. The Ministries of the Navy and War direct their own physical education programs. State offices are generally maintained for supervising physical education. Physical education is required on all education levels, and it occurs usually twice a week for periods of 30 to 45 minutes.

Physical education has been focused on gymnastics and body-building activities, but recently some emphasis has been given to activities designed to develop desirable social characteristics. Gymnastics, however, do form the basis of primary and secondary physical education at present. Encouragement of sports as a part of the required program is taking place and reflected in the programs of the more progressive schools. Some institutions already have begun to compete in sports among themselves.

At the present time in Brazil it is necessary for a group interested in a sport to secure the approval of the federal government and then form a single sport federation such as the Brazilian Basketball Confederation. A National Council of Sports was created as a department of the Ministry of Education to supervise sports governing bodies on the national level. The young men and women of Brazil have shown great interest in sport. Because the climate in most of the settled areas of Brazil is warm, swimming is a very popular sport and recreation activity. Soccer, as both a professional and amateur sport, is the most popular team game. Over 200,000 fans may be accommodated in a single stadium in Rio de Janeiro. Horse racing, other equestrian sports, and hunting are very popular leisure activities.

CHILE

Chile is a long narrow country with hot deserts in the north and mountains running into the sea in the south, accompanied by wet wooded areas along the coastline. The central part of Chile, a long central valley, accommodates the main population concentration. The people of Chile are approximately 60 per cent Spanish mestizos, 30 per cent white, and 5 per cent pure Indian. A total of nearly 9,000,000 people live in Chile.

Chile has a compulsory education system for children between the ages of seven and fifteen. The program of physical education is required on both primary and secondary levels but not at the University of Chile. Classes run about 45 minutes two or three times each week.

Joaquim Cabezas Garcia became director of the Institute of Physical and Manual Education in 1906. This agency later became a university school and now is known as the Institute of Physical and Technical Education. Garcia received his preparation in Sweden. Coupled with this was the influence of a German team of instructors who came to Chile in 1885. The formal gymnastic program consequently has always predominated, and sports assume an inferior place in the required physical education curriculum. Physical education is required two or three periods each week. In addition, the interscholastic programs in both primary and secondary schools are well organized in basketball, soccer, football, track and field, and other sports.

The emphasis on physical fitness and health stressed in schools also carries over into adult life. Many people in Chile belong to associations that have a formal tie to the National Sports Council. The Council, composed in part of government officials, concerns itself with the development of sports for adults. Other governmental bodies also are involved in the over-all sports program, and there is an apparent tendency to emphasize personal and national physical fitness.

COLOMBIA

Colombia, with both Atlantic and Pacific coastlines, containing over 19,000,000 people, is a land of contrasts—disease-infested jungles to majestic Andean peaks. Colombia is a big producer of platinum and gold and is second only to Brazil in the production of coffee. Milling cotton textiles, food processing, manufacturing clothing and chemicals, distilling liquor, and processing the country's chief exports represent a few of the industrial activities that have made great strides in the past twenty-five years.

The Ministry of Education supervises public education in Colombia. Before 1930 the Catholic church controlled the schools, but now the local boards of education, the state, and the ministry combine to finance the program. However, the Ministry of Education, for the most part, sets standards and minimum requirements on the secondary level and requires private agencies to follow them. The national government has established only a few secondary schools. On the other hand, primary education is publicly financed by state and local governments in the main. The organizational pattern is usually a 4–6 plan. Free, compulsory education between the ages of seven and fourteen is the unenforced requirement.

Elementary school terminates the education of many students. Physical education is given three times a week in elementary, secondary, and normal schools. Classroom teachers assume the responsibility for conducting these activities on the elementary level, and specialists trained in the National Physical Education School continue from that point on. Gymnastics and folk dances are given an important place in the physical education program. However, sports are becoming popular, and secondary schools organize intramural sports programs in addition to the regular class periods. Health, loyalty to the democratic way of life preserving the cultural heritage, and fitness appear as major foci of the physical education program.

ECUADOR

The small country of Ecuador has not even made an accurate survey of the wilderness of plains and jungle east of the Andes. The central area is a plateau on which most of the 5,400,000 inhabitants live, and farming is the main occupation. The coastal area produces most of Ecuador's chief exports, cacao, cyanide precipitates, gold, petroleum and other products. The main bulk of the population is either Indian or part

Indian, about 15 per cent of the population is Negro, and the few white people are landowners and control politics.

Compulsory education in Ecuador is applied only at the elementary school level, or to children up to 12 years of age. Elementary schools in urban and rural areas are of six- and four-years' duration respectively. High schools are designed so that a two-year specialized course is offered beyond a four-year general cultural curriculum. The Ministry of Education supervises almost all educational agencies.

Physical education is compulsory daily for one-half hour in elementary school and two or three hours on the secondary level. Gymnastics (rhythmic gymnastics for girls), dances, and various sports including boxing comprise the program on both educational levels. Track and field, basketball, football, tennis, and volleyball are some of the sports receiving most emphasis. Intramural and interscholastic competition have not developed appreciably.

PARAGUAY

Paraguay, a small inland republic, is a subtropical land with a small population exceeding 2,000,000 people. The land west of the Paraguay River is largely unproductive, but some authorities believe it may contain petroleum. The area east of the Paraguay River produces cotton, tobacco, sugar cane, rice, beans, corn, and other farm products. Rum, molasses, and alcohol are manufactured, and the orange groves supply about three quarters of the world's petitgrain supply, which goes into flavorings and perfumes. The native Guaraní Indians had a high standard of culture before the white men arrived, and they have freely mixed with the Spanish people. Although Spanish is the official language, Guaraní is spoken throughout Paraguay.

The Chaco War with Bolivia (1932–35) left Paraguay exhausted though victorious. Thereafter, improvements begun in health, education, and roads have been thwarted by rapid successions of government (except between 1940–48) and many internal conflicts.

Free elementary education is compulsory up to the age of 14, and it begins at the age of seven in towns and at age nine in rural areas. A Minister of Public Instruction supervises education, and, through joint operation with the National Council in Education, plans the curriculum and enforces policies. Private schools make up the secondary education program, and they continue for five years. A sixth year of specialization is available for those who intend to pursue university preparation at the National University in the capital city, Asunción.

Bodily development appears to be the focus of the physical education program which is required two periods each week. Sports and games have been introduced into the program, and the leisure use of such activities receives emphasis. An academic tradition prevails, and physical education has not gained the important place in education in Paraguay that it has in some other South American countries.

PERU

Peru has a great variety of topography and climate as it stretches from the mountain area of the Andes down to the rain forests of the West Amazon basin. The eastern area has a rich potential, but the difficulty of transportation has thwarted its exploitation. As in the time of the Inca Empire as well as during the Spanish conquest, mining still remains an important industry with gold, silver, copper, lead, zinc, and bismuth being produced. The potential for producing abundant agricultural produce is great, and the forests in Peru are extensive.

The number of natives in Peru has not been accurately determined, but it is undoubtedly true that at least half of the more than 12,000,000 population is pure Indian. The larger part of the remainder is mestizo, with a few Orientals (mostly Japanese), some Negroes, and a larger group of European whites (Spanish, German, and Italian). The Indians generally live in the east and in the mountainous areas, while the whites have established themselves in the cities and along the coastal area.

The Ministry of Public Education supervises education and is divided into six departments for administrative purposes. The Department of Physical Education and Hygiene is one of these departments and supervises the compulsory physical education program required in elementary, secondary, vocational, and normal schools. Generally, physical education is required three hours each week in secondary schools and two hours in other schools. Lima, the capital of Peru, is the home of the National Institute of Physical Education where students follow a comprehensive three-year curriculum. Entering students are required to meet certain health and physical standards.

As a complement to moral and intellectual preparation, the government encourages emphasis on physical education for school children. Gymnastics in Peru are stressed as preparatory exercises for activities in sports. In general, the needs and interests of the participants receive consideration, as does the section of the country because of the diverse climates. Tournaments to determine school champions of various sports have been organized as well as sporting expeditions in the Andes. Testing of students is frequent, and emphasis is placed upon health and body development.

Sports are organized in cities for the leisure or upper classes. Golf, polo, tennis, and swimming are some of the sports designed for, and considerably limited to, this special group. In addition, horse racing and bull fighting are popular, but all classes seem to find one way or another to enjoy these sports.

URUGUAY

Uruguay separates Brazil and Argentina, so its topography varies from the humid Argentine pampas to the South Brazilian uplands. For the most part, rain is sufficient and falls evenly throughout the year. Thus, this country with a temperate climate produces many agricultural products on a small amount of land. Raising sheep and cattle are basic to Uruguay's economy. Uruguay is a prosperous country with exceptional communication and transportation facilities. Its people are progressive and have introduced much social legislation. Child labor laws, the eight-hour work day, accident insurance, and pensions for the aged have all been effected. The 2,800,000 people are made up of about 10 per cent mestizos, practically no pure Indians or Negroes, and the rest of white European extraction, mostly Spanish and Italian.

Four directorates under the Ministry of Public Instruction and Social Welfare are organized so that each is responsible for the control of one of the following levels of education: (1) elementary and normal school, (2) industrial, (3) secondary, and (4) higher. Education in Uruguay that is provided by the state from kindergarten through the university is free of charge. Regardless of race, religion, or any other factor access to education is guaranteed to all. Six-year elementary schools predominate, but some rural schools only extend for three or four years. Secondary school curriculums are divided into two phases, a four-year general course and two-year special curriculums designed to prepare students for the universities they select. Various other types of educational institutions exist including the National University at Montevideo, the capital. Citizens and foreigners may attend all public education without cost.

The National Commission for Physical Education maintains public playgrounds, and it is to these, because of a lack of school space, that elementary school children are often taken three times weekly for physical activity. Although gymnastics receive attention, objectives relating to leisure education and social habits and attitudes become more important each year. The National Commission for Physical Education organizes and supervises sports. Many playing fields throughout the country are administered by the Commission, and the youth participate in various sports, such as basketball, football, swimming, and volleyball. Uruguay has become a vacation and recreation resort attracting many people from outside the country, and so it seems natural that the leisure aspects of physical education should be encouraged.

VENEZUELA

Venezuela is bounded by the Caribbean Sea on the north which gives it a long coastline. It has steep cliffs, waterfalls, and generally inaccessible territory in the south. The Orinoco basin is a rich cattle country, the coastal highlands in the northwest area is the main center of population, and the coast and jungle areas are extremely wet and very hot. Approximately 9,400,000 people live in Venezuela.

In northeast Venezuela astoundingly rich oil fields exist. New discoveries near Caripito make Venezuela one of the very top oil producing countries in the world. A few oil refineries have been developed, but most of it is processed outside the country. Cattle and agriculture are the leading industries, but manufacturing has developed rapidly in the last few years.

The great majority of Venezuelans are a mixture of white and Indian blood. Some mulattoes, Zambos (Indian and Negro), and Indians also inhabit the country. The powerful landowning class, although small, is Spanish for the most part.

The Ministry of Education controls and supervises the elementary and secondary schools. Only four years are available at that educational level. Secondary schools have a four-year curriculum plus a one-year course for specializing. Public education is free in Venezuela. A National Teachers College, in addition to normal schools, prepares teachers.

The National Ministry of Education has an Office of Physical Education which supervises and organizes physical education in the schools, constructs areas and facilities, prepares teachers of physical education, and promotes and organizes public sports activities with those of private groups. The program of physical education has been traditionally oriented toward preparation for the military. Gymnastic activities have predominated in the past. Recent trends indicate a swing toward considerable emphasis on sports on all levels. Basketball, soccer, volleyball, track and field, and other sports, are becoming very popular. Physical education curriculums also now include the voluntary intramural program of activities.

MEXICO

Mexico, a country of approximately 45,500,000 people, stretches south from Texas, New Mexico, Arizona, and California to the borders of Honduras and Guatemala. Three territories and twenty-eight states combine to form the administrative units of Mexico. Aridity and mountainous terrain are the curse of Mexico as they make agriculture in many parts of the country impossible. Due to an inadequate water supply, irrigating the interior is most difficult. The central plateau is the area most populated, and it offers opportunities for agriculture. The primitive means of agriculture, still used extensively in Mexico, slow agricultural developments considerably. Oil production near the city of Tampico is considerable. Homecrafts, such as pottery making and basket weaving, abound in Mexico. Industries found in the central plateau area, especially in the cities of Mexico and Monterrey, include textiles and clothing, tobacco, construction materials, paper, iron, and the brewing of alcoholic beverages.

Since Cortes undertook the conquest of Mexico in 1519 and eventually divided the country among Spaniards, there has been much stress. Even though the Catholic Church spread Christianity, there are three separate groups which never coalesced easily—the whites, the mestizos, and Indians. The revolution which lasted most of the nineteenth century gives real evidence of the unrest which has existed in the past in Mexico. Since the early 1930's, advances have been fairly steady in Mexico, and today definite progress can be noted such as: (1) better transportation, (2) political stability, (3) making the Indians an organic part of the state and increasing their literacy, (4) increased irrigation, and (5) increased industry which is leading toward self-sufficiency and an export surplus of some products.

The Constitution of 1917, which specified agrarian and labor reforms, also made educational and religious provisions which caused trouble with the church. This document ruled out religious elementary schools and placed the responsibility in the hands of the Ministry of Education. Thus, today public education is for all Mexicans, and is free, secular, and compulsory between the ages of 6 and 14, inclusive. Although each state controls its own government, the national government maintains some very direct controls over religion, public health, land, education, and other societal factors.

Physical education is required for two hours weekly in upper elementary grades, normal schools, and secondary schools. The goals of physical education deal with better physical well-being, health, leisure, education, courage and confidence, and fitness for the military. To accomplish such ends, gymnastics for boys, dancing and rhythmical gymnastics for girls, games for both sexes, and individual and team sports make up the required curriculum.

Elementary classroom teachers conduct physical education classes in many elementary schools. Specialists in physical education direct the classes in some urban elementary schools. The secondary schools in the city and many rural areas also have special physical education teachers. The Normal School for Physical Education, situated in Mexico City, prepares a carefully selected student body which undergoes comprehensive and specialized curriculum.

Health education and hygienic living have been stressed since 1922. The original Public Health Department established then has undergone certain changes and is known as the Ministry of Public Health and Welfare. This agency and the Ministry of Education work together. School health services have been established in Mexico City, dental clinics exist in some of the large cities, and medical examinations are given to teachers and pupils in other places.

Mexicans traditionally enjoy festive occasions, and folk music and colorful dances play a vital part in such activities. Dances may be either religious or light, but always colorful costumes, masks, and head ornaments add richness to the occasions. Sports have become very popular in Mexico. In addition to the games of the Mayas and Aztecs which remain, the Mexicans have long sponsored such sports as hockey, jai alai, soccer, horse racing, other equestrian sports, and bull fighting. In recent years, baseball (even professional), basketball, football, softball, and swimming are a few of the many sports which have gained additional popularity.

In general, physical education in South America is not strong, even though the countries have established some basic requirements. It will take years of effort to develop adequate programs. Some of the most important work is being accomplished through the efforts of Peace Corps personnel in deprived areas.

III

PHYSICAL EDUCATION AND SPORTS ACTIVITIES IN THE UNITED STATES

15

The Colonial Period

In the seventeenth and the first half of the eighteenth century there were but a few small colonies scattered along the Atlantic seaboard of America. By the opening of the Revolutionary War settlements had spread inland toward the mountains and a few even beyond into the Ohio Valley. By then the population of the thirteen colonies was reported to be around three million with Boston a metropolis of thirty thousand. The colonists were of divergent national origins. For the most part they were earnest, God-fearing people. A deep desire for freedom was the common cornerstone of their zeal which eventually led them unfalteringly through hardships and tribulations to the formation of a new form of government which, 350 years after the arrival in America of the first of them, is the envy of the entire world. All, in spite of their varied religious and national backgrounds, were bound together by their common worries—the unfriendly native Indians, the constant dread of French conquest, and the unjust demands of the British crown.

Throughout Colonial days the population was almost 95 per cent rural. Settlements were far apart, and as travel was by foot, horse, or boat it was difficult for people to get together. The days were filled with the struggle for existence—the conquest of the soil and of the forests, protection from the Indians, building and repairing homes, obtaining food, and preparing meals. Also, the men had to make their own tools and much of their own furniture while the women had to prepare the cloth and make the clothing and home furnishings. The children had to help in whatever way they could. Everyone was busy most of the waking hours. However, since work at arts and crafts was a necessity everyone had some form of creative work to do, and therein lay much contentment for all.

The leaders among the colonists desired a common education for all children, some of the advanced among them considering schooling for girls as well as boys. The writings of the English philosopher John Locke were well known in America, and his attack on the doctrine of the divine right of kings was a determining factor in the rising tide of thought about independence. At the same time, his *Thoughts on Education,* published in 1693, exerted such influence on the colonists that his theory of formal discipline held sway in the schools. However, in most of the land, the church had a firm hold on the school curriculum, claiming the aim of education to be solely piety and preparation for a life of hard work, and looking upon play as sin.

Lower Schools

The elementary education of boys and girls was cared for through private tutors, district schools, and public schools for paupers. Secondary education was provided for by so-called "grammar schools." In 1647 the colonies of Massachusetts Bay and Connecticut enacted laws stating that a town with fifty families should establish an elementary school and a town with one hundred families should maintain, also, a Latin grammar school. Girls rarely attended any of these schools. The teachers hired to "keep" school were quite unprepared for their task. Books were few, the school hours were long, and discipline was severe. In the elementary schools reading, writing, ciphering, and spelling comprised the curriculum. The Bible was the main textbook, and all children were taught the catechism.

Although these secondary schools were generally called "free" schools they were not free. As yet the colonists had not envisioned the idea of taxation for the support of schools, so the schools were maintained by tuition and by subsidy from the local government. In New England these schools were looked upon mostly as instruments to prepare young men for the ministry or the practice of law or medicine. Therefore, they offered courses in Latin and Greek, logic, elocution, and rhetoric, and some also offered Hebrew. For the most part only the sons of the professional classes attended. But there was, even at that early day, a "voice crying in the wilderness"—the voice of Benjamin Franklin (see p. 145). As early as 1743 in his *Proposals Relating to the Education of the Youth of Pennsylvania* he recommended that academies be organized whose aim would be to prepare young people for life in the world of their day. He called for schools with a "healthful situation" with garden, orchard, meadow, and fields and with provision for students to engage in games, running, leaping, wrestling, and swimming. Franklin founded the first academy in Philadelphia in 1749. Samuel Moody (see p. 146) followed in 1763 with the first boarding school.

In Colonial days the Latin grammar school dominated education, but after the Revolutionary War and as a result of Franklin's interest the new kind of school—the academy—became an influential part of American education. The academy was geared not to preparation for college but to preparation for life in general. Although the first academy was established in the mid-eighteenth century the idea did not "take hold" widely until the Revolutionary War was ended. Now these schools, frequently founded by philanthropists, spread rapidly and soon became the most popular type of secondary school.

In Colonial days boys and girls went to Quaker schools together wherever these schools existed, but for the most part girls did not attend school until after the Revolutionary War. However, in New England and in the Middle Colonies many young girls went to so-called "Dame Schools" where they were taught reading and writing but no arithmetic. Some authorities permitted the girls to use the boys' schools from five to seven in the morning before the boys came, and frequently girls of sixteen would be starting elementary school work while boys their own age would be attending secondary schools. Moreover, in a few localities where there was a sufficient number of girls desiring to attend secondary school, special private schools called "female seminaries" were organized. But, by the close of the Revolutionary War girls were quite generally permitted to attend all elementary schools. Also, private and day schools for girls were being established in large numbers so that many, by then, were receiving secondary education.

By 1786 many girls were coming from outside communities to attend the Moravian School in Bethlehem, Pennsylvania. In the first hundred years of its existence, over 7,000 girls came from the eastern and southern states and the West Indies to be educated there. In 1794 a coeducational school called an academy was established in Leicester, Massachusetts. The few private schools for girls that did exist at this time may be judged by the advertisement of one, which according to Monroe offered courses in "Petit Point in Flowers, Fruits, and Landscapes . . . with other embellishment for the amusements of persons of fortune who have taste."

Thomas Jefferson's bill of 1779 for the more general diffusion of knowledge opened the door for general education at public expense. In 1784 a Board of Regents was established for the State of New York, and in 1785 one for Georgia.

Higher Schools

Harvard "College," originating in 1636 from a gift of the Massachusetts Bay Company, was the first college in America. It was chartered as Harvard College in 1650, and took the designation of University in 1780.

Other colleges were established as follows: William and Mary, 1693; St. John's (Annapolis), 1696; Yale, 1701; Princeton, 1746; Washington and Lee, 1749; University of Pennsylvania, 1755 (developing from Franklin's Academy of 1749; Brown, 1764; Rutgers, 1766; Dartmouth, 1769; University of Georgia, 1785; University of Pittsburgh, 1787; University of North Carolina, 1789; Williams College, 1791; Bowdoin, 1794; Union College (Schenectady), 1795; and University of Louisville, 1798.

PHYSICAL EDUCATION ACTIVITIES

Since the responsibilities of meeting the needs of everyday life were so time-consuming in Colonial days and the post-Revolutionary War period, there was little free time for recreation. But the spontaneous urge for people to get together for companionship brought forth forms of recreational activities which, although born of their daily needs, resulted in much merrymaking for the great mass of the people. Also, some did manage to find time occasionally to engage in dance and sports. It is recorded that some boys played a form of football in the Colonies as early as 1609.

Leisure Activities

From the needs of the people to combine recreation with useful labor there arose quilting parties, corn-huskings, house- and barn-raisings. Even though the stern hand of the church was strongly felt in the land, the pious, who considered anything not connected with work or worship as a waste of time, could conscientiously join in this fun. The less pious and the young people engaged in the dances and the sports which some of the colonists had brought from the mother countries with them. Also, the need to market their products brought forth fairs, and amusements grew up around these such as wrestling matches and chasing greased pigs.

A leisure class developed around the large plantations of the South where there were slaves to do the work. Fox-hunting, horse-racing, and extravagant balls filled the leisure hours. In Philadelphia, as early as 1627, British soldiers quartered there brought to that community a form of old English pageantry, and other groups kept alive the traditional Maypole dances of England. Practically all the colonies except the strongly church-controlled ones of Massachusetts, New Hampshire, and Connecticut soon developed some forms of festivals, fairs, and pageants.

Children of Colonial days played marbles, "fives," leapfrog, hop scotch, blindman's buff, and hop-skip-and-jump. They did a lot of kite-flying and fishing, and in the spring they danced around the Maypole.

The children of the New England colonies, where the obdurate Puritans ruled both church and state, found it difficult to engage in these activities as much as they would like. The grown-ups, too, had their difficulties with stern authorities. On Christmas Day, 1621, when the Governor of Massachusetts ordered the men of Plymouth out to their daily work, the newcomers who had recently arrived on the "Fortune" excused themselves saying it was against their conscience to work on Christmas Day. So, as the Massachusetts archives tell the story:

> . . . he led away ye rest and left them: but when they came home at noone from their worke he found them in ye streete at play, openly: some pitching, ye barr & some at stoole-ball and such like sports. So he went to them and took away their implements and tould them it was against his conscience that they should play & others work. If they made ye keeping of it a mater of devotion let them kepe their houses, but ther should be no gameing or revelling in ye streets. Since which time nothing hath been attempted that way, at least openly.

Church rules or no church rules, the young people of Boston played football and squibs and in the winter threw snow balls so actively that "His Majesties Justices" passed a law in 1701 "for preventing danger by Footballs, Squibs and Snowballs." Toward the latter part of the period the boys and young men of all the English settlements played football, cricket, fives, rounders, and many other games. The village commons, or "greens" as some called them, served as the first municipal playgrounds in America. The Dutch brought to New Amsterdam their great love of skating and ninepins. They used the Old-World Dutch skates and sleds, and, in their merrymaking, both old and young were a great contrast to the dour New Englanders.

In Virginia nearly all the British sports flourished, and fox-hunting was the universal sport of a gentleman. Muster day, when all men were to report for military instruction, was an occasion for athletic competitions and games; foot races, jumping, boxing, wrestling, cockfights, and horse-racing were the main attractions at these gatherings and at the fairs and picnics. The winners received prizes and considerable notoriety. According to records at William and Mary College, the Governor of Massachusetts in 1691 issued the following proclamation:

> To the Sheriff of Surry Co. I desire that you give public notice that I will give first and second prizes to be shot for, wrastled, play at backswords, and run for by horse and foot, all which prizes are to begin on the 22nd day of April next, St. George's Day, being Saturday, all which prizes are shott for, etc. by the better sort of Virginians only, who are Batchelors.

Such meets were crude but enjoyable and were engaged in without training.

In 1792 the Methodist Episcopal Church, fearing the trends of the day, issued the following statement on play for the students attending the schools under their management.

> . . . we prohibit play in the strongest terms. . . . The students shall rise at five o'clock . . . summer and winter. . . . Their recreation shall be gardening, walking, riding, and bathing without doors, and the carpenter's, joiner's and cabinet-maker's business within doors. . . . The students shall be indulged with nothing which the world calls play. Let this rule be observed with the strictest nicety; for those who play when they are young, will play when they are old.

Dance

The early settlers brought various forms of dance to the New World with them. The British gentry brought their stately and dignified dances while the lower classes brought the jigs and reels and boisterous squares. The French brought their cotillions and quadrilles. After the Revolutionary War the few girls' schools then in existence were advertising dancing as one subject that would be taught to "the young ladies."

Sports

During the colonial years school hours were so long that there was little opportunity for boys to engage in sports. As for the colleges, the games of the students are as old as the colleges themselves, but from the very start they met with opposition from the authorities, who were quick to rule against them as harmful. As related in Princeton College archives, the boys at that school were playing some sort of ball game in 1761 as is evidenced by the outcry of the trustees of that year as follows:

> The Trustees, having on their own view been sensible of the Damage done to the President's House by the Students playing at Ball against it, do hereby strictly forbid all and any of the Sd Students, the Officers and all other Persons belonging to the College, playing at Ball against Sd President's House, under the penalty of Five Shillings, for every offense, to be levied on each Person who shall offend in the Premises.

At all events, the Princeton trustees were not forbidding the playing, merely moving it to some other setting. Providing a playing field for the boys was as yet out of the picture.

Bowling. A game called "skittles," similar to modern bowling, was played in the South in particular, surviving today in the southeastern mountain regions, no doubt brought there by the early English settlers who, judging from the many references in various of Dickens' novels to his characters' enjoyment of "skittles and beer," were addicted to both the game and the liquid refreshment.

Cricket. From an advertisement carried in the March, 1778, issue of *The Royal Pennsylvania Gazette* (Copy preserved in the New York Public Library), it is evident that the game of cricket was being played at least by the British occupation forces around Philadelphia. The advertisement was as follows: "Any person acquainted with the making of *Cricket Bats* or *Balls* may have good encouragement. Enquire of the printer." However, according to Dulles (see References) the game was being played in Virginia as early as 1709.

Football. In some colonies a form of football was played early in the seventeenth century, a game somewhat like soccer and called "long bullets." By the opening of the eighteenth century, a game then known as football was played so enthusiastically that the "freeholders and inhabitants" of Boston passed orders for "preventing danger by Foot Balls" and eighty-four years later still other orders to the effect that football was "not to be played at, or kicked through any part of the town" (according to page 11 of a town law passed September, 1701, and page 43 of a law passed in 1786).

Golf. According to a Boston News Letter of 1714, as reported by Manchester, a game called "goff" was being played in the Carolinas; and Benjamin Rush, in his *Sermons to Gentlemen upon Temperance and Exercise* of 1772, mentions "golf."

Nine-Pins. In 1714 the British Coffee House maintained a bowling green in Boston which was open to "all gentlemen, merchants and others that have a mind to recreate themselves." In New Amsterdam a green was laid out in 1732 at the foot of Broadway for the use of the public, the land being leased from the city. Bowling Green of today's New York City marks the site of these activities. Originally nine pins were used, but, because of excessive betting, the game was outlawed, and later, to evade the law, a tenth pin was added.

Rounders. The Old English game of rounders came to America with the earliest colonists and flourished through the years, gradually evolving into today's baseball, which in its present form is essentially American. According to Henderson, the earliest recognition published of the game of baseball is in *The Little Pretty Book*, published by Hugh Gaine in New York in 1762.

Shinny. The boys at Princeton College played a game "in the back common of the college" with balls and sticks which caused so much annoyance to the faculty that in 1787, as reported in the college archives, they voiced their objections declaring:

> The game is in itself low and unbecoming gentlemen Students and in as much as it is an exercising attended with great danger to the health by sudden and

alternate heats and colds and as it tends to accidents, almost unavoidable in that play, to disfiguring and maiming those who are engaged in it . . . the faculty think it incumbent on them to prohibit both the Students and Grammar Scholars from using the play aforesaid.

The diaries of the students of later years testify that the faculty prohibition was of no avail and that shinny was for many years the main college game.

Swimming. The first swimming pool in America was built on the banks of the Schuykill River at the foot of Race Street in Philadelphia in 1791. It was not a floating pool as were many later ones of that day but stationary with the bottom of the pool resting on the bottom of the river. It was called a "plunging bath." Privately owned, it had connected with it two showers and a bowling green.

Tennis. There is record that tennis, then known as court tennis, was being played in America as early as 1763. At that time the game was mentioned in the publication of *Temporary Acts and Laws of His Majesties Province,* Boston, New England.

FIRST THOUGHTS OF PHYSICAL EDUCATION

Although the colonists accepted Locke's ideas on formal discipline, they fell short of accepting his idea that vigor and discipline of the body was one of the chief aims of education. However, a few educational leaders, chief among whom was Benjamin Franklin, strongly urged recognition by the schools of the physical activity needs of children. But for the most part, physical education not only had no acknowledged place in education in Colonial days, but the educational spirit influenced by the prevailing Puritan attitudes, was hostile not only to play as sin but to all activities related to play, including sports and even physical exercises. However, particularly in New England, the boys from ten to sixteen were given military drill six days a year. But with the coming of the academies after the War of Independence, there arose an emphasis on the physical welfare of the students and the desirability, if not the necessity, of physical exercise as a part of the school program.

Noah Webster (1758–1843) in his *Address to Young Gentlemen* of 1790 said that it should be "the business of young persons to assist nature and strengthen the growing frame by athletic exercises. When it is not the lot of a young person to labor in Agriculture or Mekanic arts, some laborious amusement should daily be pursued as a substitute, . . ." Thomas Jefferson, in his writings on education, expressed his belief in the necessity of physical exercise as a part of general education. In his plans for the University of Virginia, he included provision for a gymnasium, although he made no plans for the employment of a teacher to be in charge of it. The influence of these great leaders was gradually felt, and educators began to re-evaluate their educational objectives.

EARLY PROFESSIONAL LITERATURE

Since no profession of physical education as yet existed in the early days of United States history, there was, of course, no local professional literature as such. However, there was developing a literature on physical activities which is of historic interest. From 1712 on, the first books mentioning physical activities came out in America, chief among them Hugh Gaines' *A Little Pretty Book* of 1762 which contains woodcuts of games and gives the first mention in the United States of cricket and baseball. Preceding this was Edward Blackwell's *A Compleat System of Fencing* of 1734 put out by William Parks of Williamsburg, Joseph Seacombe's *Business and Diversion Inoffensive to God* of 1739 dealing with fishing; and John Armstrong's *Art of Preserving Health,* first published in London in 1644 and reprinted for American readers in 1745 by Benjamin Franklin.

Following these were Benjamin Rush's *Sermons to Gentlemen Upon Temperance and Exercise* (published in 1772 by John Dunlap of Philadelphia), which mentions both golf and tennis; Bernard Roman's *A Concise Natural History of East and West Florida* of 1775 containing an account of lacrosse as a Choctaw Indian game; and Edmund Hoyle's *Hoyle's Games Improved* 1796, published by James Benfort of Philadelphia, containing material on tennis and quadrilles. Between 1796 and 1857 this last book ran to nineteen editions. (According to Henderson, copies of most of these books are preserved by the American Antiquary Society in Worcester, Massachusetts, the Boston Athenaenum, the Library of Congress, and the New York City Public Library.)

LEADERS IN PHYSICAL EDUCATION

Benjamin Franklin (1706–90)

America's first recorded promoter of physical education was Benjamin Franklin. His was the first voice raised in the Colonies in behalf of physical education. Not only did he as an educator interest himself and others in the kind of school and curriculum needed for the youth of the land but he also went far beyond that to offer detailed instructions and advice on setting up a physical-activity school program. He even gave instructions on the techniques of teaching some of the activities, notably swimming.

As a young boy Franklin became deeply interested in the skills of swimming. He experimented with a kite to draw himself across the water as he floated on his back and with cork paddles for his hands and feet to propel himself more effectively through the water. He investigated the problem of muscle-cramping and the physiological effects of sudden plunging into cold water. He became such an expert swimmer than when a young man he gave an exhibition of swimming in London and later gained an international reputation as an authority on the subject.

Samuel Moody (1727?–95)

Before the Revolutionary War, Samuel Moody, first headmaster of the famous Dummer Grammar School of Byfield, Massachusetts (the first private boarding school in America, which opened in 1763) became the chief exponent of physical activities as an important part of education. After Franklin he was the foremost person of this period to promote this part of the program. He, himself, taught the activities to the pupils and participated in them with the boys. Among his pupils were two signers of the Constitution, twenty members of the Continental Congress, and two Chief Justices of the Massachusetts Supreme Court.

16

Physical Activities in the Early Nineteenth Century (1800–1865)

As the western-moving settlers conquered the wilderness and settled down to establish homes and form communities, there grew up a division of labor made possible through group-living which produced some semblance of leisure time. Only those pushing ever westward still had the hard life of the early colonists. Now there developed in the settled areas new forms of leisure activities to claim the attention of the people. With the coming of steamboats and railroads, recreation took on a new form. The New York Herald in 1838 advertised round-trip boat excursions to Coney and Staten Islands and Hudson River trips with dancing and band concerts included. The quilting bees, corn-huskings, and square dancing of earlier days were still popular. Organized competitive sports had not yet come to the American scene, but there were informal games and contests to claim many participants.

By the late 1840's many Germans had come to America, bringing their Old-World ways of celebrating special occasions which set the pattern for the Fourth of July celebrations particularly throughout the Middle West with their parades, singing, bunting and flags, picnics, patriotic speeches, and reading of the Declaration of Independence. Games and contests filled the day and lasted far into the night. Freedom was indeed something very personal to these people who had so recently fled their native land to find it here in America. They threw themselves wholeheartedly into these celebrations. Czech immigrants also initiated festivals and contests. Their first sharpshooting contest was held at Washington, Missouri, in 1840 when they crowned the first United States King of the Sharpshooters.

ACTIVITIES OF PHYSICAL EDUCATION

Dance

The dances of Colonial Days were carried over into this era, and practically all schools for girls advertised dancing as one subject to be taught to the young ladies. To most heads of these schools, this alone seemed sufficient for the physical education program for girls. Mrs. Emma Willard (1787–1870), a famous woman educator of the day, set the thinking in that direction when, in a speech of 1819, she said: "Exercise is needful to the health and recreation to the cheerfulness and contentment of youth. . . . Dancing is exactly to this purpose. . . ."

Just what form of dancing was used in these school programs other than the ballroom forms of the day is not made clear; but since the dance advocates suggested the use of dancing as a substitute for calisthenics the forms used for class work, no doubt, had some calisthenic type and content, probably the forerunner of the "fancy steps" of a later day.

Gymnastics, Calisthenics, and Exercises

All three terms, gymnastics, calisthenics, and exercises, were used in this era to designate physical education activities other than sports or dancing. When the newly arrived German immigrants used the term gymnastics, they meant the German form so that the older settlers became accustomed to use the other two terms to designate exercises other than those of the German system.

German System. The great influx of German political refugees, who came to the United States in the early part of the nineteenth century bringing their love of gymnastics with them, gave this system a running head start in America. Among these refugees were three of Jahn's own close friends, who were excellent teachers and devoted followers of his theories: Charles Follen, Charles Beck, and Francis Lieber (see pp. 172–73). These three men interpreted to America the turner movment with its great fervor for freedom and its great hatred of oppression of every kind. In fact the coming of these men to America in 1824 and 1827 marked the real beginnings of a physical education program in the schools.

When a high school opened in New York City in 1825 it was announced that included in the school program would be gymnastic exercises. In that same year four leading men's colleges—Yale, Harvard, Amherst, and Dartmouth—offered instruction in gymnastics under the leadership of these recently arrived German refugees. This initial effort of the 1820's to introduce German gymnastics in America was not a sustained effort; by the 1830's this enthusiasm had died down, and the practice of gymnastics in the literary schools of the nation ceased. But the conviction that something should be done in the schools for bodily development endured in the minds of leading doctors and educators so that there remained some fertile ground ready for a revival in the 1850's and 1860's.

Swedish Gymnastics. Although little was heard of Swedish Gymnastics in America before the closing years of the nineteenth century, there are a few scattered and vague reports of its being used here and there in the 1820's. But there seems to be no firm records, such as exist concerning the use of German Gymnastics, until the announcement of the offering of a course in the Swedish Movement Cure by the Dio Lewis Institute of Physical Education in 1862 (see p. 168). Following this, but little is heard again of Swedish Gymnastics until the late 1880's, as reported in Chapter 18.

Catharine Beecher's Calisthenics. The program of useful exercise through domestic duties which was set up at Mt. Holyoke Female Seminary in 1837 was copied in many schools, but it held no appeal to many educators as a real physical education program for girls. Nor did the German gymnastics get a favorable response from women educators who felt that they were too strenuous for most girls. So Catharine Beecher (see p. 173), a fighter in her day for the education of girls, devised a system of calisthenics of her own. Adapting the word "calisthenics" from the Greek *kalos* meaning "beautiful" and *sthenos* meaning "strength" she devised a system of physical education built around twenty-six lessons in physiology and two courses in calisthenics, one for schoolroom use and one for exercises in halls (published in her book of 1831; see p. 171).

The exercises, made up of simple movements to be accompanied by music, acquired much popularity throughout the country and were accepted by many schools as a substitute for dancing. She preferred that they be practiced in a hall arranged for the purpose, but, where that was not convenient, the ordinary schoolroom would suffice. The aims were to produce grace of motion, good carriage, and sound health. This marked the first attempt of a native-born American to devise an exercise program for Americans.

In 1852 Elizabeth Blackwell (1821–1910), America's first woman graduate of a medical school, published a series of lectures on *The Laws of Life in Response to the Physical Education of Girls,* thus giving valuable backing to Miss Beecher's work.

Strength Seekers. Dr. George Barker Winship (1834–76), a graduate of Harvard, became famous throughout the United States as the advocate of heavy gymnastics. His ideas appealed to all young men who sought to have bulging muscles and great strength. From 1859 to the early seventies he toured the United States and Canada, lecturing on gymnastics and giving weight-lifting exhibitions. The Winship Gymnasium in Boston became the most famous school for strength seekers in the country. Winship's exhibitions tended to confirm the popular idea that the gymnasium was a place for strong men, prize fighters and wrestlers, and that great strength was the aim of gymnastic training and was synonymous with health and well-being. It has taken physical education almost a century to live down this concept that developed from these strength seekers.

Because of the popularity of the strength-seekers, Dr. Dudley A. Sargent (see p. 236) later called this period the "heavy-lifting phase of physical education" during which time every home and office had a "health lift." When Sargent was being considered for the position of Director of Physical Education at Harvard in 1880, this phase was still enough in the public attention that his nearest rival for the position was a man who was running a health-lift establishment in Lowell, Massachusetts.

Dio Lewis' System. Dr. Dio Lewis (see p. 174), a well-known temperance and health lecturer, attacked vigorously the popular idea that great strength was the mark of well-being and that gymnasia were primarily for gymnasts. In his writings he strove to prove that light wooden dumbbells were better suited to the real practice of gymnastics than those of iron. He took pains to destroy the common belief that free, unsupervised play of children was sufficient to develop sound and properly formed bodies. He held that a gymnastic teacher was as essential to the proper development of the body as the ordinary school teacher was to the development of the mind. Those who advocated military training for the schools, of whom there were many, found arrayed against them the promoter of the New Gymnastics as he called his system. He believed that military training not only failed to develop the upper half of the body but was conducive to rigidity and to strained positions. Also, he maintained that athletic sports, as a means of physical education, fell far short of organized gymnastics because of their overexertion of certain parts of the body and neglect of other parts.

So he devised a system of exercises for America's schools according to his own ideas. He advocated the use of music or a drum to mark the rhythm of the exercises, which should be fast enough to increase the rate of heart beat and respiration. He also originated the idea of tossing beanbags as an exercise. He preferred the beanbags to balls because they were more easily grasped with one hand. The gymnastic crown, weighing from three to one hundred pounds, was one of his contrivances. It was worn to secure erect spine and good carriage. Many of his exercises were with wands, dumbbells, clubs, and hand-rings. He claimed to have invented 500 exercises and advocated their use in place of military drill, skating, riding, and dancing.

Fig. 8. Gymnastic costumes recommended by Dio Lewis in 1862. (From Dio Lewis, *The New Gymnastics for Men, Women and Children,* 8th ed., Boston: Tickner and Fields, 1864, p. 17.)

Dio Lewis was a good salesman and engendered much enthusiasm for his system of gymnastics. He was widely acclaimed all over the country. Many magazine articles were written about him and his system. The celebrated writer, Thomas Wentworth Higginson (1823–1911), took note of him, saying in the *Atlantic Monthly* in 1861:

> Gymnastic exercises are as yet but sparingly introduced into our seminaries, private or professional, though a great change is already beginning. Until lately all our educational plans have assumed man to be merely a sedentary being; we have employed teachers of music and drawing to go from school to school to teach those elegant arts, but have had none to teach the art of health. . . . It is something to have got beyond the period when active sports were actually prohibited. It would be unpardonable in this connection not to speak a good word for the favorite hobby of the day—Dr. Lewis and his system of gymnastics; or more properly of calisthenics. . . . Dr. Winship had done all that was needed in apostleship of severe exercises, and there was wanting some man with a milder hobby, perfectly safe for a lady to drive. . . . It will espe-

cially render service to female pupils so far as they practice it; for the accustomed gymnastic exercises seem never yet to have been rendered attractive to them on any large scale and with any permanency.

Sports

The earliest settlers of Colonial days participated in many sports; these were played without organization and without universally recognized rules. But in the nineteenth century, rules were developing for certain sports, and organizations to formulate them were being established. Examples of these sports follow.

Baseball. Since its development in the latter eighteenth century, as a game apart from rounders, baseball (then spelled as two words) gradually spread throughout the then-settled part of the country. It is probable that the game was being played in most of the colleges by the 1830's, and there is a firm record that it was played at Dartmouth College in 1837. This belies the claim of Cooperstown, New York, that the game originated there in 1839. It is probable, however, that the diamond-shaped field as used today may have originated there, thus partially legitimatizing that town's claim to baseball fame, aside from the fact that it now possesses the Baseball Museum and Hall of Fame, which was established there on the basis of the earlier and now challenged claim.

Although Abner Doubleday (1819–93) is named as the originator of the game in Cooperstown, this scarcely holds up in light of the facts of his life. In 1839 he was a student at West Point, and his home was not in Cooperstown. During the Civil War he was one of the commanding generals at the Battle of Gettysburg, and he devoted much of his later life to writing and lecturing on military topics. Never did he, in his writings or lectures, show an interest in the game of baseball or make any claims for himself as originator of the game.

In the game as played in this era, base-running was done clockwise, the ball was pitched underhand, and the game was won by the team that first scored twenty-one runs. *The World Almanac* of 1966 states that the first baseball rule book was put out in 1858 by a man named Henry Chadwick (1824–1908), but according to Henderson (see references) the young Knickerbocker Club in Hoboken, made up of business and professional men, put out rules in 1845. During the fifties, however, baseball clubs increased rapidly. By 1858 there were twenty-five teams playing in and about New York City and in that year the National Association of Baseball Players was founded. This association agreed on the rules of the game and specified that the ball was to weigh six and one-half ounces and was to be ten and one-half inches in circumference. The bat might be any length but must not be more than two and one-half inches in diameter. The pitcher, who pitched, rather than threw, the ball, might stand anywhere on a line twelve feet long placed forty-five feet from the home plate. Only amateurs who had been members of the club for thirty days were permitted to play in the regular games. These were the first nationally recognized rules—the ones referred to in the *World Almanac.* During the Civil War, the clubs charged admission to the games, and the players received a share of the money, marking the beginning of professional baseball history. (For an account of early intercollegiate contests see p. 155.)

Bowling. Bowling as an indoor sport was underway at the Knickerbocker alleys in New York City in 1840; the floors of that day made of baked clay. Hoyle's 1845 edition of his game book carried information on bowling, and the following year the Providence Bowling Club in Rhode Island published its constitution and by-laws and rules.

Camping and Outdoor Education. The earliest record of camping and an attempt at outdoor education for a school group is that of the Round Hill School (see p. 162), where in the 1820's the boys were taken on weekly hikes and on an annual trip by horse and wagon when they "encamped."

Cricket. Cricket flourished in the eastern part of the country until the popularity of baseball of the Civil War period pushed it into the background. As late as 1859 a professional cricket team from the United States toured both the United States and Canada. The University of Pennsylvania had a cricket team as early as 1843, and the University of Michigan by 1860.

Football. Though the early colonists played a kicking game which they called football (an adaptation of "futballe," a game played in England as early as the eleventh century), it was not until the first half of the nineteenth century, when American collegians blended soccer with rugby and added other methods of play, that the game began to resemble the present-day game. Students at Yale University played football as early as 1807 on the public green of New Haven. Both Harvard and Yale Universities used the game to haze freshmen. By 1827 Harvard, and by 1840 Yale and Princeton, were promoting interclass matches.

The great rivalry that developed over football at Yale between the classes of '55 and '56 resulted in such controversy that it was written up and published in New Haven, starting years of such records to follow through the years between many different colleges.

Lacrosse. A game spoken of by Henderson (see references) as "primitive" lacrosse was played throughout Colonial days by Choctaw Indians of Mississippi, and in 1829 forty players were taken on an eight-month touring exhibition of the game. But acceptance of the game at large did not come until 1860, when a Canadian lawyer developed rules for the game which turned the ancient disorderly Indian game into an orderly one.

Rowing. There are records of rowing clubs on the Hudson River as early as the mid-1820's, in Detroit as early as the 1830's, in Boston by the 1840's, and on the Schuylkill River at Philadelphia and at Charleston, New Orleans, St. Louis, and Pittsburgh, by the 1850's. By then there were sufficient clubs to put on a regatta in New York in 1851 and on Lake Michigan at Chicago six years later. Several colleges also took up the sport—Harvard and Yale as early as the 1840's.

Swimming. In the early 1800's Philadelphia boasted of floating baths such as were popular at the time in France and England. They were located in the Delaware and Schuylkill Rivers and according to Watson, ". . . lay upon the water like low houses with white and yellow sides and green Venetian shutters with boatmen at hand to convey bathers to the establishment." (See references.) The walls of these houses had openings through which the river water ran to make the pools. Some were elaborate having galleries and several bath chambers.

Help for amateur swimmers was soon forthcoming from none other than Benjamin Franklin, who published *The Art of Swimming* in 1821 and followed two years later with his *Advice to Swimmers* (published in connection with Newton Bosworth's *Accidents of Human Life*), which must have been the first attempts at life-saving and safety instruction.

In 1827 Lieber opened the first swimming school in America. It was in connection with the Boston Gymnasium. John Quincy Adams (1767–1818) attended this school and became an excellent swimmer and diver.

In 1821 there was in existence an organization known as "The Humane Society," whose purpose was the restoring of life in persons apparently drowned. Aquatic activities even spread to the colleges as evidenced by the fact that in 1848 Girard College opened in Philadelphia with four indoor swimming pools, one each in the basement of the four dormitories, and one outdoor pool—all of which were planned by Lieber and were in use for over fifty years. This marked the first school in America to have a swimming pool.

Track and Field Sports. Scotch immigrants brought the "Caledonian games" to Boston in 1853, and from there they spread throughout the country until by the seventies they had become very popular. These games were the forerunners of today's track and field sports.

Sports Clubs

Aside from the baseball clubs mentioned above, other sports clubs came into existence in this era. The earliest recorded club is the Savannah, Georgia, Golf Club of 1795. Quoit clubs flourished during this era, the game having been brought to America by the English soldiers. Chief Justice John Marshall (1755–1835) is reported to have been the champion of his quoit club. The United Bowmen's Club of Philadelphia was functioning by 1830. The Czech organization of sharpshooters held its first contest in Washington, Missouri, in 1840, and a Deer Hunters Association organized in Ohio celebrated its centennial in 1958. Yale students formed the first college boat clubs in 1843, and the first intercollegiate sports association was born in 1858 when Harvard, Yale, Brown, and Trinity founded the short-lived College Regatta Association.

Intercollegiate Athletics

Although there are reports of the playing of intercollegiate games as early as the 1820's between schools located near each other, it was not until in the 1850's that contests took place for which specific reports are available. The earliest such record is of an intercollegiate rowing match held between Yale and Harvard on August 2, 1852, on Lake Winnipesaukee in New Hampshire. According to Lewis (see references), this first intercollegiate event received but little notice in the papers, although it was advertised by circulars distributed widely by the railroad company, which sponsored the event in the interest of bringing vacationers to the area, ran excursions trains for the contest, and hired a brass band to add a festive note to the occasion. In 1855 the two schools held another rowing match, this time in Springfield, Massachusetts, and again Harvard won as it had done in the first match. In 1859 the four schools that had organized the College Regatta Association staged the first intercollegiate regatta on Lake Quinsigamond at Worcester, Massachusetts. By this time much public interest had arisen in these rowing matches. Over 15,000 spectators turned out for the event, *The New York Herald* gave three and a half columns on the front page to the story, and post-game enthusiasm got so out of control that a pitched battle betwen students and police ended in the calling off of all contests for the next five years.

The second sport to enter the intercollegiate arena was baseball. The earliest record of an intercollegiate match is of a game at Pittsfield, Massachusetts, in July, 1859, when Amherst won over Williams by a score of 66 to 32. There has been preserved at Amherst College a copy of an "Extra" of the *Amherst Express* of July 1st and 2nd, 1859, which proclaims: "Baseball and Chess! Muscle and Mind!" After a report of the many preliminaries undertaken to arrange the contest the paper goes on to report the events. The Amherst players had a 90-mile journey to Pittsfield which they made the day before. The Williams teams arrived at the rendezvous the following morning having only "20 miles to overcome." The two baseball teams put up at different hotels, and the chess players were entertained by the Pittsfield Chess Club. The Williams baseball boys were dressed "in the uniform of club . . . Amherst decidely in undress." Each team furnished its own ball, Amherst's weighing two and one-quarter ounces and measuring six and one-quarter inches around, while Williams' weighed two ounces and was seven inches around. The teams from both colleges were chosen by ballot from the student bodies. It was rumored that the Amherst "thrower" was the town blacksmith, hired for the occasion. So the first gun was fired that day at Pittsfield in "intercollegiate athletics." And in that very first engagement rumor of unfair advantage lifted its ugly head.

17

Organized Physical Education in the Early Nineteenth Century (1800–1865)

By 1830 the population of the United States had increased from the three million of Revolutionary War days to ten million, and throughout the 1830's, '40's and '50's immigrants from many lands continued to pour into America at every port. To Europe, America had become "the promised land"—the home of the free. In Germany, Metternich's Carlsbad Decrees of 1819 stifled political action and instituted strict censorship of the press and supervision of universities. Through the thirty years in which these decrees were in force, German students and professors by the hundreds fled to America bringing with them their deep interest in education and freedom. Many of them, also, brought their enthusiasm for physical education, materially enriching the educational system of that period.

At this same time the Irish and Scotch-Irish were being ruthlessly suppressed by the English. From 1816 on, immigrants from Ireland poured into America in astounding numbers, reaching by 1935 an annual number of 30,000. In the hundred years from 1820 to 1920, four and a quarter million immigrants came to the United States from Ireland alone. As Wittke (see references) reminds us, these Irish and Scotch-Irish, highly individualistic, critics of the established order, hard, pugnacious, bold, and resolute, became the typical frontiersman of early days of the republic. These German, Scotch, Irish, and Scotch-Irish immigrants, as counterbalancing forces to the earlier entrenched English with their dislike of change, played a leading part in shaping a new educational philosophy for America.

As various treaties were signed by the Government opening up vast westward stretches of land to settlement, the Conestoga wagon became the symbol of westward-advancing America. The discovery of gold in California in 1848 brought a sudden rush of people to the Pacific Coast, and the Oregon, Mormon, and Santa Fe trails were developed. At last the vast territory west of the Mississippi River was being opened up to settlement. Besides the miners and professional Indian fighters and scouts who piloted the wagon trains across great plains, cowboys, too, became important in the national life, bringing to it not only their "broncho-busting" but also their own interpretation of the dances of the Tennessee and Kentucky mountain folk, which brought much recreational pleasure to the early settlers.

Women were awakening in the early nineteenth century to their opportunities for advancement, both in politics and in education. In 1848 there was held in Seneca Falls, New York, the first women's rights convention ever assembled anywhere in the world. This beginning led to opened doors for women in the world of education, bringing thoughts of careers outside the home. A side issue of the women's rights movement was the campaign for dress reform championed by Amelia Bloomer (1818–1894), editor of a popular women's magazine, which campaign led eventually through an unplanned side issue to acceptance of a type of garment that made it possible for women to dress in a manner fitting to the pursuit of a career in the teaching of physical education.

EDUCATION IN GENERAL

With the opening of the nineteenth century, elementary schools increased rapidly in number, the academies gained in popularity over the Latin grammar schools of Colonial days, and coeducation was becoming a recognized form of education. "Free public" high schools open to all children, however, were but little known in the early part of this era. In fact, as late as 1850 there were but eleven public high schools in all of the United States, and college education for women became a reality for only a very few advanced thinkers. Massachusetts in 1852 became the first state to pass a compulsory school attendance law. (It took sixty-four years for the last state—Mississippi—to fall into line.) This move brought into the schools many children who had never before attended, creating a need for changes in educational procedures and programs to take care of the special needs of these children just as the civil rights movement of today is opening doors of heretofore segregated schools to many children whose special needs call for new adjustment and programming.

Treatises and books on education by European leaders were becoming readily available in the United States. Particularly did Froebel, the German founder of kindergartens and champion of education of women, begin to have marked influence on American educational philosophy, and the theories of Rousseau and Pestalozzi called for educational programs based on the interests and needs of pupils. Many national leaders took a deep interest in the schools, in particular Thomas Jefferson, who used his great influence for the establishment of universal free schools.

In 1926 a public high school for girls was established in New York, and so many attended that it closed shortly because of lack of financial support.

Although the number of schools financed by public taxation grew rapidly between 1800 and 1850, the private schools continued to carry the great burden of the responsibility for the education of the youth of the land.

Lower Schools

In 1818 Boston added primary schools to its public school system, and followed shortly with the English High School, the first high school in America of the new free schools movement. From then on, the public high school began to replace both the Latin Grammar School of Colonial Days and the Academy of the late eighteenth century. By 1825 New York City, and by 1829 Portland, Maine, had established high schools. The movement quickly spread to Philadelphia (1838), Baltimore (1839), Cleveland (1830), St. Louis (1853), and Detroit, Chicago, and San Francisco (1856), thus spanning the continent.

In 1837 Horace Mann (1796–1859), a famous reformer in the field of education and then Secretary of the Massachusetts State Board of Education, remodeled the entire state system of education, centralizing the supervision of local district schools, eliminating religious domination wherever it still existed, and introducing new methods based on the best to be found in Europe. He insisted that common schools were to be common to all and with lay control. To supply qualified teachers for the schools, he also established the first public normal school in the country at Lexington, Massachusetts. His methods and theories were soon adopted throughout all common schools.

Heretofore secondary schools had not been considered necessary for the great mass of the people, but now the idea of universal education—at least universal male education—was growing. By the end of the era, the idea included girls as well as boys, and enrollment of girls in public schools was beginning to make serious inroads upon the enrollment in girls' private schools.

Higher Schools

In the late eighteenth century, the emphasis of education was shifted from the colleges to the lower schools. Now, in the new century, a renewed and greatly expanding trend for "higher education" began.

Following the Revolutionary War, thirteen states founded universities:

1801—South Carolina
1804—Ohio (Athens)
1807—Maryland
1817—Michigan
1819—Virginia
1820—Indiana
1820—Alabama
1831—New York
1836—Wisconsin
1839—Vermont
1839—Missouri
1844—Mississippi
1847—Iowa
1850—Utah

Many private colleges also were established in this period reaching from coast to coast, chief among them were:

1800—Middlebury (Vermont)
1813—Colby (Maine)
1831—Wesleyan (Connecticut)
1833—Oberlin (Ohio)
1841—Ohio Wesleyan (Delaware)
1842—Willamette (Oregon)
1846—Beloit (Wisconsin)
1846—Grinnell (Iowa)
1854—Iowa Wesleyan (Mt. Pleasant)

In this same period the first women's colleges were established:

Lindenwood (Missouri) starting in 1827 as a female seminary and achieving collegiate rating in 1863, to become then the second oldest women's college.
Mount Holyoke (Massachusetts) founded in 1837 as a female seminary but not achieving collegiate rating until 1893.
Rockford (Illinois) established in 1849 but not achieving collegiate rating until 1891.
Elmira (New York) started in 1851 and chartered as a college in 1853, to become the first women's college in the United States.
Vassar (New York) established in 1861 as a female seminary and acquiring collegiate rating in 1868.

Also in this period, the first coeducational college (Oberlin, in 1833) from its beginnings admitted both Negroes and women and was the first college in America to admit either. The first normal school was founded at Lexington, Massachusetts, in 1839.

Most of the colleges established in this period were founded by religious groups, and in their beginnings many were of the manual labor type of school, combining industrial training with intellectual education.

The plan seemed well suited to the growing spirit of democracy in education, because students without financial means could defray a part of their educational expenses with the products of their labor. However, it was not until the theories of Pestalozzi and Fellenberg, the two noted Swiss educators of the day, reached America that these ideas were put into practice. In 1831 the advocates of the movement for manual labor met in New York City and organized the Society for Promoting Manual Labor in Literary Institutions, and beginning in 1833 colleges founded on this idea sprang up throughout the Middle West in particular. In Indiana, the Presbyterians organized Wabash Manual Labor College in 1833 and Hanover in 1827; the Baptists founded the Indiana Baptist Manual Labor School in 1835; the Methodists, Asbury University in 1837; and the Friends, Earlham College in 1842. All these institutions long ago dispensed with the manual labor phase of their work and now exist as Wabash, Hanover, Franklin, Depauw, and Earlham.

PHYSICAL EDUCATION COMES TO THE SCHOOLS

It became somewhat generally accepted in this period that exercise and games are necessary for the proper growth of children and that the schools are responsible for the physical as well as the intellectual education of youth, so that at last the idea of physical education in the schools was spreading, though not without setbacks provoked by three distinct groups: the overly ardent advocates of manual labor as sufficient for exercise needs; those still strongly influenced by the Puritan idea that play in any form is sin; and the many scholars who felt that, although play might not be a sin, it was most certainly a waste of time.

As far as physical education for girls was concerned, there was a fourth group to speak out against it—the many who felt that girls were too frail to be expected to exercise and, besides, should not be drawn into such unseemly conduct.

The many German educators who came to America fleeing political persecution brought an enthusiasm for German gymnastics which, in its ebb and flow of popularity for more then a hundred years, greatly influenced physical education in the United States. Heretofore the English love of sports had set the pattern of physical activity, but from now on there developed the two interests—gymnastics and sports. By the close of the Civil War, gymnastics had such a strong hold that the term "physical education" (which was in use as early as 1859 according to reports of the New York State Department of Education) had come to mean to most people merely gymnastics, and there arose the custom of speaking of physical education *and* sports as if they were two different things.

Lower Schools

Many educational leaders of the day advocated that education for health, by means of regular exercise and instruction in hygiene and physiology, was necessary for complete education. The teachers, however, had no well-defined idea of the real scope and significance of the science of physical education. The popular concept was that the place for games and physical exercise was after school hours, and that special teachers were not necessary. Nevertheless, as early as 1821 the Latin School of Salem, Massachusetts, was encouraging play for its educational as well as recreational value, using simple gymnastic and play apparatus; and in 1823 a school for girls in Boston was giving its pupils some calisthenics and exercises in hanging and swinging on bars and in running and jumping.

The Round Hill School. The first recognition of physical education as a real part of a school program came when the Round Hill School was established in 1823 in Northampton, Massachusetts, by George Bancroft (1800–91) and Joseph Green Cogswell (1786–1871), two promising young scholars. (The former was later to become famous as the "father of American history," and also as the Secretary of the Navy who founded the United States Naval Academy and as United States Minister to both Great Britain and Germany, and the latter to become recognized later as one of America's brilliant scholars and as the founder of the Astor Library in New York City.)

In the Round Hill School, physical education became for the first time in United States a regular part of the course of instruction, and there for the first time also a person specifically qualified for the task was hired to teach physical education—this in 1827 when the school added to its faculty Charles Beck (see p. 172), a German political refugee, to teach both gymnastics and Latin. This also marked another first—the earliest teaching of German gymnastics in America.

From the very start, the school gave the boys a rich program of physical activities, which included archery, baseball, boxing, camping, dancing, football, hiking, running, skating, swimming, and wrestling; but these activities were carried on informally and not as a part of the school curriculum and without a specialized teacher to teach them. When Beck joined the faculty, he set up an outdoor gymnasium with apparatus such as was used in a German gymnasium, and the entire school was divided into classes, each meeting for an hour three times a week for gymnastic instruction. Beck was succeeded by Charles Follen (see p. 172), another German refugee.

Other Schools. Following this lead, about fifteen other secondary schools organized gymnastic classes for their students. When the Chauncy Hall School was organized in Boston in 1828, provision was made for exercises and games. The head master, being especially interested in the promotion of the physical welfare of the students, provided some crude apparatus for physical exercises and at recess periods took the boys to the Boston Common to play games.

In 1837 Michigan's first State Superintendent of Public Instruction called upon the teachers of the state "to know something of physical education and sound health," and in 1852, at the dedication of the Michigan State Normal School at Ypsilanti, he advocated courses in physical culture for all students. In 1860 the then State Superintendent persuaded the Michigan State Teachers Association to hold a series of institutes to prepare teachers to handle physical education classes. At this same time he was advocating that the training and care of the body should receive attention along with instruction of the mind in the arts and sciences. The work of the superintendent of schools to secure a place for physical exercise on the daily program of the schools of Boston constitutes one of the earliest efforts made by school administrators. In his school report of 1852 he said: "In addition to the exercise allowed at the time of recess each half day, all the younger children need provision for some gentle exercise as often as once in every half hour, such as riding, walking, marching accompanied with such motions of the arms as would tend to give fullness and erectness to the chest." The next year a rule that every "scholar" should have daily some kind of physical or gymnastic exercise was passed but scarcely enforced. In the annual report of 1858, the superintendent again spoke out for physical education saying: "While the intelligence is in training, the conscience and the body must not be neglected. Liberal playgrounds ought to be provided for every school at whatever cost, and they should be used." The time was ripe, however, for the enthusiasm and confidence of Dio Lewis, whose system of calisthenics was first taught in a private school in West Newton, Massachusetts, in 1860. The superintendent of the Boston schools became interested in this system and secured instruction for his teachers, so that it could be introduced into the Boston schools. The teachers were to give not more than one-half nor less than one-quarter of an hour to the exercises once during every school session. By 1862 there were seventy teachers who had had training and were giving the work to the school pupils.

In the 1850's educators were also awakening in the Middle West and on the West Coast. Many school yards of St. Louis were equipped with play apparatus which was used at recess periods, and some schools were practising "manual exercises," while in Cincinnati there were a few parallel bars, horizontal bars, horizontal ladders, and circular swings in four school yards. In 1857 the superintendent of the Cincinnati schools proposed that all teachers employed in the schools should be instructed in a system of gymnastics adapted to the several grades of the schools from the first through the sixth. A year later a department of physical education was established with a special teacher in charge of the work. A daily program of calisthenics and free play was inaugurated in 1854 in the Rincon School of San Francisco, and two years later a public exhibition of the work of the pupils consisted of exercises on horizontal bars and flying rings, and with wands, dumbbells, and Indian clubs. Several other cities made efforts to organize a system of physical training for the public schools in the fifties, but none was able to entirely overcome either the obstacles of lack of funds, facilities, and trained leaders, or the general skepticism regarding the value of the work.

Girls' Schools

In this era many people deplored the health condition of young girls and urged that physical education be made a part of their school programs. The editor of the *Boston Courier,* after attending a school festival in 1858, wrote that "not one girl in ten had the air or look of good health." Catharine Beecher in her two schools in Hartford and Cincinnati used the system of calisthenics which she had developed for girls in an effort to combat this state of affairs, and many schools adopted her system. In her *Reminiscences* there is preserved a speech which she gave in Cincinnati, in 1837, in which she said, in part:

> When physical education takes its proper place in our schools, young girls will be trained in the classrooms to move head, hands and arms gracefully; to sit, stand and walk properly and to pursue calisthenic exercises for physical development as regular school duty as much as their studies; and these exercises set to music, will be sought as the most agreeable of school duties.

In 1825 William Bentley Fowle (1795–1865) introduced into his girls' school in Boston the use of bars and pulleys at recess periods, teaching the use of the apparatus himself and reporting that his participation in the exercises with his pupils did not lessen their respect for him and that the discipline of the school was not thereby impaired. He also admonished that the household labors and walking which some schools advocated should not be used as a substitute for gymnastic exercises. (This report of Fowle's physical education work given in the *American Journal of Education* in 1826 probably marks the first published record of physical education for girls.)

Some private schools for girls of this era gave their students a physical education program that was indeed rich for that day including skating, archery, riding sidesaddle, dancing, swimming, croquet, walking, and calisthenics. A few schools, notably Mt. Holyoke Female Seminary in Massachusetts, offered physical education as early as 1837 but substituted domestic duties for a large part of the program. Nevertheless they did offer the students walking and calisthenics, the latter consisting mainly of dance steps accompanied by singing. Rockford Female Seminary in Illinois offered its students a physical education program as early as 1849.

In speaking of his work with girls, Fowle said: "My chief difficulty was in the selection of proper exercises for females. You know that prevailing notions of female delicacy and propriety are at variance with every attempt to render females less feeble and helpless."

Colleges

On the whole, college authorities evidenced little interest in the physical well-being of their students. They provided no gymnasiums and no facilities for sports. What little interest there was came from a small handful of individuals devoted to an educational ideal. A superintendent of the United States Military Academy resigned from the service in 1818 and began an agitation for the reform of the higher educational institutions of the nation, maintaining that one of the great defects of the educational system was the neglect of physical education in all the principal seminaries.

In 1826 Harvard gave permission to Charles Follen, who was then an instructor of German in the college, to organize gymnastics for the students although the activity was not recognized as a part of the educational program. On a piece of ground called the Delta, the students, directed by Follen, constructed some crude apparatus consisting of bars, ladders, wooden horses, and suspended ropes, and laid out places for running and jumping. It was a German "turnplatz" transplanted to America. The authorities also appropriated one of the vacant halls for indoor work. The student body showed great enthusiasm, and Follen had large numbers on the Delta and on the hikes and cross-country runs. At this same time the Dartmouth students set up an outdoor gymnasium "behind the college" and established cricket clubs which "covered the green during the summer."

Soon thereafter Yale, Amherst, Williams, Brown, and Bowdoin, set up outdoor gymnasiums. In many cases the faculty and students worked together to clear the ground and construct apparatus. Instructors were employed, and classes were held from two to five times per week. In addition to the outdoor gymnasium a room was usually provided for indoor work. The apparatus consisted of parallel and horizontal bars, ladders, ropes, mats, and wooden horses. Running and hiking were encouraged. In some institutions fencing and boxing were taught.

Physical Education Through Manual Labor. Throughout the 1830's and 1840's the colleges of the manual labor movement clung to their theory that manual labor was the best form of exercise and would conserve the time that participation in gymnastics would waste. These manual duties, therefore, were a substitute for physical education in all of these schools in their early years. Hence there was little progress in the development of physical education in colleges in general until in the 1850's when a nation-wide interest in the subject manifested itself and became felt in institutions of higher learning. However, this work was not given recognition as an official part of the educational program.

Amherst College Department. The President of Amherst College, who had been a pupil of Follen at Harvard, in his 1855 report to the trustees, said: "No one thing has demanded more of my anxious attention than the health of the students. The waning of the physical energies in the midway of the college course is almost the rule rather than the exception among us, and cases of complete breaking down are painfully numerous."

In 1859 the construction of a gymnasium was begun at the total cost of $15,000, and the trustees voted to establish a department of physical education, the first college department in the United States. They set forth the following requirements for the person to be selected as its head: he must be "thoroughly educated, a doctor of medicine and he must know something of gymnastics and sports and adhere to the principles that (1) the object of the gymnastics was not to learn to perform difficult feats but to keep the body in health, (2) the exercises used should be suited to all who engage in them and (3) students should be guarded against overwork in exercising." This person was to be given a seat on the faculty and the title of Professor of Hygiene and Physical Education.

Dr. Edward Hitchcock (see p. 234), recently graduated from Harvard Medical School, was selected for the post, following a brief tenure in the position by a man named John Hooker, who did not remain long enough to get a department fully established, and Hitchcock became the first officially recognized College Director of Physical Education in the United States. At the same time, he achieved the rank of Professor—the only physical educator to hold that title in any college in the United States for many years to follow. He took over his duties at Amherst in August, 1861, remaining in that post for fifty years until his death in 1911 at the age of eighty-three.

At first Hitchcock built his program around heavy gymnastics, but soon coming to the conclusion that light gymnastics, when executed rapidly, were more beneficial, he revised the program. He stressed hygienic living and regular strenuous exercise of a pleasant, recreative type, and early in his work there sponsored an intramural program of sports.

From the first year at Amherst, Hitchcock compiled statistics of measurements of the students and thus became the first physical educator in America to apply the science of anthropometry to physical education. Measurements were taken of each student upon entrance and at the close of each school year. From the findings, advice was given as to his physical education needs and special exercises were prescribed as needed. The records were kept so that the student might know how he compared with others and how he changed from year to year. It was over half a century before most physical educators caught up with Dr. Hitchcock in this phase of his program at Amherst. Also, from the very beginning of the first college department, Dr. Hitchcock called it the department of physical education, not physical training or physical culture—terms that were in popular use but finally gave way to Hitchcock's original designation.

This department was not only the first of the modern type to be organized at a college, but for twenty years it stood alone, unequalled in efficiency and professional excellence—years ahead of its day.

First College Gymnasiums. In 1820 Harvard University constructed the first college gymnasium. Although privately owned, it was maintained for the use of Harvard students. It was well equipped with German apparatus of the day. Other gymnasiums followed: Williams College in 1851—a gymnasium with baths, owned and controlled by the students; University of Virginia in 1852—a building destroyed during the Civil War; Miami University (Ohio) in 1857—a building renting for $60 a year. Harvard University, in 1859, constructed a building that cost $8,000 including the cost of equipment. This new Harvard gymnasium, an octagonal building of brick, was a gift of the class of 1822. It had two bowling alleys and dressing rooms but no baths and was opened in 1860 to all students for a two-dollar fee per term. In that same year, 1859, Princeton University built a little shack painted red which it acquired after an uprising of students in a demand for a gymnasium; and Yale University at a cost of $11,000 built a gymnasium which had a bath and bowling alleys in the basement.

In 1860 Amherst College built a two-story stone gymnasium, in 1861 Oberlin College built a men's gymnasium, in 1863 Bowdoin and Wesleyan followed suit, and in 1864 the students at Williams College raised $5,000 and erected a stone gymnasium, which, like the one built in 1851, was completely owned and controlled by them.

Teacher Training

As early as 1827, Follen at Harvard University personally prepared a few students as monitors to teach gymnastics under his supervision. This is the earliest record of an attempt at teacher training in physical education in America. Although normal schools had by now come into the educational picture, none as yet offered special courses for the preparation of teachers of physical education. However, in 1859 the New York State Normal School asked for recognition of physical education in the schools and for the preparation of teachers to handle the subject. But plans for special schools for such a purpose did not materialize until 1861. Preceding this, however, at the Pittsburgh convention of the turners in 1856, it was proposed that a normal school be established as a means of filling the demands for trained teachers. Thereupon plans were made to open a school in Rochester, N.Y., in 1861, but it was not yet in operation at the outbreak of the Civil War when the entire teaching staff and all prospective students rushed to the defense of the Union, and plans for the school were abandoned for the duration of the war.

Dio Lewis Normal Institute of Physical Education. Founded to train teachers of physical education, the Dio Lewis Normal Institute of Physical Education opened in the summer of 1861 in Boston with such a distinguished faculty that it augured well for a tie with education in general. The president of Harvard University was the school's first president, and he had a board of directors of distinguished gentlemen and an imposing faculty of four medical doctors: one as professor of anatomy, one as professor of physiology, and one as professor of hygiene, and Dio Lewis, himself, as professor of gymnastics. The school opened with fourteen pupils. It offered two full courses of ten weeks each and included two periods of gymnastic drills daily, covering a series of 200 exercises to be learned in a ten-week period. In the second year, elocution and a course in Swedish Movement Cure were added to the curriculum. By 1868 the school had conducted nine sessions and issued diplomas to 421 persons who went out to teach mainly in the large cities of New England, although some went to other sections of the United States. His graduates were greatly sought by schools and colleges. By the early 1870's Dio Lewis had turned his attention to other interests, and the school closed its doors. (Various records indicate that the school closed in the late 60's but one of the authors has seen a certificate issued by this Institute and signed by Dio Lewis under the date of 1871, which indicates that the school must have been open into the early '70's. There is also a record of a summer school of his in 1884 as mentioned on p. 239.)

Non-School Programs

The German turner groups with their ten thousand members by 1861, the private athletic clubs, the YMCA's, and the public gymnasiums that were established in this era furnished opportunities for large numbers to pursue physical activities outside the schools.

Turnverein Movement. After its popularity of the 1820's and its subsequent dying out in the 1830's, the German system of gymnastics again rose to a position of importance in the United States. In 1848 revolutionary movements again swept over Europe. In Germany, in particular, the government used a policy of reaction and suppression against those demanding a liberal form of government. As a result of this suppression, thousands of Germans migrated to the United States settling mainly in the north. They represented a high level of intellect and broad cultural interests. Deeply interested in both physical and mental development for a "chainless mind in a fetterless body" they soon, wherever sufficient numbers had collected, organized the Old-Country German gymnastic society—the turnverein.

The first such group was organized in Cincinnati, in 1848. At this time the Germans in Cincinnati still wore German peasant costumes of black velvet with red vests and big silver buttons. In that same year the second society was formed in New York City. The turnverein held its first national turnfest (outdoor gymnastic meet) in Philadelphia in 1851. Its aims were to promote physical education, intellectual enlightenment, and sociability among the members. The turnverein building was always provided with a gymnasium where classes in the German system of exercises were conducted for men, women, and children. The teachers in the early period were men who had had experience in Germany. The Know-Nothing Party, which was against all foreigners, took every opportunity to oppose the turners and even to jeer and ridicule them. But when the call came for volunteers for the Union Army the turners joined in such numbers that many societies ceased to exist, and their newly founded normal school closed.

Young Men's Christian Association. In 1851 the first YMCA in the United States was organized in Boston, seven years after George Williams (1821–1905), a London clerk, had started the movement. The growing interest in athletics and gymnastics which swept the country in the 1850's led the YMCA's to favor their promotion as "a safeguard against the allurement of objectionable places of resort," in the phrasing of the leaders of that day as reported by both Eddy and Morse (see references). At its third international convention of the YMCA's of the United States and Canada held in 1856 in Montreal, the question was raised "whether any means can be provided by the YMCA's for the physical development and promotion of the health of their members by gymnasiums, baths, etc.," but political and economic considerations of the day took precedence, and but little was done in this direction until after the Civil War other than in the establishment of boys' departments. By 1861 there were two hundred YMCA's in the country, and most supported boys' departments where exercises and games of sorts were offered.

Public Gymnasiums. Shortly after the two immigrants, Beck and Follen, arrived from Germany and began their teaching of gymnastics at the Round Hill School and Harvard University in the 1820's, prominent citizens of Boston began agitation for a public gymnasium. Dr. John C. Warren (1778–1856), Professor of Anatomy and Physiology at Harvard University, was a leader in the movement. The Board of Aldermen granted a request for a piece of ground for the purpose of establishing a school for gymnastic instruction and exercise. Money was raised by public subscription to guarantee a salary for a teacher and to provide apparatus. By September, 1826, the first public gymnasium, located in Washington Gardens, was ready, and Follen had been secured as the teacher. The gymnasium proved very popular and enrolled students until 1832. But even the expert gymnast could not keep the Boston Gymnasium alive. The novelty soon wore off, the participants became the target for the humorist and caricaturist, and the gymnasium closed its doors.

When the movement was revived some thirty years later Thomas Wentworth Higginson commented as follows in the *Atlantic Monthly* in 1861:

> It is one good evidence of the increasing interest in these exercises that the American gymnasia built during the past year or two have far surpassed all their predecessors in size and completeness, and have probably no superiors in the world. The Seventh Regiment Gymnasium in New York, . . . is 180 by 52 feet in its main hall and 35 feet in height, with nearly 1,000 pupils. The beautiful hall of the Metropolitan Gymnasium in Chicago, measures 108 by 80 feet and is 20 feet high at the sides, with a dome in the center 40 feet high and the same in diameter. Next to these probably rank the new gymnasium at Cincinnati, the Tremont Gymnasium at Boston, and the Bunker Hill Gymnasium at Charlestown, all recently opened. Of college institutions the most complete are probably those at Cambridge and New Haven. The arrangements for instruction are rather more systematic at Harvard.

With the growth of gymnasiums in the schools, colleges, and YMCA's, the public gymnasium eventually died out.

Professional Organizations

Teachers' associations had by now come into existence, and, at their meetings, physical education became a topic for discussion. In August, 1830, a convention of "Teachers and Other Friends of Education" met in Boston and organized the American Institute of Instruction. At this convention, Warren lectured on *The Importance of Physical Education,* speaking on the effects of poor ventilation, unsanitary school buildings, and improper seating, and on the relation of physical exercises to the problems of general education.

Physical Education Literature

Several books and one periodical on physical activities came off the presses in the United States in this period. Most books published in this era were on sports, but there were three books on gymnastics besides the 1831 book of Warren, *The Importance of Physical Education,* which might be called the first publication in the field of philosophy of physical education. From *Youthful Sports* of 1801 to *Medical Parlor Gymnastics* of 1859 a great variety of activities is covered. Foremost among these books are: William Turner's *Art of Swimming,* published in 1821, which included Benjamin Franklin's "Advice to Swimmers"; Charles Beck's translation of Jahn's *Treatise on Gymnastics,* published in 1828. William Clarke's *The Boy's Own Book,* Boston edition of 1829, which contains the first published mention of the game of rounders in the United States with a "diamond" indicated; Catharine Beecher's *Course in Calisthenics for Young Ladies in Schools and Families,* published in 1831 and containing sixty-two illustrations and a discussion of teaching methods and course materials, the first American book on curriculum and methods; Robin Carver's *Book of Sports* of 1834, which is the first to give rules of baseball; Chandler Robbins Gilman's *Life on the Lakes* of 1836, which gives an account of a canoe trip to the pictured rocks of the Lake Superior Region of the Canadian Border Lakes; *The Sports of Childhood,* published in 1839, containing information on archery, cricket, and the art of walking on stilts; and *The Boy's Treasury of Sports, Pastimes, and Recreation,* published in 1847, containing around four hundred engravings in addition to information on archery, golf, and hockey. In 1857 Miss Beecher published her second book, *Physiology and Calisthenics,* and in 1862 Dio Lewis put out his book, *New Gymnastics for Men, Women and Children,* which had wide circulation and ran through twenty-five editions. (According to Henderson, several of these books are owned by the New York Public Library, the Racquet and Tennis Club of New York City, and Yale University.)

The first American periodical in the physical education field was established by Dio Lewis, named *Gymnastic Monthly and Journal of Physical Culture*. It was published in Boston, beginning in December, 1861, but it did not survive long.

LEADERS OF PHYSICAL EDUCATION

For the first time in the United States there now arose leaders who fully devoted some period of their lives to the cause of physical education—three men born in Europe and one man and one woman of American origins. They are discussed chronologically according to year of birth.

The first three—German immigrants of superior education—were, beyond their training in philosophy, law, the classics, theology, political economy, and history, deeply interested in physical education. In laying the foundations of physical education in the United States, they brought to the groundwork a scholarly approach.

Charles Follen (1796–1840)

Born in Romrad, Germany, Charles Follen, a pupil and friend of Jahn, fled the country when Jahn was arrested in 1819 for his political activities. He went first to Switzerland with another of Jahn's disciples, Charles Beck. None too safe there, the two soon went to France where the Marquis de Lafayette, then a deputy in the French Chamber of Representatives, urged them to go to America. Armed with letters of introduction to Lafayette's friends, they arrived in Philadelphia in 1824. Follen, who held the degree, Doctor of Civil Laws, from the University of Geissen, soon found employment at Harvard University to teach German. Later he added the teaching of gymnastics to his schedule and soon took on the added responsibility of teaching at the first public gymnasium in Boston. Later he gave up the teaching of gymnastics and devoted his time completely to the teaching of German, ethics, and history at Harvard.

Charles Beck (1798–1866)

Charles Beck was born in Heidelberg, Germany, and procured the degree, Doctor of Theology, from the University of Tubingen. He fled to America with Follen, and almost immediately upon his arrival the head master of the famous Round Hill School procured him to teach gymnastics and Latin. This marked the first time that German gymnastics was taught in the United States. Beck left the school in 1830 to assist in the establishment of Phillipstown Academy in New York. Two years later he became Professor of Latin at Harvard University. His last years were spent as a Unitarian minister and a leader in the fight for the abolition of slavery.

Francis Lieber (1800–72)

Born in Berlin, Germany, Francis Lieber was educated at the University of Jena, where he procured the degree of Doctor of Philosophy. Also a friend of Jahn, he found life increasingly difficult in Germany and escaped to America in 1827. At that time Follen gave up his teaching at the Boston Gymnasium, and Lieber was offered the position there, where he opened the first swimming school in the United States and taught swimming while serving as editor of the first edition of the *Encyclopaedia Americana.* In the 1840's he was invited to make plans for the new Girard College which was opened in Philadelphia in 1848. Following this he took up the teaching of political economy and history and became known as America's "first academic political philosopher." His *Political Ethics,* published in 1838, and *Civil Liberty and Government,* published in 1853, marked him as one of America's top scholars.

Catharine Esther Beecher (1800–78)

Catharine Beecher born in East Hampton, Long Island; was the daughter of the well-known preacher, Lyman Beecher (1775–1863); and sister of Harriet Beecher Stowe (1811–96), author of *Uncle Tom's Cabin,* and Henry Ward Beecher (1813–87), the famous preacher and reformer. Reared in a home of unusual educational advantages, she was tutored at home by her father and did not attend her first school until she was ten years old. Twelve years later after the family had moved to Hartford, Connecticut, she opened her own private school for girls, the Hartford Female Seminary. It achieved such fame that shortly she had over one hundred pupils. Sensing that they needed an exercise program, she investigated the German gymnastics that had come into prominence in the Boston area but rejected them as too strenuous for the average frail girl of that day. Becoming interested in physiology, she combined this interest with her attempts to devise a system of exercises advisable for girls. In 1831, she produced her first book, *A Course of Calisthenics for Young Ladies*—the first manual of physical education in America—and in 1858 her second book, *Physiology and Calisthenics.* A sustained effort of twenty-seven years was required to perfect the system of exercises which she developed to produce good posture and grace.

When her family moved to Cincinnati in 1832 she opened the Western Female Seminary there and soon thereafter launched upon a career of lecturing in an attempt to sell education, in general, and physical education, in particular, throughout the East and Middle West. In 1864, she joined the staff of Dio Lewis' new school for girls in Lexington, Massachusetts, but the two soon disagreed on fundamental philosophy concerning their two systems of calisthenics, and Miss Beecher resumed her educational promotion work. She organized women's educational societies in the East to raise money to send women teachers to the Mississippi Valley as missionary teachers to start schools there. She may justifiably be claimed as the first American to originate a system of gymnastics and as the first woman physical education leader in America.

Dio Lewis (1823–86)

Dio Lewis was born in Cayuga County near Auburn, New York. Quitting school at the age of twelve, he began his teaching career three years later. When nineteen he embarked upon medical studies through a combination of a few courses at Harvard University and study in a physician's office. At twenty-eight he received an honorary degree of Doctor of Medicine from the Cleveland Medical College, and shortly thereafter embarked upon a five-year lecture career on temperance and health topics which took him all over the country.

In his travels he encountered the German system of gymnastics, but, in spite of its great popularity, he felt that it was not what the United States needed. So he devised a system of calisthenics of his own, and in 1860 he went to Boston and organized evening classes to present his system to the public. Achieving immediate acclaim, he organized his Normal Institute of Physical Education. Thus in Boston in 1861 began the first teacher-training work in this field.

In 1864 he established a school for girls at Lexington, Massachusetts, and brought Catharine Beecher to its staff. Within three years the school had three hundred pupils from various parts of the country, mostly girls of delicate constitution sent there for their health. One year later, tiring of this venture, Dio Lewis renewed his lecturing, and shortly the school closed. He now organized The Woman's Crusade, which later developed into the Woman's Christian Temperance Union, and he added Europe to his lecture itinerary.

He popularized physical education and sold the need for it to many educators who, through his influence, put it into the school programs. A man of exceedingly good looks and with much personal charm, he was a sensation wherever he went.

18

Physical Activities in the Latter Nineteenth Century (1865–1900)

In their informal leisure the people still enjoyed quilting bees, corn-huskings, square dancing, hunting, and fishing. By the 1890's bicycling, athletic contests, and prize fighting had become popular. The great German immigration to the Middle West brought to that region the love of Sunday picnics and outings, much gay music and dancing—all frowned upon so vigorously by the dominating Puritan stock throughout the Colonial period and early years of our national life. Now things began to change in America with this in-pouring of blithe spirits who did not fear the Puritan's God. Near the end of the century electric trolley cars came to the cities, and they transported the willing throngs to the amusement places that were springing up in the outlying districts.

Gymnastics became the core of the physical activity program across the land in nonschool organizations as well as in the schools. The sports and games pursued by school children and college students under their own organization and management still received but scant attention from the schools except in a few situations. However certain groups of adults now began to promote athletics and games, foreshadowing today's rich sports heritage. Here and there dancing claimed some attention—it, too, presaging an interesting future. Back in the East where pioneer days were now long since past, industrialization had set in, and great portions of the population, no longer engaged in farming, had become engaged, instead, in factory work, thus changing materially the physical development and recreational needs of the people.

With the opening of the first transcontinental railroad in 1869, the settling of the west took on new speed. The church, failing to keep pace with the westward moving settlers, began to lose its hold, and play and dance were no longer looked upon as sin except in those communities settled by the Puritan stock itself pushing westward.

Although the churches still banned card-playing, dancing, and theater attendance as evil, the old rules for strict Sabbath observance were fast disappearing.

ACTIVITIES OF PHYSICAL EDUCATION

Rhythmical, gymnastic, and sports activities as they developed in the United States following the Civil War are discussed below, and the ongoing story of their further devlopment in later periods is discussed in Chapters 21 and 23.

Dance and Rhythms

The free exercises of Catharine Beecher were performed to music, and in some schools they developed into a sort of dance form which later replaced calisthenics, but they had no permanency as did the dance forms discussed below.

Ballroom Dance. It would have been unthinkable in the nineteenth century to teach any form of ballroom dancing in a public institution. It was taught only in private schools and in dance studios. The minuet of Colonial days had about died out as a social dance by the time of the Civil War, but the Virginia reel kept its popularity. In the early part of this era the most popular dances were the schottische, polka, gallop, lancers, quadrille, mazurka, varsovienne, Newport, and gavotte. The waltz was not popular until later and then was danced only in the East for quite some time. In the 1890's when the famous band leader, John Philip Sousa (1854–1932), toured the country, his band music became so popular that its two-step rhythm popularized the new dance step, driving all other forms into the background.

Esthetic Dance. The earliest record of esthetic dance in America would seem to be a listing of this activity in the curriculum of the Normal School of the American Gymnastic Union when it opened in 1866. Just what form of dance this was is not recorded. The next mention is in 1894 of the "new esthetic dancing" taught by Melvin Ballou Gilbert (1847–1910), a famous dance master of Boston. He was the first well-known dance teacher to align himself with the schools to offer dance as a part of a physical education program. He based his work on a modified ballet form and first taught it at the Harvard Summer School of Physical Education in 1894 and a few years later at Vassar College and the Boston Normal School of Gymnastics. This form of dancing became very popular throughout the country, particularly with women.

Folk Dance. The early immigrants brought their various native dances to America, but they did not display them publicly probably because, in their eagerness to become Americanized as rapidly as possible, they did not care to give others a chance to accuse them of trying to keep their homeland customs alive in the New World. Not until teachers of physical education, themselves, went to Europe and collected the dances did they become known and used in the schools.

When Senda Berenson (see p. 333) head of physical education at Smith College studied in Sweden in the spring and summer of 1897, she collected folk dances, and upon her return home introduced them to the Smith students. This is the earliest record of this activity's being taught in a school program in America. A year or two later Anne Barr (1867–1945) visited work in Sweden and also brought back folk dances which she introduced into her program at the University of Nebraska in the fall of 1898, and at the Chautauqua School of Physical Education in the summer of 1899.

Square Dance. As the frontiers moved ever westward the pioneers carried to their new homes a form of dance brought originally from England known as country dancing which, by now, had developed several American forms of its own—the Kentucky and Tennessee mountain form; the formal one of New England; and that of the plains and the cowboys. However, square dancing did not carry over into school physical education programs in the nineteenth century. Its popularity existed in pioneer communities as the recreational dance form of the people, and it was handed down from parents to children. Thus it persisted enthusiastically in the Middle West, South, and Far West throughout the century.

Gymnastics

In the nineteenth century there were practically no public school "exercise rooms" in the United States. Class work had to be carried on in the regular schoolroom with large groups served in a small space by teachers who were unprepared to teach physical activities. A class form that must be learned by rote had to be committed to a program of formal gymnastics in order to exist at all. This form served its day and, in many places, served well in this formative period of the physical education profession. It gave children as well as many adults excellent physical fitness training, albeit a narrow program. The horse and buggy, the pony express, and the kerosene lamps of that day were inadequate, too, but while the pioneer period was passing on to the period of automobiles, railroads, electricity, and supervised play, gymnastics, as well as the other things, served their purpose well.

German System. The German system of gymnastics had gained a strong foothold by the close of the Civil War, particularly in the larger cities of the Middle West. In the 1880's Chicago alone had fourteen special teachers in its public schools to teach German gymnastics. With another wave of German immigrants coming right after the war, German gymnastics took a still firmer hold and throughout the rest of the nineteenth century was very popular. The spectacular feats of the German gymnasts created such a sensation wherever they exhibited in public school or YMCA gymnasium that Dr. Sargent labelled this era as the acrobatic stage of physical education.

Many people, though, refused to accept German gymnastics. Americans of other national strains were repelled by the intense German nationalism of the promoters of this system. Dr. Edward Mussey Hartwell (see p. 238), of Johns Hopkins University, felt it necessary to point out to these critics in his remarks at a conference in 1889 that "the fondness of the German people for gymnastics is as marked a national trait as is the liking of the British for athletic sports." Much misunderstanding has always existed about the German system which might have been avoided had the German immigrants differentiated between German gymnastics and the over-all German physical education program. To them, the word "gymnastics" embraced the over-all program, but to non-German Americans the word meant merely calisthenics and apparatus work. Americans in general do not interpret the word to embrace sports, games, and rhythms as well as free-standing exercises and apparatus work. Hence the consternation of the German Americans when the system was so bitterly attacked because it was accused of being so narrow. The true German system of gymnastics consisted of five types of activities, all evolved from Frederick Ludwig Jahn's work, namely: (1) tactics and marching; (2) free exercises with short and long wands, dumbbells, rings, and clubs; (3) "dance steps" for girls; (4) apparatus work using balance board, buck, horizontal bars, long and side horse, ladders, parallel bars, poles, ropes, round swing, suspension rings, and vaulting box; and (5) games and play—a graded set as developed by GutsMuths in 1793.

Since both the German and Swedish systems held the serious attention of both the school and nonschool groups for a rather long period, a somewhat detailed description of what they actually offered as exercise is of historical significance. In the May, 1894, *Mind and Body,* is a chart outlining the German system of gymnastics then in use in the United States. The main features of the program consisted of the following:

1. General exercises of strength, acquired through:
   a. Wrestling, weights, and putting the shot.
   b. Straining a large number of muscles to the utmost, combined with the act of exertion thus increasing "the strength and dimension of the muscle."
2. Localized exercises of strength acquired through:
   a. Calisthenics with weights—the movements frequently repeated combined with long holding.
   b. Work on horizontal bars, parallel bars, rings, or pole vaulting.
   c. Straining a small number of muscles to the utmost.
3. Exercises of skill done through "compound and flourishing calisthenics," balancing exercises, work on horse, buck, horizontal and parallel bars, far and high jump.
4. Exercises for quickness acquired through:
   a. Walking, marching, running, rope-jumping, dancing, hopping, climbing ladders or hills, swimming, rowing with moveable seat, bicycling, skating, sawing wood, mountain climbing.
   b. "Rhythmically repeated movements distributed over a great number of muscles with intention of moving forward quickly . . . or as rapidly as possible straining the activities of the heart and lungs to the utmost and causing temporary exhaustion of these organs."
5. Exercises of endurance acquired through:
   a. Exercises listed in numbers 3 and 4 above.
   b. Moderating the speed to preserve "equilibrium of different organic activities" so that the "motion may be continued for hours."
6. Exercises of attention acquired through tactics and "rhythmical motions as in May dancing, etc., where a single member is but a part of the whole."
7. Exercises of alertness acquired through:
   a. Wrestling, fencing, intricate running, and ball games.
   b. Mastering of the unforeseen and need of suddenly necessary motions on the impulse of the moment.

As this system became incorporated in our schools, track and field activities were gradually added as a start at Americanization of the program, although all parts of the offering suffered from lack of equipment, leaving calisthenics to receive the major share of attention.

Swedish Gymnastics. Although there is a record of Swedish gymnastics' being taught in a girls' high school in Boston as early as 1874, it was not until the 1880's that the system of Per Henrik Ling received sufficient attention in America to challenge the German system. Great rivalry developed between the advocates of the two forms. In fact the famous Physical Training Conference held in Boston in 1889 concerned itself primarily with discussions of the relative merits of the two systems. At that meeting Dr. Edward Hitchcock, Director of Physical Education of Amherst College, threw the weight of his influence behind the announcement of the Boston Public Schools that they were going to try out the Ling System. But Dr. Luther Halsey Gulick (see p. 321) of the YMCA school in Springfield, Massachusetts, opposed the use of either system, saying that both demanded "too much attention to detail and too much patience for what it was worth." However, he approved of the Swedish System for school children who had to exercise in the school room, but not for adults nor for free hours out of school.

The Germans held that the Swedish method was too formal, uninteresting, failed to obtain recreational values, and was very weak in social and moral training. The Swedish supporters claimed that the German system lacked scientific foundation, that too much music and rhythm accompanied the exercises and thereby prevented the maximum physical benefit from being derived, that too much emphasis was given to the recreational and not enough to the educational results, and that the system was unable to cope with problems of individual and specific weaknesses.

In light of all the arguments it is interesting to note that while a few women physical educators went to Sweden to study, no record reveals names of women as having sought foreign study or even local instruction so that they might bring the German system of gymnastics to the girls and women of America. The first American woman to study at the Royal Central Gymnastics Institute of Stockholm was Kate Campbell Hurd, M.D., the first medical director of Bryn Mawr College, who studied there in the winter of 1889–1890, followed by Senda Berenson of the Smith College faculty in 1897.

Swedish gymnastics of that period was characterized by (1) the Day's Order, (2) progression of exercises day by day and week by week from easy to difficult, from light to strenuous work, (3) use of word of command for all movements, (4) stress upon correct holding of positions, and (5) corrective or remedial effects. In fact out of the Swedish system grew the corrective gymnastics that have assumed so important a place in the school physical education program of the twentieth century. The apparatus work of Swedish gymnastics was quite different from that of the German system. In the Swedish form the following apparatus was used: high and low boom, swinging ladders, swinging and travelling rings, climbing ropes, bar stalls, rope ladders, and vaulting box. In the free-exercise part of the program no hand apparatus of any kind was used, nor was there any musical accompaniment. However, like the

German system, the Swedish system included marching, rhythms, and games.

The advocates of this system of gymnastics claimed that the functioning of the heart and lungs was the fundamental function of the body, and that Swedish educational gymnastics served to develop these organs. They were not concerned with the development of muscle strength or speed. As Dr. Claës J. Enebuske (1855–?), who held medical degrees from both Harvard University and the University of Paris and the Ph.D. from the University of Lund, Sweden, said to his pupils at the Boston Normal School of Gymnastics: "Get the heart and lungs right and the muscles will meet every reasonable demand." The Day's Order consisted of the following schedule of exercises.

1. Order movements
2. Leg movements
3. Strain bendings
4. Heave exercises
5. Balance exercises
6. Back exercises
7. Abdominal exercises
8. Lateral trunk exercises
9. Jumping exercises
10. Slow leg exercises
11. Respiratory exercises

Each lesson contained an exercise for each of the eleven items listed above and in that order. From lesson to lesson the exercises became more strenuous and difficult either by increase in the number of repetitions or by advancing to exercises requiring ever greater skill of execution. Enebuske's book *Gymnastic Day's Order According to the Ling System,* widely used throughout the United States in this era, gives three series of twenty-five lessons each, all progressively arranged from lesson one through lesson seventy-five. To show the progression in the Day's Order, Lessons 1 and 75 are aligned together below in the short-cut writing system used for Day's Orders at that time.

Lesson 1	*Lesson 75*
1. Order: Fund. std. and rest	Order movements
2. Leg: Std., ft. placing sideways	Stret. ½ horiz. std., knee bending
3. Strain bend: Std., back bend hd	Stret. bow std., alt. leg raise and heel raise
4. Heave: Wing std. position	Std. 2 arm ext. and alt. arm ext. in various directions
5. Balance: Wing stride std., 2 heel raising	Stret. ½ toe std., arm sinking sideways downward slowly
6. Back: Cross std., 2 arm rotation	½ stret. fall-out std., chg of arms and ft. with adv. in zigzag and about facing.
7. Abdomen: Std., back bending of tnk (gently)	Stret. horiz. ½ toe lean std., arm parting

8. Lateral Trunk: Std., side bending	Stret. fallout twist std., side bending and strd prone falling, alt arm and leg raising
9. Jumping: Mark time	(a) Wing toe knee bend std., spring jump in place with alt. stret of knee. (b) Std., free jp in place with facing 360 degrees.
10. Slow leg: Wing std., 2 knee bend	Stret. walk toe std., 2 deep knee bend
11. Respiratory: Std., 2 arm raising with deep breathing	Cross twist outward fallout std., arm flg sideways with chg of ft in series, alternate with std. circumduction of arms with deep breath

Delsarte System. During the early nineties the Delsarte System of Physical Culture received much acclaim, and great numbers were converted to its theories. This system took its name from its founder François Delsarte (1811–71), a French vocal and dramatic teacher. Finding that ideal poses and gestures could best be taught through physical exercises, he devised a system for use in his work. Although he had no thought of devising a system of gymnastics, many elocution and dramatics teachers accepted his methods and, adding their own ideas, evolved a system of exercises which they claimed would produce poise, grace, and health. These claims gave the Delsarte system a universal appeal entirely aside from its connection with the vocal and dramatic arts, and elocution teachers were in demand to teach this system in many girls' schools, where it was accepted as a physical education program. This system was characterized by a series of relaxing, "energizing," and deep-breathing exercises augmented by poses to denote various emotions. Related as it was to voice and speech culture, as these courses were spoken of at that time, the term "physical culture" now came into common usage in America stemming from the Delsarte system of exercises. Without sound principles back of it, this system proved but a fad, and it soon died out although it enjoyed much acclaim in its day.

Sports and Games

The post-Civil War period brought new sports to the national scene and changes to others, as is discussed in the material that follows.

Baseball. The game of baseball was popular in many army camps during the Civil War, particularly among the northern soldiers, and after the war it fast became a popular national game. By 1876 all young America was playing the game. In 1866 the ball was made smaller, the pitchers began to throw curves, and the distance and force of the batting and throwing increased to such an extent that padded gloves and masks became necessary. The overwhelming popularity of baseball hurt cricket, which had heretofore been popular particularly in those parts of the country with large settlements of English descendants. Now cricket became almost an unknown game in the United States.

Basketball. Basketball is exclusively American in its origin. Invented in 1891 by Dr. James Naismith (1861–1939), then a young teacher at the YMCA Training School in Springfield, Massachusetts, it claimed immediate popularity both as an indoor and outdoor game and as a sport for both men and women. In the first try-out game, played at the YMCA school in December, 1891, using peach baskets for goals, Naismith and Amos Alonzo Stagg (1862–1965), another young teacher, who later became a famous football coach, were captains of the two teams, while George L. Meylan (see p. 332), a visiting YMCA director, who later became Medical Director of Columbia University and a foremost leader of the camping movement, played on one of the teams. C. Ward Crompton (1877–1964), then a school boy, later to become a well-known physician, was captain of the third basketball team to be organized in New York City.

In this first game a soccer ball was used and there were nine players to a team. The peach basket was attached to the railing of the gallery running track, whereby the height of the basket was established, with an attendant on a ladder nearby to retrieve the ball after a successful throw. This clumsy set-up soon gave way to a hoop and netting, out of which the ball was poked by a long pole, and in 1906 the bottom of the netting was opened to let the ball drop through after losing its momentum. The first time the rules of this new game appeared in print was in January, 1892, when they were published in the YMCA School paper.

Naismith, trained for the ministry and later to acquire both Doctor of Divinity and Doctor of Medicine degrees, lived to see his game used by gamblers for their own ends. Not only did this grieve him, but maintaining always that basketball was a game to be played, not coached, he was ill at ease in the world of intense training and coaching that grew up around the game. The rules of the game as created by Naismith were published by the American Sports Publishing Company for the Spalding Athletic Library series and were unquestioningly accepted as the official rules of the game for boys and men. (In the early years of the game, the name was spelled as two words—basket ball—not one as today.)

Basketball for Women. In the spring of 1892 Senda Berenson at Smith College modified Naismith's rules for the use of girls, and her modified form spread rapidly throughout the country. Within the first year the girls' game had reached the University of Chicago where Stagg, who had played in the first game, was setting up that school's physical culture department as it was then called. Also in that same year, women's basketball had reached the Pacific Coast where, as well as in the Middle

West, the game was at first looked upon merely as a game for girls and grade school boys.

One of Miss Berenson's first changes was to divide the playing space into three courts, with each player to be confined to her assigned court. This gave the modified game the name "line basket ball" by which it was known in its earliest years. After a brief trial period, Miss Berenson made further modifications, such as allowing a player to hold the ball no longer than three seconds and to bounce the ball no more than three times. The rules put out in mimeograph form were sent throughout the country on request.

Shortly after Miss Berenson's modified rules became known across the country, other women produced their own modifications of the game for the use of girls, and as these various modifications differed widely from each other, confusion arose as to which set of rules was most approved by the profession.

Feeling the need of official backing of some sort for the rules, Miss Berenson (as related in the first printed guide of 1901) asked at a conference on physical training being held at the Springfield School of Christian Workers, in June 1899 under the auspices of Luther H. Gulick, that a committee be set up to study the rules of the game for girls. Dudley A. Sargent, then President of the American Association for the Advancement of Physical Education (see p. 230) was present at this conference, and he immediately appointed a committee to function under that national organization. Alice B. Foster (1866–1937), then of Oberlin College, was named chairman of the committee, with Ethel Perrin (see p. 331) of the Boston Normal School of Gymnastics, Elizabeth Wright of Radcliff College, and Senda Berenson as the other members of the committee with Miss Berenson, to serve as editor of the rules. Thus was born the first official committee on girl's sports—the Woman's Basket Ball Rules Committee of AAAPE. This move in 1899 was the first step toward what is now, several decades later, the Division of Girls' and Women's Sports of today's American Association for Health, Physical Education and Recreation.

The rules drawn up by this committee were made available in mimeographed form, but shortly the demands for copies became too great for this method of distribution, and when James E. Sullivan (1860–1914), Secretary of the Amateur Athletic Union, invited Miss Berenson to submit the rules to the American Sports Publishing Company for inclusion in the Spalding Athletic Library, the Committee accepted this offer, although the first printed guide did not come off the press until 1901.

Bicycling. The bicycle was invented in 1816 in Germany after an earlier unsuccessful attempt in France in 1769. The velocipede was developed in 1862. In 1872 came the high front-wheeler leading to the smaller wheels with chains and gears which was devised by an Englishman, and the craze for bicycling was on. "The Bicycle built for two" led to "triplets, quads, quints" and even to wheels with eight and ten saddles. Cycle racing soon became the sport sensation of the world, and the top racers were *the* athletic heroes of the day.

Women in their long, voluminous skirts of the early 1890's took to the sport, but the skirts had to be shortened. They receded to ankle length causing consternation in many communities, but that was nothing compared to the uproar that arose in every village all over the country where the bolder of the young women, abetted by liberal parents, adopted the dress reform sparked in an earlier day by Amelia Bloomer, a prominent writer, lecturer, and champion of women's rights and dress reform. The cities less stormily accepted the shortened skirts and the "bloomers" along with the bicycle-riding for girls and women.

Everyone of all ages took to wheels. On week days the streets were full of people going to work on bikes and on the week-ends full of bicycle club members who were on their own outings or following "bike" races somewhere nearby. By 1900 bicycling was the fashion of the day among all classes of people—it was, indeed, the biggest sports craze of the late nineteenth and early twentieth centuries. So many people took to wheels that bicycle speeders became a menace in the large cities, and police were mounted on bikes to catch these speeders who were endangering the lives of the other citizens at 20 miles per hour. Then, with the coming of the electric car the fad ended almost overnight—ending almost as suddenly as it arose. Bicycling then fell into its twentieth-century niche as a means of recreation for children and youth and as a means of transportation for school children and, in the earlier years of 1900, also for the working man. But while this fad lasted, in the 1890's and the first decade of the 1900's, bicycling brought splendid physical developmental exercise to the great masses of the population.

Bowling. It was not until the 1860's that bowling, popular from Colonial days on, developed into the ten-pin game and became a well-regulated sport. Beginning then, bowling clubs were organized in great numbers, and in 1875 the National Bowling League was founded. In 1895 a national reorganization was accomplished which resulted in the formation of the American Bowling Congress which revised the rules and standardized the equipment.

Football. Since 1873 football has been the most popular sport connected with college life and the most opposed and condemned; it has caused more college conferences and agreements than all other games combined. The earliest games of football were so rough and so devoid of rules that the "class rush" was substituted for it as a safer activity. As the game grew it was more like "association" football (soccer) than the present style of game. There follows a brief review of the development of football rules.

In 1869 Princeton and Rutgers played the first intercollegiate football game in America. The game was played at New Brunswick on November 6 with twenty-five players on each team. At this game yelling was introduced by the Princeton players, using an imitation of the Confederate rebel yell—a bloodcurdling cry of Civil War days. In this first match the Princeton players used the yell to frighten their opponents, but it took so much breath from the players that in the second game they asked their fellow students on the sidelines to give the yell for them. Thus started the United States custom of organized sideline yelling at games. Following this game, Columbia, Yale, Cornell, Pennsylvania, and Harvard were soon playing against each other. When Columbia and Yale played a match in 1872 they used twenty men to a team. In 1873 Princeton, Rutgers, Yale, and Columbia met together to draft a football code. The following year Harvard students organized a football team using a form of soccer rules and challenged the students of several colleges in the United States. When none accepted, they challenged the students of McGill University of Montreal, Canada, who accepted the challenge, and the game was played in May, 1875. McGill was playing rugby rules, kicking, catching, and running with the ball, which were unfamiliar to the Harvard players. The Harvard men asked them to explain their rules, and the two teams agreed to play the first half of the game by McGill's rugby rules and the second half by Harvard's soccer rules. One year later (1876) Harvard and Yale played their first match with Yale the victor. The Harvard men asked the Yale students to play by some of McGill's rugby rules to which they consented. In 1876 several colleges, not satisfied with the rules adopted in 1873, met in Springfield, Massachusetts, to revise and standardize the game. Upon the insistence of the Yale and Harvard delegates that some rugby rules be incorporated, the group acquiesced. At this time the American Intercollegiate Football Association was organized with Columbia, Harvard, Princeton, Rutgers, and Yale as members. The following year (1877) they revised the rules again, setting fifteen as the official number of players to a team.

Dr. Dudley A. Sargent, then Director of Physical Education and Athletics at Harvard, writing in *Outing* Magazine in 1885, declared that football had no peer as a physical developer but had degenerated into a brutal contest, although, as he said, it could be conducted so as to be a credit instead of a disgrace to a school.

Rowing. The sport of rowing took on new life after the Civil War. When the New York Athletic Club was founded in 1868, it built a boathouse on the Harlem River and took up the sport. In 1873 Yale built a

$15,000 boathouse to replace its smaller one of 1862. William Blaikie (1843–1904), a former Harvard crewman, became interested in the English style of rowing, which used the back and leg muscles as well as the arm muscles, and developed a style for the Harvard crews that became known as the Blaikie plan and soon produced a series of Harvard teams.

Swimming. From Frances Lieber's swimming school of 1825 grew the popularity of the "floating baths." It was in 1866, however, before Boston established its first baths and 1870 before New York City built their first of twenty-seven baths, five of which were in use up to 1904. Some of Boston's eleven floating pools and New York City's twenty-seven were for men and boys only, some for women and girls only, and some for both sexes but at different periods for each. Some had both deep and shallow pools for adults and children. Gradually, because of the changing sanitary conditions of the rivers, these pools changed to "fill and draw" type. Some converted to the use of city water and emptied into the rivers. Many of this type were in use as late as 1939.

Following the lead of Girard College of 1848, Harvard University put in the second college pool in 1880, a wooden affair. The year 1885 brought the first YMCA pool (in Brooklyn) and the first municipal pool (in Philadelphia), and the year 1888 brought the first pool for women, installed at Goucher College (in Baltimore). These pools had no showers, no water sterilization, and no hot water. They were open only in the summer and with no instruction offered. About 1896 word came from Germany that the spread of diseases could be traced to swimming pools. In the nineties Milwaukee, Utica, San Francisco, Chicago, Newark, Brookline, and Boston put in municipal pools. Of these cities, San Francisco was the first to offer instruction and Milwaukee was the first to have its pool open all the year and to have warm water and showers. After 1896 showers became a common requirement for all pools. The size of these first pools ranged from 11½ to 150 feet in width and from 20 to 300 feet in length.

Tennis. The game of court tennis, played since Colonial Days, gave way to lawn tennis when an Englishwoman, Mary Outerbridge, brought the new form of game to America from Bermuda in 1874. It was first played in the New York City area, with the Staten Island Cricket and Base Ball Club being the first organization to give the game attention. Within a year the girls at Mt. Holyoke Female Seminary were playing the game. Since women took up the game so enthusiastically, it was at first ridiculed by many as a game fit only for frail girls and women. Nevertheless, a tournament was held in Philadelphia in 1880, and the next year the United States Lawn Tennis Association was organized.

Track and Field. From the Scottish Caledonian Games, brought to America in the early Nineteenth Century, developed the track and field sports of today. The boys at Princeton were introduced to the Caledonian Games in 1873 by their Scotch physical director, George Goldie (1841–1920), and their popularity then spread into other colleges and down into the lower schools.

Other Sports. The first golf club since an earlier one in Savannah in 1795, was organized in 1888 by a Scotsman of Yonkers, New York, and it laid out a six-hole course. Shortly after this, clubs were organized in Buffalo (1889) and Philadelphia (1890). The first public golf courses were laid out in Boston, Indianapolis, and New York City around 1895. Badminton was first played in this country in 1888; the first ski club was organized in Red Wing, Minnesota, in 1886; softball was invented in 1887 at the Farragut Club in Chicago, and in that same year the first United States skating competition took place in Philadelphia; handball was first played in this country in 1888, with the first tournament put on by the Amateur Athletic Union in 1897; and volleyball was invented in 1895 by William Morgan, a YMCA physical director of Holyoke, Massachusetts, using a basketball bladder for the ball, which was exchanged shortly for the basketball itself, today's ball not coming into use until several years later.

SPORTS CLUBS AND ASSOCIATIONS

The poor physical condition of the soldiers drafted for the Civil War called for greatly increased sports in national life. This gave impetus to the rise of sports and favored adoption of physical education in the schools and colleges. Leagues of amateur and professional athletes, athletic clubs, Young Men's Christian Associations, and similar organizations contributed to the wave of enthusiasm and promoted athletic games and contests. This upsurge brought the first permanent sports clubs and intercollegiate associations.

Nonschool Sports Organizations

Although baseball clubs existed as early as 1845 (as mentioned in Chapter 16) the post–Civil War period brought a vastly increased interest in the game in all parts of the country. By 1867 there were fifty-six baseball clubs in Illinois alone and forty-two in Iowa, not to mention the many in other states. In that year the National Association of Base Ball Players was organized, and shortly after that intersectional contests sprang up. In 1869 the Red Stockings of Cincinnati turned "pro" and toured the East, winning all games. The Chicago White Stockings, Philadelphia

Athletics, and Washington Nationals were formed, and in 1871 ten such clubs played championship series. So much gambling, drinking, and corruption came to be attached to the games that professional baseball was no more than started when it became threatened with extinction. Out of efforts to lift the game to a respectable position came the National League of Professional Baseball Clubs in 1876. Other leagues soon followed, such as the American Association in 1882 and the American League in 1900.

By 1879 participation in sports had grown to such proportions that a need for standardization, control, and nation-wide promotion was felt, and the National Association of Amateur Athletes of America was organized. Its aims were to check the evils of professionalism, keep athletics on a respectable level, promote legitimate sports, define rules, and conduct competitions in an orderly and fair manner. From this organization developed the Amateur Athletic Union, which held its first meeting in 1888 in Detroit. With about 125 member clubs, it was completely reorganized in 1891, becoming a union of amateur athletic associations, rather than an organization of individual clubs. The leading nonschool sports organizations were born in this era, as follows:

1867–The National Association of Base Ball Players
1871–The Rowing Association of America
1874–The American Rifle Association
1875–The National Bowling League
1876–The National League of Professional Base Ball Clubs
1879–The National Association of Amateur Athletes of America (today's AAU)
1879–The National Archery Association
1881–The United States Lawn Tennis Association
1882–The American Association of Base Ball Clubs
1891–The Fencing League of America
1894–The U.S. Golf Association
1895–The American Bowling Congress
1895–The Athletic League of the YMCAs of North America
1900–The American League of Professional Base Ball Clubs

Intercollegiate Sports Associations

The earliest intercollegiate associations were established as follows:

1870–The Rowing Association of American Colleges (organized at the suggestion of the Harvard Rowing Club, with Bowdoin, Brown, and Massachusetts Agricultural College–today's University of Massachusetts–participating).

1873–The Intercollegiate Association for Football (organized by Columbia, Pennsylvania, Rutgers, and Yale).

1875—The Intercollegiate Association of Amateur Athletes of America (The ICAAAA, today's National Collegiate Athletic Association, organized to promote track and field in the college field; the earliest association to survive).

1876—The Intercollegiate Football Association (organized by Columbia, Harvard, and Pennsylvania to replace the 1873 association; at first a student group, but when Walter Camp (1859–1925) graduated from Yale in 1880, he continued to attend the meetings and it accepted graduate representatives from then on).

1883—The Intercollegiate Athletic Conference (the first attempt at faculty control of college sports).

1893—The American Football Rules Committee (organized to replace the Intercollegiate Football Association of 1876).

1895—The Intercollegiate Conference of Faculty Representatives (from which grew the Western Conference, today's Big Ten).

Shortly after the NAAAA (today's AAU) came into existence (in 1879), it came into conflict with the ICAAAA of 1875 (today's NCAA) as it attempted to draw college athletes under its control. Thus began a feud between the two groups which almost a century later still is unresolved.

Interscholastic Sports Associations

There was no control of high school sports until 1896 when a group of teachers in Wisconsin set up a committee to control their contests. Schools in the states of Michigan, Illinois, and Indiana soon followed suit. These efforts marked all that was done in this direction in the nineteenth century. Before organizations arose to control these sports, teachers, principals, and even janitors played on high school teams.

Women's Sports Organizations

Sports associations and clubs for women above the local level were practically unknown in the nineteenth century, and the local ones that did exist were mostly organizations of college women. As early as the 1880's, some sports clubs were in existence in some of the women's colleges, and by the 1890's in a few large universities. These were mostly bicycle, boating, tennis, and walking clubs. Bryn Mawr College united its various sports clubs into one organization in 1891, giving birth to the first Woman's Athletic Association. By 1892 the first basketball clubs had put in an appearance. In 1895 Mt. Holyoke College was presented the gift of an ice-skating rink, and the students immediately organized an ice-hockey club.

It was not until the late 1890's that basketball called forth enough enthusiasm among high school girls to support even local clubs.

SPORTS COMPETITION

Intramural Athletics

The term "intramural" as applied to sports was not generally used in this era. The word "sports" alone sufficed for all, in the lower schools referring to intramurals only, and in the colleges usually meaning only the varsity.

What few sports were carried on in the lower schools before the twentieth century were almost entirely intramural, but records of even this, are scanty. Exceptions are reports in the old files of the *Scholastic Bulletin* of the New York City Public Schools, as reported by C. Ward Crampton (see references) who tells of baseball, football, and track and field teams of the public high schools of New York City which were in action in the 1890's, sponsored by a games committee made up of representatives from each high school. The Barnard Games staged each year in mid-September by the New York City Public Schools were the great athletic event of the school year. But as everywhere else, sports for the New York City elementary school children were neglected, in spite of the organized efforts to meet the needs of the high school boys. Now and then some school in its field would offer some track or field event for the elementary school children, and this was the extent of their sports even in New York City, where many elementary schools had fine gymnasiums and excellent playgrounds.

There was much intramural sports competition going on constantly among college boys. Most of it, as in earlier periods, was organized, coached, financed, and managed by the boys themselves; in the leading colleges, however, by the closing years of this period, there were physical education departments to assist the boys in their sports. Such assistance meant including more boys than the earlier informal sports programs involved. Even in these schools, however, definitely organized intramural programs as we know them today were but a dream to be fulfilled only in the years ahead.

Interscholastic Athletics

There was but little of interscholastic athletics in the country in the Nineteenth Century. What little there was came almost entirely in the closing decade of the century and was largely pupil-inspired, pupil-controlled, and pupil-coached occurring mostly in the schools of the smaller towns where there were no physical education teachers.

Intercollegiate Athletics

The first intercollegiate contests—in rowing and baseball—which took place in the 1850's have been reported in Chapter 16. Now the first intercollegiate football game was held in 1869 as related on p. 186. Student interest in such matches grew rapidly from now on until in the 1880's such contests began to assume an important place in the over-all college life.

According to Lewis (see references), the first intercollegiate regatta following the Civil War was held by the three schools making up the Rowing Association of American Colleges—Harvard, Brown, and Massachusetts Agricultural College—in 1871, near Springfield, Massachusetts, with the Agricultural College winning. A second was held in the following year, with Amherst, Bowdoin, Williams, and Yale added to the contestants, and Amherst winning. In 1873 eleven colleges entered, but such controversy arose over the race, which Harvard won, that at the insistence of Harvard, future employment of professional coaches was forbidden. Gradually such publicity arose in connection with the regatta that college officials came to look upon these contests as great prestige builders; they drew large crowds, various localities bid for the contests, and leading newspapers and weeklies gave much attention to the sports, with front-page headlines that presaged the national publicity that would later embrace other college sports. It was rowing that first claimed such public attention for the college world.

The regatta of 1874 on Saratoga Lake, with nine colleges entered, was managed by a promoter who raised funds from railroad companies, a large hotel, and members of the Saratoga Rowing Association. It turned out to be a great social event, such as characterized the Oxford–Cambridge matches in England, and among the over 30,000 spectators was President Ulysses S. Grant. The winning Columbia team received a great welcome home in New York City. The next year's regatta, also held on Saratoga Lake, was an even greater success. Two well-known publications constructed a 30-foot tower overlooking the Lake and manned it with reporters, photographers, and telegraphers who reported the contest in full detail as it took place. At the same time, crowds gathered in hotel lobbies, in telegraph offices, and on the streets outside newspaper offices in cities and towns over a wide area for the running account of the race at Saratoga Lake. This must have been the country's first sports broadcast, foreshadowing the beginning of radio broadcasts of sports events a half century later. By the late 1870's, first Yale and then Harvard dropped out of the Rowing Association of American Colleges, and gradually rowing gave way to football as the prestige college sport.

As interest in gymnastics brought about the erection of gymnasiums, so the interest in sports now brought about the building of athletic fields. The first organized efforts at restrictions in college sports took place in this era. In 1882 a three-man faculty committee was set up at Harvard after faculty complaints that students were missing too much school work because of their games. Dr. Sargent was a member of the committee, and the following year he called a conference of other colleges for December, 1883, in New York City to consider faculty control of athletics. Nine colleges were represented at the meeting with three college presidents present.

In 1884 a committee representing twenty-two of the leading institutions attempted to secure the agreement of the college authorities to the following propositions: that athletic and gymnastic instructors shall be appointed by the faculty and not by the students; that college teams must be confined to games with college teams; that a standing committee of college representatives shall pass on the rules and regulations for conducting the contests; that no student may play on a team more than four years; and that games shall be held on college grounds only. However, these principles were not generally accepted.

Football was abolished at Harvard following a report by the president in 1885, stating that his investigating committee was "convinced that the game of football as at present played by college teams is demoralizing to player and spectators and extremely dangerous." In 1890 play between Yale and Harvard was revived, and that year Harvard won its first victory over Yale. This was a stupendous event for its day with 20,000 at the game and a special train to bring in the "fans."

With but little improvement in the contests, the President of Harvard University, following his earlier denunciations of 1885, again protested in 1894 and made proposals that stirred up great dissent among the students. The March issue of *Mind and Body* lists the three main proposals: no freshman to play in intercollegiate contests; no one to play in more than one contest a year; and intercollegiate contests to be held only once every two years. Following this, serious quarrels took place. Harvard University severed athletic relations with Yale University in 1894 and again in 1897, and with Princeton in 1897, and the U.S. Military and Naval Academies broke athletic relations with each other in 1893 and again in 1899.

But football was not the only sport used in intercollegiate contests in this era. The first intercollegiate track and field meet was held in 1874 at Saratoga, and the first intercollegiate swimming contest, including Pennsylvania, Columbia, and Yale, was held in 1897.

In 1892, when the University of Chicago was established, it immediately set up a department of physical culture and athletics. The records of its first varsity teams offer interesting study. The acting Captain of both its first football and baseball teams and a winner of the coveted "C" was Amos Alonzo Stagg who played right half back on one team and was pitcher for the other and at the same time was head of the department. Also Joseph E. Raycroft (1867–1955), the University physician, played quarter back on the first football team. But then only nineteen students came out for sports that first fall.

Non-School Competition

With the coming of railroads to all parts of the country in this era, making travel easier and less time-consuming, the several national sports associations born after the Civil War (as discussed earlier in this chapter) began to promote out-of-school competition. Inter-town, inter-city, even inter-regional and national championship contests arose now. The early 1870's brought on the first great baseball matches, which at first were limited to the larger cities of the East and Middle West. At this same time, many rowing matches developed between cities, as far west as Chicago and as far south as New Orleans. In 1879 the first national archery tournament was held in Chicago; in 1881 was the first national lawn tennis match for men, and in 1887 the first for women; the 1890's brought much intercity bicycle racing, and 1895 the first United States golf tournament, a one-day, sixteen-hole contest. But even yet, sports did not hold the general public attention enough for the development of the special sports page in the newspapers of the land. This awaited the coming of the twentieth century.

International Competition

There was but little international sports in the nineteenth century and what little there was came only after the Civil War. International contests were ushered in by the great boat race between Harvard and Oxford Universities, which was held on the River Thames near London on August 7, 1869. The course covered four miles, two furlongs. Oxford won by a half length in the time of 22 minutes and 20 seconds. This first international college contest received much acclaim both at home and abroad. One of the famous Currier and Ives prints is of this race.

According to an unidentified newspaper clipping of August, 1869 (which came to the attention of one of the authors), this race was managed from the U.S.A. side by William Blaikie (1843–1904), the young Harvard graduate who had developed the training plan for the Harvard crews. (Ten years later Blaikie, then a well-known attorney in New York City, gained nation-wide fame for his promotion of physical fitness and for his book, *How to Get Strong and How To Stay So.*)

In 1875 the one-year-old American Rifle Association sent a team to tour Ireland, Scotland, and England. Captained by Henry A. Gildersleeve—father of Virginia Gildersleeve (1877–1965), long-time dean of Barnard College—the American team won all its matches and on its victorious return was given a tumultuous welcome and a parade up Broadway. Albert G. Spalding (1850–1915), one of the earliest nationally known baseball pitchers, took two baseball teams called an "All-American team" on a grand tour of the world in 1888, introducing the American game to fourteen countries on five continents.

In 1878 Columbia College sent a crew to England where it rowed against Oxford, Cambridge, and the University of Dublin, losing all three matches.

United States Participation in the Modern Olympics. The founding of the Modern Olympics by Baron Pierre de Coubertin of France has been mentioned in Chapter 12. Although there was no such thing as an official United States team entered in the first of the modern Games held in Athens, Greece, in 1896 a few individuals from the United States entered on their own initiative or on that of some sports club. For example, James B. Connolly (1869–1957), a student at Harvard, dropped out of college to train for the Games, and entering as an independent contestant won the hop-step-and-jump event to become the first American to win in the Olympics. Other Americans won in the 100-yard dash (the winner being the only entrant in that event using a crouch start), the discus throw (although the winner had never seen a discus until he had one made to practice with a few weeks before leaving for Athens, which turned out to be heavier than the one used by the Greeks), and six other events for a total of nine wins out of twelve track and field events.

From Connolly's own report of the games, the United States athletes were the only ones who had trained for the contests, the athletes from the other countries knowing but little of such procedures. Also they were the only ones to set up a training table and keep early hours for retiring. Three Greek youths who entered the Marathon with no training and attempted to keep up a pace of eight miles an hour for a three-hour stretch died in the attempt.

Twelve nations were represented in these first Modern Olympics Games. Although no records were broken, the Games were considered an unqualified success. There were twelve bands on hand and an audience of around 80,000 until time for the finish of the Marathon race when an extra 20,000 people surged into the stadium, since this was the one event above all that held the attention of the Greek populace.

The rebirth of the Ancient Olympic Games, as conceived by Baron de Coubertin, was of a high spiritual order, aiming at a world brotherhood of man. The Baron offered an Olympic Creed—*The important thing in the Olympics is not winning but taking part. The essential thing in life is not conquering but fighting well.* He also offered an emblem (five circles intertwined representing the five major continents of the world bound together in fellowship through sports) and a motto: "Swifter, higher, stronger."

The sports offered in the first Modern Olympics were: covered court tennis, 2 events; cycling, 4; gymnastics, 8; lawn tennis, 2; shooting, 3; swimming, 1; track and field, 12; and weight-lifting, 2.

While the Americans excelled in track and field, the French excelled in cycling; the Danish and British in weight-lifting; the Germans in gymnastics; the British in tennis; and the Greeks in the Marathon and shooting. The wins of the thirty-four events offered counted up as follows: United States, 10; Germany, 6; Greece, 6; Great Britain, 5; France, 3; Denmark, 1; Hungary, 1; Ireland, 1; and Switzerland, 1.

The second Olympics was held in Paris in 1900, the closing summer of the nineteenth century. Again the United States athletes scored high in track and field events, while the other countries scored high in the other sports. Again there was no official United States team, but fifty-five athletes entered, almost as many as from all the other countries put together, each going independently or sponsored by some organization, each contestant or sponsoring group making its own arrangements and providing its own coaches independently of the others. Yale, Princeton, the University of Pennsylvania and Syracuse, Georgetown, Michigan and Chicago Universities sent representatives, each financing its own group.

In the second Games no new sports were added, but swimming, tennis, and weight-lifting were dropped, and also all cycling except the 1,000-metre race. On the other hand, ten events were added to track and field, making a total of twenty-two events for that sport alone. Also four shooting events were added, and two dropped. The total events offered were thirty-one. Of these the United States athletes won seventeen track and field events and two (of three) gymnastics events for a total of nineteen gold medals. France was the closest contender with five wins (one of them the Marathon), with Great Britain and Switzerland following with three wins each, and Hungary with one. (See Appendix, p. 399 for further information.)

In these closing years of the old century, the United States—a young nation of the New World—had, through the skills of her young athletes, much more than held her own alone against the athletic feats of all the nations of the Old World combined. Through its young athletes, the United States had won world-wide acclaim, a dramatic ending for the first full century of its nationhood.

Sports Competition for Women

From their beginnings, the women's academies and colleges favored participation of their students in sports and games as well as in gymnastics and dancing. By the 1870's American college women in particular were skating, riding side-saddle, forming walking clubs, and playing tennis. The girls at Vassar were even playing baseball. By the 1880's Wellesley College had its crews and competitive rowing on its campus lake, and Goucher and Vassar Colleges had swimming pools of sorts. By the 1890's the girls at Mt. Holyoke had an ice-skating rink; at Wells, a golf course; at Bryn Mawr, riding stables; at Vassar, an athletic field; and everywhere everyone was bicycling. With the exception of baseball, team sports were beyond the experience of girls and women until 1892, when Smith College began with basketball for women. Also the closing years of the century brought track and field sports to school girls, no doubt with an assist by the revival of the Olympics. The periodical *Mind and Body* in its November, 1895, issue reported at Vassar the first women's field day held in any college in the United States, roundly condemning the innovation as a sport for girls and women. Also at this time, gymnastics demonstrations and gymnastic-drill contests became popular, especially with college women.

For the out-of-school woman, there had long existed walking, riding, and tennis clubs and since the early 1890's bicycle clubs, but it was basketball that opened the door of team competition to women out of school. In many cities, and also in small towns, young married women and young business women organized basketball clubs, some playing in armories and some in the few YWCA gyms available by then.

Intercollegiate Competition for Women. Soon after the game of basketball was created, several women's colleges in the East that were near each other began playing the game in interschool contests, but Miss Berenson, the originator of the women's game, held out against such contests. Quoting from her biography:

> Soon there came challenges . . . from all over the East and West, and at this point Miss Berenson again proved herself a leader. With a long look ahead she foresaw that intercollegiate athletics might well become a menace to real physical education for women, she answered each letter politely, but firmly explained her reason for refusing all offers. By this stand, steadfastly adhered to, she dissipated the fear which had been at the bottom of much faculty hostility to her department.

By 1896 intercollegiate sports for women had reached the West Coast, where the University of California (Berkeley) and Stanford University were playing intercollegiate basketball. As to the situation in the Middle West, but little is known, which probably means that but little intercollegiate playing was going on before the turn of the century. Since there were but few colleges in the farther reaches of the country that supported departments of physical education before the close of the nineteenth century, it is quite probable that there is but little along this line for research workers to discover. Of the little known as of now of Middle West contests, the earliest record is of a match game played at the University of Nebraska between the University girl's basketball team and a town team from Council Bluffs, Iowa, played March 4, 1898. Out of deference to the visiting team, the first half of the game was played by Naismith's official rules; and out of deference to the host team, the second half was played by the Berenson rules for women. (An interesting side line of this first game is that the Honorable William Jennings Bryan, recently defeated for the presidency of the United States, and his wife were among the interested spectators at this game, which claimed the attention of the town's socially elite.)

There are records that the girls at Northwestern University were playing basketball in the late 1890's against Armour Institute and several nearby suburban high schools. The girls at the University of Missouri may possibly have been playing intercollegiate basketball before the close of the century, but the available records are not clear.

Interscholastic Competition for Girls. Since team sports were so new for girls and women, competition between teams was chaotic at first; college teams, high school teams, and out-of-school women's teams all played against each other indiscriminately, perhaps not so much because of a failure to understand the need for discrimination as from inability to find teams of one's own age group to challenge. If one community had a college girls' team, another had only a high school team, and yet another only a business woman's team. Except in the colleges, practically all teams were coached by men, showing the great lack of women physical education teachers of this era.

Judging fom the numerous photographs of high school girls' teams displayed in the first printed basketball guide of 1901, depicting teams from Alaska and California to the East Coast, there was wide-spread competition going on in this sport, involving, however, but a few of the sum total of girls in high schools of those years. Girls in team sports was as yet too recent an idea for it to have affected any but the most enthusiastic sports women.

19

Organized Physical Education in the Latter Nineteenth Century (1865–1900)

The United States was fast becoming the "melting pot" of the nations. It was producing a new person—the American—a blending of peoples of all nations. By 1870 the population of the United States was 38 million; by 1880, 50 million; and by 1900, 76 million. From the end of the Civil War until the close of the nineteenth century over 13 million immigrants were admitted into the country. However, by 1885 only 20 per cent of the population was foreign born. By 1880, the rural population was 71 per cent of the entire population, but, by 1890, it had dropped to 64 per cent. Nationalism had become the great emotion of the world, and the United States, because of her particularly strong belief in the equality of men and in the dignity of the individual, came to feel that to be worthy of the new nationalism all children must receive an education.

EDUCATION IN GENERAL

Whereas in 1850 there had been but eleven public schools—an American innovation—in all of the United States by the close of the Civil War most states had established public schools, and an estimated 50 per cent of the children of the nation were attending them. But the aftermath of the Civil War was as bad, if not worse, than the war itself. Particularly were conditions deplorable in the conquered South. Public schools and colleges in both the North and South were impoverished. Almost all educational work had to start anew. Libraries wherever they existed tried valiantly to fill the educational gap until schools could be re-established and teachers found to man them.

Now came a period of great educational awakening in the United States. Schools were being established rapidly in all parts of the country. The Civil War brought to the people a realization of the need to wipe out illiteracy and to give an ever-widening segment of the population an education—girls as well as boys. In fact compulsory education was born as an expression of the firm belief that every child has a right to an education.

Coeducation, too, was spreading. By 1900, 98 per cent of all public schools and 56.7 per cent of all private schools in the United States were coeducational. But a great handicap to these movements was the lack of teachers and the inadequacy of those who were teaching. Most of the teachers had no more than a high school education if, indeed, even that.

Also, by the close of the century practically all the forty-five states then in the union had established higher schools of some form—university, normal school, or agricultural college; church-dominated colleges had opened in practically all states, and eleven of today's leading women's colleges were established between 1865 and 1891.

Enrollments in the leading colleges were increasing rapidly. In the early 1800's Harvard boasted of an enrollment of 1810, and Yale had 1,180, and the University of Pennsylvania, 1,172. The University of Michigan was the first college "out West" to achieve an enrollment above 1,000, but this was not until after the Civil War. In the mid-1880's its enrollment soared to an unbelievable 1,850. But despite of the growth of the colleges, educational standards were pitifully low. The writing ability of the great majority of students in medical schools (in which they could enroll without even a high school diploma) was so poor that examinations were usually oral until President Charles Eliot (1834–1926) of Harvard in 1870, to force improvement in standards, requested his Medical School faculty to require written examinations. In many liberal arts colleges, no courses were offered in economics, history, modern languages, political science, psychology, or sociology until the close of the nineteenth century when President Eliot took the lead in getting them added to the college curriculum.

Winds of change were blowing in the field of educational philosophy. With general acceptance of the belief that every child had a right to an education, and with so many taking advantage of the opportunity, it soon became apparent to leaders of educational thought that although all children should receive an education not all require the same kind of education. Heretofore education had been, for the most part, the privilege of the advantaged few, with education for boys geared to a future in some profession, and education for girls aimed at the few seeking an education to enable them to grace a husband's home. All classes of children were now attending school, with a greatly broadened basis for future plans.

At the same time, the first settlement houses in America were established (the first in 1886 on the Lower East Side of New York City, followed shortly by Hull House in Chicago), and there soon arose a group of social workers who were influential in bringing about many innovations in the schools, such as the first school physician (1897 in New York City), school lunches, school libraries, kindergartens, and evening classes. Also, the first college department of sociology in the United States was established in 1892 in the newly created University of Chicago. Two years later John Dewey (1859–1952), a young philosophy professor, joined the University of Chicago faculty and at once became interested in the possibilities of bringing about social reforms and social progress through education. Presenting his new educational creed in *The School Journal* (LIV, 1897, pp. 77–80), it received quick acclaim and was widely circulated.

Also at this same time G. Stanley Hall (1846–1924), under whom Dewey had studied at Johns Hopkins University (where Hall had become deeply interested in problems of child development, a field as of then not yet explored), had assumed the presidency of the newly established Clark University in 1889 and there continued his interest in child development. Shortly he gave the world his famous four-volume study, *Adolescence*.

In the 1890's business and labor were both demanding that the schools give apprentice training; social workers were insisting that hygiene, domestic science, and manual arts be offered in the schools; agricultural groups were asking that courses in farming be offered; and a body of physical educators had arisen to demand that physical exercise programs be established as a part of the regular school curriculum, not only to substitute for the out-of-school lack of exercise, because of dwindling home chores of the new era, but also to meet the now recognized social needs of the child.

All of these things were to markedly influence physical education, as well as all other parts of education, in the years just ahead.

EVENTS AFFECTING PHYSICAL EDUCATION

Military Drill in the Schools

In 1862 Congress passed the Morrill Act creating the land-grant colleges of which the Universities of Cornell, Purdue, and Illinois were the earliest. In order to secure the land as an endowment the schools had to agree to teach military tactics as a part of the regular course and to require it of all male students. Following this lead scores of other colleges and universities adopted military training, too, using it as a substitute for, rather than a supplement to, physical education. Moreover, during the Civil War the military leaders of the Union took note of the excellent training and discipline of the Southern troops and ascribed it to the numerous military academies of the South. This resulted in an irresistible movement to introduce military training in the schools of the North, as soon as the war was at an end. Also, reports of the poor physical condition of over a million men recruits from sixteen to forty-five years of age who were examined during the Civil War resulted in a renewed drive for military training in the schools sparked by leading military men and statesmen—a combination of influences that gave physical education a setback still felt in some schools at mid-twentieth century.

State Legislation

In 1866 California passed the first state physical education law. It required that physical exercise be given to pupils "as may be conducive to health and vigor of body as well as mind." From then on things rested until the State Teachers Associations, the American Association for the Advancement of Physical Education (see p. 230), the Women's Christian Temperance Union, and the turnvereins of Ohio and Pennsylvania threw their organizations back of efforts in several states to procure such laws. Ohio's efforts were the first to meet with success in this renewed effort. Its law was passed in 1892, and North Dakota followed in 1899. In 1897 Wisconsin passed a permissive law.

The Birth of the Progressive Education Movement

When Francis Parker (1837–1902) became Superintendent of Schools of Quincy, Massachusetts, in 1875 and found the children trained by rote unable to apply their knowledge to anything beyond their textbooks, he began questioning the conventional curriculum and methods of teaching. He put aside the old textbooks and devised a schooling for the children based on observation of life about them, reading of current materials, nature study at first hand, and experiences in doing original writings. With a basis of learning established, he then brought back the use of the textbooks. He developed his theories still further as Supervisor of the Boston Schools and still later as principal of Cook County Normal School in Chicago. Before the 1890's his ideas were not widely recognized, but once they were made known through articles in magazines and newspapers, a growing number of educators, unhappy with the old formalism, seized upon his theories, and politicians and reformers, as well as parents and teachers, began pushing for reforms in education. Thus as Cremin points out (see references), began the Progressive Education Movement. Later John Dewey, who was so markedly to affect physical education as well as all other parts of education, was to acclaim Parker as "the Father of Progressive Education."

STATUS OF PHYSICAL EDUCATION

Physical education, as well as education in general, was neglected during the Civil War, and the advocates of physical education had to wage battle anew on every front. It was an uphill battle against the military leaders who were working to introduce military training into the schools. In the 1870's the argument of the day among educators was that of military drill versus gymnastics. Dr. Dudley A. Sargent, then head of physical education at Yale University, led the battle for gymnastics against the principals of the Boston schools, who held out for military drill. When Bowdoin College gave its students the privilege of voting between gymnastics and military drill for a requirement they stood almost unanimously for gymnastics. (See p. 237 for a similar situation at Yale.)

The calisthenics of Catharine Beecher and Dio Lewis, popular just before the war, soon began to lose their hold, but not without a last effort of Miss Beecher, who now was promoting exercises for boys as well as for girls. In an address on *Female Suffrage* given in 1870 in the Music Hall of Boston, Miss Beecher made a public appeal for trained teachers of physical education for girls in which she said:

> The department of the physical training of all the institutions should be committed to a woman of good practical common sense, of refined culture and manners and one expressly educated for this department. By the aid of both parents and teachers, she would study the constitution and habits of every pupil, and administer a method of training to develop healthfully every organ and function, and to remedy every defect in habits, person, voice, movements, and manners.

The German system of gymnastics was still receiving increased attention in many parts of the country, and by the close of the century the Delsarte and Swedish systems had put in their appearance. Throughout the nineteenth century sports and athletics still had no place in the official school or college programs. They were recognized only as the students' own after-school projects.

The 1880's and 1890's brought a period of great expansion for physical education not only in the schools but also in nonschool organizations. Many gymnasiums were built, and the schools began to demand teachers who were professionally trained. However, full-time positions were scarce, and most teachers took on two or more positions in schools, athletic clubs, or YMCA's, or coupled teaching with some other work in order to make a living. Many who had a medical degree practiced medicine on the side or, as some of the leaders did, established private schools which they maintained along with their other positions.

Although the formal physical education programs borrowed from the Europeans played a major role in schools during the second half of the nineteenth century, a new attitude toward physical education began to gain momentum. The desires of people for recreation, the popularity of organized field sports, college athletics, and a changing educational philosophy gave concern to the staunch proponents of the traditional formal program. The 1880's were years of struggles between scientific training and classical culture. It was a period of growth and expansion following the slump after the Civil War. Physical Education rode in on this wave and got a good start at that time.

The office of the U.S. Commissioner of Education reported in 1891 on the status of physical training in the schools of 272 leading cities of the United States. The figures showed that 83 cities had a special director of physical education for the entire school system, 81 others required the schoolroom teacher to teach exercises, and 108 permitted teachers to offer exercises if they so wished: 10 per cent of the schools had established exercise programs before 1887, and of those offering physical education, 41 per cent used the German system of gymnastics; 29 per cent the Swedish system; 12 per cent the Delsarte system; and 18 per cent a combination of these. At this time there were reported to be 31 gymnasiums in the schools of eleven cities of the 272 investigated.

Terminology

The term *physical culture,* used widely from the 1860's on, continued in use in some quarters as late as the 1910's with its use at its height in 1895. The use of the term does not seem strange when it is realized that interest in the classics predominated in higher education in the nineteenth century, and the word *culture* was used generally by the classicists. When the University of Chicago was founded in 1892, it named its physical education department the Department of Physical Culture and Athletics. In 1895 the University of California called its arts and science college the College of General Culture. Many colleges offered courses entitled, Religious Culture and Social Culture. Also, physical education came to many schools in those early days through the elocution departments, which called their course, Voice Culture; so it was natural for them to call the physical activity courses, Physical Culture.

The word *training* crept in when military departments were assigned the responsibility of the physical activity courses, and it was natural to make the two terms *military training* and *physical training* conform. When the social and psychological objectives came into the picture, also when the Ph.D. degree began to replace the M.D. degree in a large way among the leaders of the profession, the word *education* naturally came to the front, and the term *physical education* came into its own. It must not be forgotten that when Hitchcock in 1861 set up at Amherst College the first department in any school in the United States it was officially designated as the Department of Physical Education and that many of the physical education leaders used this term in the 1890's. By the 1920's *physical education* had become the universally accepted term.

Elementary and Secondary School Programs

Gradually a physical education program was being accepted as a "must" and introduced into the large city schools. In 1867 the Board of Controllers of Philadelphia made provision in the budget for two or three well-trained physical-exercise teachers with the class work to begin in all primary and grammar grades the following year. The teachers were required "to devote in each school room ten minutes during the course of each school session to such physical exercises as the size of the room and other circumstances might permit." Two years later they established a department of physical education with its own special teachers in a girls' high school—the first department of physical education for girls in a public school in America.

At the same time the female seminaries, all of which were of secondary school level except Elmira, were adding physical education in some form to the curriculum, and Miss Beecher renewed her campaign in behalf of physical education in these schools. Whereas in the era preceding the Civil War the emphasis of the school physical activity program for girls was on the cure of physical defects which were supposed to be brought on by too much study, in this era it became apparent that girls could stand the stress of attending school and needed, in physical education, not so much cure as prevention of ills.

The great amount of physical activity which children undertook on their own during recess periods was, except in schools with unusual teachers who assumed responsibility "beyond the call of duty," completely unsupervised. The recess periods were great fun with much physical activity wherever a few natural born leaders and a lot of lively children got together. But the timid and less venturesome were neglected, and the sort of citizenship training that came out of this play was dependent solely upon the naturally good leaders or the "bullies," as chance dictated, who would "rule the roost."

As to physical education, schools soon divided into two camps—those using the German system of gymnastics and those using the Swedish system. A few schools departed from the pattern, but the great majority adopted one of these two systems. The development from the 1870's on is discussed under these two headings.

Adoption of the German System. The following cities established physical education in their schools using the German system: Cincinnati, 1855; Cleveland, 1870; Milwaukee, 1876; Omaha, Kansas City, and La Crosse, 1885; Chicago, 1886; Davenport, 1887; St. Louis, 1888; Los Angeles, Oakland, Moline, Detroit, and Erie, 1890; Indianapolis, San Francisco, Spokane, and Dayton, 1892; and St. Paul, 1894. They procured their teachers from the Normal College of the American Gymnastic Union (NCAGU), which was the revived school started by the turners in Rochester, N. Y., just preceding the Civil War.

The story of the founding of the department in the Kansas City schools depicts the part played by the turners in the establishment of the system in the schools of America. Carl Betz (1854–98), a graduate of the four-month training course of the NCAGU, then located in Milwaukee, was appointed instructor in the Socialer Turnverein in Kansas City, Missouri, in 1885. That same year he accepted an invitation to demonstrate with a class of girls in wand and club drills before the teachers' institute. His work was well received, and all agreed that something of that kind should be a part of the schoolwork. Betz offered to direct the exercises for a few months without pay in order to demonstrate their practicability. The school board accepted his offer, and before the end of the year (1885) he was employed as director of physical education of all the schools of Kansas City, which position he held until his death in 1898.

Adoption of the Swedish System. Dr. Hartwig Nissen (1856–1924) introduced the Swedish system of gymnastics to America when he came to Washington in 1883 as Vice-Consul for Norway and Sweden. Immediately upon his arrival in Washington he began to acquaint the physicians with the value of medical gymnastics and massage and opened the famous Swedish Health Institute. Among his "patients" were prominent men such as Benjamin Harrison and Ulysses S. Grant. Next he introduced Swedish gymnastics into the Franklin School and, in 1887, among students at Johns Hopkins University. When Baron Nils Posse (1862–95), the son of a prominent family of the Swedish nobility and a graduate of the Royal Central Institute of Gymnastics of Stockholm, arrived in America from Sweden in 1885 he first visited Nissen and then went to Boston in the hopes of establishing himself there in the practice of medical gymnastics.

Mrs. Mary Hemenway (1820–94), the widow of Boston's prosperous shipping merchant, was deeply interested in the advancement of education. Her son had given the magnificent Hemenway gymnasium to Harvard in 1879, and she was prepared to give financial aid to projects in behalf of the public schools. Seeing in Swedish gymnastics possibilities for bettering the health of school children, she offered to finance the teacher training of over a hundred teachers per year provided the school board would give Swedish gymnastics a place in the school program for all pupils on an experimental basis. They consented to the project, and Mrs. Hemenway provided the services of Posse to train the teachers. By 1890 over four hundred teachers were prepared to give instruction in the Swedish system. The superintendent thereupon ordered "that the Ling or Swedish system of educational gymnastics be introduced into all the public schools of this city." Dr. Edward M. Hartwell, formerly of Johns Hopkins University, was elected to the position of Director of Physical Training and began his duties in 1891. This was the first time the title of Director was granted by a public school system for the head of physical education. Shortly Nissen was persuaded to come to Boston as Hartwell's assistant.

Following Boston's lead, many schools and colleges now adopted the Swedish system for their physical education programs. This was made possible by the Boston Normal School of Gymnastics, which was established to prepare teachers to offer this system of gymnastics to the schools and colleges of America. Thus Swedish gymnastics gained a firm hold in the schools, particularly in the New England area and in the women's departments of colleges, as the graduates of this school took positions all over the country. Within a year of its introduction in the Boston public schools alone, over 60,000 children were taking Swedish gymnastics. Until the War of 1914–1917, this system of gymnastics enjoyed great popularity in the non-German population areas of the country.

Adoption of Other Systems. In spite of the flurry of excitement over the relative merits of German and Swedish gymnastics, some schools installed physical education programs built around exercises devised by their own teachers or composed of their own revamping of the calisthenics of Catharine Beecher and Dio Lewis of an earlier day, perhaps even using the Delsarte exercises (see p. 182) which had become popular in the 1890's. And still other schools, particularly those in small towns, occasionally had teachers who had heard of exercise programs in the city schools and, wanting to give their pupils something but knowing nothing of any of these systems, contrived some drills that produced activity if not founded on anything of a scientific nature.

One "independent" of the period was Brooklyn, which set up its own school program in 1895 with Jessie H. Bancroft (see p. 329) responsible for organizing the work, which was carried on at first in a church. Miss

Bancroft had received some training both at Sargent's private school and at his Harvard Summer School of Physical Education, but she was in large measure self-taught. She devised her own set of exercises and built up a program for all the schools of Brooklyn. Shortly she was given the official title of Director of Physical Education of Public Schools—the first woman in the United States to hold such a title.

Facilities, Requirements, and Staffs. Schools were slow in supplying gymnasiums. For example, by the end of the century there was in Chicago but one elementary school that had a gymnasium, although 205 principals were requesting them. However, seven of the fifteen high schools had gymnasiums; and the others used hallways for classes with wands, dumbbells, and Indian clubs in racks on the walls. This was, no doubt, typical of the situation throughout the country.

By the end of the century many schools were requiring at least five minutes of exercise of each pupil daily or twenty minutes, two or three times a week, or a half-hour, two times a week. The most averaged fifty minutes per week. This was, indeed, quite the accepted requirement in those schools that had a program at all.

In Chicago, typical of conditions in large cities, there was as late as the 1890's only one special physical education teacher assigned to an elementary school, but there were seven other specialized teachers to supervise the physical education work given by the regular classroom teacher in the other elementary schools. These handled 30,000 pupils in thirty-four schools. Each school was visited three or four times a year by a supervisor, and those schools where the hallways were outfitted with the exercise equipment were visited as often as every four or six weeks. In the seven high schools with gymnasiums each had a special teacher of "physical culture."

Physical Education for College Men

With the close of the Civil War, physical education began to develop in earnest in many colleges. Dr. Hitchcock, at Amherst College, was setting the example for all other schools. By now the students there were having intramural athletics, but according to Hartwell, Hitchcock was firm in his denunciation of "hot and violent contests with professional gamesters," and he gave but lukewarm acquiescence to games with other colleges. Early in his work there he had instituted corrective work for those needing it.

In 1869 George Goldie, then a professional gymnast in New York City and before that a well-known athlete in Montreal, Canada, was appointed Director of the new $10,000 gymnasium at Princeton University. (He had learned gymnastics and circus stunts at a private gymnasium in New

York City which was the rendezvous of professional gymnasts.) He built his program around both gymnastics and sports. According to the *Princeton Alumni Weekly* his gym teams "could perform acrobatic stunts . . . which might have aroused the envy of P. T. Barnum." In 1873 he inaugurated the first college track meet, which was immediately named the Caledonia Games in honor of Goldie, the Scotsman, who held the Caledonian championship for all-around athletes. Also in that same year, he organized the first college amateur athletic association.

In the early 1870's, Dudley A. Sargent established a physical education program at Bowdoin College as he, himself, pursued work for the bachelor's degree. He gave all the boys free exercises varying the program the Freshman year with dumbbells, the Sophomore year with Indian clubs, the Junior year with chest weights, and the Senior year with wands and pulley weights—training in all of which he had "picked up on his own." All gymnasium classes were dismissed in the spring for military drill so Sargent went to Yale University each spring from 1872 on, and established a program for that college while he pursued his medical studies. In 1875 the Yale authorities gave the students their choice for requirement between Greek and gymnastics, and all but two selected the latter. William Howard Taft, then a student at Yale, destined later to become President of the United States, was one who elected gymnastics, and he became one of the class leaders.

Program At Harvard University. The Hemenway Gymnasium, costing $110,000, was ready for occupancy in 1879 replacing the old gymnasium of 1859. At that time Sargent was appointed to take charge of the physical education work with the title of Assistant Professor of Physical Training and Director of the Hemenway Gymnasium. He relates in his *Autobiography* that many faculty members considered the new gymnasium as a vast waste of money and resented having a college graduate placed in charge of physical education—work which they considered unworthy of a college-trained man. Sargent was charged with the task of equipping the new building, determining the policy of the department, and arranging the work. Believing that the difference in the physical make-up and physical needs of the students was too great to allow uniformity of exercise he began building a program around the individual needs of the students. He took bodily measurements of all students and also gave them strength tests which he devised. Then he prescribed exercises for each, using the many different pieces of apparatus which he invented to meet specific physical developmental needs. For many years he worked on his mechanical contrivances which came to be called "Sargent machines." They included foot, ankle, wrist, leg, and back machines, rowing and lifting machines, chest expanders, chest weights, quarter circles, and short and long inclined planes. He also used some German and some Swedish apparatus, and, at the same time, he developed a more detailed system of measurements than was being used at Amherst College. His studies along that line added greatly to anthropometric knowledge.

Dr. Sargent used photography as early as 1889 in his work, taking photographs of each student in three positions (front, back, and side) upon entrance and repeating after a period of training. This is the earliest record of the use of such a device in physical education work, almost a half century ahead of the times.

Program in Other Colleges. It was many years before other schools caught up with Hitchcock at Amherst and Sargent at Harvard. However, in 1876 Princeton organized the first college athletic association and the University of Chicago in 1893 became the first to set up a faculty committee to administer intercollegiate sports. Of the private coeducational colleges, Oberlin was the first to establish a department of physical education (1885). The University of Chicago opened in October of 1892, and its Department of Physical Culture was one of the many departments established from its very first days. Amos Alonzo Stagg was the first head of the three-fold department, which encompassed physical education for men, physical education for women, and athletics, possibly the first such tie-up in the American college world. When Clark W. Hetherington (see p. 327) established the department at the University of Missouri in 1900, he also was head over all three divisions of work, the first for a state university. Of the state universities the University of Wisconsin offered the first classes in physical education (1870), although this date does not mark the establishment of a department. For some years before an actual department of physical education with its own staff materialized, in practically all schools, physical activity classes of a sort were offered either by the students themselves or by some teacher in an academic department. The following list shows dates for the actual establishment of departments for men in state universities:

1888—California	1893—Utah	1896—Minnesota
1890—Wisconsin	1893—Illinois	1897—Ohio State
1890—Texas	1894—Kansas	1899—Iowa
1891—Indiana	1894—Washington	1900—Missouri
1891—Nebraska	1894—Michigan	

(Such dates as the ones given above are difficult to determine with any assurance of accuracy, since many school records do not differentiate men's and women's departments. In most universities, however, departments for men were established ahead of those for women, so that when two conflicting dates are offered, the earlier one probably represents the men's department and the later, the women's.)

Facilities. Many gymnasiums were erected after the Civil War, starting with the Dartmouth building of 1867 which cost $24,000. Following that Princeton replaced its earlier red shack with a $38,000 "gym," the finest of its day. Bowdoin's gymnasium had no heat, and the men dressed for class even in zero weather, changing to cotton shirts and tights and cloth slippers. Jersies and woolen sweaters were as yet unknown.

Gymnasiums were built in the Middle West in the 1870's at Washington University (St. Louis) at a cost of $7,000, at Beloit College (Wisconsin) at a cost of $5,000, and at the University of Wisconsin at a cost of $4,000, this last marking the first gymnasium building in a state university. The Yale gymnasium of 1875 had eight long bathtubs lined with zinc, which the students used only on payment of a special fee. Then 1879 brought the wonder gymnasium of the age—Harvard's $110,000 Hemenway gymnasium—followed shortly by the University of California's modest $12,000 Harmon Gymnasium and Vanderbilt's $22,000 building. During the Sixties and Seventies many colleges that could not afford gymnasiums fitted up vacant rooms as drill halls.

Fig. 9. Harvard University: Hemenway Gymnasium (1885) (Leonard and Affleck, *A Guide to the History of Physical Education,* Courtesy of Lea & Febiger).

The 1880's and 1890's brought many more college gymnasiums, most donated by wealthy alumni and ranging in cost from $10,000 to $40,000. The usual plan consisted of one large exercise floor, an examining room, a running track that could be used also as a visitor's or spectator's gallery, bath, dressing and locker rooms, and offices. A few of these later gymnasiums included a bowling alley and a small room for fencing or sparring. An indoor swimming pool was still a rarity. When the University of Chicago opened in October of 1892 and the gymnasium was completed in November, the students, under the supervision of Stagg, built the fence around the athletic field with lumber contributed by local merchants. The first football game was played on Thanksgiving Day of 1893. There were as yet no seats on the athletic field, and the students set up wooden horses with planks borrowed from buildings under construction.

When Columbia University opened its new gymnasium in 1898 it was hailed as the largest in any educational institution in the world. The main floor was 170′ × 130′ and the swimming pool 100′ long.

Staffs. Yale University listed in the catalog an instructor in physical training for the school year 1860–61 and again for 1867 through 1872. In 1867 Harvard University acquired its first teacher of gymnastics, a pro-boxing teacher. Although listed as "Instructor and Curator of Gymnasium," his name was not included in the list of regular faculty members. Amherst College gave Hitchcock the faculty status of Professor from the date of his first appointment. Later Harvard University conferred upon Sargent the rank of Assistant Professor. When Stagg went to the University of Chicago in 1892, he was given the rank of Professor and Director. The woman under him, Alice B. Foster, who was head of women's work and held the M.D. degree, was given only the rank of tutor. But in most colleges the earliest appointees to be placed in charge of the gymnasium were ex-prize fighters, weight-lifters, and janitors. In those days there were no schools in the United States preparing teachers of physical education.

Gradually men with some semblance of training in physical education became available and, taking on two or more part-time positions, managed to find full-time employment. By the close of the century, a fairly good supply of professionally trained teachers was available for the positions that did exist. The YMCA Training School furnished most of the teachers for YMCA's and the leading colleges and universities.

Salaries. Hitchcock started full-time work at Amherst in 1861 at $1,000 per year, and was raised to $1200 his second year. Sargent, at part-time employment, was paid $5 per week when he first went to Bowdoin College in 1869. Two years later the salary was raised to $500 per year. In 1872 he was paid $50 a week at Yale University on special assignment. In 1875 he asked Bowdoin for $1200 per year from which he would pay the janitor and his assistants, purchase the apparatus needed, and pay all other expenses except heat, light, and building repairs. The college refused this salary request, and he resigned. By the end of the century, Hetherington received a salary of $1800 at the University of Missouri for his full-time employment as head of athletics and physical education for both men and women.

Physical Education for College Women

As a rule physical education fared better in this era in the women's colleges than in coeducational schools. The establishment of several of today's leading women's colleges meant much to the advancement of physical education; Smith was established in 1875; Wellesley, 1876; Bryn Mawr, 1880; Randolph-Macon, 1891; the Woman's College of the University of North Carolina, 1892; Radcliffe, 1894; and Barnard, 1899. All took an important place in the promotion of physical education. From their very founding the women's colleges offered physical activity classes to their students while in most coeducational schools such classes came most belatedly long after the establishment of the schools.

First Departments of Physical Education. Vassar was the first college in the United States to offer physical activity classwork for women as a part of the school program. This was in 1868. Mt. Holyoke and Rockford Colleges had been offering work since 1837 and 1849 respectively, but neither achieved collegiate rating before the 1880's. Wellesley established its department in 1881. Oberlin College was the first coeducational college to organize a department of physical education for women (1885). According to Elliott (see References), a few state universities recognized departments for women before those for men: Indiana, Kansas, Utah, Michigan, Ohio State, and Texas. In three state universities it was the Military Department that brought about the establishment of a department for women: California (Berkeley), Nebraska, and Wyoming. State University departments for women were founded as follows:

1889–California (Berkeley)	1894–Illinois	1896–Iowa
1890–Indiana	1894–Michigan	1896–Minnesota
1890–Washington State	1894–Nebraska	1897–Ohio State
1893–Kansas	1894–Oregon	1899–Wisconsin
1894–Utah	1894–Washington	1900–Missouri

Program. The core of the college program for women was calisthenics or gymnastics with some sports hanging on as fringe activities without official college sanction. Mt. Holyoke College added to its requirement in calisthenics a daily walk of one mile in good weather and a three-quarter-hour walk in bad weather. The Dio Lewis system of gymnastics was the favored form for college women in the 1860's; in the early 1880's most women's colleges changed to the Sargent system; in 1888 Goucher College took up the Swedish system, and all the other women's colleges except Vassar swung over to this system, also; in 1890 Elmira and Rockford Colleges adopted the Delsarte system; but not one of the women's colleges accepted the German system.

However, as with men students, women organized sports activities for themselves, some times with faculty help but most frequently without. As early as the 1870's there were rowing, tennis, croquet, bicycling, and baseball clubs in action. In the 1890's golf and basketball were added to the list of activities.

The programs for women in coeducational colleges followed somewhat the pattern set by the women's colleges but the men's programs and men teachers on the same campus introduced forms of activities and a type of emphasis on methods and philosophy that differed somewhat from that originating in the women's colleges. The story of the beginnings of a department of physical education for women in a coeducational school during this era will illustrate the point. In the late 1880's, at the University of Nebraska, a group of women students urged the Military Department to give them military drill, and this it consented to do provided the girls would be content to drill indoors. In 1891, Wilbur P. Bowen (1864–1928), a mathematics teacher at Michigan State Normal School, was brought to the University to set up the Department of Physical Education for Men. The women pleaded so persistently for classwork, too, that Bowen and the new Commandant of the ROTC—Lt. John J. Pershing (1860–1948) recently graduated from West Point, who had, also, come to the university faculty in the fall of 1891—decided to do something about it. Pershing offered to teach the girls fencing and marching and Bowen to teach them dumbbell exercises and Indian-club swinging.

At the insistence of Pershing, who felt strongly that "ladies" should not be doing military drill at all and that in their physical activities they should be taught by a woman rather than a man, the Chancellor finally capitulated and the next school year (1892–93) he employed a local woman, Anne Barr, who had learned some Indian-club swinging at the local YMCA, to take over classwork for the women students on an hour-pay basis. Becoming interested in her teaching, Miss Barr went to the Chautauqua School of Physical Education the following summer and there began actual professional training (which she pursued of summers) for the position which she held for several years—first as class leader and by 1895 as Directress of the Women's Gymnasium and later as Director of Physical Education for Women. Soon physical education became a requirement of all young women for the first two years with four hours a week of activity and one of hygiene. Thus did women's physical education work get started in one state university. The story is, no doubt, typical of those of many other colleges.

Facilities. In the women's colleges, physical education classwork got under way in this period by using the out of doors, corridors, assembly halls, and store rooms. One school used a privately owned gymnasium in the local community—Radcliffe at Sargent's gymnasium. Vassar was the only college that started its physical education work with a special building constructed for the work. In 1860 it built a "Hall for Calisthenics" with footprints painted on the floor to indicate where students should stand during their exercise periods. Mt. Holyoke had a gymnasium by 1865 that cost $1900; Smith College, by 1875; Bryn Mawr, by 1885; Goucher, by 1888; and Mills College and the University of California, by the end of the century.

The coeducational colleges lagged far behind the women's colleges in procuring facilities for women students. As a rule the women were permitted to use the men's facilities on occasion, and in many schools some large room in the women's dormitory was set aside for a women's gymnasium.

Goucher College constructed the first swimming pool for women in 1888, although it did not list swimming as an activity for students until 1904; Vassar built the second pool in 1889; Smith installed a "swimming bath" in 1892 which could be used by two to five students at a time and was used for over thirty years; Bryn Mawr built its pool in 1894, and by the end of the century Radcliffe College had built one. There were no pools for women or men in any coeducational college or coeducational university of this era.

Costumes. In the 1860's the girls at Mt. Holyoke College wore for their exercise classes the Zouave trousers introduced into America by Dio Lewis for exercise periods. The Vassar girls wore a costume of gray flannel with the blouse high-necked and long-sleeved and the skirt ankle-length with bloomers underneath. Elmira College girls in 1872 wore a costume of black alpaca, lined throughout, with a "Garabaldi" waist and a skirt reaching to within ten inches of the floor with Turkish drawers underneath with elastic leg-binding and falling to the length of the skirt, with skirt and blouse trimmed in scarlet "Gilbert opera flannel."

By the 1880's shorter costumes appeared with a divided skirt; but when the bicycling craze of the 1890's brought out a new version of the costume introduced by Amelia Bloomer in the 1850's as a measure of dress reform for women, bloomers became the universally accepted costume for sports and physical education work for women.

These bloomers of a new era were made of woolen materials and were worn for all seasons of the year. They were very full, and although caught up at the knee by an elastic the folds of the material hung down to mid-calf. The blouse of the same material was long sleeved, high necked, and usually trimmed with a large sailor collar.

Staffs. Physical education in these early years was taught by teachers of other subjects who read a book or two on exercise and, from this, undertook to teach calisthenics or some dance-type activity called "fancy steps." As early as 1862 the Mt. Holyoke College catalog listed a teacher of calisthenics. The Smith College prospectus of 1874 announced that "regular gymnastic exercises in the gymnasium will be prescribed under the direction of an educated lady physician."

In the 1860's and 1870's women's departments were able to procure as part time teachers pupils of Dio Lewis who offered the first teacher-training in physical education to women in America. Wellesley College was the first to employ a full-time teacher of physical education for women, in 1881. Following its lead, other colleges began employing full-time teachers for this work: Vassar, 1883; Bryn Mawr and Oberlin, 1885; Smith, 1887; Goucher, 1888; and the University of Chicago, 1892. From then to the close of the century, many other colleges fell into line on this practice. After professional training schools for women opened in the 1880's, women teachers who were prepared for this special work became available, and schools were no longer dependent upon those who had just "picked up some superficial training on their own or had had some elocution courses that offered a smattering of training in exercises of sorts. Oberlin, the first coeducational college to appoint a woman to teach physical education, selected for the position in 1885, Delphine Hanna (see p. 329), a graduate of the Sargent School of Physical Education. Two years later she was given the title Director of Physical Education, and three years later she procured the M.D. degree. Following that, Goucher College appointed a physical education teacher from the Central Gymnastic Institute of Stockholm. Mt. Holyoke had two women teachers with the Ph.D. degree teaching gymnastics along with their special subjects, most obviously women not trained in this field. However, when these women teachers of academic subjects no longer taught gymnastics "on the side" and women trained in the field did come upon the scene, it was several decades before a Ph.D. degree again graced the women's physical education ranks. No woman physical education teacher in any women's college received recognition in academic rank of any sort in the nineteenth century. The coeducational colleges were more advanced in this respect.

Research

This period was one of great interest in anthropometric testing, which started in the United States with Hitchcock's work, at Amherst

College in 1861, based on his deep interest in ascertaining the physical-developmental needs of the students as individuals. From the very start, he used data from eight items in his research work: age, weight, height, chest girth, arm girth, forearm girth, lung capacity, and pull-up. For forty years he published, annually, anthropometric tables of Amherst men, which fill two large volumes of material. In 1873 Sargent, then a young medical student at Yale, started work on strength tests and later as a teacher at Harvard University carried it forward. From 1880 to 1886 he collected data on Harvard men, from which he devised his first anthropometric charts. Following this lead, charts were made by Jay W. Seaver (see p. 242) from the measurements of Yale men and YMCA men from 25 to 35 years of age, while research into the anthropometric measurements of women was carried on principally at Wellesley and Oberlin Colleges and the University of Nebraska. In the late 1890's the three women heads of physical education in these colleges made anthropometric charts from the measurements of 1,500 college women. Sargent's data through 1892 for both men and women college-age students was published in percentile tables, and from these, plastic figures were made and exhibited at the Chicago World's Fair in 1893, arousing much interest from the general public.

In 1890 the first athletic achievement test was born—the Pentathlon test of the Athletic League of the YMCA's of America devised by Dr. Luther H. Gulick. This is the earliest record of the use of elements of sports and games as test forms. It was the forerunner of many such tests which at the turn of the century, so markedly motivated the promotion of physical education in the schools. As developed further in the early 1900's by Gulick for the Public School Athletic League of New York City, these tests consisted of throwing for accuracy and speed, running for speed, and jumping for distance.

Teacher Training

This era marked the real beginnings of professional training in physical education in America. Immediately following the Civil War, there were but two schools in all the country that offered training in this field of work—the Normal School of the North American Gymnastic Union, then located in Chicago and turning out only men teachers, and the short-lived Dio Lewis School training women teachers. In 1878 a woman named Mary Allen opened a private woman's gymnasium in Boston, and in 1881 she offered teacher-training courses. By 1889 she had graduated seven "instructresses." From then on, she and her school are lost to the records.

In the 1880's other training schools were established. These offered a seven-month's course, which soon developed into ten months. By the

1890's all these schools offered at least two full school years of training. According to Hartwell's research, from the early 1860's to the close of the nineteenth century thirty-four normal schools of physical education were established. None, however, was of collegiate rank. (In the material that follows on teacher training work, the facts have been verified, where available, from the official records of the schools concerned.) The more notable of these schools were: 1861, the Dio Lewis Normal Institute of Physical Education in Boston which lasted but a few years; 1866, the Normal School of the American Gymnastic Union in New York City; 1881, the Sargent School of Physical Education in Cambridge; 1886, the Brooklyn Normal School of Physical Education; 1887, the Harvard Summer School of Physical Education, and the Physical Training Department of the School of Church Workers in Springfield (now Springfield College); 1888, the Chautauqua Summer School of Physical Education; 1889, the Boston Normal School of Gymnastics; 1890, the Posse School of Physical Education in Boston, and the Chicago YMCA Training School; and 1898, the New York Normal School of Physical Education, later called the Savage School.

Before teacher-training schools were established, the leading teachers of physical education were men and women trained in the field of medicine, mostly Harvard, Yale, and Johns Hopkins graduates. Before the twentieth century, the M.D. degree could be acquired without a bachelor's degree, since that degree stood only for education in the liberal arts. The medical schools gave their students the foundation courses in the biological sciences. Therefore, the curriculum of the early normal schools of physical education, manned by men and women trained in medicine, lacked the social sciences and emphasized biological sciences and medical gymnastics.

Normal School of the American Gymnastic Union. The Civil War disrupted the plans of the German turners to establish a teacher training school in Rochester, New York, in 1861. With the war at an end, the school was finally opened in New York City in 1866, open only to members of the turnverein. After three years there, it moved to Chicago with George Brosius (see p. 242), one of the foremost leaders of the turner movement, as superintendent of the school. Compelled to close because of the great fire in Chicago, the school moved again to New York City in 1872, and then in 1875 it moved to Milwaukee where it remained throughout the rest of the nineteenth century except for a two-year interval (1889–91) when it was located temporarily in Indianapolis.

During these years the course had been lengthened to require ten months of study, and it included the history and literature of physical education, anthropology, anatomy, physiology, hygiene, first aid, principles of education, the German and English language and literature, fencing, swimming, Jahn gymnastics, esthetic dancing, observation, and practice teaching. Graduates of this school taught in public schools throughout the country although most located in the Middle West. In 1878 the school graduated its first woman student, Miss Laura Gerlach, for whom there is a record that she was teaching in Milwaukee in 1883 at a salary of $450 per year.

Sargent School of Physical Education. Dr. Sargent, having become head of physical education at Harvard University, was so importuned by young women of the town of Cambridge and of Radcliffe College who desired some training in the art of teaching exercises, and by heads of schools who desired teachers trained to teach his type of exercises rather than the German system, that he took over an old carriage house, converted it into a gymnasium, and set up such a course in 1881. He offered the courses at first gratis with the stipulation that the students would actually go out to teach. At that time most people felt that if they knew a dumbbell drill, a few exercises with Indian clubs and a list of chest-weight exercises they were really professionally trained in physical education. By 1891 he had thirty pupils in his private school, and the course had developed into a thirty-two-week session for a $100.00 fee. Then he extended the course to a two-year course, the attendance doubled, and the school took on the title, Sargent Normal School for Physical Education.

Brooklyn Normal School of Gymnastics. The Brooklyn Normal School of Gymnastics was founded in 1886 by Dr. William G. Anderson (see p. 240), then Physical Director at Adelphi Academy in Brooklyn. When Anderson became Associate Director of the Yale University Gymnasium in 1892, the school was moved to New Haven and renamed the Anderson Normal School of Gymnastics. In 1896 Dr. E. Herman Arnold (1865–1929) became the director.

Harvard Summer School of Physical Education. While attending Chautauqua in 1879 (which had been established at Lake Chautauqua in New York in 1874 as a summer outing institution at which lectures were given for lay church workers), Sargent conceived the idea of offering summer courses in physical education to attract teachers during their long vacation periods. Four years later he offered the first such course in the United States in a five-week session at his then two-year old Normal School in Cambridge. This venture developed into the Harvard Summer School of Physical Education when Sargent obtained permission from Harvard University in 1887 to offer a six-weeks summer course in teacher training, open to women as well as men. In his *Auto-*

biography, he relates that, although Harvard was not too happy about opening classes to women and the granting of teacher's certificates, the authorities finally gave permission providing he would assume all financial responsibility for the project. So intense was the local feeling against Harvard's being a party to such a venture that Radcliffe College discouraged its students from attending the course and the *Boston Medical and Surgeon's Journal* opposed it and denounced Harvard for allowing such a course. In spite of the initial storm of criticism the summer school prospered and carried on for thirty-one years under Sargent's expert direction. The very first session was so successful financially, because of the unexpectedly large enrollment of fifty pupils, that he cleared $1,500, and beginning with the second session, Harvard officials took it over, relieved Sargent of the burden of collecting the fees and paying the bills, and named him Director of the Summer School of Physical Education, with salary.

Among the pupils attending the first session were Delphine Hanna of Oberlin, Helen Putnam of Vassar, Caroline Ladd of Bryn Mawr, Anna Bridgeman of Rockford, and Booker T. Washington of Tuskegee Institute.

YMCA International Training School. The YMCA International Training School in Springfield, Massachusetts (called the School for Christian Workers until 1890) was founded in 1887, establishing from its beginnings a two-year course in professional training in physical education, with Dr. Luther Gulick as its director. He immediately inaugurated a summer course as a refresher for teachers already in the field. In 1891 he set up a graduate course in physical education, the first in America, but it was short-lived. From 1891 to 1895 he also conducted a correspondence School in Physical Education, another first. In 1888, Robert J. Roberts (see p. 242), who had just completed twelve years of highly successful work as the director of the gymnasium of the Boston YMCA, joined the teaching staff. In 1895 Dr. James Huff McCurdy (see p. 329), Director of Physical Education, New York City YMCA, succeeded Gulick in the directorship of the physical training department and extended the course to three years.

In 1886 the YMCA opened the Western YMCA Secretarial Institute in Chicago and four years later added a summer course for the training of teachers of physical education under the auspices of the Springfield School—the first summer courses in this field offered west of New York State. Also in 1890 the Institute was incorporated as the YMCA Training School of Chicago, offering a two-year course. At the same time the YMCA established another training school in Nashville, Tennessee, offering training in physical education.

Chautauqua Summer School of Physical Education. The Chautauqua Summer School of Physical Education, 1888, was the second school to be founded by Anderson. In the 1890's and early 1900's the school enjoyed much popularity among teachers seeking refresher courses in a summer-resort setting as well as among teachers seeking help so that they might handle "gym" classes along with their other work The school offered work in German, Swedish, Delsarte, and "American" systems of gymnastics, and methods of teaching each system were offered.

Boston Normal School of Gymnastics. Mrs. Mary Hemenway, the Boston philanthropist, had financed the first sewing and cooking classes in the Boston public schools and the introduction of Swedish gymnastics and the training of classroom teachers to handle the work. Then in 1889 she founded the Boston Normal School of Gymnastics, to assure a continuing supply of professionally trained gymnastics teachers. This school should not be confused with the Boston Normal School, which is an older school established to train teachers in the field of general education. Mrs. Hemenway installed her secretary, Amy Morris Homans (see p. 235) as the Director of the school and Baron Posse as teacher of gymnastics, who was followed the second year by Dr. Claës Enebuske who in turn served in that capacity for several years. From the very beginning, this school was the stronghold of Swedish gymnastics in America. Wherever its early graduates went, Swedish gymnastics became the cornerstone of their programs.

In 1891 the school graduated its first class of twelve from its two-year course. Two years later it graduated forty-three with thirty others receiving a one-year certificate. The starting salary of these graduates ranged from $1,000 to $1,800, considered excellent in those days.

From the beginning the school maintained a distinguished faculty, numbering in its ranks in its earliest days the Professor of Philosophy of Harvard, the Dean of Harvard Medical School, and the Professor of Biology of Massachusetts Institute of Technology. Continuously until the school merged with Wellesley College in 1909 there were Harvard and Massachusetts Institute of Technology professors and heads of departments on the staff on a part-time basis, and, even after the transfer of the school to Wellesley College near Boston, many of these teachers were retained as special lecturers.

In its second year the school increased its staff and expanded its curriculum to include general anatomy, applied anatomy and physiology, histology, hygiene, and supervised teaching in the public schools of Boston. In the third year it added anthropometry, emergencies, general psychology, pedagogy, and voice training. To augment the activity program it added dance. In its fifth year it added to the curriculum physics, chemistry, comparative anatomy, embryology, and sanitation, all taught by Massachusetts Institute of Technology professors.

Savage Physical Development Institute. Dr. Watson L. Savage (1859–1931), teacher of physical education at Columbia University, established his institute in 1890. Eight years later he changed its name to the New York Normal School of Physical Education, and shortly after that it became known as the Savage School of Physical Education (acquiring the title officially in 1914). This school prepared many teachers for the New York City public schools.

Posse School of Gymnastics. After serving one year as head of gymnastics at the Boston Normal School of Gymnastics, Baron Posse founded his own school in Boston. Before coming to America he had been declared the skating champion of the world. He was also an excellent horseman and gymnast. Born into the Swedish aristocracy, he had been a lieutenant in the Royal Army, and up to that time had been the youngest man to be honored by the King of Sweden with the Order of VASA. He gave up the advantages of his family connections and position to come to America to pioneer in the field of medical gymnastics.

As head of his own school, he leaned heavily in his teachings upon the medical aspects of gymnastics and the principles of health education advocated by the Royal Gymnastic Institute of Stockholm. When he died in 1895, at the age of thirty-three, his widow, an American woman whom he had met in Boston, carried on the school until her retirement, after which it had a succession of directors until its demise in 1942.

Colleges and Universities. The earliest record of a teacher-training course in physical education offered in a college in America seems to be one at Wayne University, where a course to prepare elementary school teachers to handle physical education was offered in 1881. Five years later Delphine Hanna offered a one-year teacher-training course at Oberlin College—the first offered in a private college. In six years ten women had earned the certificate of this course, a special award offered by the teacher, herself. In 1892 this course was expanded into a two-year normal course, and the college recognized it by offering the certificates in its own name. In eight years thirty-five women had earned this two-year certificate.

Also in 1892 the University of Indiana, in 1894 the University of Nebraska, in 1897 the University of California, and in 1899 the University of Wisconsin started short teacher-training courses leading to a physical education certificate. In 1898 an Oberlin two-year certificate student also received the bachelor's degree, but with specialization for the degree in other fields than physical education. However, this was the first time that a student earning a two-year physical education certificate also acquired the bachelor's degree at the same time.

While Robert Clark, M.D. (1862–1945), a former member of Dr. Gulick's staff at the Springfield Training School, was head of physical education at the University of Nebraska (1894–97), succeeding Wilbur Bowen, he planned and procured official recognition for a major in physical education leading to a bachelor's degree—the first such course to be offered in a college in America. This was one of four professional courses then offered at Nebraska: Law, Teaching, Medicine, and Physical Education. The last named was put into effect in the fall of 1897. By then Clark had rejoined the staff of the Springfield School, and W. W. Hastings (1865?–1961), a Springfield graduate and holder of the Ph.D. degree from Haverford College, succeeded him in the position at Nebraska so that it was he who got the new major under way. A young woman, Alberta Spurck (1878–1954), graduated from this course in June of 1900, thereby becoming the first and only person to graduate from a college in the United States in the nineteenth century with a major in physical education leading to the bachelor's degree. (The nineteenth century did not end until Dec. 31, 1900, at the end of the final one-hundredth year.) The official University records show that this young woman had completed 52 semester hours in specialization including 24 hours in chemistry, zoology, physiology, and hygiene, and 28 hours in special physical education courses.

In 1903 Dr. Hanna made a survey of the private normal schools of physical education, and in her published report named three colleges offering specialization leading to a degree. She listed the University of California as starting its course in 1898, the University of Nebraska, 1899 (1897, however, is the correct date); and Oberlin College, 1900. (Checking in the 1950's the University of California registrar found no record of such a course at Berkeley before the close of the first decade of the twentieth century; however, in the late 1960's the University is reviewing its records and is challenging Nebraska's claim as the first. When this research is completed the final result will be made a matter of public record.)

Early Summer Courses. As noted earlier, the first summer work offered in teacher training in this field was that of Dr. Sargent in 1881, a five-week course in his newly established private school. In 1887 Dr. Gulick at the YMCA School and Dr. Sargent at Harvard started summer courses. In 1888 came the summer courses offered by Dr. Anderson at Chautauqua; in 1890, the summer courses at the Chicago and Nashville branches of the YMCA School; and in 1895, the summer courses of the Normal School of the NAGU in Milwaukee. In 1899 the University of

Wisconsin advertised in the *American Physical Education Review* a summer school in physical education to be open to both men and women. If the course materialized, it was the first such for a state university and was but short-lived.

First Talk of Standardization of Schools. In the late 1890's it was suggested in *Mind and Body*, a magazine published by the turners, that a national placement office be established to help teachers of physical education. This suggestion Dr. Hartwell hailed as novel but he proposed instead that a Commission made up of experts be set up to examine all professional training schools, especially their science courses, in order to insure conformity in fundamental knowledge and permit each school to teach beyond that whatever system of gymnastics it prefers. But nothing came of either suggestion.

Non-School Organizations

Several forces besides the schools were at work in the last half of the nineteenth century to bring physical education to all the people. The turners and the YMCA's, born in an earlier era, now materially increased their physical education activities. The Sokols and YWCA's now joined the other groups in offering activities to still more people. Private athletic clubs also came into existence, bringing sports to an ever-increasing circle of citizens. The earliest of these clubs were the Olympic Athletic Club of California, born in 1862, and the New York Athletic Club of 1868, with a building of its own erected in 1885.

North American Gymnastic Union. The 150 turner societies with their 10,000 members of prewar days and their Normal School at Rochester, New York, had been disbanded while the men fought in the Union army. Now with the Civil War at an end the NAGU was revived, and by 1872 there were 187 societies functioning. Before the 1880's little was known about the work of the turnverein in America outside German-American circles. The membership of the societies and the participation in the turnfests were confined to those of German origin. The German language was used, to a great extent, in all the activities, and no effort was made to interest other Americans in the educational, social, or gymnastic work. Throughout their history the turnverein met with vigorous hostility in some communities, for the turners were abolitionists, free-soilers, and opponents of prohibition.

During the 1880's their membership grew to 36,000 in 277 societies. They now began agitation for physical education in the public schools and contributed moral and financial support, material, publications, and leadership to that end. In some communities they purchased apparatus and placed it in the school yards. Some served as teachers free of charge in order to convince reluctant school boards of the value of their work. Their normal college demanded that its graduates be able to give instruction in the English language, that they might be prepared to enter the schools.

From 1881 on, the turner societies held turnfests every four or five years with from 1,200 to 3,400 participants in the competition. At the World's Fair in Chicago, 1893, they gave daily exhibitions of their work and distributed thousands of pamphlets. In 1894 the organization began publication of a monthly periodical, *Mind and Body*.

By 1890 the turners had over 30,000 members with 160 gymnasiums in use, reaching over 400,000 participants in their physical activities alone, at the very time when the average USA tax payer was complaining that gymnastics in the schools was but an idle luxury.

Sokols. Bohemians, as well as Germans, came to the United States in large numbers in this era, and the gymnastic enthusiasts among them organized Sokol clubs which are similar to the German turnverein—democratic, patriotic organizations for the practice of voluntary discipline aimed at both moral and physical fitness. The first American Sokol was established in St. Louis, Missouri, in 1865. Never as numerous as the German immigrants, the Bohemians did not become so widely known although the first of them came to America with the earliest Dutch settlers, having fled to Holland to escape religious persecution. The latecomers of the nineteenth century settled mainly in the Middle West and there enthusiastically pursued their physical activities—gymnastics, folk dancing, and sharpshooting.

Young Men's Christian Association. Shortly following the Civil War, the Young Men's Christian Association pushed its pre-war plans to offer opportunities to its members for physical development and promotion of health. It immediately put in the first free public baths and the first vacation schools offering carpentry, singing, and nature study, to keep children occupied during vacation periods. That same year (1866) the president of the New York City YMCA proposed a four-fold program—physical, mental, social, and spiritual—which was adopted. Three years later the first YMCA buildings with gymnasiums were erected in New York City, San Francisco, and Washington, D.C., with the Boston building and gymnasium coming in 1872. G. Stanley Hall, the famous psychologist, then but twenty-three years old and always an ardent champion of physical education, was a member of the New York City YMCA when it opened its first gymnasium.

In 1885 the Brooklyn Central Branch YMCA put in a swimming pool —the first YMCA pool in the United States. Until the YMCA school in

Springfield (see p. 220) began training teachers for the YMCA gymnasiums, the YMCA's had to use circus performers, weight-lifters, and professional athletes as part-time teachers. With the training work under way, an International Committee was established to supervise the physical education work in the YMCA's throughout the country, with Gulick serving as head of this supervisory work.

The 1890's brought historic events to the YMCA. In 1890 Gulick devised the YMCA emblem, the equilateral triangle known today the world over. In 1891 and 1895 the games of basketball and volleyball were developed in YMCA's as previously discussed, and in 1896 the Athletic League of the YMCA's of North America was founded.

By 1900, the YMCA had 294 physical directors and 22 assistant directors for 507 gymnasiums with nearly 80,000 men and 20,000 boys registered in their classes.

Young Women's Christian Association. The Young Women's Christian Association was established in the United States in this era. In 1882 the first association, which was established in Boston, set aside a nearby park for calisthenic classes and installed chest weights in the hallway of the building with a girl member of the association leading in classwork in these activities. Two years later Boston erected a new building which was the first YWCA in the country to include a gymnasium as part of the facilities, and, in 1887, the first classes in calisthenics were offered using a combination of Dio Lewis and Delsarte work.

In 1886 a national association of YWCA's was organized at a conference at Lake Geneva in Wisconsin, and in 1891 the eleventh conference created the International Board of YWCA's to send general secretaries and physical education teachers to YWCA's all over the world.

The physical education program generally in the 1890's consisted of Indian-club swinging, dumbbell drills, wand drills, "esthetic marching," and basketball. As early as 1895 the latter had become a very popular activity in the YWCA.

Movements Related to Physical Education

Although the great mass of the population still worked long hours six days per week and had but little leisure themselves, a concern was growing in this era for the welfare of children in their out-of-school periods. Out of this concern developed two important movements—the recreation and the camping movements.

Recreation Movement. As happened in so many movements in America which were for the enrichment of life, it was Boston, with its sand gardens, that started the ball rolling in the development of the playground and recreation movement. Brookline near Boston was the first town to vote public funds for a playground. This was in 1872. Chicago, in 1876, opened the first public park in America (the present Washington Park) and offered recreational facilities although without supervision. Boston in 1888 designated seven school yards as playgrounds and the following year added eleven more to these, all open to children of all ages. Also, in 1888, New York City opened its school buildings in the evenings for recreational use by the citizens, and, in 1889, Boston established several so-called "outdoor gymnasiums" for older boys and men to take care of leisure hours brought on by the shortened workday. A few years later sections were set aside in the parks for older girls and women.

Citizens of New York City organized The Outdoor Recreation League and secured from the municipal government an appropriation of about $30,000 with which twenty school yards were operated as play centers. The city then began the purchase and equipping of tracts of land at a very great cost. Seward Park alone cost $2,500,000. Jacob A. Riis (1849–1914), the leader of the Anti-Slum Movement to get children off the city streets and Secretary of the Committee on Small Parks, did more than any other person to secure adequate space for play in New York City. He was identified with the playground movement throughout his life.

The playground system of Chicago began with a vacant-lot play center managed by Hull House in 1893. Six years later New York City opened several school yard playgrounds modelled after that of Hull House, and the establishment of this type of facility quickly spread to all other parts of the country. Ten cities set up playgrounds between 1890 and 1900. In nearly all the cities the work was begun by philanthropic and humanitarian organizations; in some cases the city gave financial support, and in some it gave no encouragement whatever. The playground movement was definitely identified with the anti-slum and the social service movement.

Camping Movement. Although camping was organized to some extent in isolated situations in earlier years, as for the boys at the Round Hill School in the 1820's and at the Gunnery School for Boys in Washington, Connecticut, in 1861, the camping movement did not get a real start until after the Civil War. The first camp on record was established by a Wilkes Barre, Pennsylvania, physician at North Mountain in Luzerne County in 1875; the first church camp, by a West Hartford, Connecticut, minister on Gardner's Island in 1880; and the first YMCA camp (Camp Dudley), by the Newburg, New York, YMCA on Grange Lake—the only one of these early camps still in existence.

The first private camp—a boy's camp on Burnt Island on Asquan Lake near Holderness, New Hampshire—was established in 1881 for the specific purpose of meeting educational needs of young boys of well-to-do families who were wont to idle away their time at summer resorts with their parents. This first camp started with a program built largely around physical activities, thus setting the pattern conformed to by the camps that followed and establishing for the camping movement objectives closely akin to those of physical education itself.

Family camping became popular, particularly in the Middle West in the last decade of the nineteenth century, but it usually meant a camp site along some river or creek within horse-and-wagon reach of home.

The National Park Service. During the administration of President Grant, the government created the first National Park—Yellowstone—in 1872. Yosemite, General Grant, and Sequoia Parks were created in California in 1890, and Mt. Rainier Park in Washington in 1899. This marked the beginning of the vast national vacation and recreation areas of the United States.

Professional Literature

Literature in the field of physical education began to increase materially in this era. For the first time not only books but periodicals and reports of surveys became available from the presses of the United States and from local authors. No longer were workers in the field of physical education dependent almost solely on foreign publications.

Books. Several books achieved prominence in the field of physical education in this period. Foremost among them were: William Blaikie, *How to Get Strong and How to Stay So* (1879), which influenced several who later became prominent leaders to take up the study of physical education and which, highly popular in both Europe and the United States, ran in many editions up to 1902; DuBois-Reymond, *Physiology of Exercise* (1885), translation of Berlin edition published in *Popular Science Monthly;* Carl Betz, *Free Gymnastics,* (1887); Robert J. Roberts, *Classified Gymnasium Exercises* (1889); Nils Posse, *The Special Kinesiology of Educational Gymnastics* (1890); Claës J. Enebuske, *Progressive Gymnastic Day's Orders According to the Principles of the Ling System* (1890), which sold over 5,000 copies; *Basketball Rules,* first edition mimeographed (1894); Jay W. Seaver, *Anthropometry and Physical Examinations* (1896); W. G. Anderson, *Methods of Teaching Gymnastics,* (1898); and Senda Berensen, *Basket Ball Rules for Girls,* first edition mimeographed (1899).

Five years before the translation of *Physiology of Exercise* reached America, Hartwell wrote his doctoral thesis at Johns Hopkins University on this subject. This is the earliest record of an American writing on this topic.

Periodicals. As in the period preceding the Civil War there were several periodicals that frequently contained articles on physical education activities, but none were in any sense periodicals of the profession. But in the 1880's there appeared the *Reports of the Proceedings* of the annual conventions of the American Association for the Advancement of Physical Education covering ten years from 1885 to 1895. Then in the 1890's came an awakening, and four professional magazines were born: *Physical Education* (March, 1892–July, 1896), in four volumes with Gulick as editor (preceding this he started a YMCA magazine called *The Triangle* in June, 1891, which carried much of interest to physical education); *Posse Gymnastic Journal,* which started with the issue of December, 1892, and ran for ten years after Posse's death in 1895 still carrying articles supposedly written by him; *Mind and Body,* a monthly magazine published by the North American Gymnastic Union, starting with the March, 1894, issue (destined to last for forty years); and *The American Physical Education Review,* the official organ of the AAAPE starting in the fall of 1896 with Hartwell as "Chairman of the Magazine" (issued quarterly from 1896 through 1907, when it became a monthly periodical, and surviving today as the *Journal of Health, Physical Education, and Recreation*).

As to the first magazine, there is some confusion. Careful scrutiny of the four volumes of *Physical Education* gives no clue as to what organization, if any, backed this magazine. There is not even the mention of the editor's name, but Gulick's biographer states that he edited a magazine named *Physical Education.* It may have been the private venture of Gulick alone or of him and a group of his friends. The subscription price was $1.00 a year, and it was published by the Triangle Publishing Company of Springfield, Massachusetts. It listed an Advisory Committee made up of the profession's most distinguished leaders of that day. Hartwell was in charge of the Current Topics Department, and G. Stanley Hall, America's leading psychologist, was a frequent contributor.

Apparently the sponsorship of this magazine puzzled the people of that day for the editorial in the April, 1895, issue says:

> *Our Purpose.* There are some of our readers who have received the impression that this magazine was, or desired to give the impression that it was the official organ of the physical education department of the International Committee of the YMCA. We wish to state clearly that *Physical Education* is not the official organ of any body whatsoever, neither the International Committee Association Training School at Springfield, Massachusetts, nor American Association for Advancement of Physical Education. It stands merely for a subject—Physical Training—in its relation to the development of all-round character for manhood and womanhood.

(Issues of some of these early magazines are available in microcard from the School of Physical Education, University of Oregon. They make interesting reading.)

20

Organizations and Leaders of the Latter Nineteenth Century (1865–1900)

Although general educators before the Civil War had formed organizations to pool their interests and ideas and to promote educational standards and objectives, there was not a sufficient number of physical educators nor a profession of physical education sufficiently recognized to sustain such organizations in the physical education field until in the 1880's. By then a group of leaders had been developed, and professional organizations arose out of their coming together for mutual aid.

ORGANIZATIONS OF THE PROFESSION

The American Association for the Advancement of Physical Education

The national group known today as the American Association for Health, Physical Education and Recreation was founded November 17, 1885, as the American Association for the Advancement of Physical Education. The organization meeting was called by Dr. W. G. Anderson then a young teacher at Adelphi College in Brooklyn, who earlier approached various influential persons interested in the advancement of physical education and found them enthusiastic over the idea of a meeting. It was a gathering of such distinguished persons as the Reverend Henry Ward Beecher, William Blaikie, the New York City attorney who had written the popular book, *How to Get Strong*, Reverend T. De Witt Talmadge (1832–1902), the popular lecturer and writer, Charles Pratt (1830–1891), prosperous merchant of Brooklyn who two years later founded Pratt Institute, and leading educators, physicians, and newspaper men of New York City and Brooklyn, besides the best known physical educators of the day. At its organization meeting forty-nine members joined. At the second meeting (the first convention) in 1886, enough others joined to bring the membership to 114.

In 1892 the National Education Association, desiring to sponsor a meeting dealing with physical education, then a muchly talked of topic in educational circles, organized a Physical Education Conference to be held in July of 1893 in connection with the World's Fair in Chicago and invited Edward M. Hartwell, who was at the time of the planning President of the AAAPE, to serve as Chairman of the Conference. AAAPE thereupon gave up its own plans for a convention in 1893, and newly elected president Dudley A. Sargent and his group threw their influence back of the NEA meeting. This marked the first official recognition of physical education as a growing profession by the NEA. Two years later that organization set up a Department of Physical Education within its own organization, which functioned primarily to put on programs on the subject of physical education at its conventions. Through the years, individual leaders in AAAPE gave leadership to this NEA Department, which however was entirely without the jurisdiction of AAAPE.

At the ninth annual convention held at Yale University in 1894, professional members were listed from California, Canada, Illinois, Iowa, Louisiana, Missouri, Oregon, and Wisconsin, as well as from all the eastern states.

In 1895 at its tenth annual convention held at Teachers College, Columbia University, in New York City it voted to reorganize along the lines of the North American Turnerbund. At the same time it named Boston as the national headquarters and for the first time accepted representatives of a district as members of the national council (the Eastern District).

The destinies of the organization were in most capable hands. Five men served as president in the first fifteen years to the close of the nineteenth century—first, Dr. Edward Hitchcock, of Amherst College; then William Blaikie, the New York City attorney (the only president in the history of the organization whose vocation was not in the field of physical education); and Drs. Dudley A. Sargent of Harvard University, Edward M. Hartwell of Johns Hopkins University and the Boston public schools, and Jay W. Seaver of Yale University. Dr. Anderson, the founder of the organization, served as the first Secretary–Treasurer. Photographs of all presidents from 1885 through 1960 are shown in the *Journal of Health and Physical Education* of April, 1960. Also, all from 1885 through 1969 are listed with their years of service in Appendix A.

In 1895 professional workers in New England were called together at Clark University, and at that meeting the Physical Education Society of New England was organized as a combined several-state section of AAAPE. (At this organization meeting, G. Stanley Hall, President of Clark University, addressed the group, and Sargent gave an illustrated lecture.) This marked the first effort to organize by districts. In that same year the leaders of Ohio organized the first State Association of AAAPE, followed by one in Connecticut in 1896, which at first lasted for only two years and was not to be revived until twenty years after. A year later W. P. Bowen, then of the Normal School at Ypsilanti, Michigan, and Dr. Eliza Mosher (see p. 242) of the University of Michigan called a first meeting of physical education teachers of the state to organize a Physical Culture Section of the State Teachers Association. This section died after three years, but it marks a first attempt to develop a physical education section within a state teachers association.

The founders of AAAPE were men and women who had studied Greek, Latin, and philosophy. Their speeches reflect their intimate acquaintance with the best of literature. They brought the theories and ideas of the great thinkers of the world to bear upon their problems of the late nineteenth century. Never in the entire eighty and more years of history of this organization have there been leaders of broader intellectual and cultural background than these founding fathers. The first presidents were close friends of United States presidents, Supreme Court judges, college presidents, and leading educators and ministers of the day. Through their great breadth of interests, Hitchcock, Hartwell, Sargent, and Gulick, in particular, were nationally known outside the profession. They were members of Boards of Trustees of several colleges and recognized leaders in many well-known movements.

The problems that claimed their greatest professional attention in the early years were testing and measuring, promotion of the profession, gymnastic systems, and the place of physical education in education. Although men predominated in the membership, women were cordially accepted into the association and from the very start held elective office. At the first meeting, Miss Helen Putnam of Vassar was elected one of four vice presidents.

Society of College Gymnasium Directors

In October, 1897, Anderson and Hartwell called all men college directors of physical education who were not using the German or Swedish systems exclusively in their work to come together at New York University to talk over where America stood in regard to gymnastics. Twenty-three directors responded to the invitation and they founded the Society of College Gymnasium Directors, which through the years has wielded strong influence in physical education in the United States. This organization is known today as the National College Physical Education Association for Men. Its purpose was to "promote the physical welfare of the students in the institutions of higher learning, to make surveys and conduct research and to promote a professional spirit among its members." Hitchcock, who had served as the first President of AAAPE, now took over as the first President of this new organization. (An interesting photograph of this group assembled in convention at Yale, December, 1899, is shown in the February, 1944 issue of the *Journal of Health and Physical Education.*)

Physical Training Conference of 1889

In this period there occurred the first conference on physical education to be held outside the framework of an organized group. Known as "The Conference of 1889 on Physical Training" it was destined to be the forerunner of many equally notable conferences to follow in the twentieth century. (This first conference is fully reported, and the report, long out of print, is now available on microcard.) The conference, financed by Mrs. Mary Hemenway of Boston, was called by the Secretary of the Massachusetts State Board of Education, the Superintendent of Schools of Boston, the Presidents of Massachusetts Institute of Technology, Boston University, and Colby College, the members of the Boston School Commission, and an imposing array of leading citizens of Boston. The United States Commissioner of Education presided at the conference.

Among the thirty-four speakers at the four sessions were sixteen medical doctors, one General of the Army of the United States, one Earl from England, two Barons (one, Baron Pierre de Coubertin of France, who was touring England and America to study the sports activities, from which observations he soon thereafter developed his idea of establishing the modern Olympics), one Doctor of Laws and one a Doctor of Philosophy. Of these thirty-four speakers, five were women. The discussions and demonstrations centered around the German and Swedish systems of gymnastics. Two thousand people attended the conference, which was considered to be the most notable educational event of the era. Its success was a great boon to the advancement of physical education.

LEADERS OF PHYSICAL EDUCATION

The story of the rise of the profession of physical education is the story of its leaders who shaped the profession and advanced its cause. The list of those who materially advanced it following the Civil War is surprisingly long, considering the paucity of opportunity to prepare within this field, and the lack of incentive in the meagerness of facilities and in the ignorance of the many educators, and citizens as well, regarding the merits of this branch of education. With the passage of the years, a certain few stand out as the foremost leaders of their day. Of the men, most were educated in the field of medicine and picked up their knowledge of physical education on their own, building on their science studies. In this period, for the first time, several women leaders came into prominence. Considering the difficulties during these years for a woman to procure an education, it is surprising how many fine and capable women dedicated their lives to this branch of education, managing somehow to procure at least the fundamentals of an education. Of the several women born before 1860 who markedly advanced the profession during this era, two, like several of the men, were not trained in this field; but, unlike the men, they did not actually teach, although they used their talents and influence for the advancement of the profession. Amy Morris Homans, through her organizational and administrative talents and flair for guidance of young women, served the profession well in setting high teacher-training standards; and Eliza Mosher, a famous woman physician of that day, aligned herself closely with physical education. These leaders, both men and women, are discussed in the material that follows, in the chronological order of date of birth. Their photographs are in the Seventy-fifth Anniversary issue of the *Journal of Health and Physical Education,* April, 1960.

Edward Hitchcock (1828–1911)

Edward Hitchcock was born in Amherst, Massachusetts, where his father was a professor at the College and was later to become its third president. Edward graduated from Amherst in 1849, and after two years of teaching chemistry and natural science at a seminary nearby, he went to Harvard University, acquiring his medical degree in 1853. He then resumed his teaching until 1860, when he went to London to study comparative anatomy under the famous Sir Richard Owen, then Curator of the British Museum. In the following year, he was called to Amherst as Professor of Physical Education, to head up the newly organized department, in which he served a period of fifty years until his death in 1911. In his long directorship at Amherst, he blazed such an excellent trail that his department set a fine example for all that were to follow. (The story of that department has been told in an earlier chapter.)

Doctor Hitchcock was greatly beloved by the students and alumni, who affectionately called him "old Doc" even when he was in his middle years.

He was a genius at organizing and at seeing in the physical-exercise program a means to an end which transcended any system of gymnastics or calisthenics. He had no training in any form of gymnastics so he used the Dio Lewis system in the early days of his directorship as something tangible to start with. He immediately embarked upon research into physical measurements, thus starting the first anthropometric studies in America, which he carried on throughout his entire professional career. He was the organizing chairman of both the American Association for the Advancement of Physical Education and the Society of College Gymnasium Directors and served for two years as the first president of the former. He took the lead in the research work of both associations and was a frequent speaker at their meetings. His genius lay in his insistence upon a sound scientific basis for all his work and upon accurate and truthful observation. In this he left the profession a valuable heritage. He is a Fellow in Memoriam of the American Academy of Physical Education.

Amy Morris Homans (1848–1933)

Although not trained in the specialized field of physical education, Amy Morris Homans was one of the profession's great women leaders. Born in Vassalboro, Maine, she was educated by private tutors, as were most young girls of that day who received serious schooling. At the age of nineteen she became preceptress of a girl's seminary in Maine, and two years later went to North Carolina to become principal of two schools, one a normal school. After ten years of teaching and administrative work she became secretary to Mrs. August Hemenway of Boston. The two of them organized, and Miss Homans directed, the Boston Normal School of Household Arts which the State of Massachusetts took over two years later as the Department of Domestic Science of Framingham State Normal School—one of the first of such departments in the country. Two years later when Mrs. Hemenway founded the Boston Normal School of Gymnastics she installed her secretary as director of the school. Under Miss Homan's skillful direction and far-seeing educational philosophy the school quickly achieved leadership in the training of women. Under her management the school took the lead in acquiring collegiate status when, in 1909, it became the Department of Hygiene and Physical Education of Wellesley College. From that step she forged ahead until the department finally acquired full postgraduate status—another first in the profession.

Upon her retirement in 1918 at the age of seventy she was given the title of Emeritus Professor, the first woman in the profession to achieve this distinction. In 1909 she received the first honorary master's degree and in 1930 the first honorary doctor's degree to be conferred upon a woman in the field of physical education in the United States. She was the second woman to be elected to membership in the American Academy of Physical Education.

Until the time of her death at the age of eighty-five her counsel was continuously sought because of her rare wisdom. A woman of marked culture and refinement, she insisted upon a liberal arts education coupled with professional training. A gentlewoman in every sense of the word, she set a pattern for all women working in the profession that brooked no compromise with femininity. A woman of high courage, she was unflinching in her maintenance of high standards, and she set for her students a professional code that also brooked no compromise. A woman of dynamic personality, of unusual administrative ability, and of superior standards of thoroughness of work, she was inexorable in her insistence that students make the most of their educational advantages. All these qualities marked her as an unusual leader who demanded near perfection for her pupils yet claimed their deep respect, sincere admiration, and devoted homage.

Dudley A. Sargent (1849–1924)

Sargent was born in Belfast, Maine. He was but seven years old when his father died, and he was sent to Hingham, Massachusetts, to live with relatives. In the three years there, he had his first experience with gymnastics and liked it. Back in Belfast he entered a private school well equipped with gymnastic apparatus, and there he found a book describing dumb bells and Indian clubs and explaining how to use them. He made himself a pair of each and at the age of fourteen began in earnest his own physical development program, as he pursued his studies; at the same time he helped support himself chopping wood, lumbering, and farming, up at 6 A.M. in the winter and at 4 A.M. in the summer. At the age of fifteen he was studying Cutter's *Anatomy, Physiology and Hygiene* which he considered the most enthralling of all his school textbooks. As he grew older he took on carpentering and plumbing work to support himself, and at the same time he kept up his own physical development with gymnastic exercises he invented for himself.

When he saw a gymnastic exhibition at Bowdoin College, it interested him so much that with his chums he formed a gymnastic club, using his uncle's barn for their gymnasium; he became so proficient that he joined a circus doing an act of some of his self-taught stunts.

There he became acquainted with George Goldie (1841–1920) (later founder of the physical education department of Princeton University) and with the Harlan Brothers of the Tremont Gymnasium in Boston, stars of the acrobatic world who were being paid more per week than he earned in an entire year.

At the age of twenty he was appointed Director of the Gymnasium at Bowdoin College, where for a salary of $5 per week for the first year, and

$500 per year from the second year, he did, besides his teaching, all the janitor work for the gymnasium, setting and lighting the fires, trimming lamps, carrying water, and sweeping out.

Seeing that the boys who worked on farms and in mills and lumber yards had superior physiques, he set out to devise a program of exercises and apparatus that would give the other boys similar development. Using the muscular movements of everyday labor and sports activities he originated a system of gymnastics that was indeed "natural" gymnastics, foreshadowing that movement of the twentieth century. After teaching two years he registered in the college to study for his own degree and at this time persuaded the college to make gymnastics a requirement for five days a week, with the class work to be graded as other school subjects were. The following year, when he had to drop gymnastics for military drill in the spring term, he went to Yale to introduce his program there and thus started its physical education program. This pattern of three months of each year off for a term at Yale persisted until he procured his bachelor's degree in 1875. Armed with his degree, he asked for a salary of $1200 at Bowdoin.

Bowdoin's refusal of this request for a full-time position was an important turning point in Sargent's career, for he resigned his part-time position there and continued his work at Yale. This provided the opportunity to enter Yale Medical School. During this period, aided by his physiological studies in particular, his determination to enter upon a career in teaching physical education was strengthened and reaffirmed.

In two and a half years Sargent had completed his medical studies and also the work for the M.A. degree, and since Yale offered him only part-time employment he left and opened his own private Hygienic Institute and School of Physical Culture in New York City, working daily from 8:00 A.M. to 10:00 P.M. There he became acquainted with William Blaikie, a Harvard graduate, who was instrumental in his being appointed Director of the Gymnasium and Assistant Professor of Physical Training at Harvard University. There he developed a scientific program based on the individual needs of the students. This led to the invention of his own anthropometric and other apparatus, which by 1889 was in use in 350 institutions. Wishing his inventions to become educational tools free to all, he did not patent them, and when a manufacturer took out patents on them he caused Sargent serious trouble, which led him to regret that he had not at least "policed" his own inventions.

In the summer of 1879, before he went to Harvard, he was invited to lecture and teach gymnastics at the then one-year-old Chautauqua Summer School for Church Laymen, becoming the first of many physical educators who through the years were to teach there. In 1881 he founded his private school and in 1887 the Harvard Summer School of Physical

Education, both teacher-training projects, turning out hundreds of teachers through the years, most of whom were heads of departments in colleges, high schools, and private schools in the United States and in Canada, England, France, China, and Japan. After World War I, he established a camp connected with the Sargent School near Peterborough, New Hampshire, and there he died July 21, 1924. He is a Fellow in Memoriam of the American Academy of Physical Education.

He was a self-made man—a man of learning and culture—a man of great dignity, yet one frequently caught up in serious controversies, particularly in his efforts to "clean up" football and to bring intercollegiate athletics under faculty control. He more than any other person guided intercollegiate athletics into proper controls and regulations. He took an active part in the professional organizations and was one of the early presidents of the AAAPE and also of the College Physical Education Association.

Always a student of philosophy and the sciences, he based his work on sound scientific foundations. Always willing to speak out publicly on behalf of physical education, and an excellent speaker, he advanced the profession materially through his speeches as well as through his writings. At the famous Conference of 1889, he gave public voice to his professional credo when he said:

> One-half the struggle for physical training has been won when [a student] can be induced to take a genuine interest in his bodily condition—to want to remedy his defects, and to pride himself on the purity of his skin, the firmness of his muscles, and the uprightness of his figure.
>
> . . . . .
>
> It is more to the credit of a university to have one hundred men who can do a creditable performance in running, rowing, ball-playing, etc., than to have one man who can break a record, or a team that can always win the championship.

At this same conference, when asked what he thought were America's needs in a physical education program, he replied, "the strength-giving qualities of the German system, the active and energetic quality of English sports, the grace and suppleness of French calisthenics, the poise and precision of Swedish free movements—all of these systematized and adapted to our peculiar needs."

In 1894 Bowdoin College conferred upon Dr. Sargent the honorary degree of Doctor of Science.

Edward Mussey Hartwell (1850–1922)

Edward M. Hartwell was born at Exeter, New Hampshire, the son of a brilliant lawyer and the grandson of a surgeon. He earned several degrees—the A.B. and A.M. from Amherst, the Ph.D. from Johns Hopkins, and the M.D. from Miami Medical College of Cincinnati. He also studied at the Royal Gymnastic Institute of Stockholm and in Vienna and Bonn. Later, Amherst College conferred upon him the honorary degree, Doctor of Laws—the first such degree to be conferred upon a physical educator in America. As a pupil of Hitchcock, he became deeply interested in research, and he advanced the profession materially through both historical and biological research.

For seven years, 1883–90, he was Associate Professor of Physical Training and Director of the Gymnasium at Johns Hopkins University. In the spring of 1883 he travelled from Maine to Tennessee visiting gymnasiums for a survey of physical education for the United States Bureau of Education, producing a manuscript, *Physical Education in American Colleges and Universities*, which has through the years remained a masterpiece of historical research. Following this, in 1890, he made a third trip to Europe visiting playgrounds and school gymnasiums (in his various trips he investigated physical education work in Russia, Scandinavia, Germany and Great Britain), and the following year he became the first Director of Physical Education of the Public Schools of Boston which position he held until 1898, building a program which served as a model for all public schools for many years. In 1897 he became Secretary of the Department of Municipal Statistics of Boston serving in that capacity until his retirement in 1919.

He served the American Association for the Advancement of Physical Education as its president for five years and was a constant contributor of reports and papers, all scholarly and scientific. He gave dignity to the profession through his scholarly approach to all of his work. He is a Fellow in Memoriam in the American Academy of Physical Education.

Delphine Hanna (1854–1941)

Born in Markeson, Wisconsin, Delphine Hanna graduated from Rockport State Normal School in 1874 and for ten years taught in the grade schools of Kansas and New York. Becoming concerned about the lack of physical stamina of most pupils and teachers, she enrolled in the Dio Lewis Summer School in 1884 in the hopes of learning how to remedy this condition. Disillusioned over the lack of scientific basis of Lewis' physical education theories, she transferred to the Sargent School, graduating in June, 1885. That summer she worked with Boston orthopedic physicians to study the treatment of spinal curvature, and in the evenings she studied the Delsarte system at the Currie School of Expression. Later she incorporated the best of this system into her posture training work.

In the fall of 1885 she went to Oberlin College as Instructor in Physical Culture with the promise of living expenses but no salary and $300 to spend on equipment. She started classes in calisthenics, correctives, and "fancy steps," but the President had to be persuaded that there would be no harm in the "fancy steps" before she could proceed with them. She also offered classes to men students, and inspired several to take up physical education work. Two of these students, Thomas D. Wood and Luther H. Gulick, later became distinguished leaders in the profession. She continued her studies at Harvard Summer School of Physical Education and in 1890 procured the medical degree from the University of Michigan and after that the A.B. degree from Cornell University and A.M. from Oberlin. In 1893 she studied Swedish gymnastics at the Posse School, following that with orthopedic study in Zurich, Switzerland. Then she began giving physical examinations to her pupils at Oberlin, which led to her anthropometric research and her divising of charts for women which were widely used by other colleges and in teacher-training courses. During a year's leave of absence in the year 1895–96 she introduced girls' basketball to Colorado Springs, Colorado, which probably marked its first arrival in the Mountain states area.

In her thirty-five years at Oberlin she held the titles of Instructor in Physical Culture, Director of Physical Training, Women's Department, and, from 1903 on, Professor of Physical Education and Director of the Department of Physical Education for Women. She was the first woman in the field of physical education to be granted the rank of full professor by a private college.

She retired in 1920 as Professor Emeritus and became the first woman in the field to receive a Carnegie pension. In 1925 she was honored by election into the University of Michigan Hall of Fame. In 1931 she was among the first group to receive the Honor Award of the American Physical Education Association.

Dr. Hanna was a trail-blazer for American women in the field of physical education. She was the first woman to set up work for women founded on sound scientific procedures, to devise anthropometric charts for American women, to establish teacher's courses in a college leading to a certificate, and to set up a major in physical education leading to a bachelor's degree. (The major started at the University of Nebraska three years ahead of hers was established by a man).

William G. Anderson (1860–1947)

Born in St. Joseph, Michigan, William G. Anderson attended lower schools in Quincy, Illinois, and Boston. At the age of fourteen, he became acquainted with circus men who wintered in Quincy, Illinois, and they taught him work on the horizontal bars and the springboard. Three years later, when his family was living in Boston, he attended the Roxbury Latin School and there acquired still more skills in gymnastics at the YMCA under Robert J. Roberts. The next two years he attended the University of Wisconsin and continued gymnastics training at the outdoor gymnasium maintained there for men students. Some time during these years before 1880, he travelled in the summer with a circus in Illinois doing gymnastic stunts to help finance his schooling (as he personally related to one of the authors in the 1930's).

After two years in Wisconsin, he taught school in Clayton, Illinois, following which he became head of the physical department of the YMCA in Cleveland, Ohio. While there two years, he studied in his free time and earned the M.D. degree at the Cleveland Medical College (1883). After that he taught in Columbus and Toledo, and in 1885 was called to be Director of the Gymnasium at Adelphi Academy in Brooklyn. While there he founded the Brooklyn School of Physical Education, and also the Chautauqua Summer School of Physical Education, which he served for eighteen years. In 1892 he became Associate Director of the gymnasium at Yale, and in 1903 succeeded Seaver in the directorship, which position he held until he retired in 1932, having served Yale a total of forty years and acquiring the academic rank of professor in 1905. Concurrently with his early work at Yale and the Chautauqua Summer School of Physical Education, he served as president of the Anderson Normal School of Physical Education, the former Brooklyn school. While at Yale, by 1909, he earned the A.B., A.M. and M.S. degrees and in 1916 the doctor's degree in public health at Harvard.

He was the founder of the American Association for the Advancement of Physical Education and served as its first secretary from 1885 to 1888, taking on the position of treasurer from 1888 to 1892. He also was one of the founders of the College Gymnasium Director's Society and served as one of its early presidents. He was one of the earliest writers in the profession, producing five books and numerous articles in periodicals, mostly on medical research. He invented the ergograph and several other pieces of equipment for Yale's Department of Experimental Psychology.

The American Association for Health, Physical Education and Recreation has created the Anderson Award in his memory and conferred upon him the Gulick Award. Traveling widely in Europe, he studied research methods there and became a Fellow of the London Society of Sciences and Arts. He was a member of the American Academy of Physical Education.

Other Leaders

No account of the leaders in physical education of this era would be complete without mention of several other men and women who helped materially in blazing the trails though the professional wilderness, such as those whose brief biographies follow.

George Brosius (1839–1920). Known as "the Father Jahn of America," George Brosius, a teacher for fifty years, was the greatest leader in America of German gymnastics of his era. As the head of the Normal School of the NAGU for twenty-one years, he trained large numbers of teachers who were employed in public schools all over the country. Particularly was their influence felt in the Middle West.

Eliza M. Mosher (1846–1928). One of the leading women physicians of the United States of this era, Eliza M. Mosher, after procuring the medical degree in 1875 at the University of Michigan, practiced medicine until Vassar College appointed her resident physician in 1883. There she introduced physical examinations of women students—a first in America. She also ushered in the divided skirt, a forerunner of the bloomer of the 1890's, thus breaking down barriers to acceptance of a costume that would permit women to participate freely in physical activities. After three years at Vassar and ten more of private practice she went to the University of Michigan (1896), as its first Dean of Women and first Director of Physical Education for Women, where she organized a physical education program for the newly erected Barbour Gymnasium for Women. Immediately, the University granted her the rank of professor, the first time that any college or university conferred this rank on a Physical Director. (The University of Chicago had four years earlier—1892—been the first to so recognize its Dean of Women.) After three years there, she returned to private practice, where she gained international recognition. For twenty years she was editor of the *Women's Medical Journal.* Through her deep interest in posture training, she became a recognized authority on the subject and was a co-founder of the Posture League of America.

Robert Jeffries Roberts (1849–1920). Self-taught in private gymnasiums and libraries in Boston, Robert J. Roberts, as head of physical education at the Boston YMCA, developed a program for hygienic bodybuilding which came to be known throughout the country as the "Roberts Platform" and became the cornerstone of all YMCA physical programs. When Gulick organized the department at the YMCA Training School in Springfield, he took Roberts there with him to teach the activity classes. Shortly, however, the Boston YMCA persuaded Roberts to return there where he continued for another thirty years until his death at the age of seventy-one. He was recognized at the foremost YMCA physical director of his day.

Jay W. Seaver (1855–1915). At the age of twenty-five, Jay Seaver received the B.A. degree at Yale and three years later (1883) was appointed head of the physical education department, which position he held until 1903. As did Sargent before him, he completed the work for the M.D. degree while teaching at Yale. From its first year he was associated with W. G. Anderson at the Chautauqua Summer School, and from 1901 until his death, he served as President of the Company that controlled the school. Active in the young professional association, he was the fifth person to serve as its president and the second to serve as president of the College Gymnasium Directors Society.

William Albin Stecher (1858–1950). Outstanding physician as well as the founder of the modern departments of physical education in the public schools of both Indianapolis and Philadelphia, William Stecher was a foremost leader in the turner societies. From 1907 to 1935 he served as editor of the turner magazine, *Mind and Body.*

21

Physical Activities in the Early Twentieth Century (1900–World War II)

By the turn of the new century the United States was fast becoming industrialized. Only 40 per cent of the population was still rural, by 1927 only 29.9 per cent. Cities were becoming large beyond all dreams of the early years of the century just ended. Now the nation was populated "from sea to shining sea." Families were not as large as in the century just closed, children were spending more time in school, and much social life was taking place outside the home. The telephone, electricity, automobiles, and motion pictures were rapidly transforming the American way of life.

In spite of all efforts to keep out of World War I, the United States was finally drawn into the conflict. When the armistice was signed November 11, 1918, the war ended with the United States emerging as one of the great powers of the world. The third decade of the century came to a close with the stock market crash of October, 1929, which ushered in the great depression of the 1930's. This was the political and social setting within which physical education was coming of age, the many activities related to physical education were changing with the times, and new activities were developing to meet the new needs of a new day.

ACTIVITIES OF THE PHYSICAL EDUCATION PROGRAM

With the new century came a determined effort to bring athletics and dance into the physical education curriculum as an acknowledged part of education. This presented a challenge to the gymnastics devotees to protect their previously unquestioned monopoly of the program. The Battle of the Gymnastics Systems gave way to a new battle of gymnastics versus athletics and dance. Let us look at the status of these activities as the twentieth century got underway.

Dance

With the coming of the new century, dance gradually became solidly intrenched as a part of the physical education program, particularly in the women's departments in the colleges. By the second decade, dance festivals, May fetes, and May pageants built around the dance became popular, but following the War of 1914–18 these gradually gave way to dance interludes (programs of unrelated dances) and these in turn gave way to dance concerts, usually held indoors whereas the earlier forms had been staged outdoors.

The "dance exercises" of the 1850's and 1860's gave way to the "fancy steps" of the 1870's and 1880's. They in turn gave way to the esthetic dancing of the 1890's, which in turn gave way to such other forms of artistic expression as modified ballet and natural dancing, and after their day these bowed off the scene to make way for the so-called "modern dance." Social dance, too, had its vagaries, and various forms have come and gone with the fickleness of the other forms of dance. The more important of these will be discussed in relation to their impact on physical education of this era.

Clog and Tap Dance. A form of dance that became popular in schools in this era was clog, or tap dance as the school-used version of it came to be known. Clogging was a popular stage form in the late nineteenth century; in the 1910's children, on their own, had picked it up and had been clogging in play activities, and physical education teachers introduced this activity into the schools.

Esthetic Dance. Melvin Ballau Gilbert, who had first introduced a modified ballet called "esthetic dancing" into the schools of America through his teaching at the Harvard Summer School of Physical Education, widened his contacts through other teacher-training schools and continued his work until his death in 1910. His students took this form of dancing to the schools with them, but by the close of World War I "Gilbert dancing" as it was frequently called had passed out of the educational picture.

Folk Dance. Although the girls at Smith College since 1897, and at the University of Nebraska since 1898, had been folk dancing, it was Luther Gulick whose unyielding determination and foresight brought folk dancing into the public schools of America. In 1905 he persuaded Elizabeth Burchenal (see p. 393) to leave her position at Teachers College, Columbia University, to join his staff in New York City to organize school athletics and folk dancing for the girls. She immediately went to foreign groups in the City to gather their native dances; but this approach proved inadequate, and she then went to their original sources abroad. Summer after summer she travelled in Europe, collecting folk dances first hand, and immediately began publishing her popular collection of books of the dances of many nations. From 1908 to the 1940's she furnished the profession a total of fifteen books covering the folk dances of all countries of Europe and America.

Early in this period the Playground and Recreation Association of America organized a National Folk Dance Committee to promote folk dancing in the playgrounds of America, and in 1916 the American Folk Dance Society was organized, Miss Burchenal serving as chairman of both groups. The folk festivals which she staged with thousands of children in Central Park each spring for many years received national as well as local attention, and folk dance for school children became a recognized part of the school's physical education program. Also Miss Burchenal taught folk dance for many years at the Harvard Summer School, passing on her knowledge to teachers who gathered there from all over the country.

The teaching of folk dance has increased through the years until it has become intrenched in the physical education program while other forms of dance have come and gone. Folk dance was the one stable form of dance of this era—stable because it was rooted in the real culture of the people.

Natural Dance. As esthetic dance was coming "full circle" of the period of its popularity, a new form of dance was developing, called by some *natural dancing*, by others *interpretive dancing*, and by still others *interpretative dancing*. It developed from the earlier work of Isadora Duncan (1874–1927), America's first woman dancer of note, who achieved world-wide acclaim. She made her debut at Daly's Theater in New York City at the age of seventeen. Five years later she started a revival of the study of the ancient Greek dance. Although she developed a dance form from the choric dance of the classic Greek theater, she was not interested in reviving Greek dance as such, merely using the Greek form for the expression of emotion. She did, however, adopt the classic form of dress and custom of dancing in bare feet. She tried to bring the dance back to the people and tried to get people to dance for their own pleasure of self-expression.

At Columbia University under Gertrude Colby (1880–1960), there developed a modification of Miss Duncan's work for use in the schools which by the late 1910's and the early 1920's had completely replaced Gilbert's esthetic dance. This new form of dance was characterized by costumes of flowing draperies and bare feet and by its divorce from all ballet forms of techniques substituting much running, skipping, and leaping.

Margaret N. H'Doubler (1889–   ) developed at the University of Wisconsin a form of dance based, no doubt in its beginnings, on this natural dance form. But it was peculiarly her own concept. To her pupils and followers it was merely "the dance" although in her book, *A Manual of Dancing* (1925), she herself labeled it "interpretative dancing." She broke with former techniques and developed fundamentals of dancing as basic teaching forms. Her work won quick acclaim as her pupils presented it throughout the country. By 1926 she had organized the first major in the field of the dance to be offered by any college or university in the United States.

Modern Dance. Following World War I esthetic, interpretive, and natural dance gradually gave way to a new form, which developed from a combination of home and foreign influences. In the United States Ted Shawn (1891–   ) and his wife, Ruth St. Denis (1877–1968), established the Denishawn School of Dance in 1915, and as they toured the world with their pupils from 1922 to 1933 they evolved a form of dance that, merging with dance brought to America in 1930 by Mary Wigman (1886–   ), developed into what for want of a better name to differentiate it from the earlier forms became known as *modern dance*.

Mary Wigman, a leading dance teacher of Germany, was a pupil of Rudolph von Labam (1879–1958), a famous European dance teacher, who was an exponent of "absolute" dance to the extent of discarding all musical accompaniment. Later Miss Wigman accepted the use of percussion instruments and primitive flutes and still later allowed the return of the piano to the dance studio, provided the music was composed for the dance—not the dance for the music. This dance offers no set forms. It requires merely that the movements of the dance express something. Fundamental techniques are concerned not with form as in the ballet, but with putting the body under the control of the dancer.

American students of Miss Wigman and others brought this style of dance to a high stage of development in the United States, modifying the European to suit America's own interpretation. Notably among them, several of whom had been pupils of the Denishawn School, were Martha Graham (1893–), Hanya Holm (1899–), Charles Weidman (1901–), and Doris Humphrey (1895–1958).

As Margaret H'Doubler's form of dance gradually blended into the modern dance form, she and Martha Hill (1900–), both of whom worked in the field of education, the former at the University of Wisconsin and the latter at Bennington College and Columbia University, offered majors in the dance for the preparation of teachers. The major at Wisconsin is still functioning, but at Bennington it lasted only from 1934 to 1942. Gradually other schools developed specialization in the dance through summer courses and finally through regular college majors.

By the close of this era, the old forms of dance had completely vanished, giving way to modern dance.

Social Dance. Although ballroom forms of the dance were still taboo in most schools in the opening years of the new century, young people as well as adults engaged in the activity outside the school in increasing numbers as many churches eased their earlier prohibitions against it. As a craze for new forms of dance broke out just preceding World War I, interest in the standard ballroom forms, the two-step and the waltz, died out. The popular turkey trot led to an epidemic of other animal-named steps such as the bunny bug, the grizzly bear, the camel walk, and the fox trot. Shortly the fashionable ballroom dance leaders of that day, Irene (1893–1969) and Vernon Castle (1886–1918), brought order out of the chaos as their Castle walk, later known as the one-step, proved so popular that it became the cornerstone of all ballroom dancing and has persisted these several decades since. The Castles called their new ballroom dancing *modern dancing,* which they proclaimed in the title of their book of 1916 describing their new dances, a term in use for over a decade before the disciples of an altogether different form of dance popularized it some years later, to which form the term still applies.

Square Dance. Following World War I, after several years of eclipse, square dancing was revived. In widely scattered areas of the South and Midwest, it had never died out where the elders at their "old settlers reunions" still danced the dances of pioneer days and handed them down to their children. As late as the early 1900's, in many communities where there still remained religious objections to the waltz and two-step, this was the only form of social dance known to the young people. But to the rest of the country, square dancing had become but memories of the past until in the early 1920's Henry Ford (1863–1947), the industrialist, financed a revival that grew with the years until it had taken a firm grip on much of the country.

While Henry Ford's efforts of the 1920's and 1930's were directed towards a revival of the dignified New England form of the dance, Lloyd Shaw (1890–), a school superintendent of Colorado Springs, and many others of the South and West brought back the cowboy and southern mountain forms which were in common use in frontier days. Along with this revival came renewed interest in the old-time dances, the polka, schottisch, mazurka, and Varsovienne.

Gymnastics

As the twentieth century opened, gymnastics was the backbone of the physical education program. Sports were beginning to be approved and desired but in most places were only a sideline—not a part of the formal program. A Health-Through-Exercise Movement began after the slump in interest in gymnastics that followed the Delsarte popularity of the past era. By the 1900's many business and professional men had a growing awareness of a personal need for exercise. Without sufficient trained leadership available a host of advertising physical culturists arose to meet this demand. Announcements in the popular magazines of the period from 1899 to 1917 illustrate the point. At the same time women developed an interest in what Gulick so aptly spoke of in 1907 as "society gymnastics." This was a reaction to the Delsarte system and became very popular because of its renewed promise of Catharine Beecher's earlier dream of teaching women how to sit and stand correctly, how to ascend and descend stairs efficiently, and how to perform daily activities effectively. In the latter part of this era some schools still using gymnastics took up forms of exercises, that held the interest of women students, with hoops, balls, and ropes, which were a mixture of ideas from Finland, Denmark, and England.

The YMCA, by 1907, had developed a gymnastic program distinctly its own to meet its interpretation of the needs of American boys and men not reached by the schools. Their program was built around light gymnastics followed by a run, bath, and rub-down. They used very little heavy gymnastics in this program and gradually worked in exercises aimed toward athletic skills.

Up to 1915, 95 per cent of the colleges and universities included gymnastics in the physical education program.

Attacks on Gymnastics. The controversy of the 1890's and the early 1900's as to which system of gymnastics, German or Swedish, was better for America had by 1900 developed into a controversy as to whether either should be used. Gulick dealt gymnastics a setback when he compared the gymnastic-trained man with the athlete. The former he described as a man of overdeveloped muscles, great shoulders and chest, weak legs and heavy carriage; the latter as erect, graceful, and fleet with splendid endurance. These statements made a deep impression, for Gulick was popular with both the professional and lay public. In 1910 Wood of Columbia University advocated a program of exercises built around natural activities, sports, and games, which started a movement for what came to be called *natural gymnastics*. The following year (1911) G. Stanley Hall, the noted psychologist and friend of physical education, in his book *Adolescence* said:

> On the whole, while modern gymnastics have done more for the trunk, shoulders, and arms than for the legs, it is now too selfish and ego-centric, deficient on the side of psychic impulsion, but little subordinated to ethical or intellectual development. . . . Its need is radical revision and coordination of various cults and theories in the light of the latest psycho-physiological science.

But Sargent of Harvard, then near the end of a long and distinguished career in physical education, uttered a word of caution when he said in an address at the 1920 National Physical Education Convention:

> To condemn a thing simply because it is old or to recommend it simply because it is new, is not the best way to advance our cause. Read into physical education everything you can of the slightest value but don't read out of it the most fundamental thing of all—that is all-round *muscular exercise*.

With the general acceptance in the 1920's of the educational philosophy that the schools should educate the child for adjustment to life in general, such emphasis was brought up on the social values of all courses taught that gymnastics, whose chief claim to a place in education was at that time through its physiological values, began to suffer such a decline that by the coming of World War II only 12 per cent of the schools were giving it a place in their physical education programs.

Although many educators in general, as well as some physical educators, charged that gymnastics was too subjective to meet the needs of education and did not carry over into life situations, there still were many who felt that insofar as gymnastics served for body-building in children's growth periods, it did have a place in the schools. These exponents of physical fitness persisted in maintaining some gymnastics in the program. The activity held a firmer place in girls' programs than in boys' programs, no doubt because of boys' more intense interest in sports. The forms of gymnastics in use in this era are discussed in the material that follows. (The effect of the Progressive Education Movement on gymnastics is discussed in Chapter 22.)

German System. The turners were still the most successful agents in promoting German gymnastics in the early 1900's, making their appeal chiefly to the people of German origins. Other Americans did not stay with them long, perhaps because practice to become skillful in their form of gymnastics requires patience, thoroughness, hard work, and continued effort, and the German temperament fits that requirement. Americans of English origin wanted games in place of gymnastics in the physical education program. However, German gymnastics had a popular appeal and were carried on in and out of school, wherever there was a large German population. By 1909 the turners who were practicing German gymnastics numbered 40,000, but this marked the popularity peak, and from then on the numbers participating decreased constantly. Mills College was the first women's college to adopt German gymnastics (1902); Elmira College soon followed; but this system never achieved popularity among American college women as did the Swedish and Danish forms.

Swedish System. Since the Swedish system of gymnastics carried with it the theories of medical and corrective gymnastics, this type of gymnastics increased considerably in importance, largely as a result of the tendency to concern for individual needs. It was taught in practically all college women's departments until Danish gymnastics came in the 1920's to challenge its hold. It was also used largely in the public schools except in the strongholds of German stock. The chief exponent of Swedish gymnastics of this era was Dr. William Skarstrom (1869–1951) who was born in Stockholm, Sweden, and came to America as a young man. After graduation from the Boston Normal School of Gymnastics and subsequently procuring the M.D. degree at Harvard University, he modified the system to meet America's needs as he saw them. He reached large groups of teachers in training through his work at Columbia University and Wellesley College.

Natural Gymnastics. A new term, *natural gymnastics,* arose in the first two decades of the new century from an attempt to formulate a system of gymnastic exercises for class use built on the fundamental skills of occupational, athletic, and dance forms of movements. Wood originated and fostered the movement, and later Dr. Jesse F. Williams (1886–1966) of Columbia University, Clark W. Hetherington then of New York University (who as a student had worked with Dr. Wood at Stanford University), and Rosalind E. Cassidy (1895–), of Mills College, popularized it through their writings and teaching. This form of gymnastics was a return to the theories of Locke and Rousseau of the seventeenth and eighteenth centuries, which stressed recognition of individual differences and sought to measure a child's progress in terms of his own growth. It was also a return to GutsMuths and Jahn whose programs of play, sports, and outings had apparently been forgotten by the overly ardent advocates of German gymnastic exercises and apparatus work. And, too, it was a return to Hitchcock and Sargent of the previous era who had advocated the use of exercises adapted to the needs of the individual.

This new form of gymnastics proposed by Wood, when properly devised, would consist of movements aimed at the acquisition of not only physical strength and endurance but also physical skills which would be useful in play and sports activities and in the ordinary tasks of life. The movements of the exercises would therefore have definite aims to be attained and would not be merely ends in themselves. Also in this new form there was to be no uniformity required of the pupils, such as the old forms required at the teacher's word of command.

Danish Fundamental Gymnastics. The Danish system came to the United States in the 1920's sponsored chiefly by Americans who had studied under Niels Bukh in his school in Ollerup, Denmark. This system retained some of the formalism of the Ling Swedish system, but it substituted rhythmic action for sustained positions and precision. Although it is a strenuous form of exercise it made a greater appeal in the United States to women than to men. It enjoyed great popularity in women's departments in colleges during the 1920's and 1930's.

This system of gymnastics has largely replaced the old German and Swedish forms. Designed for the Folk Arts Schools of rural areas of Denmark, it stresses flexibility to relieve the muscle-bound condition found in the Danish youth. In the late 1920's Helen McKinstry (1878–1949), then Head of the Central School of Physical Education and later President of Russell Sage College, was the representative in America of Niels Bukh, its chief exponent. She promoted several summer sessions for American teachers who went to Ollerup to take instruction from Bukh. These teachers brought back this activity to the school and college programs. There was much enthusiasm for this form of gymnastics, and it was used widely in girls' and women's programs.

Corrective or Individual Gymnastics. Interest in medical gymnastics brought to this country by the Swedish experts of the 1880's and 1890's broadened into a highly specialized program of exercises, stemming from the Swedish System, which could be readily adapted to the school programs for correction of postural and other defects. As schools employed trained personnel for this work, special classes developed in the school programs for the benefit of pupils needing this special attention. For this, as in much of physical education, the colleges led with development, and adoption by the lower schools followed. A survey made by the United States Office of Education revealed that by 1931, out of 460 schools investigated 50 per cent were offering this work. A shortage of teachers trained in this specialized activity, however, was a factor in its lack of support, and there was also a lack of understanding of its values by parents and educators in general.

Sports

Wherever sports were given a recognized place in the departmental offerings for boys and men, the department was usually spoken of as a department of physical education *and* athletics. Even now this distinction holds in many schools, although women never have accepted this dual terminology. It was 1910 before sports were generally accepted by school authorities as a legitimate part of the school program although some physical educators themselves recognized their value in the education program and had been quietly including them in their class-hour activities for some time previous to this date. As part of the school curriculum, sports developed more rapidly in the colleges than in the lower schools.

New sports activities that came into the program in this era were hiking and other such informal activities, usually supported by outing clubs which had their birth at Dartmouth College in 1910, shuffleboard introduced in Florida in 1913, and speedball created in 1921 by Elmer D. Mitchell (1889–   ) of the University of Michigan. Judging by sales of sports equipment during this period, the ten fastest growing sports were in this order: softball, badminton, basketball, squash, football, table tennis, lawn tennis, handball, paddle tennis, and horseshoe pitching.

In this era came the first radio broadcasts of running accounts of important games, which caused much discussion "pro and con." Time proved that the broadcasts did hurt attendance as predicted but not enough to discontinue baseball broadcasts.

Baseball. At the opening of the century, professional teams began to overshadow the amateurs and claim sectional loyalties that kept the populace in a frenzy of excitement when big league pennants were being won. In 1903 the National and the American Baseball Leagues met for the first time in what they called the World Series games. As an outgrowth of these games, a year later the two leagues adopted joint rules. In the first decade of the century, before safety measures were put into effect, baseball suffered many casualties. In 1908 alone forty-two players died from injuries received on the diamond, and in 1909, thirty.

Basketball. After the turn of the century the game of basketball entered into a period of rapid growth throughout the country. Whereas in many sections of the country, notably in the Middle West and on the West Coast, girls had taken to the game first, boys and men now took it up in rapidly increasing numbers. By the close of the era, it was played all over the United States and in many foreign countries as well. Although a few professional basketball groups were first formed in 1898, it was not until after World War I that the professional game became popular. The famous Harlem Globetrotters—an all-Negro team—was organized in 1927.

As increasing numbers of unusually tall players took up the game, gaining great advantages for their teams, the center jump after each basket was eliminated and the team scored upon was given the ball (1937), in a measure neutralizing the advantage of the tall player.

Basketball for Women. The Women's Basket Ball Rules Committee, established in 1899, put out its first printed official guide in 1901. It was entitled *Line Basket Ball or Basket Ball for Women* and was published as Volume 12 of the Athletic Library Series put out by the American Sports Publishing Company. It sold for ten cents a copy and carried the name of Senda Berenson as editor. This first official guide carried articles by Theodore Hough, a well-known physiologist of the Massachusetts Institute of Technology, on the physiological effects of basketball; Luther Gulick, on the psychological effects; and Senda Berenson on the significance of the game for girls.

The 1901 rules called for five to ten players on a team. The second issue of the rules was published in 1905–1906 by A. S. Barnes and Company, the start of many years of cooperation between this publishing firm and the women's committee, and in this issue the name Line Basket Ball was dropped. Miss Berenson remained editor of the rules until 1917. By this time Julie Esbee Sullivan of Teachers College, Columbia University, was chairman of the Executive Committee on Basket Ball, and Elizabeth Burchenal, then also of Columbia University, had joined the committee to begin several years of work with this group. The second edition carried many photographs of girls' teams, among them teams at the University of Minnesota, a high school in Nome, Alaska, a YWCA in Missouri, a Turnverein group in Leadville, Colorado, and a business club group in Denver, showing the wide-spread and diverse groups that had taken up the game.

Cricket. Although cricket had all but died out in the East, it was played by the women at Wellesley College throughout the first decade of the new century. At the same time it had spread to San Francisco, and in the eary 1920's Sir C. Aubrey Smith, the famous British movie actor of that period, introduced the game to the Los Angeles area where it has flourished ever since, UCLA taking up the game in 1933.

Field Hockey. Although there is record that field hockey was played in America as early as 1897 (by men at the Springfield YMCA School), it was apparently a short-lived effort, for never have American men taken to this sport. It did come as a sport for women, however, when an English woman, Constance Applebee (1871–), came to the United States in the summer of 1901 to attend the Harvard Summer School of Physical Education and there demonstrated the game as played by her English sisters. Immediately Vassar College, followed by other leading women's colleges, adopted the sport and from them it spread rapidly to all parts of the country. It was many years, however, before high school girls played the game except in the large Eastern cities.

Football. With the coming of a new century, football began taking on importance as a sport for high school boys and college men. In the college world it gradually grew into big business, still remaining a rough game. In the 1905 season there were nineteen deaths and two hundred serious injuries on the gridiron. In the 1909 season fourteen players were killed before November first. In 1908 the California colleges abolished football, substituting rugby, and reported a marked drop in injuries to athletes. President Roosevelt's outspoken criticism of the roughness of the game led the 1906 Rules Committee to eliminate hurdling and mass formations, such as the flying wedge, and to initiate and legalize the forward pass, though it was 1913 before the forward pass was generally used.

A modification of the game, touch football, now became popular in boy's and men's intramural programs.

The 1930's brought still another modification of the game, six-man football, that shortly came into wide-spread use in high schools of small towns. Stephen Epler (1909–), then physical director and coach at the high school in Chester, Nebraska, created the new form of game and first presented it to the public in a master's thesis in the field of education at the University of Nebraska in the summer of 1934. The *Lincoln Sunday Journal and Star* published the dissertation September 2, 1934, bringing the proposed new form of the game to the attention of the public. The first match game was played October 3, 1934, in a contest between the high schools of Chester and Hebron, Nebraska, in Hebron. This immediately opened the game to the thousands of small high schools of the nation that could not produce a regulation-size team nor the regulation-size field. With a six-man team and an 80- by 40-yard field and several changes in the rules, this game required less expensive equipment and reduced the danger of injuries. The six-man game took the small high schools of the country by storm, and most high schools of America are small schools; within two years, 1,233 schools were playing this form of the game. (Epler later received from the American Academy of Physical Education a citation for this creative service to the profession.)

With improved know-how and equipment for outdoor lighting, night football, like night baseball, took on importance in this era, with the first night football games coming in 1928. The coming of night games brought greatly increased gate receipts to high schools and small colleges in particular. Perhaps the most spectacular pageantry of all night games of that time occurred at Haskell Indian Institute in Lawrence, Kansas, where as the night game was about to begin, all lights went off and a spot light picked up an Indian Chief in full war regalia silhouetted against the night sky from his pedestal on top of the high entrance arch. From the darkness of the stands below came the spine-tingling Indian war cry of the Haskell Indian students. Then the flood lights were turned on the gridiron, and the contesting teams dashed onto the field.

Golf. Interest in golf now spread country-wide. Even small towns constructed golf courses, at first all privately owned. In the early 1900's, the United States became a formidable rival of Great Britain in international matches. An American women's golf team captured the English women's championship tournament in Scotland in 1905. In the early years, due to the cost of the links, the game was confined largely to the members of private clubs. When national, state, and municipal authorities began to promote recreation and play, this movement resulted in securing the necessary land for golf courses, and placing the game at the disposal of the general public.

By 1910 there were twenty-four public golf courses in the United States, and by 1940, seven hundred, in addition to many private clubs. The United States Golf Association by then listed 1,124 clubs with a membership of over two million. The 1930's brought a craze for midget golf and golf-driving ranges, which proved a great boom to schools wishing to teach golfing skills but without facilities. Sports equipment firms reported sales of golf equipment of twenty-nine million dollars, in contrast to twelve-million-dollar sales of the 1920's. Between 1936 and 1940, the WPA constructed 207 municipal golf courses in the United States.

Softball. The intense interest in baseball brought about modifications to catch and hold the interest of the great mass of unskilled players for their own participation. In 1907 playground ball was developed in the Chicago South Park playgrounds. In 1923 rules for this game were standardized by the National Recreation Association, and by 1930 the game had evolved into the present game of softball. The Amateur Softball Association was organized in 1932. In 1934 a Rules Committee made up of NRA, YMCA, NCAA, and APEA representatives drew up official rules. The game became tremendously popular in industry, in intramural programs in the schools and small towns, and with all ages and both sexes.

Swimming. Syracuse, New York in 1900, Kansas City in 1901, and Pittsburgh in 1903 joined the ranks of cities with municipal swimming pools. Up to 1904, however, only a few offered instruction in swimming. In 1903 Chicago added to its older pools the new McKinley Natatorium, then the largest in America—50 by 300 feet.

The first bacteriological studies of swimming pool water were made in 1909. These brought about the early organization of the American Association of Hygiene and Baths in 1912, which established standards for pools (1915). The first indoor pool located above basement level (sixth floor) was at the 23rd Street Branch of the New York City YMCA. It was in this pool that the first Red Cross life-saving courses were given in 1910 and where the first tests were given in 1914.

By 1931, 25 per cent of all high schools and 1.2 per cent of elementary schools in cities of over 100,000 population had their own swimming pools. Cities of population from 30,000 to 100,000 had pools in 23.9 per cent of high schools and 1 per cent of elementary schools; towns of 10,000 to 30,000 population had pools in 14.8 per cent of their high schools; and cities of population below 10,000 had no school pools. By 1937 there were 700 YMCA's in the United States that had swimming pools with 98 per cent of them built since 1900 and the other 2 per cent built between 1885 and 1900 and still in use in 1937. By 1940 there were in the United States 8,000 pools, half of them outdoor and half indoor with 50 per cent of them built since 1925. Building came to a standstill in most of the 1930's because of the depression.

Track and Field. Track and field activities came into renewed popularity after World War I. In the early 1920's difficulties developed between the National Collegiate Athletic Association and the Amateur Athletic Union over the selection of the United States track and field athletes for the Olympic games. This brought about the establishment of the National Amateur Athletic Federation (see p. 263) which forced better representation of college organizations and of the Army and Navy.

The first national NCAA track and field championship competition was held in 1921. After that many famous Relays, such as the Drake, Kansas, Penn, and West Coast Relays, were introduced. From 1922 on, indoor meets have been popular.

Volleyball. The United States Volleyball Association was formed in 1928. The game was played almost exclusively before World War I in the YMCA's and YWCA's, but, after its introduction into the recreation programs of the armed services by the YMCA physical directors during World War I, it spread rapidly in both school and nonschool groups.

Women's Sports. Although the students of the leading women's colleges had long enjoyed a variety of sports, women in coeducational colleges also now found doors opening to sports participation. It was the coming of basketball that brought about this change. For the average high school girl, doors opened considerably later, probably because the few trained teachers went to college positions. Public schools were slow in awakening to the need of trained teachers for this work. As the women of the coeducational colleges were catching up with their sisters of the women's colleges, the latter were forging ahead with new sports. In 1901 Wellesley College started lacrosse, and Vassar, field hockey. In 1907 Smith played the first women's volleyball, and Bryn Mawr, cricket, water polo, and soccer. After World War I, in the 1920's, swimming for women took on new dimensions in colleges when water pageants and water ballets were introduced, which ultimately led to synchronized swimming.

Other Sports. The American Bowling Congress held its first championship competition in 1901. Badminton, a sport popular in Canada, did not mature in the United States until in the 1930's, when the sixty-five badminton clubs then in existence organized the American Badminton Association. Practically all the playing of this period was confined to the large Eastern cities and Detroit, Chicago, and Los Angeles. It was Douglas Fairbanks, Sr. (1883–1939), the famous moving picture star, who popularized the game in California. By 1939 Southern California had 10,000 courts, the Detroit area boasted 50,000 players, and New York State around 70,000 players, and 400 clubs had joined the Association. Also in that year the first international tournament was held with a Dane winning the men's title and a Canadian the women's title.

Handball came into popularity during the depression of the 1930's when the Works Progress Administration built 1,365 handball courts in various parts of the country, most of them of the one-wall type.

Paddle tennis also became popular in the 1930's. The National Recreation Association reported that by 1939 there were an estimated 64,000 players using the ninety-two courts at Manhattan Beach alone. The American Paddle Tennis Association was born in 1934.

In 1930 Sonja Henie (1913–   ), the famous skating star, made her debut in the United States, starting a wave of enthusiasm for ice skating. The sport had existed for years in the northern climates, but now the development of artificial-ice rinks brought it to all parts of the country all seasons of the year. Ice hockey, too, now came into prominence, and before long professional ice hockey leagues were established. The National Hockey League was organized in 1917. (The Canadians, who created the game, had been playing since 1860 and had established their League in 1890.)

After World War I skiing became a popular sport. Austrian skiers came to America as instructors, and ski trails and tows were built and ski patrols organized. According to Tunis it was estimated, in 1936, that there were 60,000 skiers in the White Mountain area alone, 88,000 in the Utah forests, 44,000 in Oregon, 110,000 in Colorado, 106,000 in Washington, and 639,000 in California. The year 1931 brought the first ski train, or snow train as it was then called. This was organized by the Appalachian Club of Boston. By the winter of 1939 ski trains running in as many as ten sections were leaving New York City on Saturdays and Sunday mornings for the Adirondacks and White Mountains. The three lone ski clubs of 1904 grew to 100 by 1930, and in 1936 the United States entered its first ski team in the Olympics.

Soccer became popular after World War I among college women and in universities with large foreign men-student enrollments. American men did not take to this game in this era.

With the know-how of the early 1920's for building all-weather courts, tennis became increasingly popular, but it was the climate conducive to year-round play that produced the better players in large numbers. By the end of the 1930's there were thousands of tennis courts in the country, of all kinds: dirt, clay, grass, wooden, asphalt, and newer compositions of many kinds.

SPORTS ORGANIZATIONS

With the coming of the new century, athletics took on such prominence in both school and national life that many organizations came into existence for their promotion and control. Some of these were already under way in the 1890's, and now new ones came into existence. The most important of these new ones (listed in the order of their founding) are discussed in the material that follows.

Public School Athletic League of New York City

In 1903 Gulick, then Head of Physical Education of the schools of Greater New York City, set up the Public School Athletic League. Although it was not a part of the school program it was sponsored by the Board of Education and also by the President of the College of the City of New York and by the Secretary of the Amateur Athletic Union. Wealthy citizens gave it financial support so that the school budget did not have to carry it. None but boys of good standing in their schools could enter the activities, and an effort was made to interest all boys, particularly those of only average ability. Early in its program the organization developed an Athletic Badge Test, and McKenzie, who had considerable skill as a sculptor, designed the first trophies.

In 1905, a Girls' Branch of the League was organized by Elizabeth Burchenal with the help of prominent women in New York City. Miss Burchenal became its first secretary and was the official instructor of folk dance and athletics. From the very start, the League refused to sponsor interschool contests. It started as did the boy's organization as a volunteer group outside the school program. However the Board of Education acknowledged it as the arbiter for all girls' athletics in the schools. In 1909, when Miss Burchenal was appointed Inspector of Girls' Athletics for the public schools of New York City, this organization became a branch of her department. Other cities that supported highly successful athletic leagues during this period were Philadelphia and Baltimore.

National Collegiate Athletic Association

Because of the great number of injuries and brutality that had developed in the game of football, serious criticism arose from many quarters at the opening of the new century. Many universities, including Stanford and Columbia, and several colleges abandoned the sport altogether. Doctors, educators, and ministers, even the President of the United States, spoke and wrote against it. In 1905 a convention of delegates from twenty-eight leading colleges, called together by the Chancellor of New York University, formed the United States Intercollegiate Athletic Association. This body was empowered to make rules and regulations governing all major sports played by colleges. At the 1916 meeting the name was changed to the National Collegiate Athletic Association, football rules were revised so that play became more open, and penalties for violation of regulations were provided. Later the organization undertook to develop rules of other sports and to control the eligibility of the players.

In 1932 it added boxing to its sports coverage, and in 1933, gymnastics, tennis, and cross country; in that same year it undertook to curb excesses in the subsidization of athletes and to improve methods of their recruitment. The first national basketball invitational tournament for colleges was held in Madison Square Garden in New York City in 1938. The following year the NCAA added basketball to its coverage and staged its own basketball championship tournament in Madison Square Garden. In 1940 it added golf, and in 1941, fencing.

Athletic Research Society

In 1907 a group of men leaders in the profession, led by Luther Gulick, Clark Hetherington, Joseph Raycroft, and Dudley Sargent, founded the Athletic Society for the improvement of physical education, recreation, and athletics in their interrelationships. In 1910 they took up the serious problem of professionalism in athletics and attacked the problem of control of amateur sports. In 1915 they set up a special committee to investigate the development of intramural sports. Following that they tackled other serious problems, making resolutions and recommendations to the proper authorities, many of which brought about improvements in sports. Following Sargent's death in 1924, this Society faded away, but it had served a good purpose and had been a powerful influence for good in athletics, particularly in bringing them under the control of physical educators in the schools.

Outing Clubs

Although many outing clubs flourished temporarily in colleges in the 1880's and 1890's, none achieved permanence. The first to claim that honor was the Dartmouth Outing Club, organized in 1910. In 1922 Smith College organized the first women's outing club to endure. From then on these clubs became popular in many colleges. They sponsored all forms of outdoor activities in all seasons of the year, many maintaining clubhouses. Also community recreation departments, YMCA's, YWCA's, and like groups organized outing clubs, some specializing in bicycling (as with the American Youth Hostel Association that came into prominence in America in the 1930's) and some in skating, skiing, and other activities.

American Olympic Association

The American Olympic Committee was created in 1911 to take charge of the participation of American athletes in the Olympic games of 1912. In 1921 it developed into a permanent organization called the American Olympic Association, with its membership made up of a federation of independent associations. It then set up the present U.S. Olympic Committee to control the U.S. Olympic teams.

Athletic Conference of American College Women

Under the sponsorship of Blanche M. Trilling (1876–1964), Director of Physical Education for Women, this organization was born at the University of Wisconsin in 1917. Women student delegates from twenty-three colleges and universities met there for a conference to discuss the problems of athletics of college women. From the beginning this organization took a stand against varsity intercollegiate athletics for women, promoting instead intramural programs for all. Throughout this period the organization held triennial conferences starting with the conference at the University of Indiana in 1921.

In 1933 the organization changed its name to the Athletic Federation of College Women (AFCW) and in its platform reaffirmed its aim to uphold the Standard of Athletics for Girls and Women as set forth by the National Section for Girls and Women's Sports.

National Section on Women's Athletics

The original Women's Basketball Rules Committee, set up under APEA in 1899, was reorganized and enlarged in 1905 under President Gulick into a National Women's Basketball Committee to set standards as well as to make rules. Senda Berenson served as editor of the reorganized committee from 1905 to 1917. Gradually the women of the profession became involved in rules for other sports and felt the need to expand into something more than a basketball group. Finally in 1917 under APEA President William H. Burdick (1871–1935), the National Committee on Women's Sports was formed to establish standards and official rules for athletics for girls and women. Elizabeth Burchenal was appointed chairman of the new committee, which kept the original basketball committee as one of two subcommittees, field hockey being the second one. A year later two more subcommittees were added—track and field and swimming. Also in 1917 the American Sports Publishing Company was given the contract to publish all women's sports rules for this committee. In 1927 the committee was advanced to the status of a section within the larger APEA, known as the Women's Athletic Section, and in 1931 its title was changed to National Section on Women's Athletics. For the next twenty years it was familiarly known as the NSWA of APEA.

National Federation of High School Athletic Associations

As early as 1896 several high schools in Wisconsin that sponsored boys' athletic associations came together and organized a state athletic association. It was several years before the idea caught on in other states, but a rush to follow suit finally started in 1903 with Indiana. From then on many states organized as follows: Iowa, Montana and Rhode Island, 1904; Illinois and South Dakota, 1905; Ohio, 1906; Nebraska, Oklahoma, and Utah, 1910; Kansas, Pennsylvania, and South Carolina, 1913; California and Oregon, 1914; Kentucky, 1917; and New Jersey, 1918. By then much dissatisfaction had arisen over contests being sponsored for high school boys by various colleges and universities and by some sports clubs and promoters without attention to eligibility rules and high school regulations, and in 1920 representatives of the state groups in Iowa, Indiana, Michigan, and Wisconsin met in Chicago and organized the Middle West Federation of High School Athletic Associations. Two years later eleven other states joined the Middle West group and established the National Federation, whose one aim was to work for the common interest in control and direction of sports for all high school boys.

One of the Federation's earliest acts was to prohibit interstate competition at the high school level other than as sanctioned by itself. By 1928 forty-two states had joined and were sponsoring their own state tournaments, as follows: basketball by all 42 states, track by 33, football by 33, baseball by 30, tennis by 20, swimming by 14, soccer by 8, wrestling by 6, volleyball by 4, and golf and skating each by 3. The work of the Federation grew, and by 1940 it was necessary to establish a national office with a full-time paid executive staff.

National Amateur Athletic Federation

Shortly after World War I, great dissatisfaction developed among parents, educators, playground leaders, youth-group leaders, and laymen in general over the trend of athletics in the United States, which were under a leadership that seemed to have no guiding principles other than to produce winning teams at any cost. National leaders in several organizations concerned with athletics came together to discuss these problems. The Secretaries of the United States War and Navy Departments, both deeply interested in the right type of athletic programs for servicemen, joined in the informal discussions. Out of this meeting developed the NAAF in 1922 with Col. Henry Breckinridge (1886–1960), a New York City attorney who was President of U.S. Navy League, as President and Mrs. Herbert Hoover (1878–1944), whose husband was at the time United States Secretary of Commerce and who, herself, was President of the Girl Scouts of America, as one Vice President and Dr. George J. Fisher (1871–1960), Executive Director of the Boy Scouts of America, as the other Vice President. Its stated aim was "to create and maintain in the United States a permanent organization representative of amateur athletics and organizations devoted thereto; to establish and maintain the highest ideals of amateur sport; to promote the development of physical education; to encourage the standardization of rules of all amateur athletic games and competitions, and to encourage the participation of men of this country in the International Olympic games." All leading organizations in the United States interested in sane sports for American youth joined the Federation which lasted until 1930. In that year it dissolved, having accomplished its main purpose—to raise the standards of American sports and to break the hold of certain sports promoters who had seized substantial control of American sports and American athletes.

Many leaders of physical education were members of the first Board of Governors of this important organization: J. H. McCurdy, Dudley Reed (1878–1955), and William Burdick, representing APEA; Blanche Trilling, representing the National Committee of Women's Sports; H. F. Kallenberg and John Brown, Jr. (1880–1961), representing the YMCA's; William A. Stecher, representing the NAGU; J. E. Raycroft and Amos Alonzo

Stagg, representing the NCAA; and George Fisher, representing the Boy Scouts of America.

Women's Division of the NAAF

In April, 1923, Mrs. Herbert Hoover called a meeting in Washington attended by over 200 women who were interested in the promotion of sports for girls and women, and they set up a Women's Division within the newly organized NAAF. Mrs. Hoover was elected Chairman of the Board, which position she gave up in 1928, when her husband became President of the United States. The groundwork of the organization was laid by the following women physical educators who were elected to membership on the Executive Committee: Helen McKinstry of the Central School of Physical Education; Dr. J. Anna Norris (1874–1958) of the University of Minnesota; Ethel Perrin, then Executive Secretary of the American Child Health Association; Blanche Trilling, of the University of Wisconsin; and Agnes R. Wayman (1880–1968) of Barnard College. Within five months the new organization had 250 members made up of institutions, organizations, and individuals. At its first annual conference held at the University of Chicago in April, 1924, the organization adopted a platform for the formation of sane and wholesome athletics for girls and women of the United States, and they worked to get acceptance of this platform in schools, in industry, in fact, in all segments of life promoting sports for girls and women. Miss Perrin served as the first Chairman of the Executive Committee, and Dr. Norris served as Chairman of the Resolutions Committee which drew up the first NAAF standards for the conduct of sports for girls and women.

At its seventh annual meeting, held in Detroit in April, 1931, it revised its platform and took a determined stand against women's participation in the approaching Olympics and in state tournaments for girls. (For a statement on the platform see p. 276.) At this time the National Board of the YWCA, the National Association for Physical Education of College Women, the Women's Athletic Section of APEA, and the Athletic Conference of American College Women joined the Women's Division to procure abandonment of all state basketball tournaments for girls. By 1938 it had 768 organization members.

Feeling as did the Men's Division of the NAAF before it, that now its purpose had been accomplished and other existing organizations could carry on, it merged its interest in 1940 in the National Section on Women's Athletics of AAHPER. In its sixteen years of battling for correct standards of sports for American women it had distributed over $106,000 donated by individuals, foundations, and trusts for their work and had spent an additional $12,000 for three years in maintenance of a Field Secretary to travel to trouble spots to help correct unfavorable conditions in women's sports. Whereas the National Section on Women's Athletics had been mainly a rules- and policy-making body, the Women's Division had set itself up as a standard-maker and a liaison group between physical educators and the lay public. Now the NSWA took over these added functions.

State Leagues of High School Girls' Athletic Associations

In the early 1920's the first State League of Girls' Athletic Associations was established in Illinois. Its purpose was to promote programs of athletics for all girls to offset the undesirable program of interschool athletics maintained in many schools for the highly-skilled few. Shortly after this leagues were set up in Colorado and Nebraska. These three state leagues advised local girls' athletic associations in high schools and helped them set up intramural programs for all girls. They established state point systems leading to local and state awards for athletic participation and achievement. By the late 1930's there were eight states supporting state leagues for girls' athletics: Illinois, Colorado, Nebraska, Alabama, North Carolina, Kansas, Iowa, and Oklahoma, founded in the order listed. Illinois, the originator of the league idea, has the most effective organization, maintaining an executive secretary and a central office in Chicago and sponsoring summer camps for its member groups. The Alabama and Oklahoma Leagues were closely related to their state departments of education, the others coordinated with the boys' state leagues of their states.

These state organizations were opposed to interscholastic competition for girls and worked instead for large-scale participation of girls in their home-school intramural programs. The state organization assisted local groups with program plans, advised on local GAA affairs, and offered state awards for unusual achievement in physical education and sports activities.

In spite of these state leagues, all school-sponsored, there were ten states in 1928 supporting state basketball tournaments for high school girls, but most of these were outside school jurisdiction and were controlled and promoted by men. In the Ohio tournament that year, there were 5,500 high schools girls entered; in Texas, 4,000 girls; and in Oklahoma, 2,000.

SPORTS COMPETITION

The twentieth century brought great increase in sports, both amateur and professional, promoted in all segments of national life through the schools, churches, industry, athletic clubs, sports associations, and all manner of such new organizations as the Boy Scouts and summer camps that were fostering activities for youth. Perhaps the greatest promoter of all of this period was the Armed Services which during World War I staged a tremendous recreational sports program with the leading men physical educators of the country working both at home with the soldiers in the Army Training Camps and in the European Theater of War with the American Expeditionary Forces.

With the great increase in professional sports, there arose a tendency among many amateur sports groups to permit amateur sports gradually to take on characteristics of professionalism. This brought about a conflict between educators in general, physical educators, and true amateur sportsmen (of whom there were many in the early decades of the century) on the one side, and on the other those who, claiming to be promoting amateur sports, were pushing athletes to win at any cost, searching for loop holes in amateur sports rules to allow a semblance of professionalism, and winking at undercover subsidization and recruitment of athletes. This brought about a soul-searching that precipitated long-drawn-out argument as to the nature of amateur as differentiated from professional sports.

From the opening of the century the Athletic Research Society, made up of leading men physical educators of the day, had sensed the rising tide of mockery of the word "amateur" in the field of athletics for college men and had waged battle against it. But with the demise of that group in the 1920's there arose an ever-increasing cause for alarm as the debasement of amateur sports spread into other sports fields beyond the college world. This alarm aroused public concern, and popular writers, ministers, educators, and sports writers, as well as physical educators and sportsmen themselves, began to raise questions: What is an amateur? What is sportsmanship?

Whereas in earlier years physical education conventions were concerned largely with arguments over the relative merits of German and Swedish gymnastics and later with discussions as to whether gymnastics should have a place at all in the school curriculum, following World War I this third great concern arose, and programs were largely given over to discussions seeking answers to those questions.

Well-known educators and writers, sportsmen and even ministers were featured speakers at many of the professional conventions, talking on these questions. Frequent arguments now arose over the English type of amateur sport of that day as representing the true amateur spirit, as compared with the American type with its ever-growing interest in championships and winning teams. A check of convention programs of this period of the American Physical Education Association and of its various districts, and of popular magazines of the day and books of this period on sports, will reveal the frequency of this topic, and a review of the articles and speeches will show the deep public as well as professional concern over keeping amateur sports in America truly amateur.

John Tunis, an amateur U.S. tennis champion of the 1920's later turned sportswriter, in his book *$port$: Heroics, and Hysterics* (see References) defined an amateur sportsman as one who "knows the thrill of real sport, of playing, not for championships, for titles, for cash, for publicity, for medals, for applause, but simply for the love of playing." Charles W. Kennedy (see References), a professor at Princeton University, defined a sportsman as:

> . . . one who loves the game for its own sake; who has a scrupulous regard for the rules of fair play and strives under those rules to pit his best against the best of an opponent whom he respects; who admires excellence in a game for its own sake and who pays an instinctive tribute of respect to excellence whether it be his own or that of an opponent; who in the stress of competition strives to the uttermost without descent to breach of rule or vindictive spirit; who hates a quitter, an alibi, or a boast; who in the course of a game preserves courage in the face of odds, and dignity, self-respect and good will in the presence of defeat; who wishes an amateur game to be played by amateurs and not by masquerading professionals; [and who acknowledges] that in the life of a great democracy he is the better man who can prove it.

With the coming of the depression of the Thirties and its accompanying curtailment of sports activities, these concerns gave way to that of survival of any programs at all as physical education, along with other subjects in the school curriculum, was attacked as merely a frill in education. The various types of sports competition engaged in during this period are discussed in the material that follows.

Intramural Competition

The intramural form of athletics preceded the intercollegiate and interscholastic forms by many years. Indeed for almost the entire nineteenth century it was the only form of sports competition for boys and men except in a few rare cases. But when extramural competition developed into a widespread movement near the end of the century, it grew to such proportions and to the neglect of all but varsity prospects that educators found it necessary to give special thought to the organization of intramurals for the mass of college men and school boys.

In Lower Schools. The earliest record of organized intramurals on a large scale in a public school system seems to be that of the Grammar School Athletic League of Philadelphia, organized in 1900 just as the nineteenth century was coming to a close. Another early record of intramurals for elementary school children is that of the first New York City Public School field day specifically put on for elementary school children by C. Ward Crampton, then head of physical training and athletics of the High School of Commerce and held in the spring of 1904 on South Field at Columbia University. Some thirty schools sent entries, and the meet was so great a success that it led to the birth of the Public School Athletic League of New York City, which was discussed earlier in this chapter.

After starting with a spectator type of program that resulted in poor responses from the parents and public, the New York City League changed its emphasis to the educational aspects of sports. Team affiliations grew up around the four classes in high school and the home rooms at the lower grade levels. The intramural idea, however, was slow to catch on in the lower schools of the country before World War I, no doubt in general because of lack of professionally trained teachers.

In 1915 the Athletic Research Society set up a committee to aid in the development of intramural sports in the schools, and by 1925 the intramural idea had filtered down into the high schools. This form of competition soon became quite popular, particularly in the large high schools where participation in the extramural program reached but a small group of students. Shortly after World War I, a form of competition developed in rural schools called Play Days, in which the children from several schools were brought together and assigned to impromptu teams, played with and against each other with no team representing any one school. This form of competition became popular in several states on a county basis and furnished much fun for hundreds of children who attended schools too small to support sports teams on their own.

In Colleges. The early intramural programs in colleges were built around class, club, and fraternity groupings. During World War I, colleges based their program on units within the Student Army Training Corps (SATC) located on the various campuses. In 1912 at the University of Chicago and in 1915 at both Michigan and Ohio State, a physical education staff member was appointed specifically to organize and administer a sports program for the many, apart from the program offered for the skilled few. According to the Athletic Research Society, by 1916, 114 colleges had such programs. The University of Michigan was the first to grant the title, Director of Intramurals; it went to Floyd Rowe (1884–1960), who later was to become Michigan's first State Director of Physical Education. In 1919 E. D. Mitchell succeeded to that position, and in 1924 he published *Intramural Athletics*, the first book on the subject. In 1928 the University of Michigan opened its Intramural Sports Building, a building devoted exclusively to these activities—the first such specialized building in the United States.

Interscholastic Competition

The story of interschool competition of the first decade of the twentieth century, in the great majority of schools, is largely the same as the story of intercollegiate competition of the late nineteenth century, namely a story of boys organizing and administering their sports for themselves, with help from interested townspeople rather than from the schools. It took the schools at least a decade into the new century to awaken to this responsibility. Once the schools responded, the story is largely that of the State High School Athletic Associations.

Intercollegiate Competition

For the earlier years of the twentieth century, football dominated intercollegiate sports, to such an extent that the story of these activities is largely the story of football. This era brought highly paid coaches, training tables, large expenditures of money for sports, and huge gate receipts undreamed of in the nineteenth century. The all-too-common attitude of the college authorities toward the student athletic sports was that they were a necessary evil, to be tolerated and at times restricted.

Quarrels such as had occurred in the 1890's over football now increased between leading schools. Many schools broke off athletic relationship, not without cause. Hetherington's *Biography* cites typical situations of this first decade of the new century when athletes were paid cash "behind the door." Many coaches were men of no educational background whatsoever, and supposedly school teams were made up of townspeople and faculty members. He reported one college game in the Middle West where seven members of the team were the town blacksmith, a lawyer, a livery man, and four railroad employees.

Theodore Roosevelt during his presidency of the United States (1901–09) remarked that "when money comes in at the gate, sport flies out the window," and called a White House Conference of football leaders and coaches in the hopes of bringing some order out of the chaos. But even that helped for but a short time. Sargent began a campaign to abolish gate receipts in the hope of eliminating much of the evil, but to no avail. No school would even try giving up gate receipts. Soon quarrels were rampant again. In 1912 and again in 1916 Harvard and Princeton Universities severed athletic relations. Many other schools were engaged in similar quarrels and breaks, but the news managed to be kept under cover. By 1914 when college sports had taken on the "win at all costs" aspect, a vocal segment among the citizenry began to speak out, comparing the English objectives of sports with our American aims built on nothing less than victory. By 1920 the condition was under such fire that the Carnegie Foundation for the Advancement of Teaching financed a survey of the situation in hopes that the facts could be ascertained and the situation improved. Their findings were published in 1929 in a bulletin entitled *American College Athletics,* and for a while it brought some improvement.

In 1928 one single contest at the Yale bowl drew a crowd of 80,000 with special trains running from several cities carrying the private cars of the affluent as well as long strings of coaches for the common herd. In that same year a sportsman journalist of the era voiced the disgust of a large segment of the citizenry over the decay of athletics when he wrote of "The Great Sports Myth"—the myth that football players are heroes of high moral qualities, "purified and made holy by their devotion to intercollegiate sports." He claimed that intercollegiate and international sports do not produce nobility of character and strengthen the bonds between nations and individuals, but produce instead "broken ankles, bad feeling, cursing, and revelry in the sanctity of dressing rooms; coarse accusations and cheap humor in the publications of a great university."

By 1930 attendance at college football games had reached the ten million mark, and the new decade ushered in the first radio broadcasts of intercollegiate games. But once more subsidization of athletes and methods of recruiting were causing serious quarrels between colleges.

Post-season bowl games had their birth in 1902, when Stanford University played the University of Michigan in Pasadena's Rose Bowl. (Today's Rose Bowl was not built until 1923.) But the idea did not catch on as an annual event until 1915, when Washington State, that year's Pacific Coast Conference champion, invited Brown University to play off a regional championship in the Pasadena bowl. This game, played January 1, 1916, started the annual event. In 1933 the Orange Bowl in Miami, in 1935 the Sugar Bowl in New Orleans, and in 1937 the Cotton Bowl in Dallas joined the Bowl series of post-season games.

Non-School Competition

The YMCA national sports program reached thousands of boys, but the AAU was the main promoter in the United States of amateur sports outside the schools. Following this organization's founding in 1888, it became powerful in the athletic world. District and national championship meets and tournaments in several sports were held under its rules and its management.

Amateur baseball came to America in a big way of summer evenings with the night lighting of athletic fields. The first night baseball game was played in Des Moines, Iowa, in 1930. In this new era, the North American Baseball Association was started, to revive and encourage small town teams and to restore the rural baseball diamond to its oldtime popularity. The Amateur Baseball Congress was established in 1933 with thirty-five state and regional associations and 2,200 teams playing under its jurisdiction.

Professional Sports Competition. League baseball grew tremendously in this period, especially so after World War I. In 1927 Babe Ruth (1895–1948) of the New York Yankees made sixty home runs and a name for himself that tops the list of America's all-time greats in sports. In 1935 the first night games were played in the major leagues. After World War I, despite an inauspicous beginning at Latrobe, Pennsylvania, in 1895, professional football finally got a genuine start. The National Football League was born in 1922 and in 1933 divided into the Western and Eastern Conferences. Beginning in 1934 the winning professional team played against a team of all-stars selected from the graduating classes of colleges throughout the United States. This classic annual game, today as then, attracts as many as 100,000 spectators.

Professional basketball did not claim particular notice until the latter part of this period, but great national interest in it did not develop until shortly before World War II.

International Competition

In this period, competition at the international level other than in golf and tennis, in which sports the United States made enviable records, consisted chiefly of participation in the Olympic Games, as given in the material that follows. (Bobby Jones (1902–) was the idol of the golf world in the 1920's and 1930's, winning the "British open" several times.)

United States Participation in the Olympic Games. With the coming of a new century, many more nations entered the Olympics; where twelve had entered the first Games in 1896, fifty-three were competing before World War II. The Games became world-wide in representation, with teams entered from Africa, South America, the Far East, the Near East, Australia, and New Zealand, and with Canada and Cuba joining the United States to represent North America. The 1904 Games were held in St. Louis; 1906, Athens; 1908, London; 1912, Stockholm; 1920, Antwerp; 1924, Winter—Chamonix, and Summer—Paris; 1928, Winter—St. Moritz, and Summer—Amsterdam; 1932, Winter—Lake Placid, and Summer—Los Angeles; 1936, Winter—Garmisch-Partenkirchen, and Summer—Berlin.

Olympic winners from the very first Games to the present have been determined only event by event. There is no official point system by which totals may be decided. However, newspaper reporters have, through the years, devised their own unofficial point system, for these games, particularly for the track and field events, and it is because of their own unofficial pronouncements that a claim is made that any country has won the Olympics. Such claims are without official sanction.

At each Olympics, new events were added within the sports already in use, and now and then additional sports were added, so that the total events offered in competition grew with the years. (For further information on this, see the Appendix, p. 400.)

In the 1904 Games, which were held in connection with the Louisiana Purchase Exposition in St. Louis, the United States team consisted mostly of athletes from athletic clubs and individual entries. College entries were conspicuously lacking, but in spite of this the United States won fifty-six out of seventy-one contests. The Games were largely a contest between rival United States athletic clubs.

Although the Games were to be held only every four years, 1906 was made an exception, and an extra Games was held in Athens in honor of the tenth anniversary of the first Modern Olympics. This was the first time the United States sent athletes as an organized United States Olympic team. There was an American Olympic Committee with President Theodore Roosevelt (1859–1919) its honorary president, and the team was financed by nation–wide contributions. This first official United States team consisted of 35 athletes who were competing against eleven other nations. The victor of each event was awarded a sprig from an olive tree in Olympia. The United States won most of the track and field events, but France, winning in many other sports, tied in total number of wins. Of the new events offered for the first time that year, the javelin throw was unknown to the United States athletes.

In the 1908 Olympics, Great Britain also had a national Olympic Committee. In the opening ceremonies, the Finns marched without a flag rather than bow to Russia and carry its flag as it was insisted upon, and the Irish athletes to their great displeasure had to march under the British flag. The much bickering that arose over the poor management and the many questioned decisions of the British officials brought about the establishment of an International Olympics Committee to govern, manage, and officiate the Games from then on, instead of leaving these responsibilities to the host country. Great Britain won 41 of the 92 events, with the United States for the first time dropping into second place.

In the 1912 Olympics, twenty-six nations entered. This was the first Games to claim front-page attention in the papers at home, also the first to use an electric timing system. The great athlete of the United States team was Jim Thorpe (1889–1953), a Carlisle Indian. An interesting ceremony in connection with these Games in Stockholm was the presentation to King Gustave of Sweden of the plaque, *Joy of Effort* (four feet in diameter), sculptored by R. Tait McKenzie (see p. 325), who at the time was President of the American Physical Education Association. The shield had been commissioned by the American Olympic Committee and was presented as a gift to the Swedish people. It was installed in the entrance to the Olympic Stadium where it is on view today.

Because of World War I, the VIth Olympiad was omitted in 1916, and by 1920 the memory of the conflict was still so fresh that Germany and Austria were not invited to send teams. This was the first United States Olympic team to which the U.S. Army and Navy contributed athletes. The leading U.S. athlete was Charles Paddock, then called the "World's Fastest Human."

In 1924 the U.S. Navy sent its athletes to the Games on a U.S. battleship, while the other members of the team crossed the Atlantic together on a commercial ship. Over 2,000 athletes from forty-five nations marched in the opening parade in Paris. The United States took 12 firsts in track and field alone plus 32 more firsts in other sports, for a total of 45 gold medals. The nearest competitor, Finland, won in 14 events; 8 of them in track and field, with its famous runner Paavo Nurmi (1897–) winning much acclaim. This year was the first that winter sports were added to the Games but the United States won only one of the eleven events. For the United States, John Weissmuller (1904–) starred in swimming. With his considerable help the United States team won 7 out of 10 events in that sport.

For the 1928 Games in Amsterdam, General Douglas MacArthur (1880–1964) was President of the American Olympic Committee. The United States team consisted of 285 athletes, among them 19 women, one of whom won 1 of the 5 women's track and field events entered for the first time. With only a total of 23 wins out of 121 contests, as against 45 of the events of the preceding Games, it was considered a poor showing for the United States, even though the nearest contenders were Finland and Germany with 11 wins each and Sweden with ten. Paavo Nurmi of Finland and Lord Burleigh of England stole the limelight in these Games.

In the Games at Los Angeles in 1932, many records were broken. As Keiran (see References) says, these Games broke all previous records for fine weather, number of spectators, and gate receipts. The last two Games set a record for number of athletes entered and number of nations represented—4,000 athletes and 45 nations. The Los Angeles Games brought only 2,000 athletes from 39 nations. But this Olympics was different, with an International Fine Arts competition and an International Folk Dance Festival arranged to run simultaneously to present to the world competition other than in sports alone. These were not, however, put on by the Olympic Committee, but by organizations concerned with the need to present a better picture of world fellowship and competition than the Olympics, with the petty bickerings and jealousies among athletes and officials that the Modern Olympics had thus far engendered. Out of 133 events offered, the United States team won 48 gold medals, with Italy the nearest contender with 12. The United States women athletes more than held their own with the men as winners. The men won 12 out of 23 gold medals in track and field, and the women won 5 out of 7.

The 1936 Olympics in Berlin brought out 5,000 athletes from 53 nations, but there was trouble before the Games were underway, for Hitler expected to dictate how they were to be managed and controlled. The International Olympic Committee informed him that the Games were the project of all the nations working together and were managed and controlled solely by the IOC representing the nations concerned, and that as Head of State of the host nation he was merely the host to the Games. When he refused to accept that dictum, the IOC informed him that it alone would manage and control the games or they would be removed to another country. Rather than lose this opportunity to preside over the Games and to show off his Third Reich to the world in this bit of pageantry, Hitler finally capitulated. For the torch-lighting ceremony to open the Games, relay runners (3,000) for the first time carried the lighted torch from ancient Mt. Olympus. As Hitler opened the Games, 3,000 pigeons were released over the stadium (as had been done in Los Angeles four years before when the Vice-President of the United States opened the Games there). In the opening parade, the athletes of the nations friendly to Nazism gave the Nazi salute as they passed Hitler's stand and were given great applause, while the others either gave the Olympic salute or merely marched by "eyes right" and were greeted with silence from the grand stand. But the United States athletes (who had gone to Berlin under the vigorous protests of much of the nation, since feeling was strong against Hitler), refusing to salute as they passed the Grand Stand, were received with whistling jeers by the overwhelmingly German crowd of 110,000 spectators. Despite this cool reception from the host country, however, the U.S. athletes won 12 of the track and field events, more than all the other countries put together and of the 145 total events won 25. But this was only second best, Germany leading with 34 wins in all. These Games of 1936 again increased the number of competing nations, athletes, and events.

The star athlete on the United States team was Jesse Owens (1913–) of Ohio State University, who won four gold medals in track and field, setting three new world records, while no other athlete won more than one. At this time, Hitler was denouncing Negroes as well as Jews, and there were ten Negroes on the U.S. team. To keep from publicly recognizing the three Negro winners on the U.S. track team he hastily left the stadium before they could be escorted to his box to receive the congratulations granted to all other winners. On another day when two more U.S. winners were Negroes he left his seat and received them under the stands away from public notice. But he steadfastly refused to receive Jesse Owens, the American athlete who in his superior physical feats and manliness refuted all of Hitler's arguments about the inferiority of the black man.

Basketball, having been an Olympic sport in 1904 and then dropped, was on the program for the second time after a thirty-two year absence, and James A. Naismith, the creator of the game, was a special guest of honor of the International Olympic Committee.

In the new century the U.S. teams won many firsts, and many seconds and thirds, in track and field, to give the United States an enviable record in that sport. They did quite well also in swimming, wrestling, rowing, bobsled running, and the United States was the only nation to win in basketball. But the U.S. athletes were outdone quite consistently in boxing, gymnastics, shooting, figure and speed skating, weight-lifting, yachting, and skiing. Before World War II the United States had not produced an Olympic winner in canoeing, cycling, curling, Greco-Roman wrestling, fencing, golf, equestrian events, racquets, soccer football, field hockey, tug-of-war, rugby, skiing (men), gymnastics (women), or foils (women).

In the eleventh Olympics held before World War II, only twice did another nation win more gold medals in the total events than the U.S., and these were in 1908 when Great Britain won 41 events to the U.S.'s 25, and in 1936 when Germany won 34 to the U.S.'s 25; in the extra Games of 1906, France and the United States tied with 12 gold medals each. (See Appendix for further information on the Games.)

Nations winning gold medals in the Olympics for the first time in this era were the following: Argentina, Australia, Canada, Cuba, Belgium, Brazil, British India, Czechoslovakia, Denmark, Egypt, Estonia, Finland, Italy, Japan, The Netherlands, New Zealand, Poland, South Africa, Spain, Switzerland, Turkey, Uruguay, and Yugoslavia.

SPORTS COMPETITION FOR GIRLS AND WOMEN

At the opening of the new century women's sports in colleges and high schools began gradually to come under the control of the physical education departments although at Bryn Mawr College students held out as late as 1929 in turning over their own control and promotion of sports to the physical education staff. With several national organizations coming into existence in this era to set standards for girls' sports competition, all adopting the slogan, "A sport for every girl and every girl in a sport," the intramural form of competition became the form approved by the profession for American girls. The principles for sports were drawn up by the leading women physical educators of the day, working through the Women's Division of the National Amateur Athletic Federation, which drew up a platform of standards, as discussed below.

Platform of the Women's Division of NAAF

Under the chairmanship of Mrs. Herbert Hoover, one of the first actions of the Women's Division after its founding in 1923 was to appoint a committee to draw up a platform of aims and principles as guides for all groups in the country promoting competitive athletics for women. Under the leadership of Dr. J. Anna Norris of the University of Minnesota, the Committee presented a platform which was unanimously adopted. Among its many provisions it included such items as the following:

1. Promote competition that stresses enjoyment of the sport and development of good sportsmanship and character rather than those types that emphasize the making and breaking of records and the winning of championships for the enjoyment of spectators or for the athletic reputation or commercial advantage of institutions and organizations.
2. Promote interest in awards for athletic accomplishment that have little or no intrinsic value.
3. Promote educational publicity that places emphasis upon sport and its values rather than upon the competitors.
4. Promote the training and employment of women administrators, leaders, and officials who are qualified to assume full responsibility for the physical education and recreation of girls and women.
5. Protect the athletic activities of girls and women from the dangers attendant upon competition that involves travel, and from their commercialization by interest in gate receipts.
6. Protect the health of girls and women through the promotion of medical examinations and medical "follow-up" as a basis for participation in athletic competition.
7. Promote the adoption of approved rules for the conduct of athletics for girls and women.

The rules of sports for women as approved by this organization were those made by the National Section for Women's Athletics of APEA. As these two groups worked together, the Women's Division was looked upon as the standards-setting body, the other as the sports-rules–making body. Both groups were working under the leadership of the profession's outstanding women.

Competition in Lower Schools

In the early years of the 1900's, girls in some high schools in all parts of the country competed in interschool activities, although the games were not organized or controlled by school authorities. Some played college teams; some, other high school teams, and some, boys' grade school teams. By 1910 girls' interscholastic basketball had become big excitement in many small towns of the Middle West and South and more than any other sport was causing "headaches" for physical education teachers and girls' leaders. Through it the girls were frequently exploited for the publicity of many small towns and a few groups of men. These groups used boys' rules and men coaches in most situations, and where women coaches were used, they were as a rule women who were not trained in the educational aspects of sports and in the care of girls in their sports participation.

Partly in imitation of the college women's athletic associations and partly to combat interscholastic games, girls' athletic associations sprang up, and, sparked by them, intramurals took the stage in most high schools. These GAA's found support and encouragement in the State Leagues which arose in the 1920's.

Competition in Colleges

From a mild start in the 1890's in a few isolated places, intercollegiate competition for women now increased in the 1900's. In the East a few colleges played intercollegiate basketball occasionally, from 1900 to the World War I period, but during the 1920's, intramural competition had almost completely superseded all such competition. In the Middle West the University of Nebraska started a program of varsity basketball in 1900 managed by a woman English teacher, playing high schools, YWCA's, and an occasional college team, but by 1906 this type of competition was replaced by an intramural program of interclass games. In the West, the University of California's Sports Past-time *(sic)* Association ran off intercollegiate matches with the University of Nevada, Stanford University, and Mills College from 1900 to 1903 when because of unfavorable publicity the school authorities put a stop to the games.

In the early 1920's about 22 per cent of the colleges sponsored some form of intercollegiate sports for women, but by 1930 only 12 per cent were engaging in intercollegiate competition while intramurals, sponsored jointly by women's athletic associations and the departments of physical education, gained in popularity.

By 1925 play days had become popular, the first held at the University of Washington as an intramural affair. The University of Cincinnati was the first to sponsor an intercollegiate play day in which girls from various colleges were scattered among many teams—no one school putting any one team into play in any activity. In other words the players played with other schools rather than against them.

This era was one of great activity in sports for girls and women. With the National Section for Girls and Women's Athletics of AAHPER, State High School Leagues, Women's Division of NAAF, and Athletic Federation of College Women all working for sports for all and play for play's sake, intramurals have become the organized form of sports for the great mass of American school girls and women.

There was but little intercollegiate competition in sports for women in this era. A survey of intercollegiate athletics for women made in 1923 was repeated in 1930 at the request of the Women's Division of NAAF. One hundred fifty-four colleges and universities were included in this second survey. The 22 per cent of colleges reporting participation in intercollegiate athletics in 1923 had dropped to 12 per cent by 1930 with only 7 per cent using the varsity-team type of competition, the other 5 per cent using only the inter-class type. Fifty-three per cent of the colleges reporting took part in play days with other schools in which the girls were mixed together in temporary teams with no team representing any one college.

Following that survey, play days took on importance and flourished for a while. Then with the coming of World War II, they gave way to the demands of the times and since then have not been revived to any appreciable extent.

Nonschool Competition

Although YWCA's, recreation centers, and like groups offered women a varied sports program, it was in this era that there first arose exploitation of girls through athletics. School girls were exploited by men's sports organizations, industrial and business groups, Chambers of Commerce, and a number of men athletic coaches, who saw that skilled girl athletes made good publicity. The AAU took the lead in organizing girls in industry for such competitive sports. Its attempt to take over the management of girls and women's competitive sports, after World War I, aroused the women leaders of physical education and many prominent lay women as well, who tried to counter its influence by the organization of the Women's Division of the NAAF. Although this organization did accomplish much in awaking the lay public to the desirability of sane and wholesome standards for sports for women, it never succeeded in breaking the AAU's hold completely, for the AAU continued to control women's competition in several fields.

In the 1920's women's national championship tournaments sprang up across the country—all man-inspired, man-managed, man-coached and man-financially-rewarded from the prowess of the worthwhile athletic "finds." Of all sports, basketball played by women caused the most controversy between physical educators (both men and women), who would keep women's sports purely in the realm of education and recreation, and those sports promoters who would push women into spectator sports with their accompanying gate receipts, win-at-all-costs atmosphere, and championships at stake. By the late 1920's the Women's Athletic Section of the American Physical Education Association and the Women's Division of the National Amateur Athletic Federation and State Leagues vigorously opposed these forces in behalf of what they called educational athletics for girls. In the 1930's the AAU became very active in this field and staged many district and national championships for women in basketball, swimming, and track and field. These tournaments were given great publicity and they brought in large gate receipts for their promoters. Interesting are the stories of how the Women's Division persuaded the AAU to accept certain standards for women's sports, to place women chaperons and nurses in women's dressing rooms at championship tournaments, replacing men trainers and "rubbers," and to give up its pre-game bathing-suit parades of contestants on the streets of the tournament city. Women educators trained in physical education waged constant war throughout this era in favor of sports for all instead of intense participation for the few. In this battle they were supported by noted men leaders who gave them courage to stand up against groups of other men who wished to exploit girls and women through sports.

International Competition

Following World War I American women became involved in tennis, golf, swimming, and field hockey on an international scale. The names of Helen Wills (1906-) in tennis and Gertrude Ederle in swimming were well known to American sports fans of this period. (Helen Wills won the U.S. Women's Tennis Singles six times in the 1920's and in 1931. In international competition she won the singles at Wimbledon eight times —1927 through 1930, 1932, 1933, 1935, and 1938, and there also won in the doubles in 1924, 1927, and 1930. She also won the French singles four times against the famous French tennis star, Suzanne Lenglin.) The tours of English, Irish, and Scotch field hockey teams to America and the return tours of American teams to the British Isles, although not receiving much public attention, were well known to all field hockey fans. But none of these sports involving women athletes held the national attention or called forth so much debate by laymen as did the entrance of American women into the Olympics, as discussed below.

Women's Participation in the Olympics. There are reports that the first entrance of women in the Olympics occurred in 1900 in Paris, but Kieran and Daley in their tables of events and winners in the Olympics (see Appendix, p. 400, and References) give the year 1904 for the first participation of women and for the sport of lawn tennis. But it was twenty years later before the U.S. team included women, and that first entry was in swimming. Other countries had entered women in swimming events since 1912. At the next Games in 1920, women from the United States joined the others and won four events out of five, for an auspicious beginning. In 1924 women tennis players were added to the U.S. team, and Helen Wills and Mrs. G. W. Wrightman overcame all opposition and, with the men tennis players, made a clean sweep of all tennis firsts for the United States. Previously to this Great Britain and France had divided tennis honors.

In 1928, with track and field for women added to the Olympic program, the United States team for this year included women athletes both in swimming and in track and field (tennis had been dropped). In 1932 women speed skaters were added to the team, who won two out of three events offered in that sport.

As with the men athletes, it was track and field that claimed the lion's share of the publicity for women. In the first offering of this sport for women, the U.S. team won one of the five events; but at the next Games in 1932, they won five out of six events in this sport, the one loss going to Poland which was represented by an American girl of Polish parentage. At this time Mildred Didrikson won two events, the 80-metre hurdles and the javelin throw, and was catapulted into the start of her spectacular public sports career. Before her death at the age of forty-two, she was acclaimed the world's greatest all-round woman athlete. At Berlin in 1936, it was a different story, with the U.S. women and Germany winning two events each and Italy and Hungary one each.

After their entry into the Games in 1920, the United States women athletes in the five Olympics before World War II won three tennis events out of three, two speed skating events out of three, eight track and field events out of seventeen, and twenty-three swimming events out of thirty-two—certainly an excellent record. But their presence on the U.S. team was questioned from many sources at home. The United States was not yet ready to accept its women in such a public role, particularly not in track and field sports.

An Olympic Protest of Leading American Women. As soon as it became known that track and field sports were to be opened to women and certain groups in the United States were pushing for a U.S. women's track team, vigorous protests were registered with the Olympic Committee by the Women's Division of NAAF, with the vigorous supporting protests of the foremost men leaders of physical education. In 1929 at its annual meeting, the Women's Division went on record as a national group of women leaders, both in physical education and the lay world, that was opposed to the entrance of American women in the Olympics of 1932, and it adopted the following resolutions:

> WHEREAS, Competition in the Olympic Games would, among other things (1) entail the specialized training of a few, (2) offer opportunity for the exploitation of girls and women, and (3) offer opportunity for possible overstrain in preparation for and during the Games themselves, be it
>
> RESOLVED, that the Women's Division of the National Amateur Athletic Federation go on record as disapproving of competition for girls and women in the Olympic Games,
>
> . . . . .
>
> WHEREAS, The Women's Division is interested in promoting the ideal of Play for Play's sake, of Play on a large scale, of Play and recreation properly safeguarded,
>
> WHEREAS, It is interested in promoting types and programs of activities suitable to girls as girls, be it
>
> RESOLVED, That the Women's Division . . . shall ask for the opportunity of putting on in Los Angeles during the Games (not as a part of the Olympic program) a festival which might include singing, dancing, mass sports and games . . . demonstrations, exhibitions, etc.
>
> WHEREAS, . . . a crisis is at hand whereby the Platform and principles of the Women's Division will be severely tested,
>
> BE IT RESOLVED, That the members of the Women's Division and all who are interested in the Federation and its ideals . . . do all in their power to spread more actively the principles advocated by this Division and to work unceasingly toward putting on for girls a program of sports and games . . . which shall (1) include every member of the group; (2) be broad and diversified; (3) be adapted to the special needs and abilities and capacities of the participants; with emphasis upon *participation* rather than upon *winning.*

The above resolutions were widely publicized and were later adopted by the National Association of Physical Education for College Women, the National Section on Women's Athletics of the American Physical Education Association, the Athletic Conference of American College Women, and the National Board of the YWCA's of America, and they were endorsed by the National Association of Deans of Women and the American

Association of University Women. In April of 1930 the Women's Division sent a petition to the International Olympic Committee urging the exclusion of women from the 1932 Olympics, calling their attention to a speech by Pierre de Coubertin, founder of the modern Games, made at the XIth Olympic Games in Amsterdam in 1928, in which he said:

> As to the admission of women to the Games, I remain strongly against it. It was against my will that they were admitted to a growing number of competitions.

But both the United States Olympic Committee and the International Olympic Committee turned a deaf ear to these appeals.

22

Organized Physical Education in the Early Twentieth Century (1900–World War II)

The new century brought a great awakening in education in America. The idea that all children should have an education and at public expense was now a generally accepted idea. As the century opened there were still fifty-seven per cent of school children whose parents were foreign born, many of them not speaking English, so that there was still much adaptation to the American way of life to be made, and the schools had come to be recognized as the cornerstone of democracy. More money was appropriated for schools, better buildings and equipment were provided, and more professionally trained teachers became available.

People now became concerned about putting into practice the best educational theories. Coeducation had become universally accepted for all elementary schools and in practically all public high schools except in some of the larger cities where the age-old custom of segregation of the sexes, at least in the high schools, was slow in dying.

The small percentage of children who attended school in the earlier years of our nation had risen markedly in the elementary schools, and the vast majority of all children of lower-grade ages were now in school; but the drop-out rate was still high for the high schools. In the school year of 1900–01 only 10 per cent of high-school-age children were attending school, but by World War II this had risen to seventy-two per cent.

At the opening of the century, the United States was still predominantly rural and small town. Before World War I, five million children were attending one-room schools wherein all grade levels were taught, and as late as 1930 over 25 per cent of high school children were attending small schools of 100–200 enrollment, and 50 per cent, schools with fewer than 100 pupils. With the coming of motor buses, the movement toward consolidation of rural schools got under way. This contributed directly to the advancement of physical education in rural areas, since such schools could support gymnasia and in-door as well as outdoor playing space.

Social studies now gained attention in the schools. John Dewey, the leading social philosopher of the time, had said in his book *School and Society,* published in 1900: "What the wisest and best parents want for their children, that must the community want for all its children." This statement aroused educators to reappraise their objectives in terms of this social philosophy. In 1918 the National Education Association proclaimed its Seven Cardinal Principles of Education, listing among them health, citizenship, and worthy use of leisure—three concerns to which physical education could so well contribute. The 1920's and 1930's in particular brought many reforms in American education.

EVENTS AFFECTING PHYSICAL EDUCATION

During this era the terms *physical culture* and *physical training* gave way to *physical education,* as this department of work became recognized as a legitimate part of education. The term had long been in use, however, in a few isolated situations, such as at Amherst College, where Dr. Hitchcock had used the term ever since the 1860's. Many forces affected physical education and aided it in procuring recognition. These are discussed in the material that follows.

State Legislation

The movement for state laws requiring that physical education be taught in the schools, which started in the 1890's, lagged in the 1900's. Up to 1914 only three more states had acted: Pennsylvania in 1901, Michigan in 1911, and Idaho in 1913. During the war eight more fell into line. Then educators in general joined forces with physical educators to hasten this process. Even President Wilson (1856–1924) had spoken out in behalf of the needs for physical training of all children. Shortly, a Committee for the Promotion of Physical Education in the Public Schools was organized, with headquarters in Washington, to push for a model state bill for physical education. Dr. John Dewey of Columbia University served as chairman of the committee, and Mrs. Ella Flagg Young (1845–1918), Superintendent of the Chicago schools and the first woman to hold the presidency of the National Education Association, served on the committee, as did Dudley Sargent and the state superintendents of education of North Carolina, California, Illinois, and Washington and two college presidents—a notable group. Sargent was commissioned to draw up a model bill, and in February of 1917 it was placed before the General Assemblies of California, Indiana, and Connecticut with the following preamble:

> We believe the time has come when the public schools can, and should, enter deliberately and purposefully upon a definite plan for the preparation of our youth physically for the exigencies of life and for all the demands of citizenship. We need to spend more money and more time upon physical training intended to develop the body so that both boys and girls may be prepared equally for the pursuits of peace and the vicissitudes of war.

This Committee started the ball rolling. By 1930 thirty-nine states in all had passed physical education laws. With state legislation came state physical education directorships set up in the state departments of public instruction. New York in 1916 became the first state to create such a position with Dr. Thomas A. Storey (1875–1943), of the College of the City of New York, in the directorship. California was the second with Clark W. Hetherington serving as state director from 1918 to 1921. By 1930 twenty-two states had state directors of physical education. (See Appendix.) The rising tide of state legislation which increased physical education work in the schools showed up the shortage of teachers in this field, and private schools, normal schools, colleges, and universities stepped up their teacher training work.

Most of the early laws required the teaching of physical education in the larger schools and made it permissive in the smaller ones. Later the laws carried provisions for time allotment and required physical education credits for graduation. Whereas the first laws specified the teaching of calisthenics and/or gymnastics, the later laws specified instead sports and rhythms. However, the crowded conditions and lack of facilities of many elementary and high schools encouraged the use of calisthenics rather than games and sports. The joyous acceptance of sports and dance into the program brought about a public awareness of and interest in physical education, which in turn brought about public support for the program.

World War I

The world-wide war of 1914–18 was spoken of as the Great War until a second one twenty-five years later, when the earlier one became known as World War I. In the conduct of this first world war, into which the United States was finally drawn after serious attempts to keep free of it, the Government recognized physical education in many ways as it turned to various national leaders for advice and help in special projects, thus advancing markedly and favorably public recognition of the profession. Also many private agencies called on physical education leaders to help in their specific endeavors related to the war. Joseph E. Raycroft, then of Princeton University, was appointed Chairman of the Athletic Division of the War Department Commission on Training Camp Activities and was sent by the Secretary of War to Europe to study conditions affecting the morale of the American Expeditionary Forces. Following this the United States Navy set up a similar commission with Walter Camp of Yale at its head. He immediately appealed through the NCAA for the colleges to loan their athletic trainers to work with aviators. Dr. Edward C. Schneider (1874–1954), of Wesleyan University, was appointed a member of the Medical Research Board of Aviation with the AEF, and Dr. Thomas A. Storey, New York State Director of Physical Education, was made Executive Secretary of the Government Inter-departmental Social Hygiene Board.

Women physical educators were also drawn into top positions of war work. Jessie Bancroft, head of physical education in the Brooklyn Public Schools, was called to serve as Chairman of the Government Commission on Training Camp Activities and President of the War-Camp Service. Elizabeth Burchenal was appointed a member of the U.S. Department of Labor's Commission of Wartime Community Services and a member of both the U.S. War and Navy Departments' Commission on Camp Activities. Dr. Clelia Mosher of Stanford University (see p. 328) was Medical Director of the Bureau of Refugees and Relief for the American Red Cross. Lillian Drew (1874–1930) of Columbia University was appointed by the Surgeon General as Supervisor of Reconstruction Aides for the War Department. Blanche Trilling of the University of Wisconsin served as one of the regional directors for the Fosdick Commission of the National Recreation Association for their recreation activities for communities located near war-mobilization camps, and Wilma Haynes (1888–) of the Dayton, Ohio, YWCA, held a similar regional directorship for the National YWCA Commission on Recreational Services.

Athletic Program of the American Expeditionary Forces

Several leaders of physical education under the sponsorship of the United States Army laid the foundation for the great athletic program of the AEF of World War I: such as J. H. McCurdy, of Springfield YMCA School; George J. Fisher, head of the Physical Department of the International YMCA; A. A. Stagg, of the University of Chicago; Paul Phillips (1865–1942), of Amherst; George Meylan, of Columbia University; E. B.

DeGroot, of the Chicago Park System; and F. L. Kleeberger (1885–1942), of the University of California (Berkeley). These men, with three hundred and forty-five others serving under them as athletic directors, reached a peak in participation in sports at rest camps of 21,710,406. When General Petain asked the United States to furnish recreation leaders to produce a similar program for the French "poilus," Meylan was put in charge of this work, and he set up 1,300 recreation centers for the French armies. After the close of the war and while the allied armies were still in France, the YMCA's, under the leadership of Dr. John Brown, Jr., organized Inter-Allied Athletic Contests—the Military Olympics—which were open to all soldiers of all allied armies. For these games the YMCA's built a 40,000-seat concrete stadium and presented it as the Pershing Stadium to the French Republic, with General Pershing himself making the presentation speech. These games, according to Friermood (see References) in progress as the Versailles Peace Treaty was being signed, did much to seal international friendships between the men of the armed forces of the Allies. Besides this work in European army camps, there were at home thirty-two great mobilization camps, each with four physical directors in charge of the recreation work for the men.

The After-Effects of Draft Figures

Thirty-three per cent of the men drafted for the United States armed services for World War I were rejected as unfit to serve. Out of the ensuing accusations and recriminations came an awakened conscience. People were now ready to give backing to a real program of physical education in the schools. This postwar impetus brought greatly expanded facilities and increased staffs. Swimming pools, football stadiums, spacious gymnasiums, and large athletic fields sprang up all over the country. A growing consciousness that physical education and athletics were for the many, not just for the few, brought a great upsurge for intramural sports and increased required work in physical education in the schools and colleges.

The Progressive Education Movement

As John Dewey's ideas on educational reforms became widely known, there developed an ever-growing group of educators who accepted them and tried to change general educational procedures to fit Dewey's philosophy. It was not until after World War I, however, that there was, even in education in general, such a thing as a formally organized group openly committed to advance the cause of *progressive education,* as this movement came to be called. The Association for the Advancement of Progressive Education was not born until 1919, when it named Charles Eliot of Harvard its honorary president and announced as its objective the reformation of the American school system. To attain this objective, it aimed to meet the needs of children, to give the child freedom to develop naturally, to attend to all things that affect a child in his physical development, and to make *interest* the child's motive of work. This meant changing the teacher from the task-master of old into a guide.

According to Cremin (see References), Dewey himself did not join this organization, although upon Eliot's death in 1926 he accepted the honorary presidency. The excesses of followers of his philosophy who came to control the association alienated many educators and parents who wanted education to find better ways of teaching traditional subjects but wished to retain the traditional subjects and also to retain hard, disciplined work, which the extremists would discard. These extremists were not pleasing to Dewey either, and he never took an active part in the work of the organization and was critical of its "outlook." He believed that essentials in education must come first and after that the refinements, but many, claiming to be followers of his theories but misinterpreting them, advocated the abandoning of much of the essentials and the offering of only the refinements of education. Dewey was deeply disappointed in these developments, and as early as the 1920's declared that his own venture to change American education had turned into a failure.

At first controlled by leaders in Eastern private prep schools, the Association for the Advancement of Progressive Education was largely ignored by leading university professors, who clung to Dewey's brand of philosophy, but in the 1930's the organization came under the control of leaders in the Teachers College of Columbia University. William Heard Kilpatrick (1871–1965), Professor of Philosophy of Education at Columbia, became the chief exponent of progressive education, and as his philosophy was somewhat different from that of Dewey the movement grew even farther away from Dewey's conception of what the education of the American child should be. Disturbed over these developments, Dewey published his book *Experience and Education* in 1938 (see References) to counteract the misunderstandings that had arisen following World War I about his theories.

Perhaps the best known of the educators who stood by Dewey's theories was Boyd Henry Bode (1873–1953), Professor of Education at Ohio State University. In 1938 he published his book, *Progressive Education at the Cross-Roads,* in which he expressed concern about the type of teacher bred by the extremists in the movement, who permitted children, in trying to follow the so-called progressive pattern, to flounder about to find their own way through the educational maze. He strongly felt, as did Dewey, that children should be helped and guided and that education must have a sense of direction.

By the coming of World War II, the progressive education movement, as then envisioned by its own organization, had come under such severe criticism by many leading educators and laymen that membership fell off materially, and in the 1950's the association died. However, the movement (which included the true followers of Dewey who did not subscribe to the excesses of the Association members within the movement) did have a great impact on education in the opening decades of the new century. It markedly changed the character of the schools, and for the better. And it also had a great impact on physical education and changed it, too, for the better.

The progressive education movement raised in the world of education talk of adjusting the school to the child, not the child to the school; teaching children rather than subjects; adapting the school to life situations; giving the child opportunity for creative self-expression; taking into consideration individual differences; and teaching "the whole child." Several of these concepts had long been recognized by a few educators. For example, in the field of physical education, Hitchcock since the 1860's and Sargent since the 1880's had been advocating attention to individual differences. Now these things were being brought to the attention of all. And as far as these ideas themselves were concerned, there was no special quarrel; the differences that arose came about over how these things were to be accomplished and what changes were required.

From the beginning of physical education in the schools of America, gymnastics had been, in most schools, the core of the program—in many, the whole of it. The changes demanded by the new philosophy seemed to many physical educators to call first of all for a complete break with the old forms of gymnastics. But this did not come about without much argumentation within the profession. A small group of physical educators, led by Thomas D. Wood of Columbia University, who also found merit in Dewey's philosophy began examining physical education in light of the new ideas. By 1910 Wood had published his book *Health and Education* (see References), in which he acknowledged the influence of Dewey on his thinking and proclaimed that through physical education the child should acquire mental, moral, and social as well as physical benefits. He pointed out that physical education had been given space and time in the educational program only begrudgingly and only with the aim of counteracting the unhealthful influences of the school day. He maintained that this was no longer enough and that the physical education program should be psychologically and socially as well as physiologically sound. Recognizing gymnastics as an activity that could still be taught readily in the space allotted for physical education in so many schools in those days and to the large-sized classes required at that time in so many schools, he did not advocate the abandonment of gymnastics but instead the substitution of a new form (see Chapter 21) to be called *natural gymnastics,* which term he used as early as 1891 when he established the department at Stanford University to be built around sports and activities related to life situations. He would retain gymnastics for its physiological values; but he would replace the old forms done in response to formal commands with this new form which would embody social and psychological objectives that were lacking in the old forms.

There soon arose a considerable body of followers of Wood for the "new physical education," but unfortunately too many teachers without a realistic understanding of either Dewey's or Wood's philosophy and disliking the old forms of gymnastics gladly seized upon the idea of natural gymnastics as a way out of a dilemma, and, lacking creative skill to formulate procedures to fit the new ideas, became involved with class periods in which the pupils had little exercise and attained little in the way of social or psychological objectives and definitely no physiological ones. They had merely wasted their time. This vacuum of attainment most certainly had not been the intent of the originator and the leading promoters of the new gymnastics, and these early failures led to a division among physical educators. One group would retain the old forms of gymnastics for their own value. Another group would keep the old forms but rob them of their old formal and militaristic aspects. A third group would replace the old forms of gymnastics entirely with Wood's natural gymnastics. A fourth group would have no gymnastics at all in the physical education program but would instead build the program around sports and dance in their various forms. In the end, this last group was the one that prevailed, although the proponents of the other three groups had their way for a brief period, each in various parts of the country, with some diehards holding out into the 1930's. None of these groups were formally organized, and one never knew for sure to which group others belonged except for the few outspoken ones of each group.

In fact never was there any such thing within the profession of physical education as a progressive education movement as such. Things were not as clear cut as that. The profession, aroused by Dewey and Wood, was groping toward something new but was not too sure as to what this new thing should be. But since gymnastics had been the only activity recognized as physical education in the schools in the century just closed, it was gymnastics that came under attack in this new day.

Upon Wood's retirement at Columbia, his mantle fell upon Jesse F. Williams; and just as Kilpatrick had not hewn to the line in following Dewey's philosophy, Williams, too, departed somewhat from that of Wood. Whereas Wood had been for retaining gymnastics in the program but in a new form, Williams in public speeches voiced disapproval of any school system that would tolerate the retention of any form of gymnastics in its program. In his book *Organization and Administration of Physical Education* (see References) he spoke of formal calisthenics and gymnastics as a deformity in physical education, for which a cure should be sought. (In this period the word *gymnastics* meant the combination of gymnastic marching, free-standing exercises, and apparatus work.) As lines came to be drawn for and against gymnastics as a legitimate part of physical education, the chief adversaries seemed to be Williams on the one side and C. H. McCloy (1886–1958) of the University of Iowa on the other. At least they were the ones who most frequently and publicly debated the topic against each other and who spoke out most emphatically in speeches and in writings, each in defense of his own theories. Both had large followings—neither stood alone. Williams and his followers were for deleting gymnastics entirely from the schools, whereas McCloy and his, though in agreement as far as getting rid of the old militaristic forms was concerned, were for retaining parts of the old which they claimed had been tested and were found to be still good for the new day. In McCloy's *Philosophical Basis For Physical Education* (see References), he said:

> . . . the monkey in us would point toward apparatus work as being as natural as basketball, merely needing to be reorganized, purged of its "exercises," and to be properly taught. . . . I am convinced that the dropping of this type of activity is not at all complimentary to our professional intelligence.

Williams berated even the setting-up exercises of the type of the Daily Dozen, popularized by Walter Camp and many others, whereas McCloy defended them as appropriate for certain people unable to exercise otherwise and insufficiently knowledgeable to devise their own forms, though he disclaimed them as a criterion for a physical education program.

As natural gymnastics developed, it soon became apparent that even this new form, as it was presented by many, was not really natural after all, since many of the exercises used did not come to children naturally, but were thought up and taught to the children by others. The old teacher-imposed, teacher-controlled exercises of the German and Swedish systems were merely replaced by new teacher-contrived, teacher-imposed exercises of a new form and with a new name, so that shortly natural gymnastics (which regretfully never had a chance to develop properly for lack of adequate teachers) faded from the program, to be replaced entirely by sports and dancing. Gymnastic apparatus of all kinds now vanished from the gymnasiums of the American schools that adopted the new philosophy, and most did adopt it. The great majority of teachers, as usually happens, avoided the extremes at both the left and right, trying out the new but not forsaking all of the old, and in the process formulated a new and greatly improved program of physical education.

Followers of the Progressive Education Movement did get rid of the calisthenics drill master, but when many schools replaced him with the domineering type of coach many complained that this was not enough. As physical education sought a reply to this new tyrant, there arose much talk of benching the coach during games, which talk did cause physical educators and many coaches as well to reappraise the function of the coach as an educator, even if the bench-the-coach idea never did get a serious following.

Another accompaniment of the Progressive Education Movement that went to absurd extremes at the hands of the Movement's radicals was the changing concept about teaching democracy. There grew up the idea that any decision made by a majority was superior to one arrived at by a minority, regardless of how greatly the balance of wisdom might be in favor of the minority. This extreme notion of the value of majority opinion on all things called forth much protest from many leaders. In physical education, C. H. McCloy spoke out on this (see References) when he said in his article, "A Half Century of Physical Education":

> I hope the next fifty years will cause physical educators to . . . seek for facts, proved objectively; [and] to question principles based on average opinions of people who don't know, but are all anxious to contribute their averaged ignorance to form a consensus of uniformed dogma.

Although much nonsense arose as to how to teach democracy and how to reorganize the school as a pattern of democratic procedure, in the end common sense did prevail in most situations; and much good came from the effort, although there still lingers in the minds of many educators and laymen the thought that too much permissiveness may not after all have been real democracy in action. Was education producing a generation that considered the rights of the individual to be above the greatest good of the greatest number? The arguments on this still rage in many aspects of national life.

The 1930 House Conference on Child Health and Protection

In November of 1930 President Hoover's White House Conference on Child Health and Protection was held in Washington, D.C. Its purpose was "to get a composite picture of this complex child, to find out how he rates physically, mentally, morally, what our rapidly changing civilization is doing to make or mar him, to determine where our social, educational, and governmental machinery is at fault in training him to his utmost capacities, and where it may be strengthened."

The conference's conclusions were embodied in a Children's Charter of nineteen aims for the children of America, one of which pledged "for every child from birth through adolescence promotion of health, including health instruction, and a health program, wholesome physical and mental recreation, with teachers and leaders adequately trained." This conference led to greatly increased interest in physical education for the schools (see References).

The Depression

In the economic stress of the depression of the 1930's, school boards, urged on by groups of citizens, ordered drastic cuts in education. The specialized subjects—music, art, home economics, and physical education—were labeled the "fads and frills" of education and came in for undue and sharp criticism and attacks. In many towns and cities these subjects were forced to bear the brunt of cuts in budgets and staffs. But thanks to the efforts of educators and citizen groups who recognized the aims of physical education and put up a fight in its behalf, physical education, on the whole, suffered no more than did the regular school subjects and was spared the drastic treatment meted out to music, art, and home economics.

STATUS OF PHYSICAL EDUCATION

Whereas in the nineteenth century the chief consideration concerning programs was the question as to what system of gymnastics to teach, attention now turned to whether the program should be built around gymnastics, or sports and dancing, or a combination of the three. Also, where previously a goodly segment of citizens had advocated military drill in the schools in place of physical education, physical education had so effectively demonstrated its values during World War I that even the War Department came to recognize it as a valuable partner of military training and openly discouraged the idea of substituting military drill in the schools for physical education.

The death knell of gymnastics as an activity in the school program was sounded largely in 1910, when the National Society for the Study of Education published its *Ninth Year Book* in which Wood of Columbia took a firm stand for sports as a substitute for gymnastics. Psychologists, led by G. Stanley Hall, and sociologists, backed him in this stand, and school authorities began to accept the idea.

In 1916 Dr. Ernest H. Arnold, in his presidential address before the American Physical Education Association, complained: ". . . the plow of physical training has scarcely drawn a furrow in the virgin soil." But by the end of this era, with the coming of World War II, that plow had made a wide swath across the land. Just how much of a swath is revealed in the many figures in the material that follows throughout the remainder of this chapter. If there seems to be a surfeit of dates and statistics it must be realized that only by dates can an item be placed in its niche in history and only by figures can one grasp the extent of growth.

Aims and Objectives

Educators, parents, and the public in general now began asking what were the aims and objectives of physical education. Although Hitchcock and Sargent in an earlier day had both voiced their own aims, the profession as an organized group had not faced up to the challenge. Now Hetherington, President of the Physical Education Department of the National Education Association, voiced for the profession the aims in this new century as: (1) organic education for vital vigor, (2) psycho-motor education for power and skill in neuro-muscular activities, (3) character education for moral, social, and spiritual powers, and (4) intellectual education acquired through free play or development of social thinking. These aims were a far cry from the single, narrow aim of the earlier eras, that of relieving the tedium of the school room.

At the same time physical education added to its aims a broader base: (1) to share in the development and carrying out of the pattern of general education—in other words, it became an integral part of education; (2) to offer a program that would become an integral part of community life through its recreational aspects.

Much talk arose over the concomitant learning to be derived from physical education activities, particularly over character education from plays and games. Frequent topics at professional gatherings for many years centered about sportsmanship. What are the elements of true sportsmanship? What is an amateur? What is a professional? Much oratory, some eloquence, much debate, some wisdom, came out of all the talk. School essays were written on the topic. Professional association presidential addresses dealt with it, and the professional literature of the period abounded in articles on the subject. What leader in the profession did not present his own definition of a true sportsman to have it checked against those of his peers for long argumentation as to just how participation in sports could be made to produce this concomitant learning in children. Even clergymen across the country discussed from their pulpits this newly recognized objective of physical education and looked hopefully to the profession to make true sportsmen of all school children now that emphasis was placed on play and games as a part of the school program.

What physical education teacher worth his mettle did not keep posted in a conspicuous place on his school bulletin board his favorite definition of sportsmanship for all to read and study. And of all that were posted perhaps none enjoyed more acclaim than the definition offered by Charles W. Kennedy on p. 267.

Lower Schools

Whereas practically none but the large city schools had organized physical education by the end of the last century and only a few small towns had added it after the turn of the century, the post-World War I period brought great and sudden growth in this branch of education. For example, Alabama, California, Ohio, and Virginia not only employed state supervisors of physical education but county supervisors as well; the entire state of Florida had but three full-time physical education teachers in 1924, but by 1927 it had 73; Indiana had but few schools in 1900 with special teachers of physical education, but by 1930 it had 802 in 477 schools; and Minnesota had only 108 full-time and 63 part-time teachers of physical education in 1924, but by 1930 it had 301 full-time and 698 part-time teachers. These are typical examples of what was going on throughout the country.

Facilities. Although gymnasiums of this new era far outnumbered those of the 1890's, building did not keep abreast with the growth of the programs. The medium-sized towns made the best showing in facilities according to the findings of the White House Conference of 1930, which reported, for example, that Ohio had gymnasiums in 80 per cent of its public schools; New York, in 62 per cent; the Dakotas, in 51 per cent; and New Hampshire, in 44 per cent.

The National Education Association through its Committee on School House Planning set up standards for physical education facilities in the schools calling for every junior and senior high school to have a gymnasium which "must be a Hall of Health with an abundance of fresh air and sunlight." The Committee on Reorganization of Secondary Education went further and recommended for every school two gymnasiums, one for boys and one for girls, and many schools strove to meet these requirements. In 1908 Detroit opened a swimming pool in its Central High School—the first high school pool in the United States. As to playing fields the Society of State Directors of Physical Education called for a field of three to four acres for every 400 pupils, and the NEA asked for fields of at least ten acres for all rural high schools.

Programs. The College Physical Education Association spent nine years on the study of a national curriculum for all grades through college and from this study set up an approved program for the elementary grades which was accepted as a national pattern. It consisted of the following: athletic games, 25 per cent of program; rhythms, 20 per cent; hunting games, 15 per cent; and 10 per cent each of self-testing activities, mimetics, free exercises, and relays combined with stunts and tumbling.

Requirements. Most state departments of education set a minimum physical education requirement in the schools, and many city and town schools set their own minimum above that. In the 1920's many schools set a minimum of 415 minutes per week of physical education classwork in the elementary schools and 300 per week in junior high schools.

A 1932 survey showed that 80 per cent of the three-year high schools required physical education for all three years and 70 per cent of the four-year schools required it all four years. This survey covered schools in forty-six leading cities in twenty-two states. No doubt, with the great increase in facilities and teachers, the percentages would run even higher if the survey had been repeated in the 1950's.

The question of granting school credit for physical education classwork was fought out seriously in this era. A survey of 582 schools of New York State in 1924 revealed that 82 per cent of the principals and superintendents were in favor of granting credit. Of the 17 per cent opposed one said, "I am opposed to giving credit for digging potatoes, etc. in lieu of Latin"; another said, "Schools are for training the young to read and write"; and yet another said, "It would be as much out of the general scheme as giving credit for eating well-balanced dinners." So it was obvious that as late as 1924 many educators still held a narrow concept of both physical education and education. However, by 1930 credit was being granted in seventeen states. From a survey of 254 school systems it was shown that 70 per cent were granting credit by that date.

Staffs. In 1903 when Gulick became the first head of the physical education department of the New York City schools he inherited a staff of thirty-six physical education teachers, the largest group in any school system in the United States at that time. Before his coming, these teachers had each been a law unto himself, going his own way alone. Now Gulick united and coordinated them into a department staff. When Ethel Perrin was appointed Supervisor of Physical Education for the Detroit public schools, she inherited a staff of three men and two women specialists. When she left that position fourteen years later, she left a staff of 360 specialists.

Most elementary schools followed the general pattern of placing the responsibility of teaching physical education upon the classroom teacher. The high schools tended to employ sports coaches for the boys, and then assign them the physical education class work; while they called upon the home economics or some other academic teacher to teach the physical activity classes for girls. But after World War I the situation improved considerably.

By 1931 Alabama, California, and Virginia were maintaining county directors of physical education as well as state directors. Indicative of the progress throughout the country are the following figures: Indiana schools from 802 physical education teachers in 1930 to 1,037 in 1932; Massachusetts schools from 211 physical education teachers and 60 school gymnasiums in 1920 to 1,100 teachers in 700 gymnasiums in 1932; and Pennsylvania schools from 153 physical education teachers in 1921 to 2,200 in 1935. Indiana schools in 1932 required all coaches of interscholastic sports in high schools to hold certificates of training in the field of physical education.

Studies of this era showed the commonly accepted standard distribution for the 40-hour-per-week teaching load of a physical education teacher to be 25 hours of teaching, 5 hours for administrative work, 5 for extracurricular activities, and 5 for consultation with pupils.

There is little information available as to salaries of this era but there is a record that in the New York City schools in the early 1900's, men physical educators were paid $1,300 to $2,400, and junior assistants, $1,000 to $1,200 per year, while the women teachers were paid $1,000 to $1,900, and junior assistants, $700 to $1,000. These would represent top salaries for the opening of the century.

Physical Education for College Men

In the early 1900's much antagonism still existed within the college faculties toward physical education as a part of the educational program. Nonetheless those colleges that had not yet developed physical education departments before the end of the nineteenth century now began to carry on the programs heretofore carried on unofficially by the students themselves.

The state universities that had not established physical education before the close of the nineteenth century fell quickly into line, with Pennsylvania leading in 1904 and Idaho in 1908. Of the several universities that first established physical education departments, fifteen maintained separate departments of physical education for men and women with five of these completely separated in all respects and ten separated but coordinated under a Division of Physical Education.

Facilities. This was a period of gymnasium building and rebuilding: funds were made available, and many fine buildings were provided. William Ralph LaPorte (1889–1954) of the University of Southern California invented the self-service locker-basket system which added much to the efficiency of dressing rooms and facilitated classwork materially. The increased popularity of indoor intercollegiate athletic sports caused architects to increase the seating capacity of the structures. Gymnasiums with a gallery running-track became popular at the turn of the century, but interest in this feature had practically died out by 1930. Not only fine gymnasiums were built in this era but also great football stadiums.

Early in this era when football was becoming "big business" in the colleges and universities, Harvard University built the first of the large stadiums (1904). It seated 23,000, an unheard-of seating capacity before this date. Yale followed in 1913 with its coliseum, so-called at first because it was not open at the ends but was enclosed like the Greek and Roman coliseums. Later it became known as the Yale Bowl. It seated 67,000. Other colleges slowly fell into line, but most stadiums of this era were not built until the 1920's. By 1920 the total seating capacity of stadiums then in existence was 929,523; by 1930 the total had risen to 2,307,000. The stadium at the University of Michigan first seated 87,500 and was later enlarged to seat 97,000; the Ohio State University stadium seated 77,000, later increased to 85,000 capacity.

As to gymnasiums of that period, the most magnificent in the United States, no doubt in the entire world, was the ten-million-dollar Payne Whitney Gymnasium at Yale University, completed in 1932. Five stories high, with an additional four stories in the large tower, each level represents some one phase of activity in the physical education program. Its beautiful entrance hall is decorated with reproductions of sculptures of athletes by R. Tait McKenzie. In its spacious quarters it can accommodate 1,200 students participating in activities simultaneously.

Requirements. The University of Pennsylvania was the first university to require all students to take courses in physical education for all four years. Beyond this, following the advice of their own Benjamin Franklin, given 150 years earlier, the authorities also made the ability to swim a requirement for graduation. The land-grant colleges lagged in their physical education offerings, because of their commitment to require military drill of all male students. By the close of the era in the other colleges and universities, physical education was quite generally required for both men and women for three hours per week for the first two years of college work.

Staff Rank. The University of Pennsylvania gave R. Tait McKenzie the rank of full professor when he was brought from McGill University in 1904 to become head of its physical education department. Following that appointment, several other colleges granted professional rank to heads of physical education departments. A study by Meylan of Columbia University in 1916 showed that out of 252 colleges surveyed, 100 granted the rank of professor to men directors of physical education, as against only 30 granting this recognition to women directors.

The College Physical Education Society reported that by 1927, 27 per cent of college physical directors had the M.D. degree; eight per cent, the Ph.D. or Ed.D. degree; 20 per cent, the master's degree as top degree; and 38 per cent, the bachelor's degree. Seven per cent had no college degree.

As to salaries after World War I, a survey of 1922 showed that while the top salaries to heads of departments were one of $10,000 and two of $8,000, 61 per cent of the 227 colleges of the survey paid the top position $2,000 to $3,500; 8 per cent, between $1,500 and $2,000; 27 per cent, between $1,000 and $1,500; and 3 per cent, less than $1,000. It is quite probable that these lesser salaries were paid to men who carried athletic coaching positions on the side and were compensated for that part of their salary from the athletic funds.

Physical Education for College Women

By the time of World War I practically all colleges and universities with women students had established departments of physical education for women. In the coeducational schools, some were placed under the men's departments, some were coordinated with them, and some were independent of them.

Many forceful women were at the helm at this time shaping the destinies of these college departments and setting the pattern of a philosophy for the physical education of women which materially affected programs in the lower schools and in nonschool groups as well as in the colleges.

Facilities. In most coeducational colleges and universities the women's physical education facilities were quite meager compared to those for the men. The women used the men's gymnasium floor and playing fields when the men did not wish to use them. But in a few colleges women were fortunate to have their own facilities. In 1900 Hearst Hall, a gymnasium for women, was built at the University of California (Berkeley). Women of the University of Texas had their own gymnasium in the basement of the Woman's Building early in this era, and the University of Washington had a small building for a women's gymnasium. The Mary Hemenway Gymnasium of Wellesley College of 1909 was then years ahead of the times in many of its details, such as central-controlled showers and costume-disinfection system. But all too frequently the women fell heir to the men's old gymnasiums when they acquired new ones, but at that it was better than none at all.

However, it was not until the 1920's that women students really came into their own in physical education facilities. The new Hearst Memorial Gymnasium at the University of California at Berkeley, built in 1927 in semi-monumental style of architecture, was particularly magnificent in its architectural design and in its scope of facilities.

Four well-designed and equipped gymnasiums were constructed for college women in the 1920's at the Universities of Oregon, Washington, and California (Berkeley), and at Smith College. Other notable buildings of that decade were those at North Carolina College for Women built in 1923, and at the Universities of Minnesota, Colorado, and Illinois.

For outdoor facilities Mills College built the first college outdoor swimming pool in 1924 to be followed shortly by the three outdoor pools for women at the University of California.

The novelty of electrically controlled doors to divide gymnasium floors came as early as 1930. One of the first was in the women's gymnasium at St. Catherine's School in St. Paul, Minnesota.

In the early 1930's several splendid gymnasiums were constructed for the women students such as those at the Universities of Texas and California (Los Angeles branch), Stanford University, and Wellesley and Oberlin Colleges. These buildings, representing Spanish Renaissance, Lombardian Italian Romanesque, Tudor Gothic, and modern types of architecture, set a new style of beauty with utility for women's gymnasiums in the United States.

Athletic fields for the exclusive use of women in coeducational institutions were first developed in this era. In the fall of 1901 the women at the University of Chicago had a hockey field laid out in an open parkway at Woodlawn Avenue and 59th Street. Since the game had come to America only that summer, this must have been one of the earliest hockey fields in the country, most certainly the first away from the Eastern college area. The women's colleges have always led all other schools in their playing space for women. In 1902 Wellesley College constructed a boathouse and bathhouse on the shores of its campus lake, and by 1929 boasted twenty-two tennis courts, several hockey fields, and a like proportion of other play areas. Smith College by 1930 led all other colleges in its outdoor facilities for women. This college maintained in one field twenty tennis courts, ten archery lanes, a running track, and in another field of twenty acres, four hockey fields, a soccer field, a baseball diamond, a golf-driving range, several badminton courts, and a bridle path. Smith College also had three outing cabins, a boathouse, a crewhouse, and riding stables.

Programs. Although women engaged in sports in colleges from the earliest days of their enrollment in these schools, they, like the men students, organized them on their own, quite apart from any officially recognized physical education classes. Wellesley College was the first of the women's colleges to accept activities other than gymnastics and rhythms as a part of the physical education required program. It was not until the 1910's that sports were accepted as a part of the all-year school programs by most colleges.

In the 1920's there was a marked increase of emphasis on corrective work (individual gymnastics) for those needing special developmental or protective measures in their exercise program. A few colleges offered this work in the 1910's, and a rare few, influenced by the Swedish Movement Cure of the late nineteenth century, offered this work in the first decade of the 1900's. The women's departments in all eras have been far in advance of the men's departments in this field of work in the United States.

Throughout this era there was a constant increase in sports offerings, also the introduction of courses in body mechanics. A survey of 1930 made in connection with research on women's athletics covering 120 colleges in all sections of the country showed that the most commonly used athletic activities were the following: basketball used in 96 per cent of the colleges; softball, in 90 per cent; field hockey, in 87 per cent; swimming, in 80 per cent; archery, in 70 per cent; track and field, in 60 per cent; and soccer, in 58 per cent. In the 1930's and 1940's, fieldball and speedball, badminton, deck tennis, and handball were added to the women's programs.

Staffs. In the 1890's a department of physical education for women was considered sufficient in size if it had one teacher with possibly one or two student assistants. By 1900, however, several women's colleges had as many as two or three full-time teachers, and by 1929 most had two or more full-time teachers. Wellesley College boasted thirteen. A few colleges employed women trained in Sweden and England but most used graduates of American schools of physical education. As to academic training, Oberlin College was the only one at the turn of the century which employed a woman teacher trained in physical education who also held a college degree. Gradually teachers with college degrees came on the scene, and by the end of this era practically all heads of women's departments in colleges held at least the bachelor's degree, and most of them had from one to two years of graduate work. The several women heads of departments who held the medical doctor's degree in this new era were trained in physical education as well as in medicine.

In the earlier century the only title recognized for a woman physical education teacher except in one or two rare cases was that of Director or Directress of the Gymnasium. Even into the 1920's many colleges conferred upon their women physical education teachers no academic rank whatsoever. On the other hand, as early as 1885 and 1895 Oberlin College and the University of Nebraska accorded the rank of instructor to their women directors of physical education. In 1896 the University of

Michigan conferred the rank of full professor on their Director of Physical Education for Women. Oberlin advanced their women's director to the rank of full professor in 1903—the first private college to grant this rank to a woman physical educator. Wellesley College, in 1909, became the first of the women's colleges to accord the head of the department of physical education the rank of professor.

Salaries for women physical education teachers ranged from $500 to $1,500 per year in the early part of this era, and after World War I increased to range from $1,000 to $4,000 in the 1920's and 1930's. These figures are for the average positions.

Costumes. The most universally accepted costume of the first part of this era was the long, full bloomers of three to five yards of woolen suiting, a middy blouse and middy tie, or a blouse of the same material as the bloomers worn with a stiffly starched dickey with complicated underarm harness to hold it in place, long, black cotton hose, heavily ribbed, and leather, orthopedic-style gym oxfords. By the 1910's a decided change came about, and in the 1920's still another so that by 1930 the woolen costume had given way completely to cotton, and the full bloomers had practically vanished from the scene replaced by scant bloomers with elastic well above the knee or by shorts.

Not until the 1930's were swimming suits of other than gray cotton permissible for school use. By this date special treatment of materials had been devised to protect against the shedding of lint and the running of dyes. Thus swimming costumes at last became attractive to women students. For girls' gymnasium suits, this period brought into use the short cotton, knicker-type, scant bloomer with sleeveless blouse, or shorts with tailored blouse. For dance, the leotards came into use—knitted material like that used in swimming suits—some with short sleeves, some long, some shortlegged and some long. Boys' costumes, too, took on a *new look* with trunks greatly abbreviated from those of earlier eras.

Research

The interest in research of the preceding century grew with the years, and the new century brought new and wider interests in testing. Whereas anthropometrical measurements and strength tests held the main interest in the earlier days, physical achievement tests and tests of cardiac efficiency now took the stage of interest, motivating for improved programs.

By the opening of the new century it had become apparent to the medical men both within and outside the profession that children, for their protection, should be classified for exercise according to the functioning of their heart and blood vessels. In 1905 McCurdy at Springfield started work on adolescent changes in heart and blood pressure, and in 1917 Schneider at Connecticut Wesleyan developed his cardio-vascular efficiency tests, which were used by the aviation services during World War I.

From the first physical achievement tests for school children (devised by Gulick for the New York City Public School Athletic League in 1904 from his earlier Penthathlon tests of the 1890's devised for the YMCA) to those given in 1928 by the National Recreation Association to 44,117 boys and girls of 450 cities, there was a great advance in testing techniques and standard-setting. The American Physical Education Association produced its athletic badge tests with established standards of achievement in 1913, and its national committee, set up under McCurdy in 1922 to work on motor ability tests, developed a physical intelligence quotient. At this same time the Playground Association presented its Athletic Badge Test consisting of, for boys, (1) arm strength, (2) jumping for distance, (3) running for speed, (4) throwing a baseball for accuracy, and (5) throwing a baseball for distance; for girls, (1) balancing, (2) running for speed, (3) throwing a baseball for accuracy, (4) throwing a baseball for distance, and (5) efficiency in fundamentals of a game, either baseball, basketball, or volleyball.

In the college field, Meylan of Columbia University devised in 1919 the first achievement tests for college men using elements of sports in running, jumping, climbing, vaulting, throwing, etc., and in the same year Agnes Wayman (1880–1968) of Barnard College presented the first such tests for college women. In 1921, Sargent first presented his Physical Test of a Man, which achieved much attention throughout the country. This test consisted of a vertical jump using the factors of height and weight with ability to overcome the force of gravity. The efficiency index for this test was arrived at by the formula of weight in pounds multiplied by height of vertical jump in inches divided by height in inches. In the 1920's Frederick Rand Rogers (1894–   ), of Boston University, started work on a physical fitness index (PFI), which although largely replaced by later tests is still in use in the 1960's. This index is the achieved strength index divided by the normal strength index for the individual's age and weight. Tables of norms for age and height were worked out for the formula.

Interest in testing and research, aimed at improvement of the profession in all of its aspects, had grown so remarkably by 1930 that 25 per cent of the schools of a national survey were found to be using a testing program of some kind whereas practically none had testing programs at the opening of the century. Written tests of knowledge came into popular use in the early 1930's, also, and have now become a recognized part of all testing programs. Also, beginning in 1930 the American Association for Health, Physical Education and Recreation established a periodical on the subject, *The Research Quarterly*.

The summer of 1924 was the first time that a course in testing in physical education was offered in a teacher-training department—Teachers College, Columbia University.

There arose such a deep interest in testing in this period that many schools plunged into it without anyone adequately prepared to do such work or to interpret it correctly; many even used the tests themselves as the foundation of their programs. Harold Rugg, a leading educator of the time, in his book of 1941 (see References) spoke of this period as one when education "was consumed with a passion for precise measurement." As he said:

> We lived in one long orgy of tabulation. . . . Mountains of facts were piled up, condensed, summarized and interpreted by the new quantitive technique. The air was full of normal curves, standard deviations, coefficients of correlation, regressive equations.

Yet out of it all, with much enthusiasm well placed, yet some misplaced, there came improvements in physical education programs with standards of performance at hand for the measurement of growth and progress.

Teacher Training

Whereas in the nineteenth century most teachers of physical education had but little technical training, many teachers of the early decades of the twentieth century did have, and more women than men teachers had a good preparation. This factor no doubt resulted from the fact that there was a preponderance of training schools for women over those for men; also, the laity considered any man sufficiently prepared to teach the subject if in his own school days he had participated in sports.

An increasing demand for more teachers brought forth more training schools and also more attention to this need by the colleges. Also, the growing demand that teachers have at least a bachelor's degree brought about the movement within the private noncollegiate normal school for affiliation with some college, which meant marked changes in many of these schools and the demise of others.

At the close of World War I there were approximately 10,000 men and women in the United States professionally trained in physical education. In 1930 ninety-three institutions of collegiate rank were offering teacher preparation in physical education, to meet the demand for trained teachers in the field. Not only schools and colleges were asking for trained personnel but also playgrounds, recreation centers, boys' and girls' clubs, YMCA's, YWCA's, all manner of youth-saving groups, hospitals, rehabilitation centers, and all branches of the Armed Services. This demand brought about greatly increased teacher training offerings. But the day of the private noncollegiate school of physical education was coming to a close. All teacher training in the field of physical education was, by the end of this era, established in the colleges and universities.

Private Non-Collegiate Schools. Practically all schools preparing physical education teachers before 1900 were private noncollegiate normal schools. Early in the new century, several new schools were established—the Chicago Normal School of Physical Education (1905), the Battle Creek School of Physical Education (1909), Bouvé-Boston School of Physical Education (1913), the American School of Physical Education in Boston (1914), Columbia Normal School of Physical Education in Chicago (1915), the Newark School of Physical Education (1917), the Central School of Physical Education in New York City (1919), the YMCA Graduate School in Nashville, Tennessee (1919), the Marjorie Webster School of Physical Education in Washington (1920), the Ithaca School of Physical Education (1920), and the Bouvé School in Boston (1925).

The first of the private schools to achieve collegiate rank was the YMCA International Training School of Springfield, Massachusetts, which acquired authority in 1905 to confer the degrees of bachelor of physical education (B.P.E.) and master of physical education (M.P.E.). In 1912, the name of the school was changed to the International YMCA College and in 1953 to Springfield College. By 1916 it had lengthened its physical education course to four years. Dr. J. H. McCurdy was head of the physical education work of the school from 1895 to 1930. In 1907 the Normal School of the North American Gymnastic Union moved to Indianapolis, Indiana, and was authorized by law to confer degrees. Under the leadership of Emil Rath (1873–1943), who served as Dean of the school from 1909 to 1934, the school widened its curriculum, and in 1941 it affiliated with the University of Indiana. The Boston Normal School of Gymnastics was the first of these private schools to seek collegiate affiliation. In 1909 it affiliated with Wellesley College, offering a five-year course for the bachelor's degree, and a two-year course in specialization open to those who already possessed the bachelor's degree. In 1917 it achieved graduate status, fulfilling the dreams of many years of Amy Morris Homans. In 1913 the YMCA Training School in Chicago achieved collegiate rating and became George Williams College.

The Anderson School (originally the Brooklyn School of Physical Education), which moved to New Haven in 1900 and became known as the New Haven Normal School of Gymnastics, took on collegiate rank in 1921 as Arnold College. In 1924 the YMCA Graduate School of Nashville achieved collegiate rating, but it closed its doors in 1937. In 1929 the

Central School of Physical Education moved to Troy, New York, aligning itself with Rusell Sage College. The Bouvé and Boston Schools of Physical Education merged in 1930 and in 1931 affiliated with Simmons College as the Bouvé-Boston School. In 1942 this joint school transferred to Tufts University where it remained until after mid-century.

In 1931 the Ithaca School of Physical Education, which had merged with the Ithaca Conservatory of Music in 1920, became Ithaca College. In 1902 the Sargent School had lengthened its course to three years, and in 1929 became a division of the School of Education of Boston University. In 1933 it became Sargent College of Boston University. In 1931 the Savage School closed its doors, and in 1943 turned its records over to New York University.

The Chicago Normal School of Physical Education became Kendall College of Physical Education in the early 1930's, and, closing its doors in 1935, turned its records over to George Williams College. The Posse School closed in 1942, ending a 52-year career. By mid-century, all the old schools of specialization in physical education had achieved collegiate rating on their own, or had affiliated with some college, or had closed their doors.

Colleges and Universities. Although a few colleges and universities, such as Wayne University in 1881, Oberlin College in 1886, and the Universities of California, Indiana, and Nebraska in the late 1890's, had offered isolated teacher training courses before the turn of the century, only two—the University of Nebraska, in 1897, and Oberlin, in 1900, had started a professional course leading to a degree, and only the University of Nebraska had graduated the first student before the close of the century (see p. 222). Shortly thereafter several colleges and universities established physical education majors as follows: Teachers College, Columbia University (1903); the State Normal School, Ypsilanti, Michigan (1907); California, Oregon, and Washington, men (1910); Wisconsin (1911); Missouri and Utah (1914); Iowa (1918); Illinois, men, Indiana, men, and Minnesota (1919); Kansas (1920); Michigan and Washington, women (1921), Texas and Illinois, women (1923); Ohio State (1924); and Wyoming (1925).

As the teacher training work in this field developed in various universities it was sponsored in some by the liberal arts colleges, in some by the teachers colleges, and in some by the schools of education. The last two named had gradually absorbed practically all teacher training in physical education, when a new form of organization arose.

By early 1920's a struggle developed in the colleges within the fields of physical education, health education, and recreation for the control of teacher preparation in these fields. The heavy requirement of "education courses" demanded by the teachers colleges, on the false assumption that all students expect to go into the public schools to teach, allows but little time for courses in allied fields, hence handicapping professional training. Under the professional school form of organization, preparation in physical education readily combines with preparation in the fields of athletics, health education, safety education, and recreation. Several universities established this form of organization, some setting up this teacher-training work in a School and others in a College of Health, Physical Education, and Recreation.

The earliest record of an attempt to set up such a school or college within a university is that of 1908, when Clark Hetherington successfully piloted through the Board of Curators of the University of Missouri a resolution calling for the establishment of such a four-year school offering a Bachelor of Science degree in Physical Education. For some reason the approved project was side tracked, and nothing came of it. Two years later Hetherington left Missouri, and it was twelve years later (1920) when the first School of Health and Physical Education within a university was established at the University of Oregon. In 1924 a similar school was established at Stanford University. Other schools of physical education were initiated at the University of Illinois in 1932, and the University of West Virginia in 1937. This era produced only one College of Health and Physical Education—this at Pennsylvania State University in 1930.

Public Normal Schools. The first public normal school to offer specialization in physical education was at Ypsilanti, Michigan. The course started in 1907 under Wilbur P. Bowen. Soon many normal schools, spurred on by state legislation, provided for specialization in physical education.

Graduate Preparation. In 1901 Teachers College of Columbia University, inspired by Dr. Wood, became the first institution to offer the master's degree with specialization in physical education, and soon thereafter a few other schools followed their lead. However, Wellesley College was the first to set up a graduate curriculum in physical education which was open only to persons who had completed full undergraduate requirements for a major in physical education.

For many years it has been accepted that Columbia University and New York University were the first schools in the United States to offer a doctoral program with specialization in physical education, both entering upon this work in 1924. But recent research by J. Edmund Welch (see References) refutes this and offers the following facts concerning the conferring of doctor's degrees with specialization in physical education: in May of 1925 Columbia University conferred the Ph.D. degree upon Frederick Rand Rogers; in August of 1925 the YMCA Graduate School of Nashville conferred the D.P.E. degree upon Glenn Gentry; in May of 1926, Columbia University conferred the Ph.D. degree upon Ethel Saxman; these were the first doctorates in this field: the first Ph.D., the first D.P.E., and the first doctorate to a woman.

By 1930 twenty-eight institutions were offering graduate work in physical education, New York University starting its program in 1925. The University of Pittsburgh and Stanford University (1929) were, according to Nash, the first institutions to offer the Doctor of Education degree for specialization in physical education; the first such degree conferred was at Pittsburgh in 1932.

Summer Schools. By 1909 the Harvard Summer School of Physical Education had developed into a specialized course covering three seasons of work to procure a certificate. Following the 1918 session it closed, although that summer it had 230 students and a staff of 48 lecturers, instructors, and assistants. This closing ended thirty-one years of service to the profession. In its thirty-one years of existence it had been a powerful force in the advancement of the profession. According to Sargent's own records it had trained 3,652 persons, who came from 1,082 different institutions, 53 countries, 232 colleges and universities, 245 secondary schools, 326 elementary schools, 72 YMCA's, 19 municipal gymnasiums, 30 athletic clubs, 27 state institutions, 4 voice-training schools, and 11 normal schools. These students were school superintendents, college professors, principals of public and private schools, lawyers, physicians, members of foreign embassies, school teachers, and athletes.

The Chautauqua Summer School of Physical Education continued for several years into the twentieth century before closing its doors. In 1903 the Savage School added summer courses for a few summers. In 1904 Yale inaugurated a summer school of physical education, but it lasted only four years. In 1909 the Teachers College of Columbia University offered its first summer courses in this field. In 1912 the New Haven School and the University of Utah joined the summer school group. After World War I, summer courses increased markedly in universities, particularly making an appeal to the classroom teacher who had been drafted to teach physical education part-time.

Specialized Training. Correspondence courses in physical education were offered by Dr. Jay W. Seaver of Yale in the opening years of the century. When these course offerings started is not on record, but letterheads carrying the date of 1903 have been seen with Dr. Seaver's name listed as President and Medical Director of the American Institute of Physical Culture—a Correspondence School of Health and Exercise. The letterhead carried the address of 29 Beacon Street, Boston crossed out with New Haven substituted.

In 1914 the University of Illinois offered its first Coaches School, and this idea spread quickly to other universities. Also, special professional courses in physical therapy were offered in some schools during World War I to meet the current need of trained personnel in that field. Following the War this specialization grew into permanent courses offered by several schools in cooperation with the physical education major.

Non-School Organizations

Physical education developed rapidly in the 1900's in nonschool organizations with the YMCA's and YWCA's leading all other groups.

Young Men's Christian Associations. The YMCA expanded its program of physical activities working with all types of community agencies to promote physical activities for young boys in particular, yet giving increased attention, also, to its offering for young adults and older men. The national organization now maintained two colleges, one in Springfield, Mass., and one in Chicago, Ill., both of which specialized in the preparation of teachers of physical education to man their so-called "physical departments."

In 1906 Dr. George J. Fisher, then a YMCA director at Brooklyn, was named head of the Physical Department of the International Committee, and in 1910 Dr. John Brown, Jr., a former YMCA Director at Montreal and New York City and just out of medical school, joined the staff of the National Board. When Dr. Fisher became Deputy Scout Executive of the Boy Scouts of America in 1919, Dr. Brown succeeded to the directorship which he held until his retirement in 1941. Under the management of these two men the international physical education program expanded remarkably.

Dr. Fisher originated the "Teach America to Swim" slogan, and in 1906 the YMCA under his direction inaugurated a mass swimming campaign, followed shortly by swim tests and awards. It cooperated with the American Red Cross in setting up the earliest first-aid classes and until 1925 the two organizations gave a joint certificate. In 1910 the YMCA interested the American Red Cross in establishing life-saving courses. In 1915 it set up its junior and senior hexathlons, and in 1916 its School of Aquatics.

Since 1896 the YMCA Athletic League, upon recommendation of the YMCA Physical Directors Society, had been affiliated with the AAU, but in 1913 it broke off relations, not to renew the alliance for eighteen years.

During World War I many YMCA physical directors beyond service age worked with the allied troops both at home and overseas. The program they offered to the servicemen was designed to occupy leisure hours through recreational sports participation aimed at developing morale and a sense of brotherhood with all other servicemen. They also worked with convalescents in hospitals, helping with muscle re-education and recreational activities. Many others worked in Community Service Camps and organized recreation programs for civilian war workers.

Following the war the YMCA started the national volleyball and indoor swimming championships in 1922, national basketball championship in 1923, and handball contests in 1925. In 1937 it held its first aquatics conference and in 1938 a Sports Championships Congress, and in 1940 it launched its Learn-to-Swim campaigns.

Throughout this period there was a marked increase in gymnasiums and athletic fields available to the public under YMCA auspices, also in numbers of trained leaders to man the facilities.

Young Women's Christian Associations. In this new era the YWCA added swimming to its activity programs, with the first classes opened at Montgomery, Alabama, and Buffalo, New York, in 1905. In 1911 they organized the first National Conference of YWCA Health Education Directors. The National Board uses the term *health education* in preference to *physical education.* The Centennial Report of 1916 stated that there were 65,000 women attending YWCA gymnasium classes, and 32,000 in the swimming classes. In thirty years the enrollment in physical activity classes had increased to 380,965.

Turners and Sokols. With the public schools assuming the responsibility for the physical training of children, the Turner and Sokol clubs now placed their emphasis on programs for adults. With the coming of World War I, so much feeling arose against Germany that it became highly advisable for groups bound together by their common German background to dissolve and to identify themselves exclusively with other Americans as Americans. This materially affected these societies and they waned markedly.

Movements Related to Physical Education

Many important movements related to physical education in various aspects of their programs originated in this era, such as the Boy Scouts of America and the Camp Fire Girls (1910), the Girl Scouts of America (1912), and the National Park Service (1911). The recreation and camping movements grew ever more important with the coming of the twentieth century.

Recreation Movement. The playground movement of 1900 helped to sell physical education to the public, and the play activities, athletics, and folk dance which were now added to the recreation program, helped immeasurably to popularize it. The promotion of recreation had become an accepted part of American life in the large cities and the groups that had previously supported settlement yards and school playgrounds broadened their activities to include municipal, state, and national recreation areas. Sums of money which were enormous for those days were spent for these ventures.

In 1900 Chicago appropriated $10,000 for the equipment of playgrounds in densely populated districts. Congress began the annual appropriations for playground work for the District of Columbia in 1905. Chicago, in 1903, voted a $5,000,000 bond issue for small recreation parks, and ten were opened in 1905. By 1910 the city was operating 65 playgrounds and bathing beaches, and its South Park system was regarded as the finest in the world. Boston, New York, and Philadelphia also made provision for playgrounds and parks. In all, more than 150 cities reported playgrounds before 1910, and many other cities had them in the planning stage. Los Angeles appointed its first Board of Playground Commissioners in 1904.

The increased interest in recreation which followed World War I brought greatly expanded facilities: play fields, swimming pools, bathing beaches, golf courses, day camps, and winter sports facilities. By 1925, 748 cities had community recreation leaders, and 688 cities had 5,121 playgrounds with 17,177 leaders representing a yearly expenditure of $1,900,000.

In the 1930's, the Work Progress Administration came into existence to relieve the unemployment problem. It covered projects for recreation in every state but Maine. It built 13,700 parks, 22,000 playing fields, 670 golf courses, 1,510 swimming pools, and built or repaired 7,930 recreation buildings.

By 1935 the WPA had undertaken the training of leaders for group recreation and had organized recreational programs in many communities throughout the country, using the leaders they had trained. These programs covered sports and games, aquatics, dancing, drama, and musical activities as well as play centers for pre-school children and therapeutic recreation for the physically disabled. By 1938 some 38,000 people were employed per month on WPA recreation projects alone, not counting those engaged in construction projects.

Public agencies created hundreds of lakes across the country for flood control, offering to millions of people an opportunity for recreational fishing and boating not available to them at the turn of the century; and public agencies also opened up over a hundred thousand miles of trails for outing activities in some one hundred and eighty million acres of public land in our national forests.

Before World War II, many other agencies were sponsoring recreation: municipal departments of recreation, municipal park boards, and public schools; such voluntary agencies as the Boy Scouts, Girl Scouts, Camp Fire Girls, youth centers, and church recreation departments; such private agencies as sports clubs and commercial recreation establishments; private schools; and such industrial recreation agencies as the UAW–CIO Recreation Department, established in 1937 with a trained physical educator at its head with the status of International Representative of the Union.

Camping Movement. With the American Indian recognized as the earliest of American campers, Indian lore has been woven throughout much of the fabric of the camping movement. Also, legends of Kit Carson and Daniel Boone gave inspiration for much of the rituals, while interest in outdoor life aroused by Teddy Roosevelt, Dan Beard (1850–1941), and Ernest Thompson Seton (1860–1946), all great outdoorsmen, gave impetus to the cause. By the opening of this century, there were an estimated 50 to 60 organized camps established in the United States, and the movement grew rapidly from then on.

In the first sixty years (from 1860 to 1920) the movement was largely a recreational one. During the 1920's it began to take on its educational stage when camping became an extension of the school. Many schools now established their own camps. Omaha, Nebraska, established its school camp in the early 1920's—one of the first such camps. The most notable of the early school camps were the Life Camps maintained by the New York City Board of Education.

The first Boy Scout camp was organized by Daniel Beard and Ernest Thompson Seton shortly after that organization came into existence, followed soon by the first Girl Scout Camp in northwestern Georgia, named Camp Lowland after their founder, Juliette Lowe. The first Camp Fire Camp was established by the Gulick family at Lake Sebago in Maine and named Wo–He–Lo after the words, Work, Health, and Love. By 1930 the camping movement had moved into the stage of orientation and responsibility. Physicians, nurses, and dieticians were added to the camp staffs and camp life became less highly organized than in the 1920's. By the late 1930's the United States was dotted with a wide variety of types of camp, such as: (1) organization camps, (2) school camps, (3) public camps, (4) private camps, (5) labor-union camps, (6) specialized camps, (7) day camps, and (8) CCC camps. This last, the Civilian Conservation Corps camp, was established during the depression of the 1930's by the federal government so that young boys could be housed, fed, and given employment in areas where they could, under supervision, help construct camps, state and federal parks, mountain trails, and recreation areas. It was a life-saver for thousands of boys who would otherwise have been thrown onto the streets unemployed during those difficult years. By the close of the era just preceding World War II, the Girl Scouts alone maintained 453 camps, with a total attendance of over 700,000 girls. Also, eighty-one cities were operating day camps.

The American Camping Association was organized in the 1930's made up of owners, directors, and leaders of various camps. The Camp Directors Association of America was founded in 1910; and the National Association of Directors of Girls' Camps in 1916, with the wife of Luther Halsey Gulick as its president. In 1924 these two organizations merged and became the Camp Directors Association, with George Meylan as its president. By then camping had become a big summer-time business in America.

American Youth Hostels. This European movement for inexpensive outings came to the United States in 1934, but it was confined mostly to the New England states and localized areas surrounding a few metropolitan centers where several hostels were established in communities easily accessible to each other by foot or bicycle. A few physical educators threw their influence and enthusiasm into this movement because of its possibilities of bringing aroused interest for hiking and biking to American youth and adults. Because of the great distances in the United States and the hazards of the highways from automobile traffic, the movement has never flourished here as in Europe.

Professional Literature

As if to make amends for the dearth of professional literature of the earlier years, many writers in the field of physical education emerged early in the new century, and many "firsts" for the United States came off the press, such as: Jessie Bancroft's *School Gymnastics and Light Apparatus,* 1900; a city school manual by Gulick, 1903; Sargent's book on philosophy and principles, *Physical Education,* 1906; Gulick's book on the same topics, 1907; then Elizabeth Burchenal's *Folk Dance Tunes,* followed in quick succession by several other books by her on folk dancing, with a total of fifteen between 1914 and 1941; Jessie Bancroft's *Games for School, Home, and Playground,* 1909, one of the professional all-time best sellers; Clark W. Hetherington's *Normal Course in Play,* 1909; and R. Tait McKenzie's *Exercise in Education and Medicine,* 1909.

The second and third decades also brought forth several firsts, such as Thomas D. Wood's *Health Education,* 1910, the book that started the modern natural gymnastics movement; Gulick's *The Healthful Art of Dancing,* 1911, which was used for over twenty years in the schools of America; the state of Michigan's *Physical Training for Public Schools,* 1912, the first state manual; Wilbur P. Bowen's *Action of Muscles,* 1912, the first on kinesiology; Fred Eugene Leonard's *Pioneers of Modern Physical Training*, 1919, and *History of Physical Education*, 1923; James H. McCurdy's *Physiology of Exercise*, 1924; and Elmer D. Mitchell's *Intramural Sports*, 1928.

It was in the 1920's that the first books by Dr. Jesse Feiring Williams came off press. For many years he was the profession's most prolific writer, producing books covering a wide range of topics, some of which came out in many editions. No one book of this era, however, ran into more editions or topped the sales figures of Neils Neilson's and Winifred Van Hagen's *Physical Education in the Elementary School* first published in 1929 as a California State Manual. Outstanding books of the 1930's were Neilson and Cozen's *Tests and Measurements*, 1930; Josephine Rathbone's *Corrective Physical Education*, 1934; Agnes Wayman's *Education Through Physical Education*, 1934, a first in organization and administration for girls and women; and Frederick Luehring's *Swimming Pool Standards*, 1939.

Many authors furnished many books on many subjects. Each succeeding decade brought forth many new authors who contributed notably to the advancement of the profession after the "firsts" on various phases of work had charted the way. A perusal of the publishers' lists in the various issues of the national organization's periodicals through the years will reveal the wealth of topics covered and the names of persons who in this way served the profession.

The two periodicals started in the 1890's, *Mind and Body* (1894) and *The American Physical Education Review* (1896), continued through this era, the former surviving until 1935. Edward Hartwell was the editor of the latter until 1900, then Luther Gulick took over and was editor from 1900 to 1902. He in turn was followed by Dr. George Fitz (1860–1934) of Harvard University, who turned the editorship over to James Huff McCurdy in 1905. The periodical had been a quarterly from 1896 through 1907, when it became a monthly. McCurdy edited the magazine through the year 1929 and in 1930 it became the *Journal of Health and Physical Education*, under the editorship of Elmer D. Mitchell of the University of Michigan. Mitchell had been Editor of the *Pentathlon* (the official organ of the Midwest Physical Education Association, which had been established in 1928 and had been produced in eleven issues). When he succeeded to the office of Secretary–Treasurer–Editor of the APEA in 1930 the Midwest group gave up its own venture, throwing its influence and support back of the new national magazine. At the same time the APEA began publication of the *Research Quarterly*.

Four new magazines were established in this era. *Physical Training* was started by the YMCA in 1901, with Gulick as its editor. In 1905 George Fisher took over the editorship; in 1924 it changed its name to

The Journal of Physical Education, and in 1926 John Brown, Jr., became its editor. The magazine *Playground* put in its appearance in 1907 as the official organ of the Playground and Recreation Association of America.

A periodical called *American Gymnasia and Athletic Record* was started in September, 1904. It was published by the American Gymnasia Company of Boston, and it claimed to be "The Only National Physical Training Publication Giving News of the Profession." The few issues available for perusal are full of interesting news of meetings, programs, and teachers—much that the other periodicals of that time did not carry. The periodical did not survive long, but while it lasted it maintained a book sales division and a teacher's exchange—both in the field of physical education.

In March, 1909, another magazine entered the field, *Hygiene and Physical Education,* edited by W. W. Hastings of the Springfield YMCA School. This magazine had purchased the mailing list of the defunct *American Gymnasia.* It carried articles on health education and hygiene as well as physical education, and its first few issues gave promise of a brilliant future in the educational field; but it, too, soon vanished from the scene. It apparently took the backing of a national organization to keep a professional periodical on its feet in those days.

23

Professional Organizations and Leaders of the Early Twentieth Century (1900–World War II)

The new century brought increased interest in the promotion and control of athletics as well as advancement in the profession of physical education so that many new organizations came into existence in the early 1900's. Also, the number of trained personnel in the field increased materially, and a new group of leaders arose to carry on the work started by the stalwart pioneers of earlier days.

PROFESSIONAL ORGANIZATIONS

Interests had become sufficiently specialized by the coming of the twentieth century to support several different types of professional organizations. The continuing history of those already in existence at the opening of the century will be discussed in the material that follows along with the history of new organizations, listed in the order of their founding. (The leading groups and their presidents through the years are listed in the Appendix.)

American Physical Education Association

The American Association for the Advancement of Physical Education, founded in 1885, changed its name in 1903 to the American Physical Education Association (APEA), in 1937 to the American Association for Health and Physical Education (AAHPE), and in 1938, to give recognition to its actual scope of many years past, including recreation, it adopted its present long name, the American Association for Health, Physical Education and Recreation, commonly spoken of as the AAHPER.

With the coming of the new century, it undertook to organize its workers into sections of interests. By 1904 it had three sections—the Section on Normal Schools and Professional Training, the Section on Gymnastic Therapeutics, and the Section on Anthropometry—and three affiliated organizations—the Secondary School Directors' Society, the Public School Directors' Society, and the Society for Research—all of which later developed into sections. At the same time it had built up a federation of local societies, some of them city groups, some state groups and one a New England regional group of several states. By 1930 it had eleven sections and five affiliated organizations. Also, it had united its many local groups into district societies with the Eastern, Middle West, and Southern districts coming into the mother organization in the order named. Shortly thereafter three new districts came into the mother organization, two new ones carrying states not heretofore represented and a third resulting from a redistricting of the earlier large Midwest group. The Northwest states joined APEA in 1931 and the Southwest states in 1934, thus bringing all of the United States into the organization. In 1934 the old Midwest group, extending from Pittsburgh to Denver, split into two groups, the portion east of the Mississippi retaining the old name and the states west of the Mississippi taking the name of Central District. Within each district the states maintain state associations, each with representation on the national council, thus reaching down to the very grass roots of the profession.

In 1937, AAHPE affiliated with the National Education Association and is now that organization's largest department. Since that date it has maintained its official offices in the NEA building in Washington, D.C.

For the first thirty-eight years of this organization, all presidents held the M.D. degree except William Blaikie, the second one, who was an attorney-at-law deeply interested in physical fitness. For the next fourteen years (1923–37) there were nine presidents, only two of whom held the M.D. degree, Frederick Maroney (1884–1958) and Jesse F. Williams; the others held neither the M.D. nor Ph.D. nor Ed. D., but all had technical training beyond the bachelor's degree. This period marks the transition years within the profession when the Ph.D.'s and Ed.D.'s gradually were taking over from the M.D.'s. Beginning with 1937 and up to the time of World War II, there were eight presidents all holding the Ph.D. except one, Margaret Bell (1888–), who, serving 1939–40, was the last president with the M.D. degree. This clearly marked the trend within the profession itself, the gradual change of the early twentieth century from the medical to the educational emphasis.

College Physical Education Association

The Society of College Gymnasium Directors of 1897 became the Society of Directors of Physical Education in Colleges in 1908 and in 1935 became the College Physical Education Association. Throughout the 1910's and 1920's it held its annual meetings in conection with those of the National Collegiate Athletic Association and the American Health Association. During World War I the Society offered the services of sixty men in fifty colleges and universities to the United States government, all experienced medical examiners and practical physical educators. It also gave serious study to the problem of the relation between the departments of gymnastics and those of athletics, which in most colleges had developed as two separate departments.

Physical Directors Society of the YMCA

There were enough men working in physical education in the YMCA's by 1903 to found the YMCA Physical Directors Society to improve the standards and enlarge the field of service in physical education in the YMCA's of America.

Playground Association of America

During this era many organizations important to physical education came into existence. In 1904 the Big Brother Movement, Inc., headed by Jacob Riis (1849–1914), leader of New York City's anti-slum movement, was born to help under-privileged boys. From it came the idea of a similar organization on the national level, and in 1906, sparked by Luther Gulick, the Playground Association of America was organized in Washington with Gulick as its first president, and Jacob Riis as vice president; Theodore Roosevelt was Honorary President. At this time there were forty-one cities in the United States with playgrounds already established. The new organization started to work for the development of year-round programs and for municipal support. It sent out field workers to conduct campaigns in cities to get playgrounds organized, and it also set up programs for playgrounds and started a drive to find leaders to man them. In 1911 it changed its name to the Playground and Recreation

Association of America (PRAA) with Joseph Lee (1862–1937), a philanthropist of Boston, known as "the father of the playground movement," taking over the presidency and continuing in that office until his death in 1937. In 1930 it changed its name once more—this time to the National Recreation Association (NRA).

National Association of Physical Education for College Women

In the spring of 1910 Amy Morris Homans invited directors of physical education in women's colleges of New England to meet at Wellesley College to discuss their mutual problems. In 1915, again meeting at Wellesley, the group enlarged to include all Eastern colleges, and they organized the Eastern College Women's Physical Directors Society. Two years later the college women physical directors of the Middle West met at the University of Chicago where they organized their district association. In 1921 the Western group organized at Mills College. Then in 1924 these three regional groups through representatives met together in Kansas City and affiliated as the National Association of Directors of Physical Education for College Women. It immediately embarked upon investigations into physical examinations of women, excuses from required work, programs, and credits. In the early days of the organization none but directors of departments were accepted into membership, but before the close of this era membership was opened to all members of the staffs of physical education for women in colleges and the word "directors" dropped from the title.

American Academy of Physical Education

An early Academy of Physical Education was organized by Gulick in 1904. This was an informal group of physical educators who desired to get together for discussion free of formalities and red tape. They met annually for an entire week in early September at the summer camp of Dr. George L. Meylan on Sebago Lake in Maine. The group of eleven included the pre-eminent men leaders of that day. The meetings produced much fine thinking for the advancement of the profession, but with the interruption of World War I and the death of its guiding spirit, Gulick, in 1918, this organization broke up.

In 1926 a new group organized the present American Academy. Three of the five original members—Clark W. Hetherington, R. Tait McKenzie, and T. A. Storey—had been members of the earlier group. The other two originating members of the new organization were Dr. William Burdick (1871–1935), of the Baltimore Athletic League, and Jay B. Nash (1886–1966), of New York University. These five selected five others to join them, and these ten selected five more the following year. This process was continued until 1930 by which time the charter membership list was completed. This group then proceeded to draw up a constitution and to get the organization work under way. Of the earlier group Dudley Sargent, Luther Gulick, and Fred E. Leonard (1866–1922) had passed away and were elected Fellows in Memoriam. The others of the earlier group were Wilbur Bowen, J. H. McCurdy, George Meylan, and Paul Phillips, who were taken into charter membership, and Dr. C. Ward Crampton who had by then left the profession to practice medicine. Later, however, he was elected to associate membership. Throughout this four-year organization period, Hetherington acted as Chairman of the group, and in 1930 McKenzie was elected its first President, serving in that capacity for many years. (The purpose of the organization is discussed in Chapter 25.)

Society of State Directors of Physical Education

By 1926 there were fourteen states with state directors of physical education, and for mutual aid they joined forces to create the Society of State Directors. As more states acquired directors, the group grew in size and importance, and as the profession widened its concerns, it became the Society of State Directors of Health, Physical Education and Recreation. This organization concerns itself with these interests in the lower schools of the nation.

Conferences on Physical Education

After World War I, many conferences were held patterned after the famous Boston Conference of 1889. The most far-reaching in its effects on physical education was one held in 1918 when the United States Commissioner of Education called sixty leaders of physical education to Atlantic City for a conference. Out of this meeting grew the formation of a National Committee on Physical Education with Dr. Thomas D. Wood at its head. It immediately established the National Physical Education Service to promote state and federal legislation on physical education programs and playgrounds in all schools under their jurisdiction. The Playground and Recreation Association accepted the sponsorship of this service, and $10,000 was contributed to finance it. James E. Rogers (1885–1959), who had been on the National Staff of PRAA since 1911, was appointed head of the service, and from then on he travelled constantly all over the United States until his retirement in 1950, promoting state and federal programs of physical education. It is impossible to fully appraise the advancement which this work brought to the profession. Following the 1918 conference, a number of important conferences related to physical education were called by special groups for special purposes quite aside from the conventions held regularly by the various professional organizations. Two of the more important special conferences were the White House Conference on Child Health and Protection in 1930 and the International Recreation Congress held in connection with the Olympics at Los Angeles in 1932.

LEADERS OF PHYSICAL EDUCATION

With the greatly increased size of the profession at the opening of the twentieth century there naturally arose a larger group of leaders than in the earlier era. Among these were many recognized above others for their foresight, wisdom, and enthusiasm which advanced the profession to a higher place in education and community life. Of these mention can be given here to only a pre-eminent few.

Time has given prominence to four leaders of physical education of this period to whom comes acclaim far beyond the confines of the profession itself, namely Luther Halsey Gulick, who brought the profession to the notice of the lay public; Thomas D. Wood, who called the profession to the attention of health education; R. Tait McKenzie, who brought recognition of the profession to the medical and art worlds; and Clark W. Hetherington, who sold physical education to general education. They are discussed chronologically by year of birth.

Luther Halsey Gulick (1865–1918)

Luther Gulick was born in Honolulu of missionary parents and as a child lived in several foreign countries, in Europe as well as in the Orient. At Oberlin College he came under the influence of Dr. Delphine Hanna, who aroused his interest in physical education. Thomas D. Wood was his roommate, and together they worked out a philosophy of physical education which in later years brought strength and advancement to the profession. After two years at Oberlin College, he went to the Sargent School to prepare to teach physical education. There he became acquainted with Sargent, starting a friendship and a professional tie that served the profession well. From there he went to a position at the Jackson, Michigan, YMCA, resigning after one year to enter upon medical studies at New York University, where he procured the medical degree in 1887. From there he went to Springfield, Massachusetts, where he established the department of physical education at the School for Christian Workers (today's Springfield College). At the same time, he prevailed upon the YMCA to establish the position of Secretary of the International Committee of Physical Education of the YMCA's, becoming the first to hold the position. After thirteen years at Springfield, he became Principal of Pratt High School in Brooklyn, which position he held from 1900 to 1903, leaving it to become Head of the Department of Physical Education of the Public Schools of Greater New York City. Previously there had been separate departments of physical education of the various boroughs of the city but all were united into one over-all department with Gulick the first to hold the directorship.

In 1907 he left the teaching profession to join the staff of the Russell Sage Foundation to work full-time for the Playground Association of America which he had founded. During this period he built his camp at Lake Sebago in Maine, which developed into the famous Gulick Camps where the Camp Fire Girls of America began. In 1913 he left the Russell Sage Foundation to take up full-time work for the Camp Fire Girls, leaving that work in 1918 to devote himself fully to the War Board of the YMCA. In this last work he went to France early in 1918, heading up the foreign war work of the YMCA. After a six-week stay, he left Dr. James H. McCurdy in charge of affairs for the Board in France with six helpers—all that were then available instead of the 300 urgently needed—and returned to the United States to conduct a recruitment campaign for the YMCA overseas workers. And it was in his Lake Sebago Camp that he loved where he died in his sleep on August 13, 1918, having gone there for a brief rest from his arduous war-work duties.

Foremost Contributions. His many important contributions to physical education, recreation, education in general, and to the enrichment of American life are unmatched in number by any other leader in the profession. He was the founder of many important movements, such as the establishment of physical education in the YMCA's of America, the Playground Association of America, New York University Summer School of Physical Education, the Department of School Hygiene of the New York Academy of Medicine, the position of Secretary of the International Physical Education Committee of YMCA's (he being the first to hold the position), and the Camp Fire Girls. Besides this he was one of the founders of the American School Hygiene Association, the Boy Scouts of America, American Folk Dance Society, and American Camping Association. Also, he was the creator of the inverted red triangle emblem of the YMCA representing "Spirit upheld by mind and body," and the inspiration for the founding of the Mother's Club of Springfield, Massachusetts, which was the forerunner of the National Congress of Parents and Teachers.

Literary Productions. He served as editor of five different magazines, four of which he founded: *The Triangle,* 1891–92; *Physical Education,*

1892–96; *American Physical Education Review*, 1900–02; *Physical Training*, the organ of YMCA, 1901–03; and *Wohelo*, organ of the Camp Fire Girls, 1914–18. Besides his editorial work he published 217 articles on both popular and professional topics in fifty different periodicals and eight handbooks, nine pamphlets, and fourteen books. Perhaps his two best known books are *Physical Education* of 1904 and *The Efficient Life* of 1907.

Honors and Important Offices. The honors conferred upon Gulick and the high offices he held in important organizations are legion. To mention but a few he was a member of the International YMCA committee, President of AAAPE for five years, a member of the American Olympic Committee, the first President of the Playground Association of America, President of American School Hygiene Association, and the first President of the Camp Fire Girls of America. Three medals are awarded in his honor: (1) The Gulick Award of the American Association for Health, Physical Education and Recreation (see Appendix), (2) the Roberts-Gulick Award of the Society of Physical Directors of the YMCA's of North America, and (3) the Gulick Medal of the Camp Fire Association of America. New York City operates a playground named in his honor. He is a Fellow in Memoriam of the American Academy of Physical Education.

Appraisal of the Man. Gulick had educational ideas in advance of his time. Before John Dewey expounded his educational philosophy, Gulick was informing his teachers that they were to teach boys and girls rather than subject matter, and as early as 1891 he introduced the use of photography to analyze movement.

When he first began his career the YMCA physical activity teachers were ex-pugilists, old soldiers, and ex-circus performers—most were non-Christian and not interested in educational ideals. He started the movement to have none but men of Christian character to teach in the YMCA's for which he was criticized as expecting too much.

He was a great individualist, essentially different from others, quick to take up new ideas and also quick to drop them, the executive type not interested in details. He had an enormous capacity for work, and his interests were wide. He had unusual drive, unusual leadership ability, unusual vision—hence he accomplished a prodigious amount of worthwhile work in the fifty-three years of his life.

Thomas Dennison Wood (1865–1951)

Thomas D. Wood was born in Sycamore, Illinois. As a student at Oberlin College he, along with Gulick, his roommate, came under the influence of Dr. Hanna who interested him in taking up the study of physical education. After graduation from Oberlin in 1888 he procured his medical degree at Columbia University. In 1891 he went to California as one of a small group who assisted David Starr Jordan in organizing the newly established Leland Stanford University. He organized and directed the physical education department, which was called the Department of Hygiene and Organic Training. At the same time he also served as the college physician.

Trying out his own theories, he set up the first physical education program at Stanford around games, sports, tumbling, and outdoor activities, calling it a program of "natural gymnastics"—first in the United States. After ten years at Stanford, with Herbert Hoover (President of the United States 1929–33) and Clark Hetherington in his first freshman class, he went to Columbia University as Professor and Director of Health and Physical Education and College Physician, which position he held for twenty-six years. At the age of sixty-two he rounded out five more years before retirement in 1932 as Professor of Health Education.

Foremost Contributions. Wood established the first professorship of health education, the first outlines for a school health program, the first graduate work in both physical education and health education in the United States and was the originator of the movement to replace foreign systems of gymnastics with natural gymnastics of American origins. He was an advocate of the study of child development and he fought to bring the attention of educators to the fact that physical education could help in the social, emotional, and intellectual development of the child as well as in its physical development. He also championed the education of the child for democratic living.

Honors and Important Offices. Wood was a Fellow of the American Association for the Advancement of Science, of the New York Academy of Medicine, and of the American Academy of Physical Education. He was the third person to receive the Gulick Award of APEA. He served the profession through many important positions in many related organizations. He organized the Joint Committee on Health Problems in Education of the American Medical Association and the National Education Association and served as chairman of the committee for over twenty-five years. He also helped develop the American Child Health Association and was a great crusader to make the schools accept their responsibility for protecting the health of school children. As Chairman of the Committee on the School and the Child of President Hoover's White House Conference of 1930 on Child Health and Protection, he put twenty-eight subcommittees to work under his direction and turned out a prodigious report.

Appraisal of the Man. As co-author of many books and contributor of major sections of various yearbooks on health and physical education, his writings have greatly enriched the profession. He was a great leader. His earnest seeking after a better life for all children and his educational philosophy advanced the professions of both physical education and health education to a marked degree.

Robert Tait McKenzie (1867–1938)

Born in Almonte, Ontario, Canada, R. Tait McKenzie achieved international fame as a sculptor, but no less noteworthy were his achievements in the fields of medicine, writing, and physical education. A delicate boy, he took up gymnastics to strengthen his physique, and he continued this training at McGill University. Becoming interested in physical education, he studied at Springfield and at the Harvard Summer School before completing his medical studies at McGill in 1892. In 1891 he was appointed Director of the Gymnasium there, succeeding James A. Naismith. In 1893 he was given the title of Director of Physical Training, at the same time serving as House Physician at the Montreal General Hospital. In 1896 he added Medical Director to his title and served one year also as House Physician to the Governor General of Canada. In 1904 he became Director of Physical Education at the University of Pennsylvania, which position he held until his retirement in 1931.

In the summer of 1907 Dr. McKenzie gave an address in London before the British Medical Association, and that fall took on the responsibilities of Professor of Physical Therapy on the medical faculty, in addition to his other duties at the University of Pennsylvania, the first such professorship in this country. Early in 1915 he offered his services to the British in their war effort and was commissioned Temporary Major in the Royal Army Medical Corps. In 1916 he became Inspector of Physical Training for Kitchener's Armies.

Literary and Artistic Productions. The best known of McKenzie's several books are: *Exercise in Education and Medicine* (1909), *The Treatment of Convalescent Soldiers by Physical Means,* and *Reclaiming the Maimed* (1918). A sculptor of international repute, several of his sculptured pieces are world famous. His *Joy of Effort,* a forty-six-inch plaque set in the wall of the stadium in Stockholm, was commissioned by the American Olympic Committee and presented to Sweden at the Olympic Games of 1912, following which the King of Sweden conferred upon McKenzie the King's Medal for distinguished service as a sculptor. His *Olympic Shield of Athletes* is the only one ever made by a sculptor. The famous Greek sculptor, Phidias, made the *Shield of Athena Parthenos,* and the Italian sculptor, Benvenuto Cellini, made three shields; but neither had produced a shield depicting athletes, although through the ages the athlete has been a popular subject with sculptors. McKenzie's *Olympic Shield,* five feet in diameter, was completed for the Olympic Games in Los Angeles in 1932 and there won the Olympic Art Award. The original is in the Mill of Kintail Museum, which is maintained near his birthplace in Almonte, Canada, and is a memorial to him. A smaller copy of the shield was made for the Olympic Games in Tokyo in 1964 and is owned by the Japanese Amateur Athletic Association. Through his many sculptured pieces he became famous in art circles as the first sculptor since the days of the Greek ascendency to use the athletic idea as his subject. Hussey's biography of him, *R. Tait McKenzie: Sculptor of Youth,* contains illustrations of his chief sculptured pieces. As early as 1904 his art work was exhibited in London at the Royal Academy. He held a one-man exhibit of his sculpturing in London in 1921 and in New York City in the 1930's.

McKenzie achieved international reputation for his British war memorials, notably one in Edinburgh in Prince's Street Gardens entitled *The Call,* one in Cambridge, England, entitled *The Homecoming,* and one in his birthplace at Almonte, Canada. Other well-known pieces of sculpture are his monuments at Harvard University and the University of Pennsylvania. A copy of his *Blighty* was a favorite desk ornament of King George V of England. Reproductions of many of his statues adorn the entrance hall of the magnificent Payne Whitney gymnasium at Yale. Altogether he produced over two hundred works of art, including twenty-five war and other memorials.

Honors and Important Offices. In 1904 McKenzie was selected as lecturer in artistic anatomy for the Olympic games held in connection with the St. Louis World Fair. He served the CPEA as president for one year, and the Academy of Physical Medicine, then the APEA, as President for four years and was one of the founders and the first President of The American Academy of Physical Education, serving from 1930 until his death in 1938. Three colleges conferred honorary doctorates upon him.

The American Academy created the R. Tait McKenzie Memorial Lectureship in his honor. The full issue of the *Journal of Health and Physical Education,* February, 1944, was devoted to his memory, containing biographical material and tributes from his vast circle of admirers. The AAHPER purchased from his estate the original of his *Column of Youth* and placed it in the national headquarters building of the National Education Association in Washington as a memorial to him.

Appraisal of the Man. No one of modern times has bound the profession to the glories of its ancient heritage as did R. Tait McKenzie through his art work. In this alone his contribution is unique. He was a gentleman of the old school, a man of culture, with a great capacity for friendship. He had a quiet dignity and a deep interest in a variety of concerns —a man of unusual personal charm and magnetism.

Clark W. Hetherington (1870–1942)

Clark Hetherington was born at Lanesborough, Minnesota. He was a member of the first class that graduated from Stanford University. Following graduation, trained in psychology, he went to Clark University as an assistant under G. Stanley Hall and there organized their laboratory in animal psychology. From 1900 to 1910 he was Professor of Physical Education and Director of Gymnastics and Athletics at the University of Missouri; and from 1910 to 1913 was a Fels Foundation Fellow with headquarters in Chicago "to foster the interests of physical education." From his Chicago office he travelled in thirty-three states, lecturing and holding conferences with lay groups interested in the moral welfare of adolescent youth. In 1913 he joined the staff of the University of Wisconsin to establish their professional training program. In 1918 he returned to California as Supervisor of Physical Education for the State Department of Education, serving as that state's first state physical director. In 1921 he received an appointment as Professor of Physical Education at Columbia University to work under his earlier teacher, Thomas D. Wood. Two years later he went to New York University to develop its department of physical education in the School of Education, establishing a four-year undergraduate program and a three-year graduate curriculum. In 1929 he returned to Stanford University on a professorship under T. A. Storey. After four years in that position, he became Consultant in Hygiene and Physical Education at Stanford until his retirement in 1938.

Foremost Contributions. Hetherington was the founder of the Missouri Valley Athletic Conference. He was also one of the founders of the Athletic Research Society, the Joint Committee of the NEA and the AMA on Health Problems in Education, the Midwest Physical Education Society, the Pacific Coast Society of Physical Education (today's South West District of AAHPER), and the American Academy of Physical Education. He was one of the chief promoters of the natural gymnastics movement. He produced several books and articles, chief among which was his book, *The School Program of Physical Education.*

Honors and Important Offices. He served as a member of the Board of Directors of the PAA, President of the Athletic Research Society, President of the Department of Physical Education of the NEA, President of the Midwest Physical Education Association, and in the four years of its organization period he served as Chairman of the American Academy of Physical Education.

He was the recipient of the Posse Medal for distinguished service in the field of health and the Gulick Award of the AAHPER for distinguished service to physical education. The University of Southern California conferred upon him the honorary degree of Doctor of Pedagogy. The American Academy of Physical Education has established the Hetherington Award in his honor.

Appraisal of the Man. As a child and young man Clark Hetherington continuously fought tuberculosis. Plagued with ill health much of his life, he triumphed over great odds. He was a stern man, uncompromising in matters of integrity, and he found much in the promotion of sports in particular that antagonized him. He was also a reticent man and to many seemed difficult of approach, yet to those who broke through the wall of reserve he offered friendliness and inspiration of a rare quality.

He was recognized as the foremost scholar and philosopher of physical education of his day. In the words of Charles H. McCloy of the University of Iowa, upon receiving the first Academy Hetherington Award: "Clark Hetherington's thinking laid the base, not only for an integrated philosophy of physical education, but also pointed the way for much scientific research which was to follow, to establish facts upon which to base further constructive philosophizing."

Others

It is not possible in a short history to give space to biographical sketches of all the leaders whose fine work notably advanced the profession of physical education in the early decades of the twentieth century. Many have been mentioned throughout this book in connection with specific activities and movements in which they played an important part. This period produced the profession's first historian, Fred E. Leonard of Oberlin College, to whom all later historians of the profession owe a debt of gratitude for his original research into the history of the development of physical education in America. Brief biographical sketches follow for a few others whose work was of special significance to the profession.

Clelia D. Mosher (1863–1940). Born in Albany, New York, Clelia Mosher was educated at Wellesley College and at Cornell, Johns Hopkins, and Stanford Universities. She was deeply interested in research and early in her medical career she challenged the all too prevalent ideas about the physical incapacities of women. As an assistant in hygiene at Stanford University she developed her studies that refuted the idea that women naturally breathe costally. Out of this study grew a deep interest in dress reform for women. From 1894 on she waged battle for abandonment of stiff corsets and the adoption of sensible shoes and light-weight clothing, and encouraged women's participation in sports. She organized girls' basketball teams and arranged game schedules for them. When she became physical examiner of women at Stanford University she developed her research in functional periodicity in women and disproved the theory that menstruation is an infirmity that must be suffered by women. Later she devised exercises for the relief of painful menstruation, which known as the "Mosher exercises" have been used for over fifty years in Europe as well as in America. Following this she was a co-inventor at Stanford of the schematograph as an aid in posture training. During World War I she went to France with the American Red Cross to work with refugee children and later became Medical Director of the Bureau of Refugees and Relief. All women owe Clelia Mosher a great debt for, through her studies, she set them free physiologically.

James Huff McCurdy (1866–1940). Graduating from the International YMCA School of Springfield, James H. McCurdy went to New York University where he procured the medical doctor's degree in 1893. In 1895 he returned to the school in Springfield and in 1900 succeeded Gulick as Director of the Physical Department which position he held for thirty years. From 1930 until his retirement in 1934 he was head of the Division of Health and Physical Education of Pratt Institute in Brooklyn. During World War I he was on leave to serve as head of athletics, medical and social services of the YMCA in France. Deeply interested in physiological research he devoted his years of retirement to studies of organic efficiency, particularly for men past middle age, war veterans, and Army and Navy fliers. Throughout his teaching career he made significant contributions to the profession in the field of physiology of exercise and published much material of value to the profession. His book on the physiology of exercise was one of the earliest in America on that subject. He devoted his adult life to the establishment of sound scientific procedures for the profession. He was a charter member of the American Academy of Physical Education. As Executive Secretary of APEA and Editor of its magazine, *The American Physical Education Review*, for twenty-four years (1906–30) he gave the national professional association the best of his talents and the best years of his life.

Jessie H. Bancroft (1867–1952). Jessie Bancroft was born in Winona, Minnesota. After one year at Winona Normal School and one at Iowa Medical College she took a few gymnastic courses in Minneapolis from a former pupil of Sargent who was located there. She then opened a school of her own and conducted "parlor classes" throughout Minnesota,

Iowa, and Illinois before attending the Harvard Summer School in 1891. In 1893 she was appointed Director of Physical Training of the Brooklyn Public Schools at a salary of $1200 per year. Ten years later she became Assistant Director of Physical Education of the schools of Greater New York City under Gulick which position she held until she retired in 1928. She produced many books and carried on much research, particularly in the field of posture. As a result of her measurements of school children she procured adjustments in school seats and desks, an unheard-of innovation for those days. She was a founder and President of the American Posture League, the first person to receive the Gulick Award of the American Physical Education Association, the first woman to be taken into membership in the American Academy of Physical Education, the first woman in the profession to produce a considerable body of professional literature, writing on posture, games, and anthropometry, and the first woman to head a large public school department of physical education. During World War I she was Chairman of the Government Commission on Training Camp Activities and President of the War Camp Community Service. Also she established the American Cooked Food Services for the American Expeditionary Forces.

Senda Berenson (1868–1954). Although Smith College had offered physical activities classes to its students from 1875 on, it was not until January, 1892, with the opening of a gymnasium building, that an actual department—then called the department of physical culture—emerged. This department was founded by Senda Berenson, who had come to America from Lithuania with her parents at the age of seven. The family settled in Boston, where Senda, concerned about her lack of physical stamina, became interested in Swedish gymnastics when that system was introduced into the Boston schools. In the fall of 1890 she persuaded the Boston Normal School of Gymnastics to accept her as a special student who would be taking the work not to become a teacher but to build up her own physique. By the end of the first year's work, she had decided to become a teacher of physical education and so returned for the second year. But at the close of the first term of her second year, Smith College offered her the opportunity to organize its department, and with the blessing of Amy Morris Homans she left school and accepted the Smith College offer.

One of her first ventures was the creation of modified rules of basketball for the use of girls. Because she herself had triumphed over long years of physical frailty, she took deep interest in the students who were physically below par. The necessity of building a firm foundation of physical fitness for all other activities became the cornerstone of her program for her students.

Although Miss Berenson is best known for her promotion of basketball for girls and her sixteen years of service as editor of its official rules, she put on a strong program of Swedish Gymnastics, standing firmly against detractors who objected to gymnastics as tending to make girls angular and ungainly. Miss Berenson, herself unusually attractive, was far from muscular and ungainly, and she gave no serious thought to those opposed to gymnastics for girls. She also introduced esthetic dancing into the program, one of the earliest ones to do so, and introduced special exercise programs for the upper-class girls who were excused from the requirement to take physical education. Early in her career she broke down all resistance of the faculty against the requirement for sophomores as well as for freshmen. Also by her tact and excellent work, she gained recognition as a regular faculty member (unusual for a woman working in physical education in those days), although she was never given academic rank. The times were not yet ripe for this.

At the very start of the enthusiasm over basketball for girls, she took a firm stand against intercollegiate competition, stressing that the game was for all the students, not just for a few who would be favored in such a program. Shortly she organized an athletic association open to all students—one of the first such in the country. She organized boating and introduced fencing, later studying fencing in Sweden under a fencing master of the Swedish Army Officers. She studied for four months at the Central Gymnastic Institute in Stockholm in the spring and summer of 1897—the second woman in America to study there, following Dr. Kate Hurd, an early graduate of the Women's Medical College of Philadephia and the first medical director of Bryn Mawr College, who had studied at the Central Gymnastic Institute in the year 1889–90.

Miss Berenson was also one of the first to offer a Field Day to the students, but she organized hers not as a contest in track and field events but as a series of game contests. For a few summers she taught at the Chautauqua Summer School, and in all probability introduced there the Swedish folk dances she had learned in Sweden in 1897. She also offered an exercise program to the mental patients at the Northampton State Hospital—perhaps one of the earliest in this field to undertake such specialized work. When she married in 1911, she resigned her position at Smith but continued to teach part-time for ten more years in a private school. The broad lane leading to today's Scott Gymnasium at Smith College is named Berenson Place in her honor.

Ethel Perrin (1871–1962). Born in Wellesley, Massachusetts, Ethel Perrin graduated in the second class of the Boston Normal School of Gymnastics. She remained at the school and taught there for fourteen years. From there she went to Smith College and then to the University of Michigan before the Superintendent of Schools of Detroit persuaded her to join his staff and organize a department of physical education for girls in one of his high schools. Up to that time their program consisted merely of basketball played by a few girls. She organized such a good program of a variety of activities interesting large groups of girls that the following year the superintendent urged her to take over the directorship of physical education for both boys and girls for all the schools of Detroit. Accepting the offer she became the second woman in the United States to head a department of physical education in a city public school system. In her first year in that position (1909–10) she had three men and three women on her staff who supervised all classwork which was carried on by the regular classroom teachers. In a few years she was able to appoint all professionally trained persons to do the teaching. Then she added health education work to her program and soon had forty specialists in that field on her staff. When she left the Detroit position in 1923 she had built up a staff of 350 physical and health educators and 15 supervisors.

From 1923 to her retirement in 1936 Miss Perrin served as Associate Director of the American Child Health Association. An ardent champion of correct standards of physical education and athletics for both boys and girls, she carried her struggles for them into work in the Women's Division of the NAAF which she helped to found. She served as first chairman of the Executive Committee. Miss Perrin was the first woman president of the Middle West Society of Physical Education, and the first woman to hold the vice-presidency of the national organization during the time it elected only one. She was the recipient of both the Honor and Gulick Awards of APEA for her distinguished service to the profession.

George L. Meylan (1873–1960). Born in Le Brassus, Switzerland, Meylan procured his medical degree from New York University in 1896 and went at once to the Boston YMCA as Medical Director. While there he secured his B.A. degree from Harvard and the diploma from the International YMCA School. In 1903 he became Professor of Physical Education and Medical Director of Columbia University where he remained until his retirement in 1929. Early in this position he earned the M.A. degree from Columbia and shortly after entered upon his long career in camp work. This culminated in his presidency of both the Camp Directors Association (1921–1923) and the United Camping Association (1927).

From March, 1907, through 1911 he served as President of APEA, the youngest person ever to hold that office. During World War I he was one of the first of many physical educators to serve overseas under the

International YMCA, organizing athletic programs and rest camps for the American Expeditionary Forces. He himself set up 1300 recreation centers for the French Army.

Elizabeth Burchenal (1876–1959). Miss Burchenal, born in Richmond, Indiana, graduated from Earlham College and the Sargent School of Physical Education. Her first position was at Columbia University where she taught from 1902 until 1905 when she organized and became Executive Director of the Girls' Branch of the Public School Athletic League of New York City. Four years later she became Inspector of Girls' Athletics for the New York City public schools, which position she held until she founded and became Executive Director of the American Folk Arts Society in 1916. In 1929 she became President and permanent Director in charge of the Folk Arts Center in New York City. Her professional contributions have been chiefly in the fields of athletics for girls and women and folk dance. In the former she served as the first chairman of the Women's Athletic Committee of APEA. This organization is today the Division of Girl's and Women's Sports. As its first chairman she started the work in the United States of establishing national standards for girls' and women's sports.

In the field of folk dance Miss Burchenal travelled widely in Europe from 1904 on, collecting and publishing dances of the people of many lands and conducting dance research. For many years she lectured and conducted institutes of folk dance throughout the United States, Canada, England, Scotland, Ireland, and Germany. For many years she was Chairman of the USA Committee on Folk Arts and a member of the International Committee on Folk Arts. She was the official delegate of the United States to the Fine Arts Section meetings of the League of Nations and, later, UNESCO of the United Nations at Geneva, Prague, London, and Paris.

In her later years Miss Burchenal was a resident Fellow of Carl Schurz Memorial Foundation and a Research Fellow of the Oberlaender Trust. During World War I she was Assistant State Inspector of N.Y. Military Training Commission and National Representative of U.S. War and Navy Departments Commission Training Camp Activities and also a member of the War Workers Committee of the U.S. Department of Labor.

Miss Burchenal was one of four women who were charter members of the American Academy of Physical Education, a recipient of both the Honor Award (1931) and Gulick Award (1953) of AAHPER. Boston University conferred upon her the honorary degree of Doctor of Science in Physical Education and she was long listed in *Who's Who In America.*

24

Physical Activities in the Mid-Twentieth Century

The greatly increased mechanization of post-World War II life over that of previous periods has still further robbed large segments of society of opportunities for physical exercise that formerly existed both in the home and at work. It has also still further increased leisure time over that of even the post-World War I period, which was in turn a marked increase over the leisure of the nineteenth century. The 14–16-hour work day of the 1880's has changed to the 6–8-hour work day of the present, and there is talk of a 6-hour work day and a four-day week. Children as well as adults have greatly increased leisure. Except in rural areas there is little opportunity for them to do hard physical labor together. Children now spend much of their out-of-school hours at movies, poring over "funnies," or watching television, instead of engaging in the informal play activity of old, so that there is a greatly increased need for organized physical activity for them both in the school and in the community. Also the need for release from the tensions that develop from the pressures of today's highly mechanized world calls for much physical-activity recreation for adults. As the way of life has changed markedly, because of the advances of technology, so physical education and sports activities have changed, too, as discussed in the material that follows.

ACTIVITIES OF PHYSICAL EDUCATION

Dance and Rhythm

Mid-twentieth century has seen a complete acceptance of modern dance in the lower schools as well as in colleges and the world of the performing arts. It has also seen a revival of square dancing. There has arisen a marked growth of interest in and acceptance of dance as a tool of education. The Dance Section that was established within the AAHPER in the early 1930's was advanced in 1965 to the Division of Dance within that organization, giving dance equal recognition with physical education in general and athletics.

Modern or Contemporary Dance. As the years have passed, *modern,* as used for the new dance form of post-World War I, has come to seem inappropriate for the new period, and the term *contemporary* has come into usage by many to replace the earlier term *modern.* John Martin, noted dance critic, in an interview on a television program on Dance of Today (November, 1967), spoke of the unfortunate new name *contemporary dance* as being as poor as the old one. He expressed the hope that some name for this form of dance might yet be devised which would not be tied to any period of time.

Since this book is concerned with the history of activities of physical education it is not necessary to discuss dance in its professional aspects, but only in its educational features.

The school and college dance concerts originating in the 1930's and 1940's still hold sway in institutions where dance is taught. The old argument of the earlier era as to where the department of dance belongs in the educational world—in the department of physical education or in that of Fine Arts—is still debated and where settled has been decided in some schools in favor of the one and in others in favor of the other. Today many institutions offer a major in dance.

With the boost given for the past several decades by Ted Shawn, noted dancer and exponent of modern dance, to the idea that dance is a worthwhile and challenging activity for men as well as women, an increasing number of men in colleges are joining modern dance classes. Also, men coaches have come to recognize the fundamental techniques of dance as excellent body-building exercises and urge their athletes to join classes in this activity.

Post-World War I, Martha Graham developed her form of modern dance around the concept that movement based on the strength and flexibility of the trunk muscles originates from the center of the body and from there flows outward to the other parts of the body. Doris Humphrey developed her form of the dance around the idea that all movement is a continuous process of fall and recovery, of losing and regaining balance. Various other leaders developed modern dance according to their own concepts of movement, but all held that dance is the vehicle through which one expresses emotion and ideas by movement. But today, according to Hahn, one of the new generation of modern dance teachers (see

References), movement is now considered an end in itself. It does not have to express anything but itself, in relation to time, space, and energy, as it explores the relation between sound and movement, between light and movement, between words and movement, and so on. In the early years of the development of modern dance, great emphasis was placed on the divorce of modern dance from all forms of stylized dancing, such as ballet. But in this new period, modern dance is taking a fresh look at such forms to acknowledge a concept all hold in common—that dance of whatever form is the art of movement with the body its sole instrument.

Square Dance

The post-World War I revival of square dancing has persisted, and following World War II it still moved forward enthusiastically. The Nebraska revival is typical of that in many other states. Lincoln, a city of a little over 180,000 population, had twenty-three square dance clubs in 1956; Omaha, twenty-nine; and other localities supported thirty-one other clubs. All are united in the Nebraska Folk and Square Dance Association, organized in the 1940's, which holds an annual state festival in Lincoln each spring with as many as 800 or more dancers on the floor at a time. In the 1950's it maintained a youth section which sponsored square dancing for young boys and girls throughout the state. Each year at its festival it featured some one nationality represented among the citizenry of the state and invited this group to put on an exhibition of its Old-Country folk dancing. This brought much pleasure to these groups in the way of friendly recognition of their Old-World culture and much of educational value to others.

This revival has been going on in all sections of the country, and not only state but also regional and national festivals are held. But in the 1960's it is not so much a revival and continuation of old dances as a creation of new present-day square dances. Many of today's square dancers create their own dances, building on the fundamental forms and figures of the old but transforming them into new patterns that form altogether different dances. In some of these new dances they use the two-step or waltz instead of the shuffle or skipping steps of the older forms. As a local club creates a new dance and passes it on to other clubs and demonstrates it at some festival, it may become popular and well known. Thus there has grown up a body of new square dances unknown to the pioneer of yesteryear, also new calls and jingles for the callers. Whereas in the old square dancing anyone gave the calls for them, there has today grown up a group of professional callers, in great demand at festivals, who travel about the country and are paid large fees for their services. In today's square dance world, it is frequently the caller rather than the dancers who receive public acclaim.

Gymnastics

Following World War II, a reaction set in against the post-World War I disapproval of gymnastics, which was voiced so strongly that gymnastics all but disappeared from the physical education program. Now has come a new appraisal of gymnastics, and once more this activity is back in the program, though in a new form. Whereas in earlier years the word "gymnastics" referred to a series of formal free-standing class exercises done in unison at a teacher's command, followed by apparatus work; today it refers mainly, at least as far as women are concerned, to the apparatus work alone. With the introduction of such new pieces of gymnastic apparatus as the high balance beam, the uneven parallel bars, and the trampoline, even the apparatus work has taken on new forms, which offer training in creativity and opportunities in the development of self-realization, through the performer's own original creation of exercise forms both on apparatus and in free-exercise routines. For this latter the student uses tumbling and acrobatic and rhythmical forms somewhat similar to modern dance techniques. Some of the free-exercise forms as done by women are called "gymnastic ballets."

The use of the high balance beam, popular today with women in particular, came to America by way of Sweden, where it was introduced into the Swedish Lingiads of 1939–49 by Madam Maja Carlquist, who was seeking a new approach to Ling's principles of gymnastic exercises and developed work on the balance beam as important in the training of women. The high balance beam is 16½ feet long and 4 inches wide and is adjustable in height up to 4 feet. Basic rules for exercise on it and a Code of Points for judging one's performance have been developed by the Federation of International Gymnastics, which governs gymnastics for the Olympic Games and other international competition. Exercises on this piece of apparatus aim at the development of grace, poise, balance, coordination, and the ability to orient oneself in space. The uneven parallel bars seem to older persons trained in earlier years on the Swedish bom to be a fairly good substitute for that old piece of apparatus which was so popular in years gone by. The trampoline is too widely known and used to need explanation. The opportunities it gives for learning to handle the body in mid-air are found in no other piece of gymnastic apparatus, and in that respect it is unique.

Some of the apparatus used in earlier years, such as the horse, buck, vaulting box, parallel bars, and flying rings, has been retained, but gone are the Swedish bom, climbing ropes and ladders, and the horizontal and vertical ladders of by-gone days. As to hand apparatus, gone also are the wands, dumb bells, and Indian clubs of the late nineteenth and the early twentieth centuries, but in their place today, at least for women, are loops, hoops, and balls used along with the free-exercise routines.

With the coming of these completely new forms of gymnastics, following a period of almost complete lack in the schools of gymnastics in any form, there is a dearth of teachers prepared to handle such work, so that there has sprung up gymnastics-training institutes to carry on until teacher-training departments catch up with the skills of teaching gymnastics in its new forms. This applies more to women than to men, for the latter never did abandon gymnastics in the 1930's, 1940's and 1950's quite so completely as did the women.

Danish Gymnastics

Wherever gymnastics of the older forms is found in the schools today, it is most probably Danish gymnastics or some closely related form. Particularly is this true for work with girls and women. This is the form that was worked into the fitness program for the Women's Army Corps and was also used in civilian fitness programs during World War II. With the close of the War, however, popularity for this form of gymnastics gradually died out, to be revived temporarily here and there where touring Danish gymnastics teams aroused enthusiasm afresh. But Danish gymnastics, popular in America in the 1920's, 1930's, and early 1940's, especially with women, has also undergone changes in keeping with the times.

Individual or Corrective Exercises. Individual or corrective exercises (formerly spoken of as corrective gymnastics) refers to the program of specific exercises formulated to meet an individual student's corrective needs that are amenable to correction by specific exercises, and not to a program of restriction within the regular school work in gymnastics, sports, or dancing. This latter, usually spoken of as "restricted" class work, is designed for those who do not need specific correction of physical faults but do need, for various reasons that show up in a medical examination, restrictions on their exercise which they can nevertheless pursue as a part of regular class activity. Many students assigned to correction need restriction in dosage of exercise, but many do not, and the corrective program should not be confused with the restricted one.

By no means do all physical education programs, even in late twentieth century, offer corrective work, since this calls for highly specialized and individual teaching. But where offered, it, too, has taken on a new look in recent years. With the return of gymnastics to the physical education program, brought about by the Physical Fitness Movement, has come a return of interest in corrective work in order to take care of the deviations of children from the normal physique. According to Rathbone and Hunt (see References), the new correctives talk of progressive resistance exercises, "circuit training" isotonic exercise, geniometry, psycho-physical wholeness but still holds to the earlier objectives of body reconditioning and neuro-muscular re-education.

The Veterans Administration now requires their corrective therapists to be graduates of an approved course in professional physical education training.

After World War II there was an awakening of interest in corrective gymnastics, stemming from the public interest in the rehabilitation program of the Armed Services. Hospitals have adopted individual gymnastics in the treatment of many ailments.

Sports and Athletics

Without question the sports program that developed slowly during the nineteenth had by the middle of the twentieth century crowded the traditional and formal required physical education program out of the schools. But despite efforts by many leaders to broaden the base of athletics in schools and colleges, football, baseball, basketball, and track and field remain the important sports for boys and men. Of these sports, football holds the number-one position with the public, and basketball is a close second. But judging by sales of sports equipment, the fastest growing sports of this era are skiing, fishing, bowling, softball, badminton, skating, bicycling, basketball, table tennis, and paddle tennis, in the order listed.

The same thing has happened in sports with regard to television as happened in an earlier period with regard to radio. At first the television broadcasts cut into gate receipts of games, and many sports managers denounced them as radio broadcasts had been denounced earlier, but in the late 1960's the crowds attending the big games are larger than ever dreamed of in earlier decades in spite of television's pull to keep many at home to watch the games in comfort.

Basketball. By the 1950's basketball had spread throughout the world, and teams from many nations compete in the sport now in the Olympic Games. In 1949 the National Basketball Association was established, marking growth in the professional game. An estimated twenty million people play this sport throughout the world. The National Collegiate Athletic Association elimination contest, the National Intercollegiate championship, and the National Invitation tournament represent the major college play-offs held near the end of each basketball season. Crowds of 15,000 people or more often attend college basketball games in various cities throughout the country. On occasion, gambling has reached out to involve college basketball players, but even with accompanying poor publicity the game continues to grow in its appeal.

Today's game is changed considerably from that of the early days when the tallest men were the height we today consider but average. In "pro" basketball teams of today, the centers range from 6 feet, 9 inches, to over 7 feet tall, the forwards from 6 feet, 6 inches, to 6 feet, 9 inches, and the guards from 6 feet, 1 inch, to 6 feet, 7 inches. In college basketball the University of Kansas in 1957 claimed the tallest man of all basketball history in their player who was 7 feet, 2 inches tall, and in the 1960's a California school boasts a player who is 7 feet, 1⅜ inches tall. Today's high school players average 5 feet, 5 inches.

Because of this great increase in the stature of athletes over that of the early 1900's, the height of the basket, which has remained unchanged through the years, is in altogether different ratio with the height of the average player. Some have advocated, although as yet in vain, that the basket be raised. However, there have been of late years several rule changes aimed at neutralizing the extra-tall man, such as widening the free-throw lane to twelve feet, prohibiting a player from guiding the ball to the basket, and adding of the center 10-second line and the bonus free throw rulings.

As late of the 1960's the two groups that have put out rules of basketball for girls and women for the many years past, the AAU and the DGWS, have joined forces and have set up a joint committee to edit and publish the rules from now on.

Bowling. According to Tunis (see References) more people engaged in bowling in the United States in the late 1940's than in any other sport. It was estimated that fifteen million people were bowling at that time with the sport holding its greatest popularity in the Midwest. By that date there were in the United States 25,000 bowling alleys with an average of eight lanes each. Since then the sport has grown to still greater popularity.

The American Bowling Congress (ABC) and the Women's International Bowling Congress (WIBC) were attacked by many individuals and groups in the late 1940's for the racial discrimination clauses in their constitutions. Industrial recreation groups particularly felt this injustice and opened an attack on these groups which paid off, for in May, 1950, the ABC at its annual convention voted overwhelmingly to remove the word "white" from their constitution and thereby opened their national tournaments to all the American people. Previous to this a judge of the Superior Court of Cook County, Illinois, found the ABC guilty of racial discrimination and fined the organization $2500 on the ground that its conduct was "violative of the provision of the Illinois Civil Rights Act." This opened the door, and the American Bowling Congress "saw the light." Immediately the women's group voted racial discrimination out of its constitution also.

Cricket. Since World War II cricket has become popular in some parts of the country, particularly on the West Coast, although in club rather than in school situations. UCLA is the one college that maintains the sport, which no doubt is supported largely there by the foreign students from such countries as India, Pakistan, and the West Indies, where the game has long been popular from early British-mandate days. The game has been played at UCLA since early 1930's and since 1960 it is recognized by the awarding of a varsity letter. By 1960 there were eight cricket clubs actively functioning in the Los Angeles area. The Westwood Cricket Club is made up of UCLA students and alumni, its first captain an American who had learned the game in Australia.

In the late 1960's there are twelve such clubs in the Los Angeles area alone, with seven playing fields at their disposal, and among them they carry on a six-months schedule of games, all played on Sundays, with three different trophy tournaments to end the season.

Field Hockey. From its beginning in the United States, field hockey has been popular in the women's colleges and prep schools in particular, with small groups in many coeducational colleges and universities, and in some high schools of the larger cities. It has never appealed to most American girls and women, but the groups that participate in it are ardently enthusiastic. The game enjoys great popularity among small groups of young women recently out of college, who join forces with similar groups from near-by cities. Several large cities and communities with many college graduates support active hockey clubs, which under the banner of the American Field Hockey Association play in tournaments and on occasion compete against visiting English, Scotch, and Irish teams.

Football. The popularity of American football in colleges is tremendous—crowds of between 90,000 and 100,000 people at a single contest are no longer rarities. The first Rose Bowl game (post-season and intersectional) occurred in 1902. Today more than 20 other bowl games have been promoted in a single season in various sections of the United States. The American Football League was established in 1959 for "Pro" football.

The budget, the efforts to lure athletes to colleges, the commercialization of football surpass that of any other sport. More coaches, in high schools and colleges, are employed for football than for any other sport. Despite occasional scandals concerning the conduct of football, it continues to grow in importance, and it is the "wealthy uncle" who supports practically all the other sports in colleges and high schools and builds the magnificent stadiums and gymnasiums. Eight-man football is a new form of the game introduced for high-school boys in this era.

Swimming. Following World War II the construction of swimming pools took on new life. Indoor pools, previously considered a "must" only for the gymnasiums in the larger cities and in the larger colleges and universities, are now installed in the schools of many smaller towns, while outdoor pools are commonplace in practically every community of several thousand inhabitants and up. Thus swimming at mid-century has become a sport for all of America, old and young. In the 1950's scuba diving was added to swim instruction, and a feature called drown-proofing was added to life-saving courses.

Other Sports. Gradually American men are taking to soccer, which as played in the United States before mid-century was almost exclusively a college women's game. At the present time thousands find valuable recreation in golf. Golf championship matches have grown from a one-day, 16-hole event of the 1890's to the 4-day, 72-hole event of today. Although riding has long been a part of the physical education program in many prep schools and colleges, especially in women's departments, it never received national organization attention until 1967, when a National Riding Committee under the AAHPER went into operation.

Ice-skating has grown to large proportions in the last two decades. The Works Progress Administration of the World War II period alone built 691 rinks throughout the country. Many modern municipal auditoriums have an ice rink, and they are spreading gradually into the college world. The large rink at the Ohio State University is in constant use by both faculty and student body.

Of all sports, skiing has the greatest participation record. In winter hundreds of thousands of skiers fill the ski trails of the mountain areas of the country, and the sport has been added to the curriculum of many colleges and universities.

Volleyball, too, has increased markedly in popularity since World War II. The international Volleyball Federation was organized in Paris in 1947. Since then there has been a marked increase in participation in this game.

Many large lakes have been created behind the man-made dams that have been built in many parts of the country since the early 1950's. These have opened up fishing and boating to millions of people. Also there are 180 million acres of public land in our national forests with 116,000 miles of trails for outing activities. The National Park Service is developing roads, trails, and camps at the price of 476 million dollars, to take care of the outing of millions of park visitors each year. It was estimated that over 80 million people visited the national parks in 1966.

Interest in sports has become so keen that more publicity is given to them in the daily papers than to any other single activity. The tendency of sports to attract spectators gives rise to considerable concern by many who desire to see people actively engaged as participants. However, those so concerned should gain satisfaction from the numbers who participate in bowling, fishing, and hunting, golf, tennis, softball, swimming, and various other sports and games. In fact a government report of 1955 showed that since World War II, participation in spectator sports had fallen off 19 per cent, while participation in individual sports had increased 34 per cent and the sale of boats, bicycles, aircraft, golf clubs, and like sports equipment had risen 137 per cent.

SPORTS ORGANIZATIONS

In the earlier years of competitive sports in this country, only a few organizations existed for their promotion and control, some for a combination of sports and a few each to cover some one sport. But at mid-twentieth century there, is a great multiplicity of associations, clubs, and leagues, covering sports participation both in and out of the school, both amateur and professional, for all age groups, for both sexes, and at all levels—local, state, regional, national, and international. To discuss them all would require a book in itself; and since this is a book on the history of physical education, the authors here discuss only new amateur organizations and the few organizations still functioning that have existed since earlier periods and have been discussed in earlier chapters and which serve amateur sports only.

Although some early organizations that served to promote and control professional sports have been discussed in earlier chapters of this book, as a part of the heritage of sports, the number and variety of such sports organizations have grown so tremendously and are so far removed from the field of education that they have been given no further consideration in this book. (The reader should review the discussions of these organizations in Chapters 18 and 21.) The sports enthusiast will readily find such further information as he may desire in current newspapers and periodicals and in books concerned with today's sports scene. The old-time amateur sports organizations discussed in this chapter fall into four groups: (1) those for out-of-school amateur sports, (2) those for college sports, (3) the NFHSHA for high school sports, and (4) those for girls and women's amateur sports.

Organizations for Out-of-School Amateur Sports

At mid-twentieth century, the AAU is the oldest of the organizations that have persisted from earlier periods to promote and control amateur sports outside the schools. Today its authority is being challenged as never before by several new organizations, each established in the interest of some one sport, only one of which is discussed below as a sampling of the several new organizations that challenge AAU's authority today.

Amateur Athletic Union. Today's AAU claims jurisdiction over all amateur sports not under the control of schools, colleges, YMCA's and a few isolated sports such as golf, tennis, and bowling, each of which is controlled by its own national organization and a few team sports such as football, ice hockey, baseball, and track and field, each of which is controlled by its own league. With these exceptions it claims control of basketball, boxing, gymnastics, handball, running, jumping, walking, weight-putting, hurdles, pole vault, swimming, tug-of-war, wrestling, weight-lifting, and volleyball. Since the disturbing days of the 1920's and 1930's, when the AAU was promoting some sports for women, it has confined itself mostly to activities for out-of-school boys and men. However, it does interest itself in a few women's sports today, some in co-operation with the Division of Girls and Women's Sports of AAHPER.

United States Track and Field Federation. History has a way of repeating itself, and as the National Amateur Athletic Federation was born in the 1920's out of the discontent of many groups with the dictatorial policies of the AAU, so today's United States Track and Field Federation (USTFF) was born in 1962 out of continued discontent with those same policies. Founded by fourteen national amateur athletic groups and twenty-one amateur athletic conferences the following charter members were largely instrumental in its birth: National Collegiate Athletic Association, National Junior College Athletic Association, National Federation of State High School Athletic Associations, National Track and Field Association, and the American Association for Health, Physical Education and Recreation. Associate members include among other groups the Athletic Institute, United States Track Coaches Association, and the President's Council on Physical Fitness. It functions under five divisions: intercollegiate, interscholastic, club and unattached groups, and allied groups.

Quoting from its publication *Record* of June, 1966: ". . . the members of the United States Track and Field Federation comprise nearly the complete sum total of the grass roots track and field programs of the nation and provide the United States its basic strength and resources in the sport of track and field." Through its member groups it actually covers over

90 per cent of all track and field athletes in the country, over 90 per cent of all track coaches and all track facilities, and over 90 per cent of all money spent on the sport. Similar organizations exist for other sports, but they are too numerous to discuss individually in a brief history of physical education.

Organizations for Intercollegiate Sports

For the many years since the birth of the NCAA in 1905, it alone controlled intercollegiate sports competition up to the time of World War II. Today this world of sports is divided into three divisions—the university division, controlled by NCAA; the small college division, controlled by the National Association of Intercollegiate Athletics; and the junior college division, controlled by the National Junior College Athletic Association.

National Collegiate Athletic Association (NCAA). Following World War II the NCAA added baseball, in 1947, and ice hockey, in 1948, to its wide coverage of intercollegiate sports. Although there are still today occasional accusations and violations of NCAA rules by some schools in the organization, and now and then some penalty declared, on the whole the NCAA maintains good order within its sphere of sports control—indeed excellent order compared to the constant bickering, charges, countercharges between colleges, the frequent discontinuance of competition between various schools, and the constant complaints of college faculties about sports competition that existed in the early years of the organization.

National Association of Intercollegiate Athletics (NAIA). In 1945 small colleges of the country that were not served in their intercollegiate athletics by the various large-institution leagues, such as the Big Ten, the Big Eight, etc., came together and united their small-college leagues (many of which are as old as the NCAA itself) into the National Association of Intercollegiate Athletics for mutual help and benefit. By the mid-1960's it had 465 college members and was sponsoring football, baseball, bowling, golf, soccer, cross country, swimming, wrestling, and track and field. Following this lead, the junior colleges have joined forces and maintain their own league, the NJCA, to foster their own competition.

The United States Collegiate Sport Council. In October of 1967 the United States Collegiate Sport Council, made up of the NCAA, NAIA, NJCA, and the National Student Association, held its first meeting. It was established to represent all colleges and universities in the United States in the *Federation Internationale du Sport Universitaire.* World university games were held in Tokyo in 1967, when schools in the United States sent eighty-eight athletes. The Department of State allocated $15,000 to help defray expenses of the United States athletes in their attending a college meet in Innsbruck, Austria, in January of 1968, and holds forth the possibility of still greater financial support to send college teams to summer games in Spain or in Portugal in 1969.

Organizations for Interscholastic Sports

As yet the world of interscholastic sports has not developed a multiplicity of organizations to promote and control it, as has the world of sports for adults. Practically all high school sports groups for boys are under the jurisdiction of the one over-all organization, the NFHSAA, which in many states controls sports competition for girls as well as for boys.

National Federation of High School Athletic Associations. Following its birth in 1920, this federation grew until by 1940 it had established a national office with a full-time executive staff.

Today the State High School Athletic Associations of all states in the union except Texas belong to this Federation including groups in Alaska and four Canadian provinces. As of 1967, over 20,000 high schools belong to the state groups that make up this organization. It checks on close adherence of all state groups to eligibility rules for all sports contests, holding all to local, district, and state level. Regional and national tournaments have never been sanctioned by the Federation.

Since World War II the Federation has brought about a reduction in size of football and baseball for high school use, set up less expensive equipment as standard, standardized officiating in high school contests, and materially raised the coaching and playing ethics. One of its chief objectives, now as in its earlier years, is to protect high school boys from exploitation in their sports. A prime concern is to protect them from groups not related to the world of education that would use them for their own publicity purposes regardless of the best interests of the boys themselves. Also strict rules have been adopted concerning the recruiting of high school boys by colleges—rules designed to protect the best interests of the high schools.

Organizations to Promote Sports Competition for Grade School Boys

Although groups of adults have existed in earlier periods to promote sports competition for grade school boys outside the school program, they have not been so numerous or so wide-spread as today. When the first of them came into existence, shortly before World War II, with sufficient strength to claim such public attention, the American Association for

Health, Physical Education and Recreation and many leaders of the medical profession and the Congress of the Parents and Teachers Association registered vigorous protests over their exploitation of young boys by adults who in order to produce winning teams were disregarding all tenets, psychological and sociological as well as physiological, of the type of sports competition suitable for grade-school-age children. The protests brought a betterment of the situation, and though still disapproved of by many adults there are today many organizations promoting such sports, such as, to name but three of them, the Little League Baseball, Biddy League Basketball, and Pop Warner Football League. These groups promote state, regional, and national matches.

Organizations for Intramural Sports

A new development in the sports field since World War II has been the establishment of the National Intramural Sports Association and the National Girls' Athletic Association, both sponsored by the AAHPER for the promotion and setting of standards for intramural sports for both college- and high-school-age groups. The first mentioned boasts of 523 school members by 1967 and held its nineteenth annual convention in 1968. The latter was created to fill the gap left by the demise of most of the earlier State Leagues for High School Girls Athletic Associations.

Organizations for Women's Amateur Sports

Although the AAU, some State High School Athletic Associations, some Women's State Basketball Leagues, various groups such as the U.S. Women's Field Hockey Association, the Women's International Bowling Congress, and the U.S. Lawn Tennis and Golf Associations control various amateur sports for women, there are today three national groups functioning exclusively for women on the over-all sports level—the DGWS, the ARFCW, and the Women's Board of the U.S. Olympic Committee.

Division for Girl's and Women's Sports. The Women's Basket Ball Rules Committee of the AAAPE of 1899 gave way in 1905 to the National Woman's Basketball Committee of the APEA, and it in turn led to the organization of a larger group in 1917 named the National Committee on Women's Sports. In 1927 this committee became the Women's Athletic Section (WAS) of the APEA. In the early 1930's it changed its name to the National Section on Women's Athletics and was known for the next twenty years as the NSWA. In 1952 it again changed its name, this time to the National Section for Girls and Women's Sports (NSGWS). But this name soon gave way to another as the organization in 1957 took on the status of a Division of AAHPER with ever-increasing responsibilities in behalf of girls' and women's sports in the United States. This group, that started out in such a small way over sixty years ago to set standards and make rules for one sport for women, has advanced through its several stages to the responsibility of setting standards and making rules for many sports for girls and women. The group is today familiarly known as the DGWS. (For its chairmen through the years see Appendix A.)

It is doubtful if there is any other group in the profession of physical education that turns out more work or engages more workers within the profession in its various projects than does the DGWS. In 1967 over 10,000 women were at work on its many and varied committees and projects, not only putting out the rules of many sports for women but setting standards for sports participation—a task handed on to it by the Women's Division of the NAAF on its demise—publicizing its activities putting on clinics, holding sports officiating training projects, to name only the more important of its many areas of work. Its earlier work along this line has grown until it now maintains local officials rating boards in forty-seven states. Since World War II the DGWS is also represented on the AAU Gymnastic, Track and Field, and Swimming Committees, and in the U.S. Track and Field and Gymnastic Federations. It is also working with the Women's Board of the U.S. Olympic Development Committee. With the Athletic and Recreation Federation of College Women, it also maintains joint committees on golf and extramural sports.

In cooperation with the Men's Athletic Division of the AAHPER the DGWS is conducting riding rating centers throughout the country and exploring the concerns of intramural sports. It also maintains official rating boards, with local boards in forty-seven states. Another new development since World War II is its promotion of clinics in various parts of the country to develop better sports skills among American women in the individual sports, such as golf, track and field, gymnastics, tennis, archery, and swimming. It also holds institutes around the country on girls and women's sports in general.

Although there are other groups in the United States that make rules for various women's sports, the profession of physical education looks upon the DGWS as the official rules-making body for sports for girls and women. In the year 1966–67 alone it put out eighteen sports guides.

Now at mid-twentieth century the DGWS has added to its many undertakings the promotion of intercollegiate sports competition for women and has set up special committees for this task. This has come about through a changing attitude of the women leaders in the profession since World War II. Although the older generation of leaders who fought to keep women and girls out of highly competitive sports have passed from the scene of action as deceased or retired, there is still a small body of young women working in the profession who cling to the old ideals of women's place in the world of sports, but they are in a very small minority, and the will of the majority rules as is the American way. True it is that times have changed greatly since World War II. We now live in a highly mobile world. It means but little more today, if as much, for people to dash off to foreign countries than it meant a couple of generations ago to travel to the farther reaches of our own country. Whereas before World War I it was common to encounter people who had never travelled beyond their own state borders, today it is rare to find people who have not travelled in other states. Today society on the whole is more concerned with and more knowledgeable about the welfare of the individual than in earlier generations. Today many more women in advanced countries of the world participate in sports than in earlier years so that they are less conspicuous and attract less attention than in earlier times. Today women take a far more prominent part in the world's work than they did even in the opening years of this century, so that their participation in sports competition that attracts much public notice is not so unusual as of old and therefore more acceptable. Also today there has developed a large body of women trained in physical education, who are capable of handling women's sports participation, so that it is safeguarded in ways that were impossible two generations ago, when there were so few women trained in such work. So it is recognized that times have changed and the attitude of the profession in regard to the participation of women in highly competitive sports situations has also changed with the times. Only time will reveal the wisdom or error of the changes. To assure the wisdom of the many changes to fit the times, the DGWS is making every effort to hold the line for standards based on sound educational principles and philosophy and urges all groups that sponsor extramural competition for girls and women to hold to the high standards such as it sets forth in its own publications. (Copies of the DGWS Sports Standards are obtainable from the AAHPER in Washington, D.C.)

In 1966 it established a Commission on Intercollegiate Sports for Women (CIAW) to promote intercollegiate sports and to be the national sanctioning body. It functions only in competition involving five or more institutions on the state, regional, and national level.

Athletic and Recreation Federation for College Women

The organization which started in 1917 as the Athletic Conference of American College Women (ACACW) took on a new name in 1933 and functioned for twenty-four years as the Athletic Federation of College Women (AFCW). At its April, 1957, conference it changed its name to the one given above, which better reflects its true purpose, namely "to further athletic interests and activities for girls and women according to the highest and soundest standards of sports and recreation."

Since 1947 the organization has held conferences biennially instead of triennially as in its earlier years. From the twenty-three schools which were represented in the charter membership, the organization has grown as of 1967 to a membership of 198 colleges and universities, including junior colleges. In recent years this Federation has aligned itself with the AAHPER, and its organizational work is under the charge of a consultant in the National office.

The Women's Board of the U.S. Olympic Development Committee. The Board of Directors of the United States Olympic Development Committee created a Women's Advisory Board in 1961, which two years later dropped the word Advisory; the Women's Board became a functioning group with the following duties: (1) to increase opportunities for girls and women to participate in sports, (2) to help women physical educators to become competent in teaching and officiating in sports, (3) to provide opportunities for women physical educators to give leadership toward properly organized and administered sports experiences for girls and women, (4) to interpret for women the place of competition in our culture, and (5) to encourage research in women's sports.

Under the sponsorship of both the DGWS and the AAHPER, the Board put on sports institutes in 1963, which were attended by hundreds of teachers from all states, who in turn put on work shops in their respective states, reaching hundreds of other teachers. The institutes in 1963 were on gymnastics and track and field; in 1965, on gymnastics, track and field, kayaking, fencing, and diving; and in 1966, on skiing and figure skating, and on coaching basketball and volleyball.

SPORTS COMPETITION

Although there has been a tremendous increase in participation in sports since World War II, there is still a tremendous interest throughout the country in watching sports competition, both professional and amateur, so that sports coverage now takes up much of both radio and television time, as well as much space in the newspapers. Also, many new periodicals have been established to cater exclusively to the sports scene. Through the promotional efforts of the many sports leagues and associations, both professional and amateur, that abound in the United States today, there is much competition going on all the year round in many different parts of the country and in many different sports, with baseball, basketball, and football, both professional and amateur, holding the limelight in public attention, and ice hockey and golf increasing greatly in the 1960's in spectator sports appeal.

Whereas in years past the seasons of various sports were well defined and did not overrun each other's schedule on the calendar, today these seasons have become so prolonged to meet public interest that the closing dates of one sport's season now overlap the opening dates of another sport's season. It has become common place to have baseball and football games claiming public attention at the same time in early fall, football and basketball in early winter, and basketball and baseball in early spring.

Since World War II the U.S. State Department has used athletes as goodwill ambassadors to various foreign countries and has sent athletic coaches to backward countries to help them set up athletic programs and to prepare teams for Olympic and other international competition.

Intercollegiate Athletics

Some physical educators believe that the emphasis on winning which pervades athletic competition in many schools and colleges will, if not curbed, lead to the eventual deterioration of athletic competition. There is, also, much concern in education circles over the subsidization of athletes and a growing desire that all colleges follow the example set by the Ivy League schools.

In the college Ivy League (Brown, Columbia, Cornell, Dartmouth, Harvard, Pennsylvania, Princeton, and Yale) the members of the football teams are students in every sense of the word—not men brought in to play in various sports. Strictly amateur, these teams nonetheless draw large crowds and hold student, as well as public, interest.

These Ivy League colleges play round-robin schedules with each other, completely under the control of the academic authorities. There are no athletic scholarships. No student who was subsidized as a high school player is eligible to play on these college teams. Each player must be working in earnest toward a college degree, and there are no snap courses for athletes. Players receive the same consideration for scholarships as do all other students. The amount of scholarship granted to an athlete is determined by educational authorities and not by coaches or athletic directors. All gate receipts from games go into the college treasury.

The 1933 effort of the NCAA to curb excesses in subsidization of college athletes failed to improve conditions, so it set up a new committee, which drew up a Sanity Code that was adopted in 1948. This Code covered such matters as amateurism, institutional control, academic standards, financial aid, and recruiting. However, when several colleges were accused of violating this code in 1950, and the necessary two-thirds vote to expel could not be procured, charges were dropped, and the Sanity Code became ineffective. Since then there have been continuing efforts at reforms but all have been ineffective in curbing abuses.

The post-season interregional games as well as the in-season games within the various regions, have become enormous business today, all under NCAA jurisdiction. In early 1968 talk arose within that organization about national championship games in college football. Many college stadiums have been enlarged in recent years to accommodate the greatly increased crowds that turn out for games.

An interesting new development has arisen in the late 1960's in the college sports field that reminds how history does at times repeat itself. In several colleges where intercollegiate sports competition has been dropped, club sports have arisen since 1965, all student-originated, student-managed, student-financed as was the situation with college sports in almost the entire nineteenth century. In the fall of 1967 there were thirty-six such college clubs playing games against other colleges. The members of these clubs hire the coaches, buy their own equipment, carry their own insurance, arrange their own pep rallies. Most of the colleges where these sports clubs exist permit the boys to use the college playing fields. At Marquette University the coaching staff of 1967 consisted of three high school coaches and a dental student.

Interscholastic Athletics

Early in this era there developed interschool competition for elementary schools which called forth protests from the medical profession, many school administrators, and physical educators. At its convention in 1947, AAHPER adopted resolutions advocating the abolition of interschool competitive athletics for elementary school children. In spite of this open opposition, little league football, basketball, and baseball is sponsored by private organizations for the benefit of boys twelve years of age and under. In the summer of 1951, little league baseball was being played in thirty-seven states. The national championship games attracted over 10,000 people. Thousands of boys participate in these sports each year, and the number competing is increasing. Unfortunately, educational guidance is frequently lacking in the conduct of these programs.

Competition at high school level is controlled by the National Federation of State High School Athletic Associations. Highly organized by today, this Federation has splendid control of all interschool sports competition for high school boys. It opposes athletic competition on the national level but does sanction sectional events provided they are held in strict observance of Federation rules on distance to be traveled, type of sponsor, and extent to which the event might interfere with smaller events that will include greater participation. It permits no international competition without the sanction of the National Federation and permits no tournaments to determine a national or regional championship. It also prohibits post-season all-star games. It prohibits the transportation of high school boys to colleges for try-outs for future considerations and all interviews with high school athletes except in the school guidance office.

The Federation frowns upon the signing of school boys to professional sports contracts, and one state, Washington, has even passed a law against such activity on the part of professional sports groups. Also, the Federation has definite standards for interschool contests, to which all its member schools subscribe. As of 1964–65 it was sponsoring thirty-three sports, ranging from archery to wrestling.

March is tournament month all over the United States for high school boys' basketball. In 1964–65 the most schools participating in any one activity in state programs were 19,112 schools in basketball, with 639,755 boys entered in the state tournaments. There were 15,524 schools entered in the various state track and field meets, with 512,271 boys taking part; and 13,248 schools in the state baseball tournaments, with 357,145 boys participating. On the other hand, there were only two schools entered in a field hockey tournament engaging 40 boys. These were Canadian schools. Over-all in 1964–65 there were 2,891,930 high school boys engaged in various sports activities in the various state tournaments conducted by the state associations of the National Federation. Communities throughout the nation have become interested in having their high schools sponsor winning football, basketball, baseball, and track teams. This has made it possible to erect large gymnasiums, playing fields, and stadiums in which public school students participate. Support for such ventures has come from public taxation, school bonds, or donations from businessmen.

Intramurals

Although intramural athletics have grown tremendously at both the college and high school levels, it was reported in 1949 in the proceedings of the 54th Annual Convention of AAHPER that, of 113 elementary schools surveyed, only 46 per cent provided intramural sports programs for the elementary school children. So there is much room for growth in the years ahead. Practically all colleges, large high schools, and a high percentage of smaller high schools now offer a varied intramural program of sports. Today most students in college find some opportunity to satisfy their desire to engage in athletic contests of a recreative nature.

International Sports Competition

Today there is much international competition in sports going on all over the world, promoted by a great variety of organizations and sponsored by a great variety of interests. A check with the sports pages of the leading newspapers will give news of those that engage American athletes.

Of all of these international contests, none arouses so much national interest as the Olympic games that are held every four years. The discussion of international sport that follows will be confined to this alone.

Olympic Games. Because of World War II, no Games were held in 1940 and 1944. Since then they have been held as follows: 1948, Winter–St. Moritz, and Summer–London; 1952, W–Oslo, and S–Helsinki; 1956, W–Cortina, and S–Melbourne; 1960, W–Squaw Valley, and S–Rome; 1964, W–Innsbruck, and S–Tokyo; 1968, W–Grenoble, and S–Mexico City.

Due to the intransigeance of United States sports promoters as much as to that of any other nation, the 1948 Winter Games were mostly verbal battles of charges and countercharges of unfair advantages being taken, which rendered the Games a farce as far as the promotion of world brotherhood of man was concerned. The Summer Games went better. In the aftermath of the war so recently ended, Great Britain, in spite of the wreckage of its major city and much of the countryside and in spite of its food shortages and transportation difficulties, was host to the athletes of the world. The English refused to permit any competition on a Sunday, and according to Kieran, unlike the Germans who had played their national anthem 480 times during the 1936 Games in Berlin, the English played theirs only twice—at the opening and closing ceremonies. Out of the 151 events run off, the United States won 40 gold medals, with Sweden the closest contender with 21. Six thousand athletes took part in the Games, representing 59 nations, the largest number of athletes (not to be surpassed until sixteen years later) and the most countries ever entered. The war-torn world was apparently happy to turn its attention once more to sports. Of all the athletes, perhaps none won more acclaim than Bob Mathias, the 17-year old youth from the United States who won the decathlon. He won it again in the next Olympics, breaking his own 1948 record.

The Olympics of 1952 was the first time an American held the presidency of the International Olympic Committee—Avery Brundage (1887–) of Chicago. The ceremony of lighting the torch at the opening of the summer Games at Helsinki was unusual in that after thousands of relay runners had carried the torch (which had been lighted at the Temple of Zeus on Olympia) across Europe, over the Baltic Sea, across Sweden and into the Arctic Circle, Laplanders there with the use of magnifying glasses lighted a fire from the rays of the Midnight Sun to blend with the flame from the torch. Added to this bit of drama was the selection of Paavo Nurmi, the famous Finnish runner of thirty years before, to be the final runner to enter the stadium at the opening ceremony to light the flame on its high peristyle. Again as in so many other Games the United States team won the lion's share of gold medals, 43, Russia following with 23.

At these Games Russia demanded and was given separate housing for her athletes and those of her satellite nations apart from the other nations in the Olympic Village. Up to 1952 sport followers had employed an unofficial point system by which they determined an unofficial winner of the Olympics—10 points for a first place; 5 for a second, and 4, 3, 2, and 1 for third through six places. With the Americans usually winning so large a share of firsts, the Russians decided that first place should be awarded only 7 points and proposed that their point system be adopted by the Congress of the International Athletic Federation as official, but this request was rejected. Since the Russians had won so many second and third places their point system indicated Russia as winner of the Olympics and the Russian papers so announced it.

The 1956 Olympics were a different story for both the Russians and the United States. This time the Russians won 33 gold medals, to 29 for the United States. This was the first time the Games were held in the Southern Hemisphere. The Russians and their 510 athletes were served notice that there would be no separate housing for them—all would be housed together in the Olympic Village. The political situation was so bad in so many parts of the world at this time that Egypt, Lebanon, Iraq, Spain, the Netherlands, Hungary, and Switzerland withdrew from the Games, some in protest to Russia's presence and others in protest to the countries of the Suez Canal attack. The United States, with 427 athletes on its team, and Australia, with 360, added to Russia's still larger group, almost turned the Games into a three-way contest, with these three countries taking over 50 per cent of the gold medals. Russia entered the Winter Games for the first time this year and stole the show there. With the summer victories added, Russia easily was proclaimed victor of the 1956 Olympics. This was the fourth time in the history of the Modern Olympics that the United States had not led all other nations—in 1906, at the extra unofficial Olympics, the United States tied with France; in 1908 Great Britain led; in 1936, Germany led; and now in 1956, Russia led. In the 14 Games including those of 1956, the United States had been top scorer ten times. Once more, as in London eight years before, no competition was held on a Sunday. Melbourne does not even allow newspapers to be printed on a Sunday.

By now other nations had improved in the sports-training techniques and had become a serious challenge to the sports supremacy of the United States. One U.S. athlete who equalled the record set by Paavo Nurmi, the famous Finnish runner of earlier Olympics, was not good enough in 1956 to win even a bronze medal. The U.S. Olympic Committee now established the U.S. Olympic Development Committee, in the hope of stemming this tide of challengers from other countries. At about this time the International Olympic Committee made a study of the athletes entering the Games, which showed the following as arranged from Jokl (see References):

1. By race: The black athletes excel in sprints, hurdles, jumping, and boxing, whereas the yellow-browns excel in swimming, and the white in technically differentiated sports. (The U.S.S.R. used no yellow-brown athletes on their teams, although many such are among their citizenry.)
2. By climate: The cold countries produce more high-class athletes, although some "hot belt" athletes are superior.
3. By age: Age of an athlete means but little in performance. The youngest and oldest seem equally good. (Germany took 900 teen-age athletes to Rome in 1960).
4. By sex: Men and women both reach top-level capacity earlier and retain it longer in the post-World War II period than they did even twenty, forty, or even one hundred years ago.
5. By size of country: In relation to size of population to draw from for athletic competition, the Scandinavian Countries rank above both the U.S. and U.S.S.R. in athletic achievement.

The 1960 Olympics in Rome were historically dramatic, with the marathon race starting at the foot of the steps leading up to the Capitol; passing the Colosseum, dating from 80 A.D., where gladiators fought; and out into the country, by way of the Appian Way, dating from 312 B.C., where Caesar's Legions marched. The gymnastic events were held in the ancient Baths of Caracalla, the equestrian sports in the famous old Borghese Gardens. For the other sports, Rome built ten new stadiums, a large gymnasium, two sport palaces (including seven swimming pools), and an Olympic Village to house 8000 athletes. Again the Russian team led, with 51 gold medals to the U.S.'s 37.

The 1964 Olympics were the first to be held in the Orient. Japan at Tokyo played the host nation superbly. U.S.S.R. led for the third consecutive time, taking 41 gold medals to the U.S.'s 37. (The Russian athletes are civil servant athletes, the stars subsidized by the Soviet government. As such they are in the control and pay of the government.) To match some of the historical pageantry of the preceding Games in Rome, the Japanese Olympic Committee hoped to have the lighted torch for the opening ceremonies to come by land from Mt. Olympus over Central Asia's historic and ancient Silk Route, but since a goodly part of that route passes through Red China the idea had to be abandoned.

Although ninety-four nations competed in the 1964 Olympics, the bickering and quarrels such as accompanied the Olympics of the early twentieth century seem to have taken on less importance, and the friendships of the athletes to have taken on greater significance. As Bush, a news reporter (see References), put it:

> Whom shall we believe, the . . . sports writer, chuckling over . . . petty offenses which quickly melt away, or the athletes who form friendships and treasure pleasant memories for a lifetime?

Many nations won their first Olympic gold medals after World War II: such as Bulgaria, Ethopia, Iran, Jamaica, Luxemburg, Mexico, Peru, Rumania, and Russia. (For further information on USA participation in the Olympics see the Appendix. A comparative study of first and best records through the years in various track and field and swimming events, as shown there, makes an interesting inquiry, especially a comparison of women's records of today compared with those of men in the early Olympics in the same events.)

Controversies over National and International Sports Competition

Although there have been controversies through the years over domestic competition in many sports, none has been so prolonged as the one over the control of track and field sports in international competition, which for over sixty years has claimed the attention of high government officials as well as the sporting public. Since the first Modern Olympic Games in Paris in 1896, track and field sports have held the special attention of the public and the major emphasis and publicity of all Olympic sports.

A review of the history of the control of this sport gives a picture of today's situation and of the contending organizations that claim jurisdiction over it. The first extramural track meet on record in the United States was an intercollegiate meet held at Saratoga, New York, in 1874. The following year several colleges banded together to organize the Intercollegiate Association of Amateur Athletes of America (IAAAA), which took over control of intercollege sports competition. In 1905 this organization gave way to the United States Intercollegiate Athletic Association (USIAA), which was founded through the auspices of several college presidents who were demanding reforms in sports competition. This organization in turn developed into today's NCAA.

In the meantime, the amateur sports clubs that existed in the 1870's outside the then so very small world of college sports banded together and organized the National Association of Amateur Athletes of America (NAAA). This was in 1879, four years after the IAAAA came into being to control college competition. In 1888 the NAAAA developed into today's AAU, which by 1900 claimed jurisdiction over all amateur sports in the country, including college sports already covered by the IAAA. This brought about disputes that flared up intermittently until in 1907 representatives of high schools (for by then athletics had developed in this field), colleges, YMCA's, and Boys Clubs came together to discuss how they could protect their athletes from the AAU's attempts to take them over. The AAU was demanding that for the privilege of competing in any amateur extramural contest an athlete must take out membership in the AAU, and pay the membership fee and also an entry fee for each contest. The AAU was so well entrenched by then that it could enforce its dictums. To protect their own athletes from this management, the other group now added to their earlier group representatives from playgrounds, social centers, Turners, and the U.S. military forces and organized the Athletic Research Society (see p. 260). In 1910 it appointed an official committee to challenge the AAU. In 1912, the AAU became a member of the International Amateur Athletic Federation and as the first organization in that body from the United States, acquired the American franchise in that organization for all United States international competition, which it still holds today.

After fruitless years of meetings between AAU and Athletic Research Society, the latter called for the formation of a Federation to consist of all groups of amateur athletes and through union might be able to break AAU's control of amateur sports. In 1921 the NCAA tried to interest the AAU in joining these other groups, so that all would work together, but the AAU was not interested. Thereupon the other groups went ahead without the AAU and organized the National Amateur Athletic Federation (see p. 263) to place the control of amateur athletics on a democratic basis consistent with the ideals of our nation. At this same time the AAU had undertaken the promotion of women's amateur sports along its usual lines so that in 1923 the Women's Division of the NAAF (see p. 264) was established to enlist the help of women physical educators and all women interested in the welfare of American girls and women in their sports experiences. Although these two groups (the NAAF and its Women's Division) were short-lived, they alerted the leaders and citizenry of the nation to the unfavorable situations then existing in sports competition of the youth of the land.

In 1928 the Western Track Coaches Association disagreed with the AAU over control of their own track athletes, as a result of which a movement was started to form a democratic organization that would speak for all track and field athletes of the United States. But matters drifted during the depression. In 1936 the NCAA urged the American Olympic Association to change its constitution to give better representation to athletes from the college world, who by then were beginning to dominate the track and field sports. But things still drifted, and World War II came and went. Throughout the late 1940's and 1950's, controversies multiplied. Finally, in 1960 the AAU brought down the wrath of the International Basketball Federation on its head by trying to deny United States college basketball teams the privilege of playing a touring Swedish amateur team. Following this the NCAA cancelled its Articles of Alliance, drawn up some time before with the AAU, and refused from then on to recognize the AAU's suspension of athletes. In early 1962 the NCAA attempted to bring about a reconciliation with the AAU, but after several meetings, when the AAU refused permission for any other group to attend meetings even as observers and insisted upon a union in which the AAU would have 32 out of 50 votes on the Foreign Relations Committee, the NCAA abandoned all hopes for reconciliation. Then the other groups decided to organize the U.S. Track and Field Federation. The AAU was invited to be one of the organizing groups, but it refused to attend the organization meeting. Later it was invited to join the new Federation, but it declined the offer. Following this, increased controversies arose, so that the federal government stepped in and requested that the AAU, the new Federation, the U.S. Olympic Committee, and other interested parties meet in Washington in October of 1962 for open discussion of their difficulties. At this meeting the Washington Alliance agreement was reached as to *closed* and *open* meets and other moot points of contention, and the agreement was referred to the boards of each group concerned for ratification. The USTFF approved the agreement at once but the AAU rejected it. Then the U.S. Attorney General, Robert Kennedy (1925–1968), was drawn into negotiations. This step resulted in the Olympic House Coalition, which was accepted by the representatives of both the AAU and the USTFF. This plan gave equal voting power to the two groups and established a coalition governing body for all U.S. track and field athletics, which was commissioned to petition the International Amateur Athletic Federation for recognition as the U.S. governing body for track athletics. But within a few weeks, the AAU rejected the plan. Then President Kennedy (1917–1963), himself, stepped in and requested arbitration by General Douglas MacArthur, to which the USTFF agreed but the AAU objected. But the MacArthur meeting was held anyway in January of 1963, and a four-point program was drawn up, which among other things set up an Olympic Eligibility Board of three men each from the USTF and the AAU and recommended that following the 1964 Olympic Games the President of the United States arrange a meeting of all amateur athletic groups to draw up a permanent plan for the control of amateur sports. That fall, the USTFF issued a notice that its athletes could take part in all amateur meets without the necessity of joining the AAU and paying its membership and entrance fees and obtaining AAU travel permits. This notice was approved in advance by General MacArthur. In 1964, as a result of the MacArthur Agreement, the amateur athlete who was not a school or college athlete, known as an *open* athlete, was also freed from the necessity of joining the AAU in order to compete and was granted the privilege of affiliating with a club of the National Track and Field Association, which is a member of the USTFF. Thereby, *open* athletes can enjoy the advantages of the coaching, facilities, and competition of this national federation.

Then in 1966, as the U.S. efforts in track and field appeared to be jeopardized by continuing controversy, the Vice-President of the United States was empowered to select an arbitration panel, which was made up of a distinguished labor arbiter and attorney of New York City, a former Commandant of the U.S. Marines, a former famous U.S. Olympic champion sprinter, a nationally known newspaper editor, and a Harvard Law Professor who had served as United States Solicitor General under President Kennedy. But in spite of many meetings of this group, the controversies are still unresolved.

Sports Competition for Girls and Women

Since World War II, as in earlier periods, public interest in sports competition still lies mainly with men's sports. Only an infinitesimal number of girls and women go out for the sports that involve gate receipts and "spectatoritis" with their resultant objective of winning at all costs and the settling of important championships, and girls' sports do not make sensational news and so are not played up in the papers. Only a very few American girls and women are of public sports interest. Also, not many women's sports teams achieve even state-wide attention, let alone national. However, many small towns throughout the country still develop considerable interest and excitement, over girls' high school basketball teams in particular, and in a few states carry this on to state-wide attention. But for the great majority of American girls, participation in sports competition is confined to the intramural scene and to the out-of-school world.

This does not mean that American girls and women are not interested in sports. Intramural records from schools and colleges, youth centers, and community centers belie that thought. In all these organizations, much in the way of girls' sports goes on constantly—mostly dual and individual sports, since the great majority of American girls and women prefer them to team sports.

The mottoes of the first group of women who organized and promoted sports for girls and women of America were, "A sport for every girl and every girl in a sport" and "Play for play's sake." These mottoes of the early twentieth century are not heard so frequently today, although a check with many women leaders in physical education who are teachers first and coaches only second, shows that they still have them in mind.

Intercollegiate Competition. Although there is in late 1960's but little intercollegiate sports competition for women going on in the United States, as compared to the enormous programs of intramural sports carried on in hundreds of schools all over the country, that little occurs mostly in the individual sports. The rigid attitude of the women trained in physical education of the early twentieth century has given way to a more flexible position, so that intercollegiate competition is more readily accepted today than in earlier years. With the establishment of the Commission on Intercollegiate Sports for Women under DGWS control, there will no doubt be considerable growth in such sports in the near future. The Commission will sanction only such competition as will involve only full-time college students, is open to all such students of each college involved, and involves five or more colleges and is not held to select all-star teams or as a clinic.

In 1967 the Commission sanctioned two events, an intercollegiate archery meet in Arizona and a swimming meet at the University of New Mexico. In 1968 it sanctioned a college women's golf tournament and planned for 1969 an intercollegiate gymnastic meet and a track and field meet, and for 1970 a swimming meet and badminton and volleyball tournaments. This changed attitude has come about with improved facilities and programs and a larger body of professionally trained women to promote and control these sports. There is still, however, a large group of women leaders who would have sports competition for women in the intramural form only, others who approve of extramural competition but in individual sports only, others who approve of it also in a few selected team sports if held to strict standards of participation and conduct, and a few who would let down all bars, opening competition for girls and women into a world of sports comparable to that now engaged in by men and boys.

Interscholastic Competition. At mid-century ten states (Arkansas, Georgia, Iowa, Louisiana, North Carolina, North Dakota, Oklahoma, South Carolina, Tennessee, and Texas) maintain state tournaments for high school girls in basketball, which are supported mostly by the small towns of the state. Nine states, through their State High School Athletic Associations, prohibit all interschool athletics for girls: Alabama, Colorado, Illinois, Nebraska, New York, Oregon, Utah, Wisconsin, and Wyoming. Nine other states prohibit only interschool basketball for girls, and several others, while not prohibiting, do discourage such activities. In Kentucky interschool sports for girls are permitted only in swimming and tennis, and in Oklahoma only in softball.

Non-School Competition. Many girls and women outside the schools engage in sports competition today, no doubt a larger percentage than in any other period of our history. These activities are sponsored by YWCA's, YMCA's, church leagues, sports clubs, and recreation organizations of great variety. Archery, basketball, bowling, golf, field hockey, shooting, skiing, softball, swimming, tennis, and volleyball each claims a large following today. Never have American girls and women been so sports-participation minded, and never before have interests, both public and private, made facilities for women's sports so readily available.

Olympic Competition. In speaking of women in Olympics John Kieran and Charles Daley, two top-flight sports writers (see References), spoke of them as follows: ". . . women's events, a branch of the Olympics which usually evokes loud yawns from the customers and other disinterested folk." This remark was made in connection with their story of the 1948 Games in Amsterdam. Since then it seems that most probably there are fewer yawns and fewer disinterested folk. Beginning with 1956 the women entering the Games have been younger than in previous years, and the majority of United States women contestants have come from the college field rather from industry, as had been the case in previous games. Also, the United States has produced since then some remarkable women athletes. However, this in no way means a discounting of such women athletes of previous years as Helen Wills in tennis and Helene Madison in swimming.

The sports open to women in the Olympics of today are track and field, swimming, foils, gymnastics, figure skating, and skiing. In this period, Russian, Hungarian, and Australian women have outshone the U.S. women athletes (in 1952 and again in 1956), but the U.S. women eclipsed all others in the 1948, 1960, and 1964 Olympics in the number of gold medals won. In the 1960 Olympics Wilma Rudolph was the only member of the U.S. team to win 2 gold medals. (In the 1964 Games a Russian woman won four gold medals—all in speed skating.) Women skaters had taken part in the Olympics in 1908 and again in 1920, and from then on it was 1956 before a U.S. woman skater won a gold medal in that sport, but the triumphs of American women in skating in the recent Olympics has surely wiped out all memory of a lack of medals in the past. The one gold medal won by a U.S. athlete in the 1968 Winter Olympics was won by Peggy Flemming (1947–) in figure skating.

Sports Halls of Fame

There are many sports halls of fame scattered throughout the country, the earliest and most notable of which are located in New York, New Jersey, Massachusetts, Connecticut, Ohio, and Florida, as discussed here. The Baseball Hall of Fame established in Cooperstown, New York, in 1939 was the earliest. Since then a College Football Hall of Fame has been established at New Brunswick, New Jersey, where the first intercollegiate football match was played in 1869 between Rutgers and Princeton. The professionals' Football Hall of Fame is in Canton, Ohio. The Basketball Hall of Fame was established in Springfield, Massachusetts, in 1965 at the site of the birth of the game in 1891. The Swimming Hall of Fame was established in 1966 at Fort Lauderdale, Florida. It consists of an Olympic pool, a building housing many exhibits on swimming, a swimming research library, a collection of films covering all aspects of swimming. The first annual international swim meet was held there in December of 1966, at which time the first twenty-one swimming immortals were inducted into the Hall of Fame.

The National Art Museum of Sport is located in New Canaan, Connecticut. Robert J. H. Kiputh (1890–1967), famous swimming coach at Yale University, was the first chairman of its Board of Trustees. The International Olympic Museum, established at Lausanne, Switzerland, by the International Olympic Committee, is a repository of pictorial and documentary displays concerning the history of the Modern Games.

25

Organized Physical Education in the Mid-Twentieth Century

Following World War II there was a marked increase in the United States in awareness of and interest in world problems. Where the tendency following World War I had been toward the isolationism that kept the United States out of the League of Nations, the situation now was quite different. The new generation of leaders accepted the fact that the United States had become a world power and thus had responsibilities to the rest of the world. It now led in the creation of the United Nations, which held its 1945 organization meeting on our own West Coast and on our East Coast found its permanent home. Within this organization, developed the United Nations Educational, Scientific and Cultural Organization (UNESCO), which has had world-wide effect on the advancement of education.

Also during and following the war, a great population movement began, from the rural areas to the large cities, as the country changed to a society that was largely industrial. As a nation we had become enormously wealthy, which affected all segments of society as the standard of living rose to heights but little dreamed of only a few decades before. At the same time there was a great increase in population, affecting education in many ways. The following figures on the number of children enrolled in the public schools at various periods reveal the situation:

1900–15,503,000 1960–36,087,000
1930–26,678,000 1965–43,851,800
1969–50,000,000 (est.)

These figures, however, do not represent population increase alone. Some of the enrollment increase has been due to an increase in the percentage of children seeking an education. Figures on the education of the draftees of World War I compared to that of the draftees of World War II show a marked increase in educational interest between the two generations as follows:

	WW-I Draftees	WW-II Draftees
Average number of years in school	7	10
Percentage completed high school	20	47
Percentage with one year in college	5	16

A larger percentage of youth is attending school than ever before in our country's history, more than in any other land of the world. The changed educational philosophy of post-World War I is now being still further changed by the Civil Rights Movement that arose in the 1950's. Equal educational opportunity for all became the new objective, which brought with it much turmoil in many communities as Negroes backed by many whites began the struggle for their right to an education equal to that of whites, just as one hundred years before, women backed by many advanced thinkers among the men were waging the same battle for the right of girls to an education equal to that of boys.

As the post-World War I Progressive Education Movement collapsed following World War II it nevertheless left an impact for the better on education. In the end Dewey's tenet—what the wisest and best parents wish for their children, that must the schools wish for all children—has strongly affected education, so that schools of today are far better even though far different from those of the early twentieth century. There has arisen a concern, never so widely or loudly voiced before, for the welfare of all children, the mentally retarded, the blind, the crippled, all children who are disadvantaged in any way, economically or physically, and this concern is reaching into the schools and many other aspects of life.

The collapse of the Progressive Education Movement came not as a rejection of Dewey's philosophy, but as Cremin (see References) points out, from struggles between the factions that arose within the Movement itself. With radicals in their midst seizing power, the Movement appeared ridiculous. They talked of education for the "whole child," and through "creative expression," but never made it clear to their followers just what they meant in terms of actual teaching; and the Movement failed to produce a body of teachers who could answer these questions satisfactorily for themselves and might therefore work out teaching techniques that would satisfy not only their own philosophy but would at the same time satisfy parents and the public. The poor teaching techniques that grew up around this Movement were as bad for the children as the old formalism and mass teaching had been, although in a quite different way. For these reasons the Movement failed to get the support of laymen, and in the 1950's the Progressive Education Association closed its doors.

As Merle Curti (1897–), one of America's foremost historians, said (see References):

> . . . many critics hold . . . that progressive education has been responsible for the disappearance from our schools of good old-fashioned mental discipline . . . that [it] has destroyed the American school as an intellectual institution. . . . What passes for progressive education is often the outer shell rather than the substance of Dewey's philosophy. . . . Dewey did not reject reason; he tried to sharpen rationality by urging that assumption be tested and verified, that experience be relived and critically reconstructed in terms of new situations.

As the passing years give perspective, it appears that the complaints of much of the citizenry that Dewey's philosophy caused the disappearance from the schools of mental discipline were misplaced and that it was the radicals among his followers who, misinterpreting Dewey's philosophy (as he himself in his book of 1938 insisted that they had), caused the disappearance. Dewey's philosophy, where correctly interpreted, brought about awakened social consciousness that has strongly affected education in America for the good. At the same time there is developing a swing back to an appreciation for discipline in all facets of life. The two together are bringing about an educational philosophy, acceptable to the majority of parents and educators, which is being strongly felt in mid-twentieth century.

There is also a growing appreciation that disadvantaged children can be awakened and can handle a school curriculum of higher quality than heretofore considered possible, so that children can be raised up to higher standards of education instead of standards lowered mistakenly in their favor.

EVENTS AFFECTING PHYSICAL EDUCATION

Physical education, as all other branches of education, was deeply influenced by the Progressive Education Movement of the twentieth century, and now that the Movement, controversial as it was, has died out, physical educators can look back and see that it brought about many worthwhile changes, chief of which was an acceptance of sports and dance as a legitimate part of a physical education program and not merely to be tolerated as a side issue promoted by pupils themselves. But today physical educators are taking a new look at gymnastics, which was crowded out of the physical education program largely to make way in the preceding period for sports and dance. Now physical educators are returning to their earlier acknowledged responsibility toward all children —a responsibility peculiarly their own—that of developing in each child the aspects of physical fitness that depend upon participation in physical activity for its accomplishment. Accompanying this renewed acknowledgement, is the recognition of gymnastics as having intrinsic values in the development of physical fitness and as such having a place in the physical education program.

World War II

Out of nine million registrants examined for the armed services of the United States in early 1943, almost three million (one third) were found to be unfit for any form of military duty. However, because of improved techniques of examinations and diagnosis since 1917, many were rejected who would have been accepted in World War I. Indeed more men were rejected for World War II than were accepted for World War I. But those who were accepted were soft and flabby and in need of conditioning. The chief of Athletics and Recreation of the Services Division of the United States Army had this to say at the War Fitness Conference in 1943:

> Our physical programs in high schools have been a miserable failure. Physical education through play must be discarded and a more rugged program substituted. We must assume our share of the responsibility for the unnecessary loss of American lives. Many of our boys have perished because of the accumulation of fatigue, the lack of endurance, stamina, and certain abilities. You read about the men who struggled through swamps and jungles and over mountains for days and days before reaching safety, or survived in rubber boats for many days before being rescued. They had the strength and stamina to survive such ordeals, but you don't read about the hundreds that did not have such strength and stamina. They did not live to make a report.

The military called on physical educators and trained coaches to man the Armed Services' physical training and athletic programs and to head physical reconditioning programs with trained physical educators, both men and women, on their staffs.

By 1943 there were 232,000 women wearing the uniform of our Armed Services—the first women in United States history to be accepted for military duty. In September, 1944, the Surgeon General's office reported to the National Civilian Advisory Committee of the Women's Army Corps an unusually large number of rejections due to excessive weight and a general lack of strength, flexibility, and endurance of those women who were accepted. (At the same time the Harvard Fatigue Laboratory conducted a series of fitness tests on college women and found that of the group that was considered to be fit, only 22 per cent had even average strength and endurance.) Those who were accepted for the WAC were given a rigorous program of conditioning as outlined in the *WAC Field Manual of Physical Training.*

Following this, women enlisted in the WAVES, Marine Corps, American WAF, and the Medical Corps, and they, too, were found equally lacking in strength and endurance. Other women left their homes by the thousands to work in industry, to help replace the men called to the armed services, and to do their bit for the war effort. Their softness and general lack of physical fitness showed up at once. The Labor Department reported that there were sixteen million women working in industry in the summer of 1943, working a ten-hour day for seven days a week. Some were working on night shifts, some were loading freight cars, others were driving heavy trucks or welding and walking cat walks in shipyards. American women in such large numbers had never before been called upon for such physically difficult tasks.

Also during the War large numbers of American women and men entered the service of the American Red Cross and were sent throughout the world wherever our Armed Forces were stationed. The assignment of many of these was to organize recreational activities. Also the United Services Organization (USO) functioned in all communities where Armed Forces Camps were established. Other organizations took over the promotion of recreation for the war workers in industry. After the close of the war, many of these organizations became somewhat permanent, because our Armed Forces are even yet maintained in many parts of the world.

World War II demands on man power tended to deplete the recreation leadership force, but community recreation, nevertheless, realized the contributions it needed to make toward the total war effort and forged ahead. By 1946 over 1,700 communities spent over $50,000,000 annually and employed over 30,000 leaders, some 5,000 of them full time. These advances continued into the period immediately following the war. By 1949 the paid leadership force increased to nearly 50,000 leaders, with nearly 6,000 employed full time.

Physical Fitness Movement

John B. Kelley (1888–1960), a distinguished citizen of Philadelphia and a former University of Pennsylvania and Olympic athlete, who had been intensely interested in fitness from his early youth and was deeply shocked at the draft information of World War II, appealed to President Roosevelt for immediate action to correct this situation among civilians as quickly as possible. In 1942 the President set up a Division of Physical

Fitness under the Office of Civilian Defense and appointed Mr. Kelley head of this new Division. District divisions were immediately set up along the lines of the various Army Service Commands with two co-directors, a man and a woman, appointed as District Directors in each Service Command. Several of the regional directors appointed were physical educators. Frank Lloyd (1897–1957) of New York University was appointed Chief of the Physical Fitness Division of the Federal Security Agency with headquarters in Washington, D.C., and William L. Hughes (1895–1957) of Columbia University was appointed Chief Consultant.

This movement brought about a change in attitude in regard to athletics in both the Armed Forces and the schools. In the colleges eligibility rules were relaxed to permit freshman and transfer students to participate at once; intensive participation of all students in sports was encouraged. The United States Office of Education organized the Victory Corps for school children with achievement tests and insignia for physical fitness activities and held regional institutes to promote the work.

With World War II at an end, the enthusiasm for fitness died down, but then people were aroused in the early 1950's by the publication of rejection figures of the new draftees. The head of Selective Service reported in 1952 that one and a half million of the 18½-to-26-year-olds were rejected for the draft. Then come the Kraus-Weber tests of minimum muscular fitness of school children, the results of which were first published in 1953. They showed the poor fitness records of American school children compared with European children. These tests consist of six tests of key muscle groups which show up the abilities required for healthy living. They were developed from a fifteen-year study of patients with low-back pain made by Dr. Hans Kraus (1905–), Associate Professor of Physical Medicine and Rehabilitation of New York University. Designed to measure one's ability to participate effectively in activities required for everyday living, these are not supposed to be tests of high levels of muscular fitness. As these were given to 4,264 United States school children and 2,870 European children from comparable urban and suburban communities, 57.9 per cent of the United States children failed the tests compared to 8.7 per cent of the European children.

Once more John B. Kelley alerted the President of the United States to the need for a physical fitness movement. Immediately when President Eisenhower's attention was called to this report, he ordered a special White House Conference on the subject which was finally held in June, 1956. Following this the AAHPER held a Fitness Conference in Washington in September, 1956, and President Eisenhower established a President's Council on Youth Fitness and a President's Citizens Advisory Committee on the Fitness of American Youth. Later President's Conferences on Fitness of Youth were held in 1957 at West Point and in 1958 at Fort Richie, Maryland. In February of 1961 the Department of Health, Education, and Welfare held a Conference on Youth Fitness, for which it called upon the profession of physical education for help from the early planning stage. Following this the Council on Youth Fitness produced a booklet, *Youth Fitness*, that was widely circulated throughout the nation. It carried a suggestion for a school-centered program of fitness building, calling attention to the use of calisthenics as a way to develop fitness quickly, but stressing that the fitness program should not consist only of calisthenics. Shortly all states had established state fitness programs, although a few, notably Oregon, since 1945, and California, were already at work on such projects.

The situation of American Youth as of mid-twentieth century showed that 40 per cent of men entering the Armed Services in World War II could not swim as far as 50 feet and that drownings were second in all accidental deaths, after motor accidents, with most occurring in the 15–20-year range.

Following President Eisenhower's lead, President Kennedy carried on his Council on Fitness for Youth and his Citizen's Advisory Committee, naming Charles B. "Bud" Wilkinson (1916–), nationally known football coach, as Special Consultant to the President on Physical Fitness. He also issued, in July of 1961, a *President's Message to the Schools on Physical Fitness of Youth* that urged expansion of physical education programs and facilites, as he said, "to give a high priority to a crusade for excellence in health and fitness," and he set aside April 30–May 6, 1961, as National Youth Fitness Week. Following this many states held state fitness conferences, and others held clinics and workshops on fitness. The AAHPER set up fitness tests for the schools.

Following President Kennedy, President Johnson carried on this movement, naming Stan Musial (1920–), the baseball star, as his Special Consultant to succeed Wilkinson, and for administrative purposes he placed the Council under the Department of Health, Education, and Welfare. In 1967 Lt. Commander James A. Lovell, Jr. (1928–), an NASA astronaut, was appointed Special Consultant on Physical Fitness to the President. In 1966 President Johnson established the President's Physical Fitness Award, which was sponsored by the AAHPER and the Council on Physical Fitness. In 1967, 50,000 boys and girls in the 10–17-year range qualified for the award, with schools from all states, the District of Columbia, and Puerto Rico participating.

Foreign Service

Since World War II, world-wide opportunities for foreign service have opened for physical educators, coaches, and athletes of the United States through Fulbright Professorships, Special Services assignments, and the like, and more recently through the Job Corps and Peace Corps, all of which have claimed the attention of hundreds of Americans.

State Legislation

As of 1968, forty-five states were maintaining within state departments of education some person to be responsible for the state program for physical education in the schools. Most doing this special work full time are recognized as state directors of health, physical education and recreation, but some look after physical education only as an adjunct to other unrelated work; some look after both physical education and athletics; some, physical education and health education; and some, health education only. Some are designated as supervisors, some as consultants, some as bureau chiefs of HPER, some as coordinators of HPER, some as specialists in physical education, although the title *state director* seems to be the most commonly used.

Of the few states that do not give recognition to physical education at the state education department level, Montana names no one on the state superintendent's staff to take physical education under his wing. New Hampshire assigns whatever is to be done about physical education to the consultant on secondary school services; North Dakota, to the assistant superintendent; and Wyoming, to the director of instruction. At the other extreme from Montana are Ohio, which names four state directors in this field (one a woman), and Washington, two (one a woman as supervisor of health education and the other a man as supervisor of physical education and recreation). Only two states, Connecticut and Hawaii, have a woman director of all health and physical education.

Most states have a state law requiring that physical education be taught in the schools, but they vary widely in regard to the number of times a week and number of years of the requirement. In 1967 a group in the California legislature attempted to drop a part of the state physical education requirement, but their efforts were defeated. In some states, where the law is merely a permissive one, the department of education merely appoints a state director, procures budget support for his work, and goes forward without a time allotment set by law.

STATUS OF PHYSICAL EDUCATION

Today many physical educators are questioning the early twentieth century terminology, which in the term *physical education* supplanted the nineteenth century *physical culture* and *physical training*. Many are proposing that the term movement education replace the older forms. But as of the late 1960's this idea has not been generally accepted. As Ziegler (see References) points out, it is the experimentalist within the profession who objects to the old terminology and the realist who does not object to staying with the old term. As in all other branches of education, physical education has its pragmatists, realists, idealists, reconstructionists, experimentalists, and essentialists. They counterbalance each other, and together at mid-century are producing a physical education quite different in many respects from that of any preceding era—a kind of physical education that can be judged best only by the years that are ahead.

There is evidenced today a growing social consciousness within physical education, as in all branches of education, that embraces greater thought than heretofore for the education of the crippled, the blind, the mentally retarded, the economically deprived, and the malnourished—for all subnormal children. From the earliest days of the profession of physical education, there have always been a few who have striven to aid such children in their physical development, but these were isolated situations, not a specific concern of the schools. However, the physically crippled child has received some special attention from as early as the 1890's, when the Swedish System of gymnastics came to this country, bringing with it the medical aspects of rehabilitation through exercise; but this was the concern almost exclusively of hospitals and private clinics, which undertook to train physical educators in the specialization of physical therapy work. Following this lead, a few schools did employ specialists in corrective work and did what they could for the school children who needed such help but not so far as to be hospital or private clinic cases.

Today, awakened by Dewey's philosophy of the early twentieth century, education is accepting the challenge of education for *all* children; and physical education is taking a renewed interest in both the physically and the mentally handicapped. Special training in physical development for the various forms of abnormality is being devised in training schools.

Lower Schools

In spite of the great increase in physical education in the schools of America after World War II, the U.S. Office of Education reported that in 1956 less than 50 per cent of all secondary school boys and girls were receiving training in physical education. Ninety-one per cent of the 150,000 elementary schools had no gymnasiums, and 90 per cent had less than the five acres for playing area recommended by the profession in 1930. Also, only 1,200 out of 17,000 communities had full-time recreation leadership, and less than 5 per cent of the children were getting camping experience. A later survey reported by Schneider (see References) claimed that only 23 per cent of the lower grades surveyed were meeting the generally accepted requirement of 15 minutes of exercise each school day, exclusive of recess periods, and that California was the only state requiring of grades 7–12 one physical education class period daily. An AAHPER survey of the late 1950's showed that 80 per cent of junior high schools and 60 per cent of senior high schools were requiring physical education but two or three times per week. However, "Bud" Wilkinson, as head of AAHPER's Lifetime Sports Education Project, reported in the mid-1960's that 90 per cent of all institutions that sent representatives to the several Project clinics reported their schools had accelerated their programs. A survey of what actually is in progress was to be made by Wilkinson in 1968. Aside from these figures, information for the 1960's is difficult to come by.

Facilities. In the late 1940's a national movement developed for War Memorials that would be living tributes to the war dead, such as community recreation buildings and youth centers, and many of these were constructed. The memorials in some communities took the form of playgrounds outfitted with equipment requiring no supervision and having no right or wrong way to be used, such as dodger mazes, pipe tunnels, jump platforms, and mounds of earth to dig into and climb over.

A new development of facilities of this era in large cities is the high school field house for interscholastic sports—a building apart from the school gymnasium. Also many high school gymnasiums are being constructed with special rooms for corrective gymnastics, and for the past many years open showers have been approved for girls' dressing rooms.

Programs. Mid-twentieth century programs of physical education are considered excellent only if they contain a wide variety of activities chosen from aquatics, camping, combat activities, body mechanics, equitation, dancing in various forms, festivals and pageantry, free play, games, hiking, stunts, and sports of all kinds—group, individual and dual. Many schools now also maintain programs of recreation for the student body. The usual plan is to place the responsibility for administering the recreation program in the physical education department.

Closely allied to recreation is school camping. The gains in school camping in the past two decades have been tremendous. In 1951 there were approximately ninety school districts including nearly two hundred schools which sponsored some type of school-camp program. Physical educators have taken great interest and much responsibility in this movement.

At mid-twentieth century the most common weekly requirement is still the old one of three periods per week, although many schools hold to a daily requirement. River Forest Township High School at Oak Park, Illinois, with its separate gymnasiums for boys and girls, sets the standard of five hours per week for all four years, which standard is maintained by many of the best high schools.

Colleges

With the rapid growth of new colleges throughout the country in the 1960's and an equally rapid increase in enrollment in the established colleges and universities, physical education, as all other departments in colleges, is "straining at the seams." By 1967 it is estimated that one new college per week is added to the collegiate world, while the state universities are proliferating through the opening of new branches. New junior colleges also are being established in scores of communities. In 1967, according to Howe (see References), there were an estimated six million students enrolled in standard colleges and universities, with another one and a half million more in junior colleges. (California alone supports eighty junior colleges.) Since World War II, however there has developed a tendency to cut or drop the requirement in physical education. This has become an actuality in several colleges and universities.

In a survey of 1960–61 (reported by Oxendine) of college physical education programs, it was shown that 84 per cent of those surveyed (and the survey included institutions of all sizes) have a requirement in physical education. Of these, 5 per cent had a requirement for 4 years; 3 per cent, for 3 years; 68 per cent, 2 years; and 25 per cent, 1 year. Of those institutions with a requirement, 76 per cent give credit for the work, with the larger institutions predominating in this group. Fifty per cent of the institutions of over 5,000 enrollment have a swimming requirement for all students.

Facilities. Some magnificent gymnasiums both for men and for women have been built since 1950, and a few fine ones have been built for the joint use of both men and women. Two of the latest in this last group are the two-million-dollar gymnasium at New York State University Teachers College at Cortland, dedicated in 1954, and the million-dollar gymnasium completed in the early 1950's for the new Riverside Branch of the University of California. The University of Southern California built a coeducational gymnasium in 1925 which is still an excellent building, but it did not at that time establish a trend. Whether the two modern coeducational buildings will now start a trend remains to be seen.

Since World War II a splendid addition to the women's gymnasiums is the gymnasium at the University of North Carolina, Greensboro, completed in 1952 and named after Mary Channing Coleman (1883–1947), who was the second woman to hold the presidency of the AAHPER and was for many years Director of Physical Education at the University. She organized and developed a department that achieved considerable national recognition. Another and more recent woman's gymnasium is the one at the University of Nebraska, completed in 1968 at a cost of a little over two million dollars.

Many fine stadiums also have been built in colleges and universities and even in some high schools in mid-century. The Ivy League schools today have stadiums seating from 15,000 (Dartmouth) to 71,000 (Yale), supporting undergraduate enrollments of only 2,500 (Brown) to 10,000 (Cornell). Many state universities have enlarged their stadiums of pre-World War II years, most handling crowds of from 30,000 to 60,000.

Academic Degrees of Staffs. Graduate degrees are the rule today for physical education teachers in colleges and are common in high school faculties. As the top degree, the M.D. of the early years of the profession has given way to the Ph.D. and Ed.D. The year 1939–40 marked the last time that a person was elected to the presidency of the national professional organization holding the M.D. degree rather than one of the others. Today it is obligatory in most colleges and universities for the head of the department of physical education to hold either the Ph.D. or the Ed.D. degree and for the other staff members to hold the master's, although in many institutions several staff members hold the doctor's degree.

Research

A constantly growing number of members of the profession are entering upon research work in this field, following the lead of the early pioneers who, holders of the medical degree, naturally turned to physiological research, and even today this research far outstrips the sociological and historical. Particularly productive in research in physical education among the many leaders who were especially active both before and after World War II but are now deceased are the following three: Frederick W. Cozens (1891–1954), of the University of California (Berkeley), who received the Ling Foundation Medal, the Medal of Merit of the Ministry of Social Welfare of Czechoslovakia, and the Gulick Award of the AAHPER in recognition of his services to the profession; Edward C. Schneider of Connecticut Wesleyan whose cardiovascular tests were used in the service of aviation during the World War II; and Charles H. McCloy, Research Professor, University of Iowa, who as special consultant to both the U.S. Army and Navy during World War II carried on much research work for them. As a prolific worker and writer in the field of research, McCloy was recognized by four honorary doctorates and the Gulick Award of the AAHPER. He also received from the American Academy of Physical Education, besides their Hetherington Award, a special citation for his productivity in research. His writings include a dozen books in English and a great number of articles in periodicals published in nine different languages.

Today's activity in research is a far cry from the lonely efforts of Edward Hitchcock at Amherst College in those days of one hundred years ago when he alone recognized that physical education must stand or fall on the research work that furnishes its foundation. The national professional association maintains both a Research Section and a Research Council, the latter coordinating its work with that of various other organizations. In 1967 it voted to add to its national office staff a Consultant in Research and is taking under advisement the establishment of either a Research Institute or an Educational Information Center. It is also in the late 1960's materially increasing the size of its *Research Quarterly* in an attempt to keep abreast of the enlarged accumulation of reports of research.

Professional Preparation

At the turn of the century there were only two institutions of collegiate rank offering professional preparation in physical education leading to a degree, the University of Nebraska and Oberlin College. By 1930 the number had risen to 93; by 1955, according to the U.S. Office of Education, to 532; and by 1965, according to Hewitt, to 539. Three institutions of the 1965 group were offering professional preparation in health education only, two in recreation only, and 307 in physical education only. Ninety-seven others were offering preparation in both health education and physical education, another 40 in both recreation and physical education, and another 90 in all three fields. These institutions are located in every state of the Union and in the District of Columbia, some offering only an undergraduate major in the department of physical education; some offering also graduate work there; others functioning within a university as a school or college of physical education, combined with health and recreation training at both graduate and undergraduate levels; and some offering highly specialized training leading to work with the subnormal or in the field of dance. The world of professional education in physical education is a changed world since the turn of the century, even since World War II.

This era has produced several conferences on professional preparation, all sponsored by the AAHPER, some on undergraduate and some on graduate preparation. Out of these has developed self-evaluation checklists for the training program and for the institutions involved, and also a directory of institutions offering professional preparation. From these conferences has come an approach at standardization and an upgrading of specialization.

Today in some quarters there is renewed talk (as there had been in the 1920's following the lead of Wellesley College, which required five years for a major in physical education) of making the requirement five years for a bachelor's degree with specialization in this field. The talk claims justification in the curtailment of cultural subjects that occurs in a four-year program when the heavy science requirements added to the heavy physical activity requirements cut a student's time available for valuable liberal arts courses to a minimum. From others comes talk of requiring all physical education majors to complete a full academic major as well as the professional one, which also would tend to extend undergraduate work into a fifth year.

To further the work in upgrading professional education, the AAPHER retains membership in the Associated Organizations for Teacher Education (AOTE).

Present Status of the Early Private Schools of Physical Education. Collegiate affiliation of the early private schools of physical education is still in progress at mid-century. In 1953 Arnold College (originally the Brooklyn Normal School of Gymnastics, later the Anderson School, later still the New Haven Normal School of Gymnastics) affiliated with the University of Bridgeport, retaining its status as Arnold College. The Bouvé-Boston School of Physical Education, which affiliated first with Simmons College and then transferred to Tufts University, became as of July of 1964 the Boston-Bouvé College of Northeastern University. The Boston Normal School of Gymnastics, which had affiliated with Wellesley College in 1909 starting the move for ties with established colleges came to the end of its long and distinguished career in 1953, when Wellesley College decided to return to the status of a pure liberal arts college, divesting itself of professional training departments. So after sixty-four years of service to the profession (1889–1953), the last thirty-four at graduate level only, the old school bowed off the professional scene. In 1967 Sargent College of Boston University was renamed the Sargent College of Allied Health Professions to reflect its broadened scope, which has embraced physical therapy as of 1951; therapeutic recreation, 1960, occupational therapy, 1963; and a graduate program in physical therapy, 1966.

Today's Schools and Colleges of Physical Education. Since World War II, schools and colleges of health, physical education, and recreation have increased materially. Nine new schools have joined the four established in the previous era. They are located at Washington and Ohio State Universities, the Universities of Washington, Indiana, Connecticut, Minnesota, and Massachusetts, and Illinois State College at Macomb. Seven new colleges have now joined the one of the previous era. They are located at the Universities of Florida, Utah, Maryland, and Illinois (its school of 1932 developed into a college in 1957), Brigham Young University, Texas Women's University, and Boston-Bouvé College of Northeastern University. The two last named colleges give the profession its two women deans.

Specialization in the Dance. Following the lead of the University of Wisconsin in the 1920's and Bennington College and Connecticut College for Women of the 1930's, the idea of a dance major in the school curriculum developed but slowly. As such majors were established across the country, however, there soon arose the question of placement, whether in the physical education or fine arts department, or neither, with dance developing as a school by itself. Various institutions have settled the problem in their individual ways. Outstanding offerings of this era are the Summer School of Dance at Connecticut College and the Dance Department of the Julliard School of Music. By 1947 seventeen colleges and universities were offering a major in dance; by 1967 the number had increased to fifty. Besides these, sixty-three other institutions were offering courses in dance concentration, and twenty, a dance minor. Of these many majors, some are in the field of educational dance, others in the field of the performing arts. Also as of 1967, twenty-nine schools were offering summer schools of dance.

Graduate Work. According to a report of the U.S. Office of Education, 37 per cent of the institutions offering professional training in physical education in the 1950's were offering work at the graduate level, 28 per cent at the master's level, and 9 per cent at the doctorate level. A decade later, according to Hewitt, 70 per cent of the institutions offering professional training in this field are offering master's degrees, and 20 per cent, the doctor's degree. These figures show a marked increase in just one decade in graduate work offered in this field. A study of the institutions offering graduate work raises some doubts as to the quality of the graduate work being done, when one contemplates the inadequacies of size of staff, facilities, and equipment available in some of these schools. How much of this so-called graduate work is actually of graduate level, rather than merely more undergraduate work following the bachelor's degree, the profession needs to determine for the protection of its professional standing in the world of education.

Accreditation. Previously the American Association of Colleges for Teacher Education (AACTE) had been the accrediting body for departments and schools offering professional preparation, but in 1954 its accrediting functions were transferred to the National Council of Accreditation of Teacher Education (NCATE), and in 1960 the AAHPER voted to place itself under its accrediting jurisdiction. Now the AAHPER recognizes only those teacher-training programs approved by this organization, and urges state departments of education and the National School Board Association and local school boards to hire only physical education teachers who are graduates of departments, schools or colleges of physical education approved by the NCATE.

By 1964 the NCATE had reevaluated 99 per cent of all institutions previously accredited by the AACTE. In 1965, of 722 institutions offering professional training in this field, 300 were not accredited and 422 were.

Trained Personnel. Whereas by the end of World War I there was an estimated 10,000 men and women in the United States professionally trained in the field of physical education, by 1950 the number had risen to 76,000. In the year 1952–53, 6,230 men and 2,250 women received bachelor's degrees with a major in this field or in combination with health education and recreation; 1,539 men and 650 women, the master's degree; and 60 men and 47 women, the doctorate. Were comparable figures available for the 1960's, they would without doubt show a marked increase over the figures of the 1950's.

Non-School Organizations

The groups that have through the years carried on physical education activities outside the schools still function, the native groups with ever increasing vigor, with the Old World groups increasingly vanishing as each succeeding generation becomes more fully absorbed into American life.

Young Men's Christian Association. As in World War I, the YMCA, through its physical department, again rendered valuable services to the nation in World War II. It developed physical fitness programs for men drawn into the war effort outside the Armed Services, and both at home and abroad assisted in morale-building through their recreational programs. In peacetime as well as wartime, the YMCA promotion of athletic games in foreign countries has tended to bring people of different countries together in informal situations so that they understand each other better. At home the YMCA is one of the most powerful forces working for racial integration. Its physical education program offers unusual opportunities in this direction.

This era, as the preceding one, has seen great advances in physical education activity in the YMCA. Notable achievements have been the following:

1944—National YMCA handball tournament in St. Louis
1946—National YMCA volleyball tournament in Chicago
1951—International YMCA Physical Education Centennial in Cleveland
1952—National YMCA amateur sports competition
1953—856 YMCA Learn-to-Swim campaigns
1954—Third National YMCA Aquatics Conference
1955—YMCA Research Committee assignment of $1,800 for physical education research
1955—National YMCA Fitness Clinic in New York City
1956—Fourth World YMCA HPER Consultation in Melbourne
1958—YMCA Pan-American Physical Education Congress in Chicago
1964—Fifth National YMCA Aquatics Conference at Lake Geneva
1966—YMCA Aquatics and Scuba Commission workshop in Indianapolis
1966—1,573 YMCA Learn-to-Swim campaigns, with 354,231 persons passing the tests

In the twenty-two years, 1943–65, the YMCA's of the country increased by 49.9 per cent and the number of its physical directors doubled.

The YMCA has materially increased its service to women and girls, particularly in communities where there are no YWCA programs. About 70 per cent of all newly established associations make provision for them in their sports and recreational offerings.

Young Women's Christian Association. The rapid growth of the YWCA physical education program has been accompanied by a broadening of the activities to include recreation and social activities. In the mid-fifties activities in canteens, lounges, swimming pools, and gymnasiums attracted over 380,000 participants. This number had increased to over 615,000 by 1967, when there were 426 communities in the United States supporting YWCA's, 206 of them owning their own swimming pools and 204 using other pools on a rental basis. Over 300 full-time physical education teachers manned their physical education activities programs, assisted by a large number of part-time and special instructors. The 1967 enrollment in gymnastics, dance, and sports classes was 228,000, and in aquatics classes, 387,700, showing a great service to the communities where this organization functions. Through its camping program the YWCA plays hostess to thousands of others who seek enjoyment of the out-of-doors.

Turners and Sokols. The turner and Sokol groups in the United States are mostly third, fourth, and even fifth generation Americans thoroughly assimilated into American culture. These people have turned their attention to the American recreation movement and are ardent supporters. In only a few places are groups of Old-World descendants banded together still practicing the Old-World gymnastics. American Sokols still hold a slet (Sokol Olympics) every six years when gymnasts and athletes of the United States and Canada of Sokol descent come together, as they say, "to reaffirm their faith in a free and democratic way of life."

Movements Related to Physical Education

The camping and recreation movements have grown remarkably in this era.

Recreation Movement. Recreation in the United States today is sponsored by many agencies: public, private, voluntary, commercial, industrial, and of the Armed Forces. In 1946 there were 1,488 cities and towns in the United States maintaining playgrounds. Philadelphia alone constructed thirty-six new ones in the 1950's. By 1957 there were 200 full-time industrial recreation directors in the country. In 1956, thirty million people visited our National Parks, and the number rose to one hundred thirty million by ten years later. The activities of the National Recreation Association have multiplied so markedly since the last war that it has materially increased its headquarters staff. In 1965 it changed its name to the National Recreation and Park Association (NRPA) and the following year changed the name of its official magazine from *Recreation* to *Parks and Recreation.* The Association has come to mean or to stand for many things to the communities spread throughout the United States. Some of the services provided include: personnel service to serve private, voluntary, and governmental agencies; special consultant services for all phases of areas and facilities; service to industrial concerns engaged in recreation; consultant and correspondence services to agencies and individuals; special publications about problems concerning recreation; publication of their magazine; annual convention or congress for the professional leaders in the field; and research on various aspects of recreation.

Camping Movement. By 1950, ten thousand camps of many kinds served from three to five million boys and girls and adults each summer in the United States and Canada. At that time there were 2,000 camps registered as members of the American Camping Association, which sets standards for camp organization and management. By the 1950's a few state departments of public instruction were maintaining summer camps for school children. The Kellogg Foundation assisted the Michigan Department establish its camps. Soon after that, labor unions organized camps for the children of both employees and employers, and many new types of specialized camp arose such as music camps, pioneer-life camps, cardiac camps, diabetic camps, problem children camps, and crippled children camps. World War II brought into prominence the day camp, which proved popular in the large cities, where much was available in way of facilities, furnishing low cost camping to many children who could not hope to attend other types of camp.

Professional Literature

By the opening of this era the profession was receiving great impetus from the many publications that were coming off the press in this field. A perusal of publisher's notices given in each issue of the *Journal of Health and Physical Education,* year by year, from 1930 to date gives an idea of the great wealth of material that has become available. With the January, 1949, issue of the *Journal of Health and Physical Education* the word *Recreation* was added to its official title. (The Association, itself, had added the word *Recreation* to its official title in 1938–39.)

Films and Microcards. A new development of this era has been the production of films and microcards. There are available through the Athletic Institute over 2,000 16-millimeter sports films. The AAHPER has films for loan or purchase at its national office. Many schools produce their own film strips. The School of Health and Physical Education of the University of Oregon carries on a microcard publication project as a nonprofit service to the profession. The productions are, for the most part, unpublished research materials and doctoral dissertations, scholarly books that are now out of print, and periodicals of historical value which are no longer available. The school furnishes, on request, a catalog of all their microcards with prices.

PROFESSIONAL ORGANIZATIONS

American Association for Health, Physical Education and Recreation

The original American Association for the Advancement of Physical Education (AAAPE) of 1885 is "going strong" as it approaches its centennial year. Its interest groups, starting in 1904 with three sections, and reaching eleven in 1930, grew so numerous that in the 1940's they were combined into divisions: physical education, health education, and recreation, and each section was assigned to some one division with each division head recognized as a vice president of the organization. By 1967 the divisions have grown to eight and the sections under them, to thirty-two.

This is a marked extension of the horizons of the profession. (The sections within the various divisions and the numerous committees of the Association are listed annually in the October issue of the *Journal of Health, Physical Education and Recreation.)* Also the organization maintains two editorial boards and a national office staff of twenty-four heads of office divisions.

Many national organizations are affiliated with the Association, and it is the mother organization of six district and fifty state associations. The membership in 1885 was 49; it rose to 1,089 by 1905; to 3,022 by 1925; to 6,479 by 1935; to 10,193 by 1945; to 20,000 by 1954; and to 41,756 by 1967 with an additional 7,892 institutional and agency subscriptions to the two official periodicals.

The original objectives of the Association stated in 1886 hold good today: "To disseminate knowledge concerning physical education, to improve the methods . . . to bring those interested in the subject into closer relation with each other." But today it has added the interests of health education and recreation to its main concerns.

In 1960 the Association celebrated its seventy-fifth anniversary at its April convention in Miami Beach. That month's issue of the *Journal* was devoted to the story of its seventy-fifth-year history and to biographical sketches of its early leaders.

Beginning in 1965, the Association has sponsored a Life-Time Sports Education Project headed by "Bud" Wilkinson. The project was set up on a three-year trial basis, and through its many clinics it has brought about such a marked increase of interest in life-time sports in school programs that its continued support is assured. As of 1968 the Association has a Territorial organization, the Guam Association of HPER.

National College Physical Education Association for Men

The original Society of College Gymnasium Directors of 1897 became the Society of Directors of Physical Education in Colleges in 1908 and the College Physical Education Association in 1935, and in the 1960's it took on the long title above. By 1960 it had a membership of 675, representing 45 states and 320 colleges and universities. For over seventy years it has been a strong influence in the promotion of the best interests of the profession.

National Association of Physical Education for College Women

From the small group of sixteen women physical directors (representing three district groups previously established) who were present when this organization was formed in 1924, it has grown to a membership of 1,481 as of May, 1967, representing over 200 colleges and universities from all sections of the country with membership open to all college women staff members. It has developed into a working organization with over 10 per cent of the members actively at work on committees promoting improved physical education for women in colleges. For the past several years the organization has sponsored workshops which have been held biennially.

American Academy of Physical Education

From the group of charter members of 1930 this organization has grown slowly until by 1968 it had a membership of 98 active members, 35 fellows emeriti, 51 fellows deceased, and 9 fellows in memoriam. It also had 25 associate members from related professions and 46 corresponding fellows from 23 foreign countries, covering all parts of the world except Africa and the Middle East. Through its many foreign contacts, it serves as a liaison group between physical educators of America and those of the rest of the world. Its "steadfast belief in the integrity of physical education as a significant attribute to the perpetuation of American culture" is the keystone of its functioning.

Conferences on Physical Education

Since World War II, national and international conferences on health, physical education, and recreation have increased materially. The more important ones have been the following: National Facilities Conference, National Conferences on Undergraduate Professional Preparation, International Congresses on Physical Education, Recreation and Rehabilitation, International Congresses of Physical Education for Girls and Women (the first held in Copenhagen in 1949, followed by Congresses in Paris in 1953, London in 1957, Washington, D.C., in 1961, and Cologne in 1965), National Conference on Graduate Study, National Mobilization Conference on Physical Fitness and Youth, National Workshop on Recreation, AAHPER Conference on Physical Education for College Men and Women, International Congress on Essentials of Physical Education for Youth, National Conference on Intramural Sports for College Men and Women, National Conference for Education for Leisure, National Conference of City Directors of Physical Education, Health and Recreation, Anglo-American Workshops on Movement Education (the first two held in England), and National Conference on Physical Education of the Mentally Retarded.

Today there are several international organizations sponsoring the promotion of physical education. Chief among them is the International Council of Health, Physical Education, and Recreation, which held its twelfth gathering in Abidjan, Ivory Coast, in the summer of 1969.

Joint Council on International Affairs

In the late 1940's, twenty-two national organizations working in health, physical education, and recreation united their efforts in international affairs through the establishment of their Joint Council on International Affairs. The AAHPER office in Washington serves as headquarters for the Council. Its purpose is four-fold: (1) to serve as a clearing house for information, projects, and services; (2) to stimulate interest in international affairs concerning U.S. fields of endeavor, (3) to be an organized group prepared to act in international projects and conferences, and (4) to represent the profession as a whole in exchange of news, and exchange of persons, publicity, and hospitality.

National Foundation for Health, Physical Education and Recreation

Articles of incorporation of the National Foundation for Health, Physical Education and Recreation were legally recorded June 21, 1966. This is a private, non-profit corporation open to membership by both individuals and groups, sponsored by the AAHPER, and created to receive and administer funds for the advancement of the profession in behalf of mankind. Specifically it aims in part "to stimulate and promote educational activities of national and international significance related to the three fields [and] to establish and develop libraries, archives, and museums, encyclopedias, bibliographies, and other resources required by the three fields. . . ."

American College of Sports Medicine

The American College of Sports Medicine was founded in 1954 and incorporated in 1955 by a group of physicians, physical educators, and physiologists for the purpose of promoting scientific studies in relation to the effect of sports on health and fitness, of cooperation with other groups concerned with human fitness, and of initiating and encouraging research on the subject. It holds workshops (frequently in conjunction with the annual convention of the AAHPER), makes postgraduate education in sports medicine available and publishes a scientific journal dealing with human fitness. The permanent office is located on the University of Wisconsin campus.

LEADERS OF PHYSICAL EDUCATION

The number of leaders in the field of physical education has grown tremendously since World War II. All parts of the country are now covered by well-trained and effective men and women who are working in its service.

The American Association for Health, Physical Education and Recreation confers four types of awards in recognition of leadership in the profession: (1) the Gulick Award, established in 1923 in memory of Luther Halsey Gulick and conferred upon one physical educator a year for unusually significant leadership to the profession; (2) the Anderson Award, established in 1949 in memory of William G. Anderson, and conferred upon two or more persons a year who work in allied fields and have rendered distinguished service to physical education; (3) the Honor Award, established in 1931 and conferred upon several persons each year in recognition of notable leadership and (4) the R. Tait MacKenzie Award, established in 1968.

Since the inauguration of its Awards, the American Association for Health, Physical Education and Recreation has from 1923 through 1969 conferred the Gulick Award on thirty-four persons, and from 1949 through 1959, the Anderson Award on twelve other physical education leaders. (Information about and photographs of Award Fellows are found in the volume of the *Journal of Health, Physical Education and Recreation* for the year of the award. Also biographical material on the more notable of these leaders appears in *Who's Who in America*, and other biographical publications in their various editions, particularly in those issues just preceding a person's retirement. A perusal of the Appendix lists of presidents of various professional organizations and recipients of awards will reveal the names of many leaders of the profession.)

APPENDIXES

Appendix A

Associations, Officers, and Awards

AMERICAN ASSOCIATION FOR HEALTH, PHYSICAL EDUCATION AND RECREATION

Presidents

Under the name: American Association for the Advancement of Physical Education

1885–87 Edward Hitchcock (1828–1911)
1887–90 William Blaikie (1843–1904)
1890–91 Dudley A. Sargent (1849–1924)
1891–92 Edward M. Hartwell (1850–1922)
1892–94 Dudley A. Sargent (1849–1924)
1894–95 Jay W. Seaver (1859–1915)
1895–99 Edward M. Hartwell (1850–1922)
1899–1901 Dudley A. Sargent (1849–1924)
1901–3 Watson L. Savage (1859–1931)

Under the name: American Physical Education Association

1903–7 Luther H. Gulick (1865–1918)
1907 (March on) through 1911 George L. Meylan (1873–1960)
1912 through 1915 R. Tait McKenzie (1867–1938)
1916 Earnest H. Arnold (1865–1929)
1917, '18, '19 William H. Burdick (1871–1935)
1920, '21, '22 Dudley B. Reed (1878–1955)
1923, '24, '25 Carl L. Schrader (1872–1961)
1926, '27, '28 Charles W. Savage (1869–1957)
1929, 1930 Frederick W. Maroney (1884–1958)
1931 & 1932 (Jan.–Apr.) Mabel Lee (1886–)
1932–33 Jesse F. Williams (1886–1966)
1933–34 Mary Channing Coleman (1882–1947)
1934–35 Strong Hinman (1893–)
1935–36 Agnes R. Wayman (1880–1968)
1936–37 William G. Moorhead (1886–1954)

Under the name: American Association for Health and Physical Education

1937–38 Charles M. McCloy (1886–1959)

Under the name: American Association for Health, Physical Education and Recreation

1938 (Apr.–Sept.) Neils P. Neilson (1893–)
1938–39 Frederick W. Cozens (1890–1953)
1939–40 Margaret Bell (1888–1969)
1940–41 Hiram A. Jones (1899–1945)
1941–42 Anne Schley Duggan (1905–)
1942–43 Jay B. Nash (1886–1965)
1943–44 August H. Pritzlaff (1894–)
1944–46 William L. Hughes (1895–1957)
1946–47 Helen Manley (1894–)
1947–48 Vaughan S. Blanchard (1889–)
1948–49 Ruth Evans (1908–)
1949–50 Carl L. Nordly (1901–)
1950–51 Dorothy S. Ainsworth (1894–)
1951 (Apr. 20–22) Frank S. Stafford (1903–51)
1951–52 Bernice R. Moss (1906–)
1952–54 Clifford L. Brownell (1895–)
1954–56 Ruth Abernathy (1908–)
1956–58 Ray O. Duncan (1906–1967)
1958–59 (Jan.–Mar.) Pattric R. O'Keefe (1902–59)
1959 (Mar. –Apr.) Arthur A. Esslinger (Acting President)
1959–60 Arthur A. Esslinger (1905–)
1960–61 Minnie L. Lynn (1902–)
1961–62 Arthur S. Daniels (1906–1966)
1962–63 Anita Aldrich (1910–)
1963–64 Ben W. Miller (1909)
1964–65 Catherine L. Allen (1909–)
1965–66 Rueben B. Frost (1907–)
1966–67 Leona Holbrook (1909–)
1967–68 Joy W. Kistler (1898–)
1968–69 Mabel Locke (1907–)
1969–70 John M. Cooper (1912–)

Secretary-Treasurer-Editor

1907 through 1929 James H. McCurdy (1866–1940)
1930 through 1938 Elmer D. Mitchell (1889–)

Executive Secretaries

1938–43 Neils P. Neilson (1893–)
1943–48 Ben W. Miller (1909–)
1948– Carl A. Troester, Jr. (1917–)

Recipients of Gulick Awards

1923 Luther H. Gulick (Posthumous award)
1924 Jessie H. Bancroft
1925 Thomas D. Wood
1926 Thomas A. Storey
1928 Clark W. Hetherington
1929 George J. Fisher
1939 Jesse F. Williams
1940 Jay B. Nash
1944 Charles H. McCloy
1945 William G. Anderson
1946 Ethel Perrin
1947 Blanche M. Trilling
1948 Mabel Lee
1949 Elmer D. Mitchell
1950 Elizabeth Burchenal
1951 William Ralph LaPorte
1952 Charles W. Savage
1953 Frederick W. Cozens
1954 William L. Hughes
1955 Carl L. Nordly
1956 Rosalind E. Cassidy
1957 Clair V. Langton
1958 Helen Manley
1959 Delbert Oberteuffer
1960 Dorothy Ainsworth
1961 Neils P. Neilson
1962 Clifford Lee Brownell
1963 David Kingsley Brace
1964 Ruth Glassow
1965 Ruth Abernathy & Elwood Craig Davis
1966 (None)
1967 Arthur A. Esslinger
1968 Minnie L. Lynn
1969 Arthur H. Steinhaus

Recipients of Anderson Awards

Physical Educators only listed. Since 1960 only persons working in allied fields have been honored with this award.

1949 Mazie V. Scanlon
1951 Helen Manley, Seward C. Staley, and Arthur H. Steinhaus
1952 Bernice R. Moss, and Agnes R. Wayman
1953 Margaret C. Brown, and Thomas E. McDonough
1954 Elwood C. Davis, Clair V. Langton, and James E. Rogers
1959 C. Ward Crampton

Recipients of Honor Awards

The recipients from 1931 through 1964 are listed in the January, 1965, Journal of Health, Physical Education and Recreation. *For later awards, see the various issues of the magazine for each year.*

Recipients of R. Tait McKenzie Awards

1968 Mabel Lee
1969 Leona Holbrook and Frank D. Sills

AMERICAN ACADEMY OF PHYSICAL EDUCATION

Charter Members

According to numbers assigned to fellows:

1. Clark W. Hetherington
2. R. Tait McKenzie
3. William H. Burdick
4. Thomas A. Storey
5. Jay B. Nash
6. Carl L. Schrader

7. James H. McCurdy
8. Jessie H. Bancroft
9. Wilbur P. Bowen
10. Dudley B. Reed
11. Howard S. Braucher
12. Amy Morris Homans
13. William A. Stecher
14. Earnest H. Arnold
15. George L. Meylan
16. (Cancelled)
17. William Ralph LaPorte
18. Charles W. Savage
19. John F. Bovard
20. Paul C. Phillips
21. Arthur S. Lamb
22. (Cancelled)
23. John Brown, Jr.
24. J. Anna Norris
25. E. C. Schneider
26. Elmer D. Mitchell
27. Charles H. McCloy
28. Elizabeth Burchenal
29. Arthur H. Steinhaus

Presidents

1926–30 Clark W. Hetherington (organizing chairman)
1930–38 R. Tait McKenzie
1938–39 Mabel Lee (Acting President)
1939–41 John Brown, Jr.
1941–43 Mabel Lee
1943–45 Arthur H. Steinhaus
1945–47 Jay B. Nash
1947–49 Charles H. McCloy
1949–50 Frederick W. Cozens
1950–51 Rosalind E. Cassidy
1951–52 Seward C. Staley
1952–53 David K. Brace
1953–54 Neils P. Neilson
1954–55 Elmer D. Mitchell
1955–56 Anna S. Espenschade
1956–57 Harry A. Scott
1957–58 Charles C. Cowell
1958–59 Delbert Oberteuffer
1959–60 Helen Manley
1960–61 Thomas E. McDonough
1961–62 M. Gladys Scott
1962–63 Fred V. Hein
1963–64 Carl Nordly
1964–65 Eleanor Metheny
1965–66 Leonard Larson
1966–67 Arthur A. Esslinger
1967–68 Margaret Fox
1968–69 Laura Huelster
1969–70 Harrison Clarke

PRESIDENTS OF THE NATIONAL COLLEGE PHYSICAL EDUCATION ASSOCIATION FOR MEN

1897 Edward Hitchcock
1898 Jay W. Seaver
1899 Dudley A. Sargent
1900 William G. Anderson
1901 R. Tait McKenzie
1902 Paul C. Phillips
1903 Watson L. Savage
1904 R. Tait McKenzie
1905, 1906 George L. Meylan
1907, 1908 Thomas A. Storey
1909 R. Tait McKenzie
1910, 1911 Amos Alonzo Stagg
1912 Fred E. Leonard
1913 W. A. Lambeth
1914 James Naismith
1915 Charles W. Savage
1916 C. V. Young
1917, 1918 Joseph E. Raycroft
1919, 1920 Edwin Fauer
1921 Frederick W. Luehring
1922 Edgar Fauver
1923 James H. McCurdy
1924 John Herbert Nichols
1925 William H. Geer
1926 Dudley B. Reed
1927 A. W. Marsh
1928 Jesse F. Williams
1929 A. I. Prettyman
1930 William Ralph LaPorte
1931 T. N. Metcalf
1932 O. F. Cutts
1933 George E. Little

1934 William L. Hughes
1935 C. L. Brewer
1936 E. L. Mercer
1937 W. J. Livingston
1938 Harold S. Wood
1939 L. C. Boles
1940 Harry A. Scott
1941 Oliver K. Cornwell
1942 Elwood C. Davis
1943 Carl P. Schott
1944 Delbert Oberteuffer
1945, 1946 A. W. Marsh
1947 Carl L. Nordly
1948 Lloyd M. Jones
1949 Louis F. Keller
1950 Glenn W. Howard
1951 Thomas E. McDonough
1952 F. J. Hoeter
1953 Elmer D. Mitchell
1954 William F. Meredith
1955 Seward C. Staley
1956 E. B. Smith
1957 Arthur S. Daniels
1958 John H. Shaw
1959 C. O. Jackson
1960 Raymond Snyder
1961 Joy W. Kistler
1962 Richard E. Jamerson
1963 Karl Bookwalter
1964 John E. Nixon
1965 Arthur Weston
1966 Richard Donnelly
1967 Louis E. Alley
1968 Charles Kovacic
1969 David O. Matthews
1970 Chalmer Hixon

PRESIDENTS OF THE NATIONAL ASSOCIATION OF PHYSICAL EDUCATION FOR COLLEGE WOMEN

1924–25 Lydia Clark
1925–26 Alice Belding
1926–27 Mabel Lee
1927–29 Mary E. Gross
1929–32 Gertrude E. Moulton
1932–34 Ruth Elliott
1934–37 Rosalind E. Cassidy
1937–41 Dorothy S. Ainsworth
1941–43 Elizabeth Kelly
1943–45 Elizabeth Halsey
1945–47 Gertrude Manchester
1947–49 Helen W. Hazelton
1949–51 Irene A. Clayton
1951–53 Pauline Hodgson
1953–55 Laura J. Huelster
1955–57 Ruth M. Wilson
1957–59 Lucille H. Verhulst
1959–61 Esther French
1961–63 Wilma Gimmestad
1963–65 Leona Holbrook
1965–67 Celeste Ulrich
1967–69 Marion R. Broer
1969–71 Catherine L. Allen

PRESIDENTS OF THE SOCIETY OF STATE DIRECTORS OF HEALTH, PHYSICAL EDUCATION, AND RECREATION

1926–27 Carl L. Schrader
1927–28 William H. Burdick
1928–29 Allen G. Ireland
1929–30 E. W. Everts
1930–31 Elliott V. Graves
1931–33 William G. Moorehead
1933–34 Neils P. Neilson
1934–35 C. J. Prohaska
1935–36 G. K. Hendricks
1936–37 Jessie R. Garrison
1937–38 W. H. Orion
1938–39 Hiram A. Jones
1939–40 Harry Edwards
1940–41 Jess W. Hair
1941–42 Bernice R. Moss
1942–43 Alice G. Aldrich
1943–44 Harold K. Jack
1944–45 Frank S. Stafford
1945–46 George W. Ayars
1946–47 Thomas C. Ferguson
1947–48 Charles E. Spencer
1948–49 Paul E. Landis
1949–50 Ray O. Duncan
1950–51 Julian W. Smith
1951–52 Verne S. Landreth
1952–53 Ellis H. Champlin
1953–54 Robert Yoho
1954–55 Harley Robertson

1955–56 Elmer B. Cottrell
1956–57 George J. Sirnio
1957–58 Vaughn Hall
1958–59 Raymond Maguire
1959–60 Zollie Maynard
1960–61 George H. Grover
1961–62 Orlo Miller
1962–63 Herbert Spencer
1963–64 William E. Noonan, Jr.
1964–65 Lewis Spears
1965–66 Edwin G. Rice
1966–67 Robert L. Holland
1967–68 Howard Schaub
1968–69 Harold J. Schreiner
1969–70 Carl Knutson

CHAIRMEN OF DIVISION FOR GIRLS AND WOMEN'S SPORTS

Under the name: Women's Basket Ball Rules Committee.

1899–1905 Alice B. Foster

Under the name: National Women's Basket Ball Committee.

1905–1917 Senda Berenson

Under the name: National Committee on Women's Sports.

1917–21 Elizabeth Burchenal
1921–25 Blanche M. Trilling
1925–27 Katherine Sibley

Under the name: Women's Athletic Section.

1927–30 Florence A. Somers
1930–31 Helen W. Hazelton

Under the name: National Section on Women's Athletics.

1931–32 Grace Jones
1932–34 Grace B. Davies
1934–36 Eline Von Borries
1936–38 Elinor Schroeder
1938–40 Jane Shurmer
1940–42 Ruth D. Atwell
1942–43 Alice Shriver
1943–46 Anna S. Espenschade
1946–48 Alfreda Mosscrop
1948–49 Martha A. Gable
1949–52 Laurie Campbell

Under the name: National Section for Girls and Women's Sports.

1952–54 Josephine Fiske
1954 (June–Dec.) Aileene Lockhart
1954 (Dec.)–56 Grace I. Fox
1956–58 Mabel Locke

Under the name: Division for Girls and Women's Sports.

1958–59 Jane A. Mott
1959–60 Thelma Bishop
1960–61 Anne Finlayson
1961–62 Sara Staff Jernigan
1962–63 Katherine Ley
1963–64 Marguerite Clifton
1964–65 Betty F. McCue
1965–66 Phebe M. Scott
1966–67 Frances McGill
1967–68 Lucille Magnason
1968–69 Alyce Cheska
1969–70 E. Ann Stitt

PRESIDENTS OF EASTERN DISTRICT ASSOCIATION OF AAHPER

1919–21 Carl L. Schrader
1921–23 Frederick W. Maroney
1923–25 William H. Geer
1925–29 Charles H. Keene
1929–31 Jesse F. Williams
1931–33 Marjorie Bouvé
1933–35 Jay B. Nash
1935–37 Franklin Gray
1937–39 Hiram A. Jones
1939–40 Alice C. Aldrich
1940–41 William L. Hughes
1941–42 William F. Meredith
1942–44 Ruth Evans
1944–46 George W. Ayars
1946–47 Mazie V. Scanlon
1947–48 Clifford L. Brownell
1948–49 Dorothy S. Ainsworth
1949–50 Thomas C. Ferguson
1950–51 Minnie L. Lynn
1951–52 John W. Shaw
1952–53 Ethel T. Kloberg
1953–55 Lloyd M. Jones
1955–56 Karl C. H. Oermann
1956–57 Marion E. Purbeck
1957–58 William M. Grimshaw
1958–59 Elizabeth McHose
1959–60 Jack F. George
1960–62 Ruth Byler
1962–63 Elmon L. Vernier
1963–65 M. Dorothy Massey
1965–66 George H. Grover
1966–67 Margaret Coffey
1967–68 Frank Sills
1968–69 Catherine Comeau
1969–70 Burris F. Husman

PRESIDENTS OF MIDWEST DISTRICT ASSOCIATION OF AAHPER

The Middle West

When the present Midwest and Central Districts were one.

1912–13 Clark W. Hetherington
1913–17 Dudley R. Reed
1917–18 Ethel Perrin
1918–19 Wilbur P. Bowen
1919–20 Martin I. Foss
1920–21 Charles W. Savage
1921–23 W. J. Monilaw
1923–26 J. Anna Norris
1926–27 Margaret R. McKee
1927–28 E. C. Delaporte
1928–29 (Jan.) Loren Post
1929 (Feb.–Apr.) Mabel Lee (Acting President)
1929–30 Mabel Lee
1930–32 Emil Rath
1932–33 Strong Hinman

The Present Midwest

1933–34 Margaret Bell
1934–35 Guy S. Lowman
1935–36 Helen N. Smith
1936–37 John McCollough
1937–38 Laurentine B. Collins
1938–39 William K. Streit
1939–40 Helen W. Hazelton
1940–41 August H. Pritzlaff
1941–42 Grace M. Griffen
1942–43 Ben W. Miller
1943–44 Iris Boulton
1944–46 Robert Nohr
1946–47 Gertrude E. Moulton
1947–48 Leon G. Kranz
1948–49 Edwina Jones
1949–50 Lou H. Hollway
1950–51 Anne Finlayson
1951–52 Clarence Biedenweg
1952–53 Carolyn Bookwalter
1953–54 Paul E. Landis
1954–55 Margaret A. Bourne
1955–56 Arthur H. Steinhaus
1956–57 Hester B. Bland
1957–58 King McCristal

1958–59	Beatrice Baird	1964–65	Patric L. Cavanaugh
1959–60	Jack B. Daugherty	1965–67	Candace Roell
1960–61	Naomi Allenbaugh	1967–68	Nelson G. Lehsten
1961–63	G. Lawrence Rarick	1968–69	Marilyn Hinson
1963–64	Gelinda E. Vescaloni	1969–70	Charles Peter Yost

PRESIDENTS OF CENTRAL DISTRICT ASSOCIATION OF AAHPER

1933–34	Charles H. McCloy	1952–53	Leonard R. Marti
1934–35	Clare H. Small	1953–54	Wilma Gimmestad
1935–36	Louis E. Hutto	1954–55	R. B. Frost
1936–37	Edna McCullough	1955–56	Jean Bontz
1937–38	Alfred O. Anderson	1956–57	Edwin R. Elbel
1938–39	Elizabeth Halsey	1957–58	A. Gwendolyn Drew
1939–40	Willard N. Greim	1958–59	Frank D. Sills
1940–41	Helen Manley	1959–60	Anita Aldrich
1941–42	James H. Morrison	1960–61	John B. Van Why
1942–43	Gertrude M. Baker	1961–62	Hazel Dettman
1943–44	Carl L. Nordly	1962–63	Henry Shenk
1944–46	Germaine G. Guiot	1963–64	Helen Slocum
1946–47	Louis F. Keller	1964–65	Louis E. Alley
1947–48	Elizabeth Graybeal	1965–66	Barbara Forker
1948–49	L. P. Washburn	1966–67	Carl Wear
1949–50	M. Gladys Scott	1967–69	Laura Mae Brown
1950–51	Merle Henre	1969–70	Clem Thompson
1951–52	Mabel J. Shirley		

PRESIDENTS OF SOUTHERN DISTRICT ASSOCIATION OF AAHPER

1927–29	A. D. Browne	1949–50	Solon B. Sudduth
1929–30	Jackson R. Sharman	1950–51	Margaret McCall
1930–31	Elliott V. Graves	1951–52	Charles E. Spencer
1931–32	Mary C. Coleman	1952–53	Elizabeth Moore
1932–33	David K. Brace	1953–54	Gilbert L. Hermance
1933–34	Caswell M. Miles	1954–55	Caroline Sinclair
1934–35	Jessie R. Garrison	1955–56	C. J. Alderson
1935–36	Harry A. Scott	1956–57	Elizabeth Autrey
1936–37	Harold T. Taylor	1957–58	Guy W. Nesom
1937–38	Alfreda Mosscrop	1958–59	Ethel Martus
1938–39	Thomas E. McDonough	1959–61	Lloyd L. Messersmith
1939–40	Anne Schley Duggan	1961–62	Sue Hall
1940–41	Lynn B. Sherril	1962–63	Taylor Dodson
1941–42	Ethel J. Saxman	1963–64	Grace Fox
1942–43	E. Benton Salt	1964–66	Willis J. Baughman
1943–44	Katherine W. Montgomery	1966–67	Frances Mays
1944–46	Oliver K. Cornwell	1967–68	Troy Hendricks
1946–47	Mary Ella Soule	1968–69	Esther White
1947–48	Joy W. Kistler	1969–70	Kenneth Miller
1948–49	Helen Corrubia		

PRESIDENTS OF NORTHWEST DISTRICT ASSOCIATION OF AAHPER

1930–31 J. Fred Bohler
1931–32 Henry M. Foster
1932–33 Paul R. Washke
1933–34 Henry H. House
1934–35 Ruth Weythman
1935–36 John F. Bovard
1936–37 Eva Jurgensohn
1937–38 Madeline Larson
1938–39 Earl E. Boushey
1939–40 Helen G. Smith
1940–41 A. C. Pelton
1941–42 Virginia L. Shaw
1942–43 Clair V. Langton
1943–44 Mary Gross Hutchinson
1944–45 Lestle Sparks
1945–46 Eva M. Seen
1946–47 Edwin Graham
1947–48 Dorothea M. Lensch
1948–49 G. Spencer Reeves
1949–50 Grace Houghton
1950–51 Leon Green
1951–53 Agnes L. Stoodley
1953–54 George J. Sirnio
1954–55 Mabel Locke
1955–56 Glen E. Galligan
1956–57 Harold Alterowitz
1957–58 Robert W. Bergstrom
1958–60 Ruth Wilson
1960–61 Golden Romney
1961–62 Vernon S. Sprague
1962–63 Marion R. Broer
1963–64 Paul Smith
1964–65 Roger Wiley
1965–66 Jessie Puckett
1966–67 Clair Anderson
1967–68 Margaret Aitken
1968–69 Eric Kirkland
1969–70 Maxine Rowan

PRESIDENTS OF SOUTHWEST DISTRICT ASSOCIATION OF AAHPER

1934–36 William R. LaPorte
1936–38 Charles Davis
1938–39 Louise S. Cobb
1939–40 Catherine A. Worthingham
1940–41 Bernice R. Moss
1941–42 James W. Coleman
1942–43 Mrs. Leo Cleaves
1943–44 John F. Bovard
1944–45 Glen Worthington
1945–46 Hazel J. Cubberly
1946–47 Alice Oakes Bronson
1947–48 Verne S. Landreth
1948–49 Luell Weed Guthrie
1949–50 Frank R. Williams
1950–51 J. E. Marti
1951–52 Elwood C. Davis
1952–53 Dudley S. DeGroot
1953–54 Catherine A. Wilkinson
1954–55 H. B. Hunsaker
1955–56 Glenn W. Arnett
1956–57 Ruth I. Russell
1957–58 John M. Cooper
1958–59 Lois Downs
1959–60 Lawrence E. Morehouse
1960–61 John Barrier
1961–62 Conrad Moll
1962–63 Arthur Broten
1963–64 Theo Redman
1964–65 Raymond Snyder
1965–67 Tillman Hall
1967–68 Mickey Miller
1968–69 Barbara West
1969–70 Edwin Long

HONORARY DOCTOR'S DEGREES CONFERRED UPON PHYSICAL EDUCATORS

1851–M.D. to Dio Lewis by Cleveland Medical School
1894–Sc. D. to Dudley A. Sargent by Bowdoin College
1898–LL.D. to Edward M. Hartwell by Amherst College
1899–LL.D. to Edward Hitchcock by Amherst College
1921–LL.D. to R. Tait McKenzie by McGill University
1928–D.F.A. to R. Tait McKenzie by the University of Pennsylvania

1930—Pd.D. (Doctor of Pedagogy) to Amy Morris Homans by Russell Sage College
1933—LL.D. to Amos Alonzo Stagg by the College of Wooster
1934—LL.D. to Clelia D. Mosher by Mills College
1935—Pd.D. to Clark W. Hetherington by the University of Southern California
1936—LL.D. to William G. Anderson by Battle Creek College
1938—LL.D. to R. Tait McKenzie by St. Andrews University, Scotland
1939—D. Sc. to Jesse F. Williams by Rollins College
1939—LL.D. to Mabel Lee by Coe College
1942—Pd.D. to Agnes R. Wayman by Russell Sage College
1943—D. Sc. in P.E. to Elizabeth Burchenal by Boston University
1944—LL.D. to Helen McKinstry by Skidmore College
1947—D. Sc. to Charles H. McCloy by Marietta College
1949—D. Sc. in P.E. to Anna Hiss, Ruth Evans, Francis M. Greene, William L. Hughes, and F. R. Aquino by Boston University
1949—D. Sc. to Catherine A. Worthingham by Boston University
1950—L.H.D. (Doctor of Humane Letters) to Rosalind E. Cassidy by Mills College
1950—L.H.D. to Katharine Sibley by Syracuse University
1952—Sc. D. to Seward C. Staley by Springfield College
1953—LL.D. to Ellis H. Champlin by Ithaca College
1953—D.Pd. to John Lawther by Westminster College
1954—LL.D. to William Ralph LaPorte by Pepperdine College
1954—LL.D. to G. Ott Romney by Montana State College
1955—D. Sc. to Charles H. McCloy by Grinnell College
1955—D. Sc. to William L. Hughes by Springfield College
1956—D.P.E. to Mabel Lee by George Williams College
1956—Sc. D. to Dorothy Ainsworth by Smith College
1957—Lit. D. to Charles H. McCloy by George Williams College
1958—D.P.E. to Charles H. McCloy by The College of Medicine, University of Toronto
1960—LL.D. to Harry C. Good by Indiana Central College
1967—D. Sc. to Aileene S. Lockhart by the University of Nebraska
1967—D. Sc. to Thomas E. McDonough by Eastern Kentucky University
1967—D. Sc. to Liselot Diem of Germany by Springfield College

EARLY STATE DIRECTORS OF PHYSICAL EDUCATION

1916—New York, Thomas A. Storey
1918—California, Clark W. Hetherington
1918—New Jersey, Frederick W. Maroney
1918—Maryland, William Burdick
1919—Michigan, Floyd A. Rowe
1920—Alabama, O. C. Bird
1922—Connecticut, Allen G. Ireland
1922—Massachusetts, Carl L. Schrader
1922—Missouri, Henry S. Curtis
1922—Pennsylvania, Charles H. Keene
1923—Minnesota, E. W. Everts
1925—Virginia, Elliott V. Graves
1926—Delaware, P. S. Prince
1926—Ohio, Clifford L. Brownell
1927—Florida, Caswell Miles
1929—Illinois, Louis Kulcinski
1930—Texas, R. N. Sandlin

In 1929 Jessie R. Garrison was appointed Acting Physical Director for the State of Alabama succeeding Jackson R. Sharman, and two years later she became Director—the first woman to hold a state directorship.

Appendix B

The United States and the Olympic Games

The information in the following charts has been arranged from the official records of winners in the Olympic Games from 1896 on, as given in Kieran and Daley's book—see References—and in the various editions of the *World Almanac* and *Information Please Almanac*.

THE OLYMPIC GAMES AND GOLD MEDALS WON

Number & Year of Olympiad	No. of Nations Entered	No. of Athletes Entered	No. of Events Offered, all Sports	No. of Nations Winning Gold Medals	No. of Gold Medals Won by U.S. Athletes	No. of Gold Medals Won by Nearest Contenders
I—1896	12	285	34	9	10	Germany and Greece—6 each
II—1900			31	5	19	France—5
III—1904			71	4	56	Germany—6
1906	(unofficial, to celebrate 10th anniversary)		61	16	12	France—12 (tied)
IV—1908			92	12	25	Great Britain—41 (led)
V—1912	26		92	15	21	Sweden—20
VI—1916	(World War I intervened)					
VII—1920			135	19	37	Sweden—20
VIII—1924	45	2,000	126	21	45	Finland—14
IX—1928	43	4,000	121	28	23	Finland and Norway—11 each
X—1932	39	2,000	133	20	48	Italy—12
XI—1936	53	5,000	145	21	25	Germany—34 (led)
XII—1940	(World War II intervened)					
XIII—1944	(World War II intervened)					
XIV—1948	59	6,000	151	24	40	Sweden—21
XV—1952	69		154	28	43	U.S.S.R.—23
XVI—1956	74	4,000	151	27	29	U.S.S.R.—33 (led)
XVII—1960	84	5,400	171	28	37	U.S.S.R.—50 (led)
XVIII—1964	94	6,600	195		37	U.S.S.R.—41 (led)
XIX—1968	19S–37W	8,498	207	30	46	U.S.S.R.—34

SPORTS USED IN MODERN OLYMPICS

Sport	1st Used	Last Used	Sport	1st Used	Last Used
Basketball	1904	1904	Skating, figure	1908	
Revived	1936		Women	1908	
Bobsledding	1924		Skating, speed	1924	
Boxing	1904		Women	1932	1932
			Revived	1960	
Canoeing	1936		Skiing	1924	
Curling	1924	1936	Women	1936	
Cycling	1896		Soccer	1906	
Equestrian	1912		Swimming	1896	
Fencing	1900		Women	1912	
Women	1924		Tennis, covered court	1896	1912
Field Hockey	1920		Women	1908	1912
Golf	1904	1904	Tennis, lawn	1896	1924
Gymnastics	1896		Women	1904	1924
Women	1928		Tobogganing	1960	
Ice Hockey	1920		Track & Field	1896	
Judo	1964		Women	1928	
Lacrosse	1904	1908	Tug-of-War	1906	1920
Pentathlon	1912		Weight-lifting	1896	
Winter	1948	1948	Volleyball	1964	
Polo	1908	1936	Women	1964	
Racquets	1908	1908	Wrestling	1904	
Roque	1904	1904	Greco-Roman	1906	
Rowing	1904		Yachting	1908	
Rugby Football	1920	1924			
Shooting	1896				

TOP U.S. GOLD MEDAL WINNERS, TWO OR MORE, BY YEARS

1896 T. E. Burke–2
E. H. Clarke–2

1900 Ray Ewry–3
A. E. Kraenzlein–4
J. W. B. Tewsbury–2

1904 C. N. Daniels–2
Ray Ewry–3
George Eyser–3
Archie Hahn–3
Anton Heida–3
E. A. Henney–2
H. L. Hillman–3
O. L. Kirk–2
J. D. Lightbody–2
Myer Prinstein–2
Beal Wright–2

1906 Ray Ewry–2
Paul Pilgrim–2
M. J. Sheridan–2

1908 Ray Ewry–2
M. W. Shepherd–2
M. J. Sheridan–2

1912 R. C. Graig–2
Norman Ross–2

1920 J. B. Kelly–2
Norman Ross–2

1924 Clarence Houser–2
H. M. Osborn–2
Vincent Richards–2
John Weissmuller–2
A. C. White–2
Helen Wills–2

1928 P. Dejardens–2

1932 Mildred Didrickson–2
Irving Jafee–2
Helene Madison–2
John A. Shea–2
Eddie Tolan–2

1936 Jesse Owens–3

1948 None

1952 Tommy Kono–2
Andrea M. Lawrence–2
Patricia McCormick–2

1956 Patricia McCormick–2
Bobby Morrow–2

1960 Al Oerter–2
Wilma Rudolph–2

1964 Don Schollander–2

1968 Mike Burton–2
Charles Hickcox–2
Claudia Kolb–2
Debbie Meyer–2

U.S. GOLD MEDAL WINNERS IN MORE THAN ONE OLYMPICS

Richard Button, 2, 1948 & 1952
Lee Calhoun, 2, 1956 & 1960
Glen Davis, 2, 1956 & 1960
Ray Ewry, 10, 1900, 1904, 1906, & 1908
Morris Fisher, 2, 1920 & 1924
J. J. Flanagan, 2, 1904 & 1908
Archie Hahn, 4, 1904 & 1908
Clarence Houser, 3, 1924 & 1928
Duke Kahanamokua, 2, 1912 & 1920
Patricia McCormick, 4, 1952 & 1956
Bob Mathais, 2, 1948 & 1952
Martha Norelius, 2, 1924 & 1928
Al Oerter, 5, 1956, 1960, 1964 & 1968
M. J. Sheridan, 5, 1904, 1906 & 1908
Myer Prinstein, 3, 1900 & 1904
Ralph Rose, 2, 1908 & 1912
John Weismuller, 3, 1924 & 1928
Malcolm Whitfield, 2, 1948 & 1952

TOP U.S. OLYMPIC GOLD MEDAL WINNERS, THREE OR MORE

10–Ray Ewry: 3 each, 1900 & '04; & 2 each, '06, '08
5–M. J. Sheridan, 1, 1904; 2 each, '06 & '08
4–Archie Hahn, 3, 1904; 1, '08
4–A. E. Kraenzlein, 1900
4–Patricia McCormick, 2 each, 1952 & '56
5–Al Oerter, 2, 1960; 1 each, '56, '64 & '68
3–George Eyser, 1904
3–Anton Heida, 1904
3–Harry L. Hillman, 1904
3–Cris Houser, 2, 1924; 1, 1928
3–Myer Prinsten, 2, 1904; 1, 1900
3–Jesse Owens in 1936
3–John Weissmuller, 2, 1924; 1, 1928

FIRST AND BEST RECORDS SET IN THE OLYMPIC GAMES IN TRACK AND FIELD AND IN SWIMMING

Event	1st Record	Year	Nation	Best Record	Year	Nation
TRACK AND FIELD—MEN						
100 meter run	12s	1896	U.S.	10.0s	1964	U.S.
200 meter run	22.2s	1900	U.S.	20.3s	1964	U.S.
400 meter run	54.2s	1896	U.S.	45.1s	1964	U.S.
800 meter run	2m:11s	1896	Gr. Br.	1m:44.3s	1968	Australia
1,500 meter run	4m:33.2s	1896	Gr. Br.	3m:34.9s	1968	Kenya
5,000 meter run	14m:36.6s	1912	Finland	13m:39.6s	1956	U.S.S.R.
10,000 meter run	31m:20.8s	1912	Finland	28m:24.4s	1960	U.S.
Marathon	2h:55m:20s	1896	Greece	2h:12m:11.2s	1964	Ethopia
110 meter hurdles	17s	1896	U.S.	0m:13.3s	1968	U.S.
400 meter hurdles	57.6s	1900	U.S.	49.3s	1960	U.S.
30,000 meter hurdles	10m:2.4s	1920	Gr. Br.	8m:30.8s	1964	Belgium
400 meter relay	42m:4s	1912	Gr. Br.	39s	1964	U.S.
1,600 meter relay	3m:27.2s	1908	U.S.	3m:0.7s	1964	U.S.
Pole vault	10′ 9¾″	1896	U.S.	17′ 8½″	1968	U.S.
Running high jump	5′ 11¼″	1896	U.S.	7′ 4¼″	1968	U.S.
Running broad jump	20′ 9¾″	1896	U.S.	26′ 7¾″	1960	U.S.
Running hop, skip & jump	45′	1896	U.S.	55′ 3¼″	1964	Poland
16-lb shot	36′ 2″	1896	U.S.	66′ 8¼″	1964	U.S.
16-lb hammer throw	167′ 4″	1900	U.S.	240′ 8″	1968	Hungary
Discus throw	95′ 7½″	1896	U.S.	212′ 6½″	1968	U.S.
Javelin throw	175′ 6″	1896	Sweden	295′ 7¼″	1968	U.S.S.R.
Decathlon	7,724,495 pts.	1912	Sweden	8,193 pts. (Revised 1964)	1968	U.S.

Event	1st Record	Year	Nation	Best Record	Year	Nation
TRACK AND FIELD—WOMEN						
100 meter run	12.2s	1928	U.S.	11s	1960	U.S.
200 meter race	24.4s	1948	Netherlands	23s	1964	U.S.
400 meter race	—	—	—	52s	1964 and 1968	Australia and France
800 meter race	2m:16.8s	1928	Germany	2m:1.1s	1964	Gr. Br.
Running high jump	5′ 3″	1928	Canada	6′ 2¾″	1964	U.S.S.R.
Long jump	18′ 8½″	1948	Hungary	22′ 2″	1964	Gr. Br.
Shot put	45′ 1½″	1948	France	59′ 6″	1964	U.S.S.R.
400 meter relay	48.4s	1928	Canada	43.6s	1964	Poland
800 meter hurdles	11.7s	1932	U.S.	10.5s	1964	Germany
Running high jump	5′ 3″	1928	Canada	6′ 9¾″	1960	Rumania
Discus throw	129′ 11⅞″	1928	Poland	191′ 2¼″	1968	Rumania
Javelin throw	143′ 4″	1932	U.S.	198′ 7½″	1964	Rumania
SWIMMING—MEN						
100 meter race	1m:22.2s	1896	Hungary	53.2s	1960	Australia
400 meter race	6m:16.2s	1904	U.S.	4m:9s	1968	U.S.
1,500 meter race	22m:48.4s	1908	Gr. Br.	16m:38.9s	1968	U.S.
100 meter backstroke	1m:16.8s	1904	Germany	0:58.7s	1968	East Germany
200 meter breaststroke	3m:9.2s	1908	Gr. Br.	2m:27.8s	1964	U.S.
SWIMMING—WOMEN						
100 meter race	1m:22.2s	1912	Australia	59.5s	1964	Australia
400 meter race	6m:2.2s	1924	U.S.	4m:31.8s	1968	U.S.
400 meter free style relay	5m:52.8s	1912	Gr. Br.	4m:02.5s	1968	U.S.
100 meter backstroke	1m:23.2s	1924	U.S.	1m:7.7s	1964	U.S.
200 meter breaststroke	3m:33.2s	1924	Gr. Br.	2m:44.4s	1968	U.S.

TUCKER, THOMAS GEORGE. *Life in Ancient Athens.* New York: The Macmillan Co., 1906.

VAN HOOK, LARUE. *Greek Life and Thought.* New York: Columbia University Press, 1937.

WHIBLEY, LEONARD. *A Companion to Greek Studies.* London: Cambridge University Press, 1905.

Chapter 3: The Romans

CUBBERLEY, ELLWOOD P. *The History of Education.* Boston: Houghton Mifflin Co., 1920.

FOWLER, WILLIAM WARDE. *Social Life at Rome in the Age of Cicero.* New York: The Macmillan Co., 1909. Chap. x.

GIBBON, EDWARD. *The History of the Decline and Fall of the Roman Empire.* New York, 1845. Vol. I.

GRAVES, FRANK P. *History of Education Before the Middle Ages.* New York: The Macmillan Co., 1909.

HALLE, JENNIE. *Buried Cities.* New York: The Macmillan Co., 1922.

HIRTH, GEORG. *Das Gesamte Turnwesen.* Leipzig, 1893. Band I, pp. 5–230.

JOHNSTON, HAROLD W. *Private Life of the Romans.* Chicago, 1903.

MONROE, PAUL. *Source Book in the History of Education for the Greek and Roman Period.* New York: The Macmillan Co., 1901.

SANDYS, SIR JOHN E. *A Companion to Latin Studies.* London: Cambridge University Press, 1921. Articles on Education, Public Games, and Medicine.

SCHRADER, CARL L. "The Baths of Old," *Mind and Body* (May, 1916), 97–103.

SUETONIUS. *Lives of the Cæsars.* Boston: Allyn & Bacon, Inc., 1903. Bk. VI, art. 12, on Nero's games.

TACITUS, CORNELIUS. *Annals.* Art. xiv, secs. 20–21. Contains note on the introduction of Greek games to Rome.

THOMAS, EMILE. *Roman Life Under the Cæsars.* New York, 1899. Chap. iv.

VIRGIL. *Æneid.* Book V. Account of funeral games.

Chapter 4: The Dark Ages

ADAMS, GEORGE B. *Civilization During the Middle Ages.* New York: Charles Scribner's Sons, 1922.

BINTZ, JULIUS. *Die Leibesübungen des Mittelalters.* Gütersloh, 1880.

GRAVES, FRANK P. *History of Education During the Middle Ages and the Transition to Modern Times.* New York: The Macmillan Co., 1910.

KINGSLEY, CHARLES. *The Roman and the Teuton.* London, 1901.

MONROE, PAUL. *A Text-Book in the History of Education.* New York: The Macmillan Co., 1920.

MUNRO, DANA C. *The Middle Ages.* New York: The Century Co., 1926. Chap. iii.

———, and WHITCOMB, M. *The Middle Ages and Modern Europe.* New York: The Century Co., 1903. Chaps. xii and xv.

TACITUS, CORNELIUS. *Germania* (Loeb Classical Library). London, 1920. Treats of the lives of the early Germans.

THATCHER, O. J., and MCNEAL, E. H. *Source Book for Medieval History.* New York, 1907. Chap. viii.

WORKMAN, HERBERT B. *Evolution of the Monastic Ideal From the Earliest Times Down to the Coming of the Friars.* London, 1913.

Chapter 5: The Age of Chivalry

ADAMS, GEORGE B. *Civilization During the Middle Ages.* New York: Charles Scribner's Sons, 1922.

BINTZ, JULIUS. *Die Liebesübungen des Mittelalters.* Gütersloh, 1880. This work includes all popular sports.
CORNISH, F. WARRE. *Chivalry.* New York: The Macmillan Co., 1901.
DORAN, JOHN. *Knights and Their Days.* New York, 1856.
MONROE, PAUL. *A Text-Book in the History of Education.* New York: The Macmillan Co., 1920.
MUNRO, DANA C. *The Middle Ages.* New York: The Century Co., 1926. Chap. xii.
———, and WHITCOMB, M. *The Middle Ages and Modern Europe.* New York: The Century Co., 1903. Chaps. xiii and xiv.
STRUTT, JOSEPH. *The Sports and Pastimes of the People of England* (reprint). London, 1898.
TAPPAN, EVA MARCH. *When Knights Were Bold.* Boston: Houghton Mifflin Co., 1911. Elementary.
THATCHER, O. J., and MCNEAL, E. H. *Source Book for Medieval History.* New York, 1907. Chap. vi.

Chapter 6: The Renaissance

ASCHAM, ROGER. *The Scholemaster.* EDWARD ARBER, ed. (Heath's Pedagogical Library.) Boston, 1898. Vol. XXXII.
BOGENY, *et al. Die Geschichte des Sports Aller Völker und Zeiten.* Leipzig: Seeman, 1925. Lieferung 3.
COMPAYRE, JULES GABRIEL. *The History of Pedagogy.* Boston: D. C. Heath & Co., 1892. Chap. v.
ELYOT, SIR THOMAS. *The Boke Named the Gouvernour* (Everyman's Library). London, 1885. Bk. I, secs. 16–20, on exercise and dancing. III, 22, on diet.
EULER, KARL. *Die Geschichte des Turnunterrichtes.* Berlin, 1881.
GRAVES, FRANK P. *History of Education During the Middle Ages and the Transition to Modern Times.* New York: The Macmillan Co., 1910.
LAURIE, SIMON S. *Studies in the History of Educational Opinion From the Renaissance.* London: Cambridge University Press, 1903.
LEONARD, FRED EUGENE, and AFFLECK, GEORGE B. *A Guide to the History of Physical Education.* Philadelphia: Lea & Febiger, 1947.
QUICK, R. H. *Essays on Educational Reformers.* New York: D. Appleton Co., 1898. Chaps. i and ii.
WOODWARD, W. H. *Vittorino Da Feltre and Other Humanist Educators.* London: Cambridge University Press, 1921.

Chapter 7: Realism

BOYKIN, JAMES C. "Physical Training," *Report of the U.S. Commissioner of Education, 1891–92,* I.
COMPAYRE, JULES GABRIEL. *The History of Pedagogy.* Boston: D. C. Heath & Co., 1892. Chap. vi.
GRAVES, FRANK P. *A Student's History of Education.* New York: The Macmillan Co., 1915. Chaps. xiv and xv.
LOCKE, JOHN. *Some Thoughts Concerning Education.* London: Cambridge University Press, 1902.
MILTON, JOHN. *Tractate on Education* (Harvard Classics, Vol. 13). New Haven: Yale University Press, 1928.
MONTAIGNE, MICHEL DE. *The Education of Children* (Harvard Classics, Vol. 32). New York: G. P. Putnam's Sons, 1910.
QUICK, R. H. *Essays on Educational Reformers.* New York: D. Appleton Co., 1912. Chaps. v, vi, viii, x.
WATSON, FOSTER. *On Mulcaster.* (Report of U.S. Commissioner of Education, 1904, Vol. I.)

Chapter 8: The Age of Enlightenment

BARNARD, HENRY. *Memoirs of Eminent Teachers and Educators in Germany.* Hartford, Conn., 1878. See article on Basedow.

DAVIDSON, THOMAS. *Rousseau and Education According to Nature.* New York, 1898. Chaps. iv–vii.

EULER, KARL. *Die Geschichte des Turnunterrichtes.* Berlin, 1881. See article on GutsMuths.

HIRTH, GEORG. *Das Gesamte Turnwesen.* Leipzig, 1893. Band I, pp. 330–62 and 519–23; III, 534–45.

LEONARD, FRED EUGENE, and AFFLECK, GEORGE B. *A Guide to the History of Physical Education.* Philadelphia: Lea & Febiger, 1947.

LEONARD, FRED E. "Johann C. F. GutsMuths," *Mind and Body* (Jan., 1911), 321–26.

QUICK, R. H. *Essays on Educational Reformers.* New York: D. Appleton Co., 1912. Chaps. xiv, xv.

ROUSSEAU, J. J. *Émile; or, Treatise on Education.* Tr. W. H. Payne. New York: D. Appleton Co., 1892.

SIEBERT, ALBERT. "The Development of Physical Education in Germany," *Mind and Body* (Nov., 1909), 249–53. Brief historical survey to 1909.

Chapter 9: Germany since 1800

AYRES, L. P. *Open Air Schools.* Rev. New York: Sage Foundation, 1910. Chaps. i, ii.

BOYKIN, JAMES C. "Physical Training," *Report of the U.S. Commissioner of Education, 1891–92,* I.

DIEM, C. "Development and Aims of Physical Education in Germany," *Journal of Health and Physical Education,* XIX (June, 1948), 390.

EULER, KARL. *Die Geschichte des Turnunterrichtes.* 1881. Contains complete account of German physical education to 1880.

GARDINER, ROLF. "Rhythmic Gymnastics in Germany," *Mind and Body* (Dec., 1925), 776–80.

GASCH, RUDOLPH. *Geschichte der Turnkunst.* Leipzig, 1910.

———. *Handbuch des Gesamten Turnwesens und der Verwandten Leibesübungen.* Leipzig, 1928.

HARTWELL, EDWARD M. "Physical Training in American Colleges and Universities." Bureau of Education; Circular of Information, No. 5, 1885, pp. 157–85.

———. "On Physical Training," *Report of the U.S. Commissioner of Education, 1898,* 523–39.

HIRTH, GEORG. *Das Gesamte Turnwesen.* Leipzig, 1893. Contains writings of Jahn, Spiess, and their contemporaries.

JAHN, FRIEDRICH L. *Die Deutsche Turnkunst.* Berlin, 1847.

LEONARD, FRED EUGENE, and AFFLECK, GEORGE B. *A Guide to the History of Physical Education.* Philadelphia: Lea & Febiger, 1947.

LEONARD, FRED E. *Pioneers of Modern Physical Training.* New York: Association Press, 1915. Chaps. i, iv, vii.

MCKENZIE, R. TAIT. *Exercise in Education and Medicine.* Philadelphia: W. B. Saunders Co., 1923. Chap. vii.

METZNER, HENRY. *A Brief History of the American Turnerbund.* Pittsburgh, 1924.

Physical Education Around the World, 1966. Indianapolis: Phi Epsilon Kappa.

PROHLE, HEINRICH. *Friedrich Ludwig Jahn's Leben.* Berlin, 1872.

RATH, EMIL. "Physical Education in Germany," *Mind and Body* (Feb., 1923), 389–94.

RUHL, HUGO. *Entwicklungsgeschichte des Turnens.* Leipzig, 1912.

SPIESS, ADOLPH. *Turnbuch für Schulen.* Basel, 1847.

ZWARG, LEOPOLD. "The Play and Sport Movement in Germany," *Mind and Body* (Feb., 1915), 485–88.

Chapter 10: Scandinavia since 1800

BUKH, NIELS. *Fundamental Gymnastics.* Tr. Emily Andrews and Karen Vesterdal. New York, 1928.

HARTWELL, EDWARD M. *The Principal Types of Physical Training Compared.* Boston: Damrell and Upham, 1892.

———. "On Physical Training," *Report of the U.S. Commissioner of Education, 1898,* I, 539–48.

KNUDSEN, K. A. *A Textbook of Gymnastics.* Tr. Ruth Herbert and H. G. Junker. Philadelphia, 1923.

LEONARD, FRED E. *Pioneers in Modern Physical Training.* New York: Association Press, 1915. Chaps. ii, iii, viii.

MCDOWELL, HILDA. "Ollerup Gymnastik Folkhojskile," *Mind and Body* (July, 1921), 668–70.

MCKENZIE, R. TAIT. *Exercise in Education and Medicine.* Philadelphia: W. B. Saunders Co., 1923. Chap. viii.

"Physical Education in Scandinavia," *School and Society,* XLIII (April 18, 1936), 548–49.

"Physical Education in Schools," *Bulletin of the International Bureau of Education,* No. 88, 3d quarter (1948), p. 118.

POSSE, BARON NILS. *Handbook of School Gymnastics of the Swedish System.* Boston, 1902.

STECHER, W. A. "Niels Bukh and His Danish Team," *Mind and Body* (Dec., 1923), 303–4.

SUMPTION, DOROTHY. *Fundamental Danish Gymnastics.* New York: A. S. Barnes & Co., 1927.

Chapter 11: Great Britain, Australia, New Zealand, and Canada

BESANT, W. *London in the Nineteenth Century.* London: A. & C. Black, Ltd., 1909.

BROWN, H. A. "Physical Training in English Schools," *Mind and Body* (October, 1900), 176–79.

———. "French National Gymnastic Festival, Bordeaux," *Mind and Body* (August, 1905), 178–79.

COLGAN, KATHERINE. "Open Air Schools in London," *Mind and Body* (September, 1909), 179–81.

CORBIN, JOHN. *School Boy Life in England.* New York: Harper & Bros., 1898.

CURTIS, HENRY S. "Play in the English Schools," *Mind and Body* (May, 1911), 127–30.

GEM, A. H. "Physical Education in School and After," *Journal of Education* (London), LXXX (1948), 608–09.

GLOSS, GEORGE M. "Our Australian Neighbors," *Journal of Health and Physical Education* (June, 1947), 380.

GRAVES, JOHN. *Policy and Progress in Secondary Education (1902–1942).* London: Thomas Nelson & Sons, Ltd., 1943.

JACOB, A. GERTRUDE. "Health Work in London," *Mind and Body* (September–October, 1926), 204–12.

LOCKART, A. D. "Teachers and Teacher Training in Australia," *School and Society* (June, 1947), 695–98.

MACLAREN, ARCHIBALD. *A System of Physical Education.* Oxford: The Clarendon Press, 1885.

PLEWES, DORIS W. "Affiliated Organization: The Canadian Physical Education Association," *Journal of Health and Physical Education* (May, 1946), 273.

SAVAGE, H. J. *Games and Sports in British Schools and Universities.* New York: Carnegie Foundation, 1927.

SHANN, F. *Canberra System of School Athletics.* Victoria, Australia: Melbourne University Press, 1948.

"Training in Leisure Time Standards, Standards to Aim At," *The Times Educational Supplement* (London), August 10, 1940, p. 313.

Chapter 12: Other European Countries

BELBENOIT, G. "Sports and Physical Education," *Journal of Health and Physical Education* (April, 1948), 251–52.

BROWN, M. C. "Gymnastic Reunion in Prague," *Journal of Health and Physical Education* (May, 1939), 270.

EDGERTON, N. B. "Soviet Education Today," *Institute of International Education News Bulletin* (March, 1956), 6–10.

KINLOCH, J. L. "Education in the U.S.S.R.," *Educational Digest* (October, 1955), 4–6.

"International Conference on Physical Education," *Journal of Health and Physical Education* (November, 1932), 15–64.

MALLINSON, V. "Education in Belgium Today," *Journal of Education* (London), August, 1954, 361–63.

———. "Education in France Today," *Journal of Education* (London), April, 1954, 161–63.

"Physical Education in the Schools of Belgium," *School and Society* (December 25, 1937), 818–19.

PURVIS, W. A. "School System in France," *The Times Educational Supplement* (London), March 4, 1955, p. 232.

Report of the International Congress, Physical Education, Recreation, and Rehabilitation. London: Ministry of Education, 1948.

REISS, L. W. "Physical Education in Czechoslovakia," *Journal of Health and Physical Education* (February, 1932), 42.

ROUCEK, J. S. "Education in Bulgaria," *School and Society* (December 8, 1934), 775–78.

SCHROEDER, L. C. "Physical Education and Sports in Europe," *American Physical Education Review* (November, 1929), 516–21.

STALEY, S. C. "Sports in Europe," *Journal of Health and Physical Education* (October, 1931), 3.

WOODY, THOMAS. "Sokols; 1948," *Journal of Health and Physical Education* (June, 1948), 342–43, 393.

World Survey of Education, III: Secondary Education. New York: International Document Service, a div. of the Columbia University Press, 1961.

Chapter 13: Japan, China, India, and South Africa

BAUER, LUCILLE. "Japanese Dances for Children," *Journal of Health and Physical Education* (May, 1935), 17.

BHOUDE, R. B. "Indian Sports in Olden Days in Madras," *Mind and Body* (October, 1935), 100–104.

JOKL, ERNST. "A Scientific Syllabus of Physical Education for Small Children," *South African Journal of Science* (December, 1938), 407–11.

———. "Medical Research in Physical Education in South Africa," *Research Quarterly* (March, 1949), 88–109.

LEWIS, TEDFORD P. "Health, Physical Education, and Recreation in Lebanon and the Near East," *Journal of the American Association of Health, Physical Education, and Recreation* (March, 1949), 159–61, 210–13.

MCCLOY, C. H. "Physical Education Around the World, What We Can Learn from Other Nations," *Journal of Health and Physical Education* (February, 1947), 69.

WEGTHMAN, RUTH. "Relay Races from Japan," *Journal of Health and Physical Education* (October, 1935), 34.

Chapter 14: South America and Mexico

BRICKMAN, W. W. "Education in Latin America," *School and Society* (June 26, 1948), 479–87.

CASTILLON, O. F. "Physical Education in Mexico," *Journal of Health and Physical Education* (May, 1943), 11.

CHOPLIN, R. I. "Education in Paraguay," *Journal of Secondary Education* (May, 1948), 300–303.

"Columbia Physical Education," *World Education* (January, 1941), 67.

EBAUGH, C. D. "Education Among Our Latin American Neighbors," *American School Board Journal* (August, 1947), 33–35, (September, 1947), 35–37.

———. "Education in Chile" (U.S. Office of Education, Bulletin 1945, Number 10.) Washington, D.C.: U.S. Government Printing Office, 1945.

———. "Education in Ecuador" (U.S. Office of Education, Bulletin 1947, Number 2.) Washington, D.C.: U.S. Government Printing Office, 1947.

———. "Education in Peru" (U.S. Office of Education, Bulletin 1946, Number 3.) Washington, D.C.: U.S. Government Printing Office, 1946.

FURBAY, JOHN H. "Education in Colombia" (U.S. Office of Education, Bulletin 1946, Number 6.) Washington, D.C.: U.S. Government Printing Office, 1946.

GOYOSE, LAMBERTO A. "Physical Education for Pan-American Cooperation," *Journal of Health and Physical Education* (June, 1942), 356.

SALAS, ROSARIO, and BRAVO, JORGE. "Physical Education in Chile," *Journal of Health and Physical Education* (September, 1949), 478–79.

Chapter 15: The Colonial Period

CLOYD, D. E. *Benjamin Franklin and Education.* Boston: D. C. Heath & Co., 1902. Pp. 40–41.

COLLINS, VARNUM LANSING. *Princeton.* New York: Oxford University Press, 1914. P. 208.

DUNNING, EDGAR D. "The Oldest Boarding School in America," *Nation's Schools,* XVI (Dec., 1935), 14–18.

EARLE, ALICE. *Child Life in Colonial Days.* London: Macmillan & Co., Ltd., 1926.

FRANKLIN, BENJAMIN. "Proposals Relating to the Education of Youth," *Report of U.S. Commissioner of Education,* I (1902), 182–85.

———. *Autobiography.* New York: Holt & Co., 1916.

GOODSELL, WILLYSTINE. *The Education of Women.* New York: The Macmillan Co., 1923.

HARTWELL, EDWARD M. "Presidential Address," (1892) *Proceedings of AAAPE, Index 1885–1895,* No. 9, 13–40. Contains some history of early schools.

HENDERSON, ROBERT W. *Early American Sport.* New York: A. S. Barnes and Co., 1953. Pp. 25–34, 95–96, 116–25, 155–56, 224.

JESSON, CARL A. "Three Centuries of Secondary Education," *School Life,* XX (January, 1955), 98–99.

MCKENZIE, R. TAIT. "Benjamin Franklin—Illustrious Pioneer in Physical Education," *Journal of Health and Physical Education,* VII (1936).

MANCHESTER, HERBERT. *Four Centuries of Sport in America.* New York: The Derrydale Press, 1931.

MUNROE, PAUL. *Founding of American Public School System.* New York: The Macmillan Co., Vol. I, 1940.

SEYBOLT, R. F. *Source Studies in Colonial Education: The Private School.* (Bulletin no. 28.) Urbana: Bureau of Educational Research, College of Education, University of Illinois, 1925.

SHARF, J. THOMAS, and WESTCOTT, THOMPSON. *History of Philadelphia, 1609–1884.* I & II. Philadelphia: L. H. Everts & Co., 1884.

TUNIS, EDWIN. *From Colonial Living.* New York: The World Publishing Co., 1957.

WEAVER, ROBERT B. *Amusements and Sports in American Life.* Chicago: The University of Chicago Press, 1939. P. 112.

WITTKE, CARL. *We Who Built America.* New York: Prentice-Hall, 1939.
WOOD, THOMAS D., and BROWNELL, CLIFFORD. "Discipline of the Methodist Episcopal Church," *Source Book in Physical Education.* New York: The Macmillan Co., 1925. P. 352.
WOODY, THOMAS. *A History of Women's Education in the United States.* II. New York: Science Press, 1929.
———. *Educational Views of Benjamin Franklin.* New York: McGraw-Hill Book Co., 1931.

Chapter 16: Physical Activities in the Early Nineteenth Century (1800–1865)

BAKER, HENRY L. *Football: Facts and Figures.* New York: Rinehart & Co., 1945. Pp. 9–11.
BEECHER, CATHARINE. *Educational Reminiscences and Suggestions.* New York: J. B. Ford & Co., 1874.
BELL, JOHN. *A Treatise on Baths.* Philadelphia: Barrington & Haswell, 1850.
BOYKIN, JAMES C. *Report of U.S. Commissioner of Education on Physical Training,* Vol. I, 1891–92. Pp. 451–600.
BROWN, ELMER E. *The Making of Our Middle Schools.* 3d. ed. New York: Longmans, Green & Co., 1907.
DULLES, FOSTER RHEA. *America Learns To Play.* New York: Appleton-Century-Crofts, 1965.
HENDERSON, ROBERT W. *Ball, Bat and Bishop.* New York: Rockport Press, 1947. Pp. 163–65.
———. *Early American Sport.* New York: A. S. Barnes & Co., 1953. Pp. vii, viii, 34, 95–96, 195.
HUTCHINSON, JOHN L. *Principles of Recreation.* New York: A. S. Barnes & Co., 1949.
KELLY, ROBERT. *American Rowing, Its Background & Tradition.* New York: G. P. Putnam's Sons, 1933. Pp. viii, xvii, 25, 73, 101, 162.
LEWIS, DIO. *The New Gymnastics for Men, Women, and Children.* 8th ed. Boston: Ticknor and Fields, 1864. Pp. 17, 48.
LUTZ, ALMA. *Emma Willard, Daughter of Democracy.* Boston: Houghton Mifflin Co., 1929.
MCKENZIE, R. TAIT. "Physical Education at Girard College," *Mind and Body* (Sept., 1923), 197–203.
RICHARDSON, LEON BURR. *History of Dartmouth College,* 1932.
SARGENT, DUDLEY A. "Beginnings of Physical Education in America," *American Physical Education Review,* XXV (Nov., 1920).
SPALDING, A. G. *America's National Game.* New York: American Sports Publishing Co., 1911.
TUNIS, JOHN. *Sports for the Fun of It.* New York: A. S. Barnes & Co., 1940. P. 34.
WATSON, JOHN F. *Annals of Philadelphia and Pennsylvania in the Olden Times.* Philadelphia: Leary, Stuart & Co., 1900. Vol. III.
WINSHIP, GEORGE. "Autobiographical Sketches of a Strength-Seeker," *Atlantic Monthly* (Jan., 1862), 102–15.
WOODY, THOMAS. *The History of Women's Education in the United States.* New York: Science Press. I & II, 1929.

Chapter 17: Organized Physical Education in the Early Nineteenth Century (1800–1865)

Amherst College. Springfield: Association Press, 1919.
BEECHER, CATHARINE. *Educational Reminiscences and Suggestions.* New York: J. B. Ford & Co., 1874.
BENNETT, BRUCE L. "The Making of Round Hill School," *Quest,* Monograph 4 (April, 1965), 53.

BENNET, CHARLES A. *A History of Manual and Industrial Education to 1870.* Peoria: Peoria Press, 1926.
BROWN, ELMER. *The Making of Our Middle Schools.* 3d ed. New York: Longmans, Green & Co., 1907.
BRUCE, H. A. *Women in the Making of America.* Boston: Little, Brown & Co., 1912.
CREMIN, LAWRENCE A. *The Transformation of the School.* New York: Alfred A. Knopf, 1961. Pp. 10, 126, 128, 279.
DEGROOT, DUDLEY S. *"A History of Physical Education in California—1848–1939."* Doctoral Dissertation. Stanford University, 1940.
EASTMAN, MARY F., and LEWIS, CEILIA CLARK. *The Biography of Dio Lewis.* New York: Fowler & Wells Co., 1891.
EDDY, GEORGE SHERWOOD. *A Century With Youth.* New York: Association Press, 1904. A history of the YMCA from 1844 to 1904.
FOLLEN, E. L. *Life of Charles Follen.* Boston: Thomas H. Webb & Co., 1844.
FOWLE, WILLIAM BENTLEY. "Medical Intelligences," *American Journal of Education,* 1820, pp. 698–99.
"Frances Lieber," *National Encyclopedia,* Vol. 6, 1935, p. 230.
HARTWELL, EDWARD M. *Physical Training in American Colleges and Universities.* Circular No. 5. Washington, D.C.: U.S. Bureau of Education, 1885.
GOODSELL, WILLYSTINE. *Pioneers of Women's Education in the United States.* New York: McGraw-Hill Book Co., 1931. Discusses educational theories of Emma Willard, Mary Lyon, and Catharine Beecher.
LEONARD, FRED EUGENE. *Pioneers of Modern Physical Training.* New York: Association Press, 1915.
MCKENZIE, R. TAIT. *Exercises in Education and Medicine.* Philadelphia: W. B. Saunders Co., 1909. P. 82.
MILLER, KENNETH D. "Stearns, Hitchcock, and Amherst College," *Journal of Health and Physical Education,* XXV (May–June, 1957), 29–30.
MORSE, RICHARD C. *The History of the North American Young Men's Christian Association.* New York: Association Press, 1918.
MUELLER, GROVER. "A Hundred Years of Physical and Health Education in Philadelphia," *Report to Philadelphia Board of Education, 1938.*
NEW YORK STATE DEPARTMENT OF EDUCATION. "Back in 1859," *Physical Education Bulletin No. 39* (May, 1935).
PERRY, THOMAS S. *Life and Letters of Francis Lieber.* Boston: James R. Osgood & Co., 1882.
PHILLIPS, PAUL C. "Historical Data Regarding Construction of College Gymnasia," *American Physical Education Review,* XXX (Oct., 1916), 434–35.
RICHARDSON, LEON BURR. *History of Dartmouth College.* Hanover, N.H.: College Publications, 1932.
WARREN, JOHN C. *The Importance of Physical Education, Lecture No. 1.* Boston: American Institute of Instruction, 1831.
WITTKE, CARL. *We Who Built America.* New York: Prentice-Hall, 1939, p. 54.
WOODY, THOMAS. *A History of Women's Education in the United States.* New York: Science Press, 1929. I, pp. 329–42, and II, p. 601.

Chapter 18: Physical Activities in the Latter Nineteenth Century (1865–1900)

American Physical Education Review, XII (Apr., 1897), 97, and XIII (Dec., 1898), 318. News items on Columbia University and the Brookline swimming pool.
BARBOUR, R. H. *The Book of School and College Sport.* New York: Paine Press, 1904.
BARROWS, ISABEL. *Conference on Physical Training—1889.* Boston: George Ellis Press, 1899. Pp. 21, 32–34.
BENNETT, BRUCE L. *Dudley A. Sargent.* Doctoral Thesis. University of Michigan, 1948.

Berenson, Senda. "Basket Ball for Women," *Physical Education,* Sept., 1894, p. 106.

Bishop, Emily. "Americanized Delsarte Culture," *AAAPE Proceedings, 1885–1895,* No. 9 (1892), 80–96.

Clark, Ellery H. "The Olympic Games," *American Physical Education Review,* (Sept.–Dec.), 1896, 14–22.

Crampton, C. Ward. *The Public School Athletic League of New York City.* Sept., 1936. Unpublished paper, a copy of which is in the AAHPER Archives.

Davis, Parke H. *Football, the American Intercollegiate Game.* New York: Charles Scribner's Sons, 1911.

Durivage, F. A. "A Visit to François Delsarte," *Atlantic Monthly,* XXVII (1871), 613.

Enebuske, Claës. *Progressive Gymnastics Day's Orders.* New York: Silver Burdette & Co., 1890.

Gildersleeve, Virginia C. *Many a Good Crusade.* New York: The Macmillan Co., 1954. P. 21.

Hangar, G. W. *Public Baths in The United States.* U.S. Bureau of Labor Bulletin No. 54, Sept., 1904.

Hartwell, Edward M. "Early History of Physical Education in the United States." In Presidential Address, 1892, *INDEX, 1885–1895, AAAPE,* No. 9, pp. 13–40.

Hill, Edith Naomi. "Senda Berenson," *Supplement to Research Quarterly* of APEA, XII (Oct., 1941), 658–65.

Kieran, John. *The Story of the Olympic Games—776 B.C.–1936 A.D.* New York: Frederick A. Stokes Co., 1936.

Kindervater, A. G. "Early History of Physical Education in the Public Schools of America," *Mind and Body,* XXXIII (Jan., 1926), 97–105.

Kistler, George. "Historical Sketch on Intercollegiate Swimming Association," *Intercollegiate Swimming Guide,* 1915–1916, p. 39.

Leonard, Fred Eugene, and Affleck, George B. *A Guide to the History of Physical Education.* Philadelphia: Lea & Febiger, 1947.

Lewis, Guy M. "America's First International Sport—The Regattas of 1852 & 1875," *Research Quarterly* of AAHPER, Vol. 38, No. 4 (Dec., 1967), 637.

Luehring, Frederick. *Swimming Pool Standards.* New York: A. S. Barnes & Co., 1939. P. 23.

Martin, Henry B. *Fifty Years of American Golf.* New York: Dodd, Mead & Co., 1936. P. 46.

Menke, F. G. *Encyclopedia of Sports.* New York: A. S. Barnes & Co., 1947.

Naismith, James. "Basket Ball," *American Physical Education Review,* Vol. 19 (1914), 339.

National Federation of State High School Athletic Associations. *Handbook, 1964–1965.*

Nevins, Allan. *History of American Life—III: The Emergence of Modern America.* New York: The Macmillan Co., 1927. Pp. 221, 226, 239.

Rinsch, Emil. *History of the Normal College of American Gymnastic Union of Indiana University—1866–1966.* Bloomington: Indiana University Press, 1966.

Savage, Howard J. *American College Athletics.* New York: Carnegie Foundation for the Advancement of Teaching, Bulletin No. 23, 1929. P. 20.

Schmidt, F. A. "Physiological Treatise of the German System of Gymnastics," *Supplement to Mind and Body,* I (May, 1894), chart between pp. 10 and 11.

Schwinn, Frank W. *The Story of the Bicycle and Its Contribution to Our Way of Life.* Chicago: Arnold Schwinn & Co., 1945. Pp. 31–51.

Spalding, Albert G. "Story of Women's Basket Ball Rules Committee," *Women's Basket Ball Guide.* New York: American Sports Publishing Co., 1901.

———. *America's National Game.* New York: American Sports Publishing Co., 1911.

Stagg, Amos Alonzo. *Physical Culture and Athletics.* University of Chicago Decennial Publications, Vol. I. Chicago: University of Chicago Press, 1904.

Stebbins, Genevieve. *Delsarte System of Expression.* 6th ed. New York: E. S. Werner, 1902.

SULLIVAN, JAMES E. "First Athletic Clubs in the USA," *American Physical Education Review,* VIII (March, 1903), 268.

TUNIS, JOHN. *Sports for the Fun of It.* New York: A. S. Barnes & Co., 1940.

WAYAND, ALEXANDER M. *The Saga of American Football.* New York: The Macmillan Co., 1955.

World Almanac, Readers Digest Publications, 1965.

Chapter 19: Organized Physical Education in the Latter Nineteenth Century (1865–1900)

AINSWORTH, DOROTHY. *History of Physical Education in Women's Colleges.* New York: Columbia University Press, 1927. Pp. ix, 24, 27.

BANCROFT, JESSIE. "Pioneering in Physical Education," *Supplement, Research Quarterly* of APEA, Oct., 1941, pp. 672–75.

BARROWS, ISABEL. *Conference on Physical Training—1889.* Boston: George Ellis Press, 1899. Pp. 62–66.

BENNETT, BRUCE L. *Dudley A. Sargent.* Doctoral Thesis, University of Michigan, 1948.

BOSTON PUBLIC SCHOOL TEACHERS. *Memorial Services In Honor of Mary Hemenway.* Boston: George Ellis Press, 1899. Contains material on the founding of the Boston Normal School of Gymnastics.

BOYKIN, JAMES C. "Physical Training," *Report of U.S. Commissioner of Education,* Washington, D.C.: Government Printing Office, 1891–92.

"Brief Outline of Life and Work of Delphine Hanna," *Supplement—APEA Research Quarterly,* Oct., 1941, pp. 646–52.

BRONSON, ALICE O. *Clark W. Hetherington—Scientist and Philosopher.* Salt Lake City: University of Utah Press, 1958.

BROSIUS, GEORGE. *Fifty Years Devoted to Physical Culture.* Milwaukee: Germania Publishing Co., 1914.

CALIFORNIA STATE SUPERINTENDENT OF PUBLIC INSTRUCTION. *Second Biennial Report* (Appendix E) Revised School Law, March 24, 1866, Sec. 55.

CHAMPLIN, ELLIS. *The YMCA Training School.* Paper read at 75th Anniversary Convention of AAHPER, 1960.

CRAWFORD, IDA B., and MITCHELL, VIOLA. *Camp Counseling.* 3d ed. Philadelphia: W. B. Saunders Co., 1961.

CREMIN, LAWRENCE A. *The Transformation of The School.* New York: Alfred A. Knopf, 1961. Preface, pp. 22–63, 98, 100, 116, 129–33.

DOGGETT, LAURENCE. *Man and a School.* New York: Association Press, 1943. Story of Springfield College.

EDDY, GEORGE SHERWOOD. *A Century with Youth.* New York: Association Press, 1944.

ELIOT, CHARLES W. *A Late Harvest.* Boston: Atlantic Monthly Press, 1924.

ELLIOTT, RUTH. *The Organization of Professional Training in Physical Education in State Universities.* New York: Teachers College, Bureau of Publications, Columbia University, 1927.

FELLOWS, E. H. "The Founding of Physical Education in the Public Schools of Kansas City, Missouri," *Index—Proceedings, AAAPE—1885–1895.* No. 2, p. 9.

GOODSELL, WILLYSTINE. *Pioneers of Women's Education in the United States.* New York: McGraw-Hill Book Co., Inc., 1931.

GULICK, LUTHER H. "Physical Education in the YMCA," *Proceedings,* AAAPE, 1891.

HANNA, DELPHINE. "The Present Status of Professional Training in Normal Schools," *American Physical Education Review,* VIII, No. 1 (March, 1903), 293–97.

HARTWELL, EDWARD M. *Physical Training in American Colleges and Universities.* Washington, D.C.: U.S. Bureau of Education, Circular No. 5, 1885.

———. *The Rise of College Gymnastics in the USA.* Washington, D.C.: Government Printing Office, 1886. Special report of U.S. Bureau of Education given at World's Industrial and Cotton Centennial Exposition in New Orleans, 1884 & 1885.

———. "The Condition and Prospect of Physical Education in the United States." *Index—Proceedings, AAAPE—1885–1895,* I, No. 9 (1892), 13–40.

HINES, THOMAS. *History of the Posse School of Gymnastics.* Paper read at the 75th Anniversary Convention of AAHPER, 1960.

HITCHCOCK, EDWARD, and SEELYE, H. H. *Anthropometric Manual.* Amherst: Press of Carpenter and Morehouse, 1893.

HOUSTON, RUTH ELLIOTT. *Modern Trends in Physical Education Facilities of College Women.* New York: A. S. Barnes & Co., 1939. P. 43.

KINDERVATER, A. G. "Early History of Physical Education in The Public Schools of America," *Mind and Body,* XXXIII (Jan., 1926), 97–105.

LEE, JOSEPH. *Normal Course in Play.* New York: A. S. Barnes & Co., 1926. P. 225.

LEE, MABEL. *Survey of Founding of Departments of Physical Education for Women in State Universities,* 1947. Unpublished.

LEONARD, FRED EUGENE, and AFFLECK, GEORGE B. *A Guide to the History of Physical Education.* Philadelphia: Lea & Febiger, 1947. Pp. 273, 329.

LUMLEY, ALBERT E. *Edward Hitchcock.* Paper read at 75th Anniversary Convention of AAHPER, 1960.

MCCURDY, MRS. PERRIS. "Physical Training at Mt. Holyoke," *American Physical Education Review,* XIV (March, 1909), 139.

MITCHEL, ELMER D., and MASON, BERNARD. *Theory of Play.* New York: A. S. Barnes & Co., 1948.

MUELLER, GROVER. "A Hundred Years of Health and Physical Education in Philadelphia," National Physical Education Service, *News Letter,* No. 114, Nov., 1938.

NEWS ITEMS, *AAAPE Index—Proceedings—1885–1895; American Physical Education Review,* Vol. 3 (Dec., 1898), 38; Vol. 8 (March, 1903), 268; Vol. 28 (March, 1923), 116.

"Ohio State Law on Physical Education," *Mind and Body,* VII (March, 1900), 12–15.

PHILLIPS, PAUL C. "Historical Data Regarding the Construction of College Gymnasia." *American Physical Education Review,* XXI (Oct., 1916), 434.

Princeton Alumni Weekly, March 10, 1920, 514–15.

Princeton University and Her Sons, Vol. 2, 339.

RINSCH, EMIL. *History of the Normal College of the American Gymnastic Union of Indiana University—1866–1966.* Bloomington: Indiana University Press, 1966. P. 22.

SARGENT, DUDLEY A. *Autobiography.* Philadelphia: Lea & Febiger, 1927. Pp. 196–98, 207.

SEAVER, JAY W. *Anthropometry and Physical Examinations.* New Haven: Dorman Press, 1896, P. 14.

SEELYE, L. CLARK. *The Early History of Smith College, 1871–1910.* New York: Houghton Mifflin Co., 1923.

STAGG, AMOS ALONZO. *Physical Culture and Athletics.* University of Chicago Decennial Publications, Vol. I. Chicago: University of Chicago Press, 1904. Pp. 336–72.

WELLESLEY COLLEGE, *Calendar, 1878–79.*

WILLOUGHBY, W. W. "History of Secondary Schools in the United States," *Report of the Commissioner of Education—1891–92.* Washington: Government Printing Office, 1894. P. 920.

WILSON, ELIZABETH. *Fifty Years of Association Work Among YWCA's.* New York: National Board of YWCA of U.S.A., 1916.

WITTKE, CARL. *We Who Built America.* New York: Prentice-Hall, 1939. Pp. 201, 222, 235.

YMCA. *Brief Review of Background and Progress in National YMCA Physical Education.* Exhibit E, March 31, 1955. Mimeographed material sent out from national office.

Chapter 20: Organizations and Leaders of the Latter Nineteenth Century (1865–1900)

ANDERSON, W. G. "The American Association for the Advancement of Physical Education," *American Physical Education Review*, XXV (Nov., 1920), 312.

BARROWS, ISABEL. *Conference on Physical Training–1889.* Boston: George Ellis Press, 1899. For Sargent quotations see pp. 66–68. The addresses reported in this book carry great significance for today's student.

BENNETT, BRUCE L. *Dudley A. Sargent.* Doctoral Thesis, University of Michigan, 1948.

BRINK, B. DEANE. *The Body Builder, Robert J. Roberts.* New York: Association Press, 1916.

BROWN, MARGARET, and BEIDERHASE, JOSEPHINE. "William G. Anderson," *Journal of Health, Physical Education and Recreation*, Vol. 31, No. 4 (April, 1960), 34.

"Delphine Hanna," *Supplement to Research Quarterly of APEA*, Oct., 1941.

"Edward Mussey Hartwell," *National Cyclopedia of American Biography.* New York: James J. White & Co., 1929. XX, 132–33.

"Edward Hitchcock–A Tribute," *American Physical Education Review* (June, 1908), 368.

"Eliza Mosher–In Memoriam," *American Physical Education Review*, XXXIV (April, 1929), 134.

FINGELS, M. *"Biography of William Stecher,"* Master's Thesis, Temple University, 1934.

KERR, A. M. "Dr. W. G. Anderson," *Journal of Health and Physical Education*, VI (April, 1935), 31.

LEE, MABEL, and BENNETT, BRUCE L. "This Is Our Heritage," *Journal of Health, Physical Education and Recreation*, Vol. 31, No. 4 (April, 1960), 25–33, 38–48, 52–58, 62–73, 76–86.

LEONARD, FRED EUGENE. *Pioneers of Modern Physical Training.* New York: Association Press, 1915.

"Life of Eliza Mosher," *The Medical Woman's Journal*, XIV (Oct., 1922), 253.

LUMLEY, ALBERT E. *Edward Hitchcock.* Paper read at 75th Anniversary Convention of AAHPER, 1960.

LYNN, MINNIE L. "Delphine Hanna," *Journal of Health, Physical Education and Recreation*, Vol. 31, No. 4 (April, 1960), 51.

MCKENZIE, R. TAIT. "William G. Anderson," *American Physical Education Review*, XXXIV (1920), 311, 363.

MAKECHNIE, GEORGE K. "Dudley Allen Sargent," *Journal of Health, Physical Education and Recreation*, Vol. 31, No. 4 (April, 1960), 36.

MILLER, KENNETH D. "Edward Hitchcock," *Journal of Health, Physical Education and Recreation*, Vol. 31, No. 4 (April, 1960), 35.

———. "Stearns, Hitchcock, and Amherst College," *Journal of Health, Physical Education and Recreation*, XXV (May–June, 1957), 29–30.

NEWS ITEMS, *American Physical Education Review*, Vol. 1 (1895).

NICHOLS, J. H. *Oberlin College, Delphine Hanna and Fred E. Leonard.* Paper read at 75th Anniversary Convention of AAHPER, 1960.

"Organization of Ohio State Physical Education Association," *Mind and Body*, VII (April, 1895), 38.

PHILLIPS, PAUL C. "Dr. Edward Hitchcock," *American Physical Education Review*, XVI (March, 1911), 217.

Princeton University and Her Sons, Vol. 2, p. 339.

Proceedings of AAAPE–1885–1895.

RATHBONE, JOSEPHINE. "Amy Morris Homans," *Journal of Health, Physical Education and Recreation*, Vol. 31, No. 4 (April, 1960), 37.

SARGENT, DUDLEY A. *Autobiography.* Philadelphia: Lea & Febiger, Publishers, 1927.

———. "Tribute to Edward M. Hartwell," *American Physical Education Review*, XXVII (March, 1923), 116.

SCOTT, HARRY A. "The Society of Directors of Physical Education in Colleges," *Journal of Health and Physical Education,* III (April, 1932), 3.

SKARSTROM, WILLIAM. "Life and Work of Amy Morris Homans," *Supplement to Research Quarterly of AAHPER,* Vol. 2, No. 3 (Oct., 1941), 615–27.

"Tributes to Dudley A. Sargent," *American Physical Education Review,* XXIX (1924). This issue of the magazine carries several tributes by many different people under the one title.

WASHKE, PAUL. *History of the American Physical Education Association.* Doctoral Dissertation, New York University, 1943.

WELCH, J. EDMUND. *Edward Hitchcock, M.D., Founder of Physical Education in the College Community.* Greenville, N.C.: Published privately, P.O. Box 2043, 1966.

Chapter 21: Physical Activities in the Early Twentieth Century

AINSWORTH, DOROTHY. *History of Physical Education in Women's Colleges.* New York: Columbia University Press, 1927.

ALBRIGHT, SYDNEY. "Wickets Sprout in WLA," *Independent Press,* Los Angeles, July 10, 1960.

American Physical Education Review, XV (1910). Reports of Efforts at Athletic Reforms.

ANDREWS, EMILY. *Fundamental Gymnastics of Nils Bukh.* New York: E. P. Dutton & Co., 1928. Translated, rearranged, and adapted for use in America.

ATHLETIC RESEARCH SOCIETY. "Report of the Committee on Intramural Sport," *American Physical Education Review,* XXIII (April, 1918), 198.

BALLANTINE, HARRIET I. *The History of Physical Training in Vassar College—1865–1915.* Poughkeepsie: Lansing & Boas, 1915.

BERENSON, SENDA. "Basket Ball For Women," *Physical Education,* Sept., 1894, p. 106.

BRAMMEL, P. ROY. *Health Work and Physical Education.* U.S. Office of Education Bulletin No. 19, Monograph No. 28, 1932. Pp. 79–80.

BRONSON, ALICE G. *Clark W. Hetherington—Scientist and Philosopher.* Salt Lake City: University of Utah Press, 1958.

CRAMPTON, C. WARD. *The New York City Public School Athletic League.* Sept. 1, 1936. Unpublished paper, a copy of which is in the AAHPER Archives.

DORGAN, ETHEL. *Luther Halsey Gulick.* New York: Teachers College, Bureau of Publications, Columbia University, 1934.

GRIFFITH, JOHN L. "Annual Report of NAAF," *American Physical Education Review,* XXXIV (March, 1929), 156.

GULICK, LUTHER H. *Physical Education.* Philadelphia: Blakiston's Sons & Co., 1907.

———. *The Healthful Art of Dancing.* New York: Doubleday, Page & Co., 1911.

HALL, G. STANLEY. *Adolescence.* New York: Appleton-Century Co., 1901. Pp. 200–7.

H'DOUBLER, MARGARET M. *Dance and Its Place in Education.* New York: Harcourt, Brace Co., 1925.

HETHERINGTON, CLARK W. "Fundamental Education," *Journal of Proceedings and Addresses of the National Education Association,* XLVIII (1910).

JORDAN, DAVID STARR. "Letter From the President of Stanford University," *American Physical Education Review,* XV (April, 1910), 282.

KENNEDY, CHARLES W. "Self-Control and Chivalry Through Sport," *Sportsmanship,* June, 1929, p. 5.

LUEHRING, FREDERICK. *Swimming Pool Standards.* New York: A. S. Barnes & Co. Pp. 23, 34.

KIERAN, JOHN, and DALEY, ARTHUR. *The Story of the Olympic Games, 1896–1956.* New York: J. B. Lippincott Co., 1957.

LEE, MABEL. "The Case For and Against Intercollegiate Athletics for Women and the Situation As It Stands Today," *Mind and Body* (Nov., 1923) and *American Physical Education Review,* XXIX (Jan., 1924).

———. "The Case For and Against Intercollegiate Athletics for Women and the Situation Since 1923," *Research Quarterly of APEA,* II (May, 1931), 93–127.

MARSH, AGNES L. *Dance in Education.* New York: A. S. Barnes & Co., 1926.

MITCHELL, ELMER D. *Intramural Athletics.* New York: A. S. Barnes & Co., 1939.

NATIONAL FEDERATION OF HIGH SCHOOL ATHLETIC ASSOCIATIONS. *Handbook.* Chicago: NFHSAA, 1966. Gives history of development of the organization.

"News Reports on Injuries to Athletes," *American Physical Education Review,* XIV (1909), 645.

"Report of the Athletic Program of the AEF," *American Physical Education Review,* XXV (March, 1920), 116.

RICHARDSON, LEON BURR. *History of Dartmouth College.* Hanover, N.H.: College Publications, 1932.

SARGENT, DUDLEY A. "History of Intercollegiate Athletics in the United States," *American Physical Education Review,* XV (April, 1910), 252.

———. "Speech at APEA Convention," *American Physical Education Review,* XXV (Nov., 1920), 365.

SAVAGE, HOWARD J., *et al. American College Athletics.* Carnegie Foundation for the Advancement of Teaching, Bulletin No. 23, 1929.

SCHWARTZ, MARGUERITE. "The Athletic Conference of American College Women," *Journal of Health and Physical Education,* VII (May, 1936), 297.

SEFTON, ALICE. *The Women's Division of NAAF.* Stanford: Stanford University Press, 1941.

SPALDING, A. G. "The First Women's Basket Ball Rules Committee," *Official Women's Basket Ball Guide.* New York: American Sports Publishing Co., 1901.

STAGG, PAUL. *The Development of NCAA and Its Relation to Intercollegiate Athletics in the U.S.A.* Doctoral dissertation, New York University, 1946.

"Stephen E. Epler Fathered Six-Man Football," *Lincoln State Journal & Star,* Sept. 2, 1959.

TUNIS, JOHN. "The Great Sports Myth," *$port$: Heroics and Hysterics.* New York: John Day Co., Inc., 1928. Pp. 16–35.

———. *Sports for the Fun of It.* New York: A. S. Barnes & Co., 1940. Pp. 139, 245.

VEEN, JAN. "Mary Wigman's 80th Birthday," *Journal of Health, Physical Education and Recreation,* Vol. 38, No. 2 (Feb., 1967), 55.

WAYMAN, AGNES. "The Women's Division of NAAF," *Journal of Health and Physical Education,* III (March, 1932), 3.

WHITTEN, C. W. "History of the National Federation of High School Athletic Associations," *Journal of Health and Physical Education,* Vol. IV, No. 5 (May, 1933), 6.

WOOD, THOMAS D., and CASSIDY, ROSALIND E. *The New Physical Education.* New York: The Macmillan Co., 1927.

Chapter 22: Organized Physical Education in the Early Twentieth Century

AINSWORTH, DOROTHY. *History of Physical Education in Women's Colleges.* New York: Columbia University Press, 1927.

American Physical Education Review, XXIV (May, 1919), 303–305. Editorial on War Department's stand on military drill and physical education.

American Physical Education Review, March, 1918, p. 182; and May, 1919. News of Professional Leaders and their war work.

ARNOLD, E. H. "Presidential Address," *American Physical Education Review,* 1916, p. 492.

BODE, BOYD HENRY. *Progressive Education at the Cross Roads.* New York: Newson & Co., 1938.

Bovard, John, and Cozens, Frederick. *Tests and Measurements.* Philadelphia: W. B. Saunders Co., 1930.

Bronson, Alice. *Clark W. Hetherington—Scientist and Philosopher.* Salt Lake City: University of Utah Press, 1958.

Clarke, H. Harrison. "The Extent of Graduate Study in Physical Education in the U.S.A.," *Journal of Health and Physical Education,* V (April, 1934), 33.

Commission of NEA on Reorganization. *High School Buildings and Grounds.* Washington: Bureau of Education, Department of Interior, Bulletin No. 23, 1922. P. 11.

Cooper, Frank Irving. "Report of Committee," *School House Planning.* Washington, D.C.: NEA, 1925. P. 144.

Crawford, Ida B., and Mitchell, Viola. *Camp Counseling.* Philadelphia: W. B. Saunders Co., 1950.

Cremin, Lawrence A. *The Transformation of the School.* 2d ed. New York: Alfred A. Knopf, 1961. Pp. 141, 197, 213, 221.

Dewey, John. *School and Society.* Chicago: University of Chicago Press, 1900. Pp. 10, 19.

———. *Democracy in Education.* New York: The Macmillan Co., 1916.

———. *Experience and Nature.* Chicago: Open Court Publishing Co., 1925.

———. *Experience and Education.* New York: The Macmillan Co., 1938.

Dinsmore, Avis, and Gates, Edith. "The National Association of Employed Officers of the YWCA," *Journal of Health and Physical Education,* IV (Jan., 1933).

Dorgan, Ethel. *Luther Holsey Gulick.* New York: Teachers College, Bureau of Publications, Columbia University, 1934.

Elliott, Ruth. *Organization of Professional Training in Physical Education in State Universities.* New York: Teachers College, Bureau of Publications, Columbia University, 1927.

Friermood, Harold T., *et al. Continuing the Centennial Observance Through YMCA Programs.* New York: National Council of YMCA's, 1944.

Hetherington, Clark W. *School Program in Physical Education.* Yonkers, New York: World Book Co., 1922.

———. "Fundamental Education," *American Physical Education Review,* Vol. XV (Dec., 1910), 329.

Houston, Ruth Elliott. *Modern Trends in Physical Education Facilities for College Women.* New York: A. S. Barnes & Co., 1939.

Kennedy, Charles W. "Self-Control and Chivalry Through Sports," *Sportsmanship,* June, 1929, 5.

Kiputh, R. J. "The Payne Whitney Gymnasium of Yale University," *Research Quarterly of APEA,* IV (March, 1933), 131.

La Porte, Ralph William. *The Physical Education Curriculum.* College Physical Education Association, 1937.

Lee, Mabel. "Survey of Athletic and Gymnastic Costumes Used by American Girls and Women," *Research Quarterly of AAHPER,* III, No. 1 (March, 1932). Includes a survey of college women's programs.

———. *Survey of Founding of Departments of Physical Education for Women in State Universities,* 1947. Unpublished.

McCloy, Charles H. *Philosophical Basis for Physical Education.* New York: F. S. Crofts & Co., 1940. P. 97.

———. "A Half Century of Physical Education," *Physical Educator,* Oct., 1960, p. 91. Published posthumously.

McCurdy, James H. "Survey of the Status of Physical Education," *American Physical Education Review,* XXII (Oct., 1917), 441.

Meylan, George. "The Status of Physical Education in American Colleges," *American Physical Education Review,* XXI (March, 1916), 155.

Nash, Jay B. *The Administration of Physical Education.* New York: A. S. Barnes & Co., 1932.

———. *Interpretations of Physical Education,* Vol. I: *Professional Preparation.* New York: A. S. Barnes & Co., 1935. P. 332.

National Office of the YMCA. *A Brief Review of Backgrounds and Programs in a National Study of YMCA Physical Education.* March 31, 1955.

———. *Centennial Report,* 1916.

Pangburn, Weaver. "Play and Recreation," *Annals of American Academy of Political and Social Sciences,* Nov., 1940, 126.

"Report of the Athletic Program of the AEF," *American Physical Education Review,* XXV (March, 1920), 116; and XXII (June, 1917), 382.

"Report of Committee for Physical Education in the Public Schools," *American Physical Education Review,* XXII (Feb., 1917), 113.

Rinsch, Emil. *History of the Normal College of the American Gymnastic Union of Indiana University–1866–1966.* Bloomington: Indiana University Press, 1966.

Rogers, Frederick Rand. *Physical Capacity Tests.* New York: A. S. Barnes & Co., 1931.

Rugg, Harold. *That Men May Understand.* New York: Doubleday Doran & Co., 1941, p. 182.

Sargent, Dudley A. *Autobiography.* Philadelphia: Lea & Febiger, 1927.

———. *Physical Education.* Boston: Ginn & Co., 1900. Pp. 66–71.

———. "A Physical Test of a Man," *American Physical Education Review,* XXVI (April, 1921), 188–94.

Stagg, Amos Alonzo. *Physical Culture and Athletics,* University of Chicago Decennial Publications, Vol. I. Chicago: University of Chicago Press, 1904.

Steiner, Jesse F. *America at Play.* New York: McGraw Hill Book Co., 1933. Pp. 88–92.

Tunis, John. *Sports for the Fun of It.* New York: A. S. Barnes & Co., 1937.

Welch, J. Edmund. "The YMCA Graduate School of Nashville." Paper presented at Research Section of AAHPER, St. Louis, Mo., March 30, 1968.

White House Conference of 1930 on Child Health and Protection. New York: Century Co., 1931, Forward and Children's Charter.

Williams, J. F. *Organization and Administration of Physical Education.* New York: Macmillan Co., 1924, p. 9.

Wood, T. D. *Health and Education.* (Part I of the 9th Yearbook of National Society for the Scientific Study of Education.) Chicago: University of Chicago Press, 1910.

Works Progress Administration. *A Study of WPA Recreation Projects.* Washington, D.C.: Federal Works Agency, 1940.

Chapter 23: Professional Organizations and Leaders in the Early Twentieth Century (1900–World War II)

Ainsworth, Dorothy, *et al.* "Women College Directors Society," *Journal of Health and Physical Education,* Vol. 6, No. 5 (May, 1935), 3.

American Academy of Physical Education. *Archives.* Mimeographed material.

"Senda Berenson," *Supplement, Research Quarterly of APEA,* XXII (Oct., 1941), 658.

Bronson, Alice. *Clark W. Hetherington–Scientist and Philosopher.* Salt Lake City: University of Utah Press, 1958.

Carkin, Janice. *Biographies of Five Women Gulick Award Recipients.* Doctoral thesis, Stanford University, 1952. Contains biographies of Jessie Bancroft, Elizabeth Burchenal, and Ethel Perrin.

Dorgan, Ethel. *Luther Halsey Gulick.* New York: Teachers College, Bureau of Publications, Columbia University, 1934.

Fisher, George, and Nash, Jay B. "The Luther Gulick Award," *Journal of Health and Physical Education,* XVII (June, 1946), 302.

Gulick, Luther H. "The Academy of Physical Education," *American Physical Education Review,* XV (May, 1910), 342.

HAZELTON, HELEN. "Seventeen Years of Progress—Women's Rules and Editorial Committee of APEA," *Journal of Health and Physical Education,* V (April, 1934), 11.

HOWARD, GLENN W. "The College Physical Education Association," *Journal of Health and Physical Education,* XVII (Sept., 1946), 19.

HUSSEY, CHRISTOPHER. *R. Tait McKenzie—Sculptor of Youth.* London: Country Life, Ltd., 1929.

LASALLE, DOROTHY. "Thomas D. Wood, M.D.—A Great Leader," *Journal of Health—Physical Education—Recreation,* XXII (Nov., 1951), 28–30.

———. "Thomas D. Wood," *Journal of Health, Physical Education and Recreation,* Vol. 31, No. 4 (April, 1960), 61.

LEE, MABEL, and BENNETT, BRUCE L. "This Is Our Heritage," *Journal of Health, Physical Education and Recreation,* Vol. 31, No. 4 (April, 1960), 25–33, 36–47, 52–59, 62–73, 76–86.

LEYS, J. F. "R. Tait McKenzie," *Journal of Health, Physical Education and Recreation,* Vol. 31, No. 4 (April, 1960), 48.

"James Huff McCurdy," *Journal of Health and Physical Education,* XI (Oct. & Dec., 1940), 476, 619.

"R. Tait McKenzie," *Journal of Health and Physical Education,* XV (Feb., 1944). The entire issue of the magazine is devoted to articles about the man.

MCKENZIE, R. TAIT. "The American Academy of Physical Education," *Journal of Health and Physical Education,* Vol. 3, No. 6 (June, 1932), 14.

NASH, J. B. "Luther Halsey Gulick," *Journal of Health, Physical Education and Recreation,* Vol. 31, No. 4 (April, 1960), 60.

SCOTT, HARRY. "The Society of Directors of Physical Education in Colleges," *Journal of Health and Physical Education,* Vol. I, No. 4 (April, 1930), 3.

SCHRADER, CARL. "History of the Society of State Directors of Physical Education," *Journal of Health and Physical Education,* Vol. IV (Oct., 1933).

Supplement to Research Quarterly of APEA, XII (Oct., 1941). Contains biographies of Jessie H. Bancroft, Clelia Mosher, Ethel Perrin, and Senda Berenson.

"Twentieth Anniversary of the National Physical Education Service," *Journal of Health and Physical Education,* IX (Sept., 1938), 424.

"Tributes to Luther Halsey Gulick," *American Physical Education Review,* XXIII (Oct., 1918); and XXVIII (Sept.–Oct., 1923). The latter volume contains tributes to many different persons.

WASHKE, PAUL R. *The Development of The American Association for Health, Physical Education, and Recreation and its Relationship to Physical Education in the United States.* Doctoral dissertation, New York University, 1943.

Chapter 24: Physical Activities in the Mid-Twentieth Century

ALBRIGHT, SYDNEY. "Wickets Sprout in WLA," *Independent Press,* Los Angeles. July 19, 1960.

CONNERY, DONALD. "Tokyo Changes Face for Asia's First Olympics," *Sports Illustrated,* May 8, 1961, 38.

BUSH, CLARENCE A. "Witnesses for the Olympiads," *Christian Science Monitor,* July, 1936, Magazine Section, p. 3.

D. G.W.S. "National Intercollegiate Athletic Championships for Women," *Journal of Health, Physical Education and Recreation,* Vol. 39, No. 2 (Feb., 1968), 24.

———. "Statement on Competition for Girls and Women," *Journal of Health, Physical Education and Recreation,* Vol. 37, No. 7 (Sept., 1966), 36.

DRURY, BLANCHE JESSEN. "Place of Gymnastics in a Physical Education Program." Paper read at the National Institute on Girl's Sports, University of Oklahoma, Nov. 3–9, 1963.

GALENPUL, DAN. *Information Please—Almanac.* 23rd ed. New York: Simon & Schuster, 1968. Covers Olympics, 1896–1968.

HAHN, INA. "Modern Dance for Modern Times," *Wellesley College Alumnae Magazine,* Jan., 1968, 22.
"A History of Discontent," *A Statement for the Record.* United States Track and Field Federation, 1964.
JOKL, E., *et al.* "Research on Olympic Athletes," *Journal of Health, Physical Education and Recreation,* Sept., 1956, 41.
KIERAN, JOHN, and DALEY, ARTHUR. *The Story of the Olympic Games—1896–1956.* New York: J. B. Lippincott Co., 1957.
LONG, LUMAN H. *World Almanac.* New York: New York World Telegram and Sun, 1966.
NATIONAL FEDERATION OF HIGH SCHOOL ATHLETIC ASSOCIATIONS. *Handbooks 1964–1965, 1966–1967,* and *1968.*
The Position of the United States Track and Field Federation in the Current Controversy. Ann Arbor: USTFF, March, 1967.
"Progress of the Swimming Hall of Fame," *Journal of Health, Physical Education and Recreation,* March, 1960, 83.
"Rah! Club! Rah!" *Newsweek,* Nov. 6, 1967, 82.
RATHBONE, JOSEPHINE, and HUNT, VALERIE V. *Corrective Physical Education.* Philadelphia: W. B. Saunders Co., 1965.
ROBBINS, JHAN, and JUNE. "Biggest and Most Beautiful Olympics," *Winnepeg Free Press,* July 2, 1960; as reported in *Readers Digest,* Aug., 1960, 106.
SAVAGE, HOWARD J., *et al. Current Developments in American College Sports.* Bulletin No. 26, Carnegie Foundation for the Advancement of Teaching, 1951.
SCOTT, PHOEBE, and ULRICH, CELESTE. "Commission on Intercollegiate Sports for Women," *Journal of Health, Physical Education and Recreation,* Vol. 37, No. 10 (Oct., 1966), 10.
TUNIS, JOHN. *Sport for the Fun of It.* Rev. ed. New York: The Ronald Press Co., 1958. Pp. 9–21, 32, 109, 115, 139, 243–46.
VALENTE, PHYLLIS PIER. "The Dance in American Colleges," *Journal of Health and Physical Education,* XX (May, 1949), 312.
VAN DALEN, D. B., *et al. World History of Physical Education.* New York: Prentice-Hall, 1953. P. 487.
WILLIAMS, J. F. *Principles of Physical Education.* Philadelphia: W. S. Saunders Co., 1927.
WILSON, KENNETH. "The Olympic Games," *Journal of Health, Physical Education and Recreation,* Vol. 32, No. 7, Part I (Oct., 1961), 24.

Chapter 25: Organized Physical Education in the Mid-Twentieth Century

Background and Progress in National Study of YMCA Physical Education. Leaflet—Exhibit E. New York: National YMCA, March 31, 1955.
BANK, THEODORE P. "Physical Fitness From the Standpoint of The Army," *Proceedings, National War Fitness Conference,* 1943. P. 29.
BROER, MARIAN. "For Fitness Vary Your Program," *Journal of Health, Physical Education and Recreation,* Sept., 1956, 16.
CLARKE, HARRIET L. "Functional Physical Test of College Women," *Journal of Health, Physical Education and Recreation,* Vol. 14 (Sept., 1943), 359. Report of Harvard Fatigue Laboratory tests.
CREMIN, LAWRENCE A. *The Transformation of the School.* 2nd ed. New York: Alfred A. Knopf. 1961.
CURTI, MERLE. *American Paradox.* New Brunswick, N.J.: Rutgers University Press, 1956. P. 63.
DANIELS, ARTHUR S. "The Profession in 1961," *Journal of Health, Physical Education and Recreation,* Sept., 1961, 22.
DEWEY, JOHN. *Experience and Education.* New York: The Macmillan Co., 1938.

"Directory of Institutions Offering Professional Preparation Programs in Health, Physical Education and Recreation," *Journal of Health, Physical Education and Recreation,* Oct., 1965, 21.

"Fitness in Action—Report of the States," *Journal of Health, Physical Education and Recreation,* Sept., 1961, 39.

FRIERMOOD, HAROLD T. "Highlights and Issues in YMCA Physical Education—Past and Present." Paper presented April 24, 1967, to YMCA Curriculum Consultation at Lake Geneva Conference.

HERSEY, MAJOR GENERAL LEWIS B. "Inside Story of the Rejection Rates," *Journal of Health and Physical Education,* XXIV (Jan., 1953), 9.

HEWITT, JACK. "Status of Graduate Faculty," *The Research Quarterly,* XXXVII (Oct., 1965), 236.

HOWE, HAROLD (U. S. COMMISSIONER OF EDUCATION). Report of Speech given before the National Student Association at College Park, Md., Aug. 22, 1967, as reported in *United States News and World Report,* Sept. 4, 1967, 14.

KRAUS, HANS, and RUTH P. HERSCHLAND. "Muscular Fitness and Health," *Journal of Health, Physical Education and Recreation,* Dec., 1933. This article reports the difference between American and European Children.

KRAUS, HANS, and PRUDDEN, BONNIE. "Minimum Muscular Fitness Tests In School Children," *The Research Quarterly,* 25:2 (May, 1954), 178–88.

LEE. MABEL, and BENNETT, BRUCE L. "This Is Our Heritage," *Journal of Health, Physical Education and Recreation,* April, 1960. In five parts.

National Board of the YWCA letter to authors dated April 22, 1967, giving statistics on the YWCA physical education program of 1966–67.

National Foundation for HPER, *Journal of Health, Physical Education and Recreation,* Jan., 1967, 70.

OXENDINE, JOSEPH. "Service Program in 1960–61," *Journal of Health, Physical Education and Recreation,* Sept., 1961, 37.

"Physical Fitness," *Journal of Health, Physical Education and Recreation,* Sept., 1956. The entire issue is devoted to the topic of fitness.

"President's Message to the Schools on Physical Fitness of Youth," *Journal of Health, Physical Education and Recreation,* Sept., 1961.

Physical Fitness Through Physical Education for the Victory Corps. Washington, D.C.: U. S. Government Printing Office, 1943.

ROWNTREE, LEONARD. "Education, Health, and Physical Fitness," *Journal of Health and Physical Education,* XIV (Sept., 1943), 370.

SCHNEIDER, ELSA. *Physical Education in Urban Elementary Schools.* Washington, D.C.: U. S. Government Printing Office, 1959.

STITT, LOUISE. "Problems of Women in Industry," *Proceedings of Victory through Fitness Workshop.* NAPECW, June, 1943. P. 21.

U.S. OFFICE OF EDUCATION. *Preparation in Health Education, Physical Education, and Recreation, Year 1952–1953.* Washington, D.C.: Government Printing Office, 1954.

WAR DEPARTMENT. *WAC Field Manual of Physical Training, FM 35–20,* July, 1943, 15.

ZIEGLER, EARLE FREDERICK. *Philosophical Foundations for Physical, Health and Recreation Education.* New York: Prentice-Hall, 1964.

Index